Real Estate Marketing & Sales Essentials: Steps for Success

Dan Hamilton 2nd Edition

Real Estate Marketing & Sales Essentials: Steps for Success

Second Edition

Dan Hamilton

Executive Editor: Sara Glassmeyer

Project Manager: Arlin Kauffman, LEAP Publishing Services

Print and Digital Project Manager: Abigail Franklin

Art and Cover Composition: Chris Dailey

Cover Image: © Shutterstock / Rawpixel

Interior Image Credits

Chapter 1 © Shutterstock / Brocreative

Chapter 2 © Shutterstock / STILLFX

Chapter 3 © Shutterstock / Evgeny Atamanenko

Chapter 4 © Shutterstock / Zbynek Jirousek

Chapter 5 © Shutterstock / Sergey Nivens

Chapter 6 © Shutterstock / Minerva Studio

Chapter 7 © Shutterstock / Andresr

Chapter 8 © Shutterstock / Pavel L Photo and Video

Chapter 9 © Shutterstock / BlueSkyImage

Chapter 10 © Shutterstock / EPSTOCK

Chapter 11 © Shutterstock / bikeriderlondon

Chapter 12 © Shutterstock / Ollyy

Chapter 13 © Shutterstock / Florin Burlan

Chapter 14 © Shutterstock / Monkey Business Images

Chapter 15 © Shutterstock / Dragon Images

Chapter 16 © Shutterstock / Maryna Pleshkun

Chapter 17 © Shutterstock / Monkey Business Images

Chapter 18 © Shutterstock / Mopic

© 2015, 2006 OnCourse Learning

ALL RIGHTS RESERVED. No part of this work covered by the copyright herein may be reproduced, transmitted, stored, or used in any form or by any means graphic, electronic, or mechanical, including but not limited to photocopying, recording, scanning, digitizing, taping, web distribution, information networks, or information storage and retrieval systems, except as permitted under Section 107 or 108 of the 1976 United States Copyright Act, without the prior written permission of the publisher.

For product information and technology assistance, contact us at
OnCourse Learning and Sales Support, 1-855-733-7239.

For permission to use material from this text or product.

Library of Congress Control Number: 2015934882

ISBN-13: 978-1-62980-009-7

ISBN-10: 1-62980-009-0

OnCourse Learning
3100 Cumberland Blvd., Suite 1450
Atlanta, GA 30339
USA

Visit us at **www.oncoursepublishing.com**

Dedication

Thanks to all the real estate brokers, managers, students, and salespeople for their help in this project.

Special thanks to:
My mother, who passed away between the two editions of this book. She always wanted to write a book, and she got to live it vicariously through me—she was very proud. I also thank my dad. I miss them both tremendously.

My daughter for a lifetime of love. She has always been there for me and supports me in all my endeavors.

My wife, Laurie, for all her love.

My brother and his family, what a joy you all are to be around.

Contents

REAL ESTATE MARKETING &
SALES ESSENTIALS   vii

1   REAL ESTATE PROFESSIONALISM AND ETHICS   1

2   CHARACTERISTICS OF SUCCESSFUL SALESPEOPLE AND TIME MANAGEMENT   30

3   TECHNOLOGY FOR THE REAL ESTATE PROFESSIONAL   63

4   PSYCHOLOGY OF MARKETING   92

5   MARKETING STRATEGY   104

6   LAW OF AGENCY AND ALTERNATIVE REPRESENTATIVE AGREEMENTS   124

7   PROSPECTING FOR SELLER APPOINTMENTS   139

8   SELLER LISTING PROCEDURES   198

9   PROSPECTING FOR BUYERS   256

10   BUYER LISTING PROCEDURES   272

11	OBJECTION HANDLING TECHNIQUES	291
12	CLIENT FOLLOW-UP	321
13	CONTRACT WRITING	331
14	NEGOTIATING AND CLOSING	339
15	AFTER ACCEPTANCE	360
16	FINANCING	370
17	REFERRALS	381
18	DECEPTIVE TRADE PRACTICES ACT AND THE CONSUMER PROTECTION ACT	398

APPENDIX 411

Buyer Client Questions	412
Additional Buyer Questions	414
Contracts for a For Sale by Owner	416
Documentation Needed at Loan Application	417
Fair Trade Items (Seller)	418
Comparison of FSBO and Broker	418
Hamilton's Rules of Real Estate	419
Keys to a Smooth Closing	420
21 Steps to Marketing Your House	423
Net Proceeds to the Seller	425
Newcomer's Packet Requirements	426
Open House	427
Checklist for a Successful Open House	427
Arrive at House 30 Minutes Before Open House	429
17 Questions that Help Your Property Sell Faster	430
Information Needed for a CMA	431
Real Estate Services	432

Scripts for All Occasions	434
A Real Estate Transaction Step by Step: From Listing through Closing Summary	487
Professionalism Checklist	488
My Goal Plan	492
Goals	493
ANSWERS TO SUMMARY QUESTIONS	494
GLOSSARY OF REAL ESTATE TERMS	501
INDEX	511

Real Estate Marketing & Sales Essentials

Steps for Success

Overview of Book

At its most basic level, real estate marketing involves selling or promoting real property. However, it also includes the marketing of the real estate salespeople and the company they represent. When time and effort are put into a solid marketing plan, it pays off: Buyers and sellers are identified, sales are generated, and the real estate company and salespeople make money. *Real Estate Marketing and Sales Essentials* will take an in-depth look at the marketing of real estate; this book will provide not only a solid foundation for new salespeople who are just getting started, but it will also provide a fresh perspective for real estate veterans who are looking to improve and reignite their careers. We will look at the basics of the real estate industry, what has and hasn't worked in the past, and the latest trends in real estate. *Real Estate Marketing and Sales Essentials* will make the most out of your career when it is read in its entirety, followed step-by-step, and then referred to periodically as a refresher.

Objectives of This Book

The purpose of *Real Estate Marketing and Sales Essentials* is to teach you, the real estate professional, how to have an exciting and rewarding career while making money. The objectives of this book are as follows:

- To develop a day-to-day procedure for success
- To express the characteristics of a real estate professional
- To design and implement a prospecting plan
- To examine multiple opportunities for prospecting
- To design and implement a marketing plan
- To discover new and innovative marketing ideas
- To explore each marketing idea in depth
- To analyze the cost of marketing
- To simplify the closing process for all involved
- To manage clients after the transaction

New to This Edition

The real estate industry is constantly changing and this new edition has been updated to include the latest marketing ideas the industry is currently using. The book now encompasses updated information on the Internet, social networking, and trends of communication. The book addresses new and better techniques for prospecting for those individuals who might want to buy or sell real estate.

Chapter 1 Real Estate Professionalism and Ethics

This edition explains the aspects of attitude, including: the Emotional Aspect, the Cognitive Aspect, and the Behavioral Aspect. It includes a discussion on the latest ways a person can control his or her attitude, because attitude is fundamental in real estate sales.

Chapter 2 Characteristics of Successful Salespeople and Time Management

This edition provides an updated definition of a goal and explains how goal setting is of utmost importance to a real estate salesperson who dreams of becoming successful. Revisions and clarifications occurred in the business planning section to allow for a smooth transition into the making of an individual business plan for a real estate agent.

Chapter 3 Technology for the Real Estate Professional

Chapter 3 was revised to reflect updates in technology. Social media now has an entire segment that addresses sites such as Facebook, LinkedIn, and Twitter. This chapter now addresses the use of personal webpages, YouTube videos, and blogging.

Chapter 4 Psychology of Marketing

Marketing philosophy is now addressed in greater detail. The seven steps in creating a great marketing philosophy are included: 1. Customer-orientation, 2. Marketing Research, 3. Complete a Wants and Needs Analysis, 4. Marketing Planning, 5. Critical budgeting, 6. Integrated Marketing, and 7. Customer Satisfaction. The chapter continues with a look at the six dominant buying motives in the real estate industry.

Chapter 5 Marketing

This chapter was modified and improved in great detail. Added to this chapter are specific steps to aid in developing an overall Personal Marketing Strategy, which include: Understanding Your

Business, Promoting the Perception of Ability, Cultivating the Right Relationships and Decision Making. This section features examples of properly written Personal Marketing Strategies. Personal Marketing Plans, Personal Marketing Budgets, Personal Marketing Projects, and Personal Marketing Campaigns are all addressed and updated.

Chapter 6 Law of Agency and Alternative Representative Agreements

The Intermediary section was updated and expanded with the latest agency law as reference. The rest of the chapter includes minor changes and clarifications.

Chapter 7 Prospecting for Seller Appointments

Chapter 7 now discusses using technology to hold meetings or give presentations remotely instead of in person. This chapter revises the definition of Active and Re-Active Prospecting, adding new ideas using the latest technology and deleting ideas that are no longer in favor among the real estate establishment. Geographic Marketing is included and Farming was eliminated. Geographic marketing is expanded and emphasized as a money-making opportunity. This chapter also includes Multiple Geographic Marketing and Business Marketing. The chapter concludes with a revised look at getting Referral Company business.

Chapter 8 Seller Listing Procedures

Minor clarifications have been made in the area of Market Analysis and the use of technology in the Seller Presentation. This chapter further expands the meaning of a Wants and Needs Analysis. The chapter concludes with an overview of how technology has changed the way real estate professionals promote their listings to other real estate professionals and to the general public.

Chapter 9 Prospecting for Buyers

The ideas for prospecting for buyers in this chapter are all revised to indicate the latest techniques used in the marketplace today. Prospecting by telephone is addressed, but not advocated, while emailing and texting is addressed as the current, acceptable means to prospect.

Chapter 10 Buyer Listing Procedures

This chapter adds a great deal of information on the importance of real estate professionals asking more questions of the clients. The revisions expand the necessary skills of noticing and reading verbal and non-verbal buying signs.

Chapter 11 Objection Handling Techniques

The Objection Handling Techniques chapter provides an expanded look at the definition of a condition and the identification of a condition when presented. Probing questions were defined more properly.

Chapter 12 Client Follow-Up

The main changes in this chapter include the addition of technology to the need for client follow-up. E-newsletters are addressed, as well as other uses of the Internet.

Chapter 13 Contract Writing

The changes in this chapter are for clarification purposes.

Chapter 14 Negotiating and Closing

Negotiation is defined in greater detail. The effects of technology on closing procedures, including "virtual document signing" and secure document transfers, are now addressed. Applications for smart phones and tablets are addressed.

Chapter 15 After Acceptance

Each item previously examined is revised and expanded including Septic Systems, Well Inspections, Environmental Assessments, Structural Engineer's reports, and Radon Gas Inspections.

Chapter 16 Financing

Several different types of financing are now included in this revision. The Full Amortized loans are addressed in detail. Partially Amortized loans and budget loans are now in this material. Under creative financing, the Adjustable Rate Mortgage, Package Mortgage, Blanket Mortgage and the Reverse Annuity Mortgage are all now addressed in this new edition.

Chapter 17 Referrals

Incoming and outgoing referrals are defined and addressed with different points from the previous material emphasized. The information necessary to have a complete buyer referral is now listed. The same is listed for a seller referral. Rental referrals are addressed for the first time with this revision. How to handle incoming referrals is expanded to look at the characteristics of a great referral specialist to the steps necessary to correctly handle an incoming referral.

Chapter 18 Deceptive Trade Practices Act and The Consumer Protection Act

Punitive damages are defined with this revision and additional questions are asked in this material.

About the Author

Dan Hamilton has held a broker's license since 1989 and has several years of experience as a full time real estate company owner. During this time, he has earned a reputation for integrity, both with his peers and with his clients. He has owned and operated three real estate offices and driven those offices to the top ten in the region.

Dan developed the Hamilton Real Estate Education School. This school has helped numerous real estate professionals obtain and maintain their real estate education throughout their career. Dan is a certified lead trainer for licensure and renewal, certified by the

Texas Real Estate Commission to teach all CORE courses. He has logged over 23,000 hours teaching real estate SAE courses and over 7,000 hours in real estate MCE courses. He has also authored multiple textbooks and papers on real estate.

Dan has been the guest speaker for multiple meetings and conventions, including the Texas Association of REALTORS®. He has served on the education committee for multiple associations, and he holds Graduate REALTOR® Institute (GRI), Instructor Training Institute (ITI) and Certified Real Estate Instructor (CREI) designations. He served on the board of the national Real Estate Educators Association (REEA), and he was the president of the Texas Real Estate Teachers Association (TRETA). Dan Hamilton is currently a Texas agency rep with Alliant National Title.

Dan Hamilton
E-mail: mainbroker@aol.com

Chapter 1

Real Estate
Professionalism and Ethics

Chapter Overview

This chapter covers the aspects of ethics, including the National Association of REALTORS® code of ethics and a personal code of ethics. There will be questions, and you must provide the answers. You will be more informed on the concepts of ethics and how they apply to your personal life as well as your business life.

In this chapter you should be able to recognize professionalism and act in accordance with being professional. You will also understand the power that a positive mental attitude has in relation to professionalism. Finally, you will be aware of the designations the real estate profession offers interested salespersons.

Key Terms

Affirmation:
The act of affirming or the state of being affirmed, assertion. Something declared to be true, a positive statement or judgment. Self-talk. These are beliefs about you.

Attitude:
A position of the body or manner of carrying oneself. This is how you act.

Designations:
Nomination or appointment. A distinguishing name or title.

Ethickos:
Moral.

Ethics:
A set of principles of right conduct.

Ethos:
   Character.

Features:
   The overall appearance of the services offered. Refers to an aspect of a quality real estate salesperson.

Performance:
   The way in which someone functions. It is the Primary Operating Characteristic. Refers to an aspect of a quality real estate salesperson.

Quality:
   Degree or grade of excellence. Having a high degree of excellence.

REALTORS®:
   A service mark used for a real estate agent affiliated with the National Association of REALTORS®.

Reliability:
   Capable of being relied on, dependable. Refers to an aspect of a quality real estate salesperson.

Serviceability:
   Ability to give long service, durable. Ease in handling problems. Refers to an aspect of a quality real estate salesperson.

Subconscious:
   The part of the mind below the level of conscious perception.

Timeliness:
   Occurring at a suitable or opportune time; well timed. Prompt response. Refers to an aspect of a quality real estate salesperson.

Real Estate Professionalism

Introduction

The phrase "Real Estate Profession" is interesting. Real estate salespeople enjoy speaking this phrase, but all need to perform as professionals. Being professional is important for self-worth and to obtain top income. A real estate salesperson should strive to maintain professionalism at all costs. When some people enter the real estate business, they are afraid to tell their friends because they feel that they do not have a "real job." This "job" is "real" because the person in the real estate field feels and acts professional, not because of what others think. The question a professional real estate salesperson should ask is: "Why would someone choose to do real estate business with me?"

My dad was once given some bad advice. He was told that to be a good father and husband he should work with one company until he retired; then that company, in turn, would take care of him and his family. This simply is not true. My dad was fired twice in his life. In both instances, the companies he was working for were sold, the new companies brought in new management staff, and my dad was let go. The last time he was fired, he was in his fifties and could not find another job. I finally asked him to join my real estate company as my maintenance man; it broke my heart to know he couldn't find work to make ends meet. For a man with his education and will to work, he could have done much better.

When I am asked why I chose real estate, my response surprises most people. Most people who join the real estate business do so for money and/or flexibility. I, however, chose to pursue a real estate career for job security. I didn't want to end up like my dad. He was lied to and misled. I wanted a career that could not be taken from me, one that was limited only by me. If my current broker let me go today, I would be back online within an hour. I know how to sell and once you have acquired that skill, it cannot be taken from you. You now have the confidence and peace that comes from job security.

Sometimes people ask me how many hours per week I typically work. My response is: "How do you define work?" I define it as "doing something when you would rather be doing something else." Considering that definition, I do very little work. When I am in front of sellers or students, or at a closing with buyers of their first home, there is no other place I would rather be while making money. Have you ever heard of someone winning millions in the lottery and their first remark is, "I can't wait to get back to work because I love it so much!"? That would be my first thought, and that attitude is what it takes to be successful in real estate. It should be what you strive for. I had a garden once, and I loved to go out and enjoy the earth. However, one day that garden started to become "work" for me; it was no longer something I enjoyed and so shortly after, it was gone. That is what I am talking about—making sure you what you are doing isn't "work" but rather something you love.

One last point I want to make before we get started: Have fun in the real estate business! I had forgotten how depressed real estate salespeople can be until I did an office meeting for a manager friend of mine. In the meeting the real estate salespeople were complaining about this or that; I didn't hear one positive comment from any of them. Too many real estate salespeople begin their careers in such a serious frame of mind that they don't realize how fun it can be. Don't be so serious that you lose your edge. Learn to laugh at yourself and your situation. I have taught CE (Continuing Education) classes to experienced salespeople who want to renew their licenses. In these classes I have seen some very distraught and depressed people. These are the people who no longer have fun in real estate. Their positive attitudes are gone.

Attitude

Attitude is a position of the body or manner of carrying oneself. It is what we carry with us. It is always there, whether good or bad. It should consist of genuine concern. This is how you act. You should convey an attitude of trust and always give others your undivided attention. The good news is that we control our attitudes, and we have the power to change our attitudes. Have you ever been in a good mood, only to have it ruined when someone makes negative comments? Bam—where did our good mood go? On the other hand, have you ever been having a lousy day when a friend stops by and, with just a smile, brightens your day? Notice the words I used: a "friend" and "someone." Who do you want to be, the "friend" or the "someone"? Watch people, notice which person everyone likes to be around. Who is always being asked to lunch? Who never speaks up at a meeting and yet is always asked his or her opinion? What is his or her mood?

There are several different aspects of attitude:
First, there is the **emotional aspect**: How does the situation make you feel? Second is the c**ognitive aspect**: What are your thoughts and belief about the situation? And lastly, the **behavioral aspect**: How does your attitude toward the situation influence your behavior? Understanding the aspects of attitude can help you control it and use it to your benefit, instead of allowing it to control you.

Obvious Attitudes vs. Obscure Attitudes
Attitudes can be obvious, meaning they can clearly be seen by others and by you. Obscure attitudes are much less evident, but they can be as powerful an influencer of behavior and beliefs as obvious ones. In order to know your attitudes, you must first know yourself.

Attitudes are based on past experiences, knowledge, and other people. Sometimes attitudes are formed by what we *THINK* is true. The experiences tell us how to behave. If we have been bitten by a dog, our attitude toward dogs may be less than favorable. If we have had a woman reject our proposal, then we may believe that all women will reject us. These attitudes toward situations are both positive and negative. If we touch a stove and it burns us, we could form the attitude that stoves are bad and for the rest of our lives eat cold food. Or we could adopt a healthy attitude, one that recognizes that the function of the stove needs to be respected: It *COULD* burn us, but it makes our food much better.

The following illustration is accurate concerning attitude:

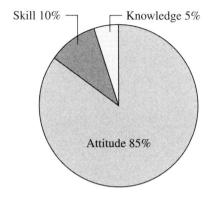

Success in the real estate business is 5 percent knowledge (what you know), 10 percent skill (how you perform), and 85 percent attitude. Your attitude determines how much success you will have in the real estate business.

REMEMBER:

God made the day; we decide whether to make it good or bad. Attitude is just an outside sign of what is going on inside. If you change your belief on the inside, your attitude will also change. And what you think is what you bank.

A positive mental attitude is as important an aspect of real estate as the best education, but no one is immune to an occasional attack of the "downers." Unfortunately, being in a bad mood is a luxury not available to salespeople trying to make a connection with a client.

> *"Your attitude, not your aptitude, will determine your altitude."*
> —Zig Ziglar

Here is a list of possible remedies for the downers:

- Don't appear "down" when you feel down. Hold your head up and act and talk as though you feel great . . . always. As Mary Kay Ash, founder of Mary Kay, Inc., famously said: "Fake it until you can make it!" Stay out of the office when you can't be positive.

No need to infect other productive real estate salespeople with your negative attitude; come back when things look brighter.

- Don't think or talk about unpleasant things, as they appear to be at the moment. Do something to make those things better. Change your outlook, and the unpleasant things will change.

- Don't dwell on the negative. Negativity is like a downward spiral where one negative thing leads to another. Only you can change this. The opposite is also true: Positive thinking is an upward spiral.

- Don't be one of those people who experiences some minor negative event and dwells on it all day long, blowing it out of proportion and allowing it to consume an entire work day. It's okay to think about, talk about, and envision things the way you'd like them to be. You should accept the truth of each situation, but then separate the truth from the unrealistic negatives. Ask yourself how the bottom line of your company would be affected if everyone had the same attitude as you. Do you like the answer? Carefully distinguish between what's actually happening and what you think is happening, and then be aware of what you think about it.

- Don't make a self-fulfilling prophesy out of your negative thoughts. A self-fulfilling prophecy is when you don't want something to happen so bad that all you think about is the negative until it actually happens. It is like the coach who told the baseball pitcher not to throw the fastball inside to the next hitter. All the pitcher could think about was not throwing the fastball inside, and sure enough, he threw it inside and the batter crushed it for a home run.

- Don't sit around the office doing nothing. Do get moving. Do something—anything. You could drive by neighborhoods and look for "for sale by owner" signs or investment properties. Better yet, fast walk those same neighborhoods. Physical activity is a natural mood lifter, as well as a helpful diversion.

- Don't judge yourself too harshly or expect perfection of yourself. Be as patient with your shortcomings as you are with those of your best friends. Recognize and reinforce in yourself and others the behavior you approve of before criticizing faults.

My motto is as follows:

Learn from your mistakes and leave them behind. Learn from your successes and keep them with you.

- Don't be a target for the negative people in your life. Avoid such people when you can and when you can't avoid them, refuse to be affected by their depressive conversation and attitude.

Circumstances may be (and often are) matters of chance, but the moods that accompany them are, for the most part, matters of choice.

> *"Never despair, but if you do, work on in despair."*
>
> —*Edmund Burke*

Activity literally breeds activity and that breed's productivity! A top executive was asked what advice he would give a person looking to be a success. The executive answered, "Fail faster." Failure is not the problem; the problem is being so afraid to fail that you do nothing. And nothing gets no thing.

One last thought on attitude: Don't think of yourself as inferior to others, regardless of who or what they are. See yourself as a very special, unique, and worthwhile human being. According to Eleanor Roosevelt, "No one can make you feel inferior without your consent." These beliefs about yourself are your own affirmations.

Affirmations

Affirmations are defined as the act of affirming or the state of being affirmed, assertion. Something declared to be true, a positive statement or judgment. Self-talk. These are beliefs about you. Don't accept unhappiness as a normal, unavoidable state of affairs. Remind yourself that when you are unhappy it is because your thoughts and self-talk are inappropriate. (Happiness is the normal state of being, and any deviation is abnormal!) You control the things around you. I once heard that we are where we are because that is where we want to be. Our thoughts, positive or negative, put us where we are today. If we actually do not like our place in life, all we have to do is mentally change it.

Affirmation is a sophisticated way to say "self-talk." Everyone talks to himself or herself, whether or not they choose to admit it. Napoleon Hill states, "Whatever a person can conceive and believe, he can achieve." This clearly notes Hill's belief in self-talk.

> Keep your thoughts positive because your thoughts become your words;
>
> Keep your words positive because your words become your behaviors;
>
> Keep your behaviors positive because your behaviors become your habits;
>
> Keep your habits positive because your habits become your values;
>
> Keep your values positive because your values become your destiny.
>
> *Gandhi*

The brain is made up of a complex group of neurons that direct the way we feel, act, and react. The brain can be broken into two parts, the conscious and the subconscious. The conscious brain is the thinking brain. You are reading this material and understanding it with the thinking brain. The subconscious brain is the part of the mind below the level of conscious perception. The subconscious is active under the control of the conscious brain. The subconscious brain is always listening and observing. Right now, is there a clock, fan, or some other noise going on while you are reading this? Could you hear it before I mentioned it? If not, it is because the subconscious brain is filtering those noises out. The subconscious motivates us. So we need to ask, how can we motivate the subconscious, which in turn will motivate ourselves? The interesting thing about the subconscious is that it cannot tell the difference between imagination and reality.

One summer I worked with my dad at a manufacturing plant that made paint for the stripes on roadways. It was a powder paint that, when heated, would melt into a liquid that could be sprayed on the road. The yellow paint had lead in it. I wore a hardhat, a coverall for my clothes, work boots, gloves, and a face mask. The average temperature in the warehouse was over 100 degrees in the summer. I had to be at work at 6 a.m., and I worked till 4 p.m. My job was to take 50-lb. bags of this powder and place them on pallets. That was it, and I hated every minute of it—with a passion. I was in college at the time, and this was the best summer job I could get. I endured this torture day in and day out. I did not even have the energy to eat, and I lost a lot of weight. One day I noticed a rash on my left arm. After a couple of days, it spread down my side to my left leg. I finally went to the doctor. He did a series of tests and then asked, "What is going on in your life?" I wasn't sure where he was going with the question, so I just began talking. When I finally mentioned how much I hated my job, he asked me why I didn't quit. When I told him that I didn't want to embarrass my dad (he was in management, not on the line), he wrote a prescription that read, "Quit your job." He explained that I was not allergic to anything. The rash was all in my head; I created it by my thoughts.

I challenge you now to look at your arm and try and get a rash. It can't be done. But I did it. My sincere affirmations gave me what I had asked for. Affirmations do not need to know how, but what, and what I wanted was out of that job. Affirmations program the subconscious by relating information to it that has not yet become reality. "I feel good, I feel fine" repeated often will make you feel good even if you did not feel that way in the beginning. Affirmations must be

1. stated in the present tense.

2. stated with intense emotion.

3. stated repeatedly throughout the day.

4. stated in a positive format.

5. believable.

You have many beliefs about yourself, not just one. These beliefs are what control the real use of your potential, at the level of your self-esteem and self-image. When you learn to change these beliefs, you can expand the use of your skills. You have unlimited potential within you. The way you think determines the way you act. If you grew up thinking of yourself as shy, then you are shy. If you see yourself as naturally overweight, you might lose a few pounds. But soon you will creatively gain back those pounds you lost because you see yourself as an overweight person.

At one time in my life I believed that I could not remember people's names. My subconscious mind granted me my belief. I could be introduced to a person and ten seconds later could not remember his or her name. What is interesting is that my subconscious mind had done what I had commanded, even though it was not actually what I wanted.

Do not underestimate your sarcastic humor; your subconscious mind does not get it. Have you ever seen a person that continues to say something about himself in a sarcastic way and becomes more and more like that? The reason for this is that the subconscious mind gives you what you ask for whether or not you really want it. My subconscious mind would interrupt my thinking with other thoughts like: "What should I say next?" or "I wonder if there is spinach in my teeth?" All of these thoughts limited my ability to remember the name. One day I determined that I would remember people's names. I began working on my self-talk. I concentrated on telling myself that I was great at names. As a result, I began listening differently. Someone would say a name and in my mind, I would repeat it several times. Every

> *"I am NOT a product of my circumstances, I AM a product of my decisions."*
>
> —Stephen Covey

time I saw that person, I would repeat the process. In a short period of time I was great at remembering names. Now I can enter a classroom and within an hour, I have every person's name saved in my memory.

Many professional athletes use affirmation and visualization along with practice to help them play at peak form. They visualize the perfect athletic feat over and over again.

The same can be true for you and business. If you rehearse the future over and over in your mind and see yourself performing perfectly, you will dramatically increase your chances of making that future reality.

Affirmations work on you, but you should not neglect your service to others. The best way to think of others is to ensure your service is of the highest quality. Always strive to improve the quality of your service.

Quality Service

Quality is defined as having a high degree or grade of excellence. Improving quality is on everyone's mind these days, but you don't need a crash course to upgrade the quality of your efforts. A slow but steady approach is more likely to be effective in the long run. There are many programs out there, including Total Quality Management, Quality Control, Quality Service, and Continuous Quality Improvement, but the main objective is to ensure that your clients are not only satisfied with your service, they are thrilled with it.

Stanley Marcus's father, the founder of Neiman Marcus, gave Stanley some valuable advice early in his career. It was advice that later helped build Neiman Marcus into a first-class store. A woman ruined a dress she had worn just once and wanted her money back. While Stanley argued that the woman had obviously abused the dress herself and that the manufacturer wasn't going to help pay for it, Stanley's father told his son to give the woman her money back. He said that the woman wasn't doing business with the manufacturer; she was doing business with Neiman's. His father told Stanley that it had cost more than $200 to get the customer, and that he didn't want to lose her over a $175 dress. He also told Stanley to refund the money with a smile. Over the years, the woman ended up spending more than $500,000 at Neiman Marcus.

Having thrilled clients means they will not only come back, but they will pass your name onto their friends. Here are a few ideas:

- **Begin by beginning.** Don't procrastinate; do whatever you can to increase your quality and efficiency. The hardest part of reworking yourself is to get started. Don't allow yourself to get distracted by things that try to hinder you from doing your business better. If you don't start now, when will you?

- **Keep an open mind.** I once read that many people's minds are like concrete, "thoroughly mixed and permanently set." Don't be that person. Working on one project may trigger ideas that will help improve quality in other areas of your work. Put your new ideas into action and test them.

- **Start simple.** Don't put too much pressure on yourself by over-preparing or tackling a huge problem. Get realistic about what you can do. Real estate is a personal business, so concentrate on how to make YOU better.

- **Practice continual improvement.** No matter how efficient you become, always look for ways to get better. Minor improvements might have beneficial effects on other areas of your work. Remember that the process never ends. To be successful, you've got to dedicate yourself to pursuing quality endlessly. It's not easy, but in these tough competitive times, it's necessary. This book has been revised many times and will continue to be improved.

The following are some aspects and examples of quality:

PERFORMANCE—*Primary Operating Characteristic*
("I know that my real estate salesperson performs and behaves just as he or she should.")

FEATURES—*Services Offered*
("The features, characteristics, and attributes of my real estate salesperson are all that anyone could ask for.")

RELIABILITY—*Trust in the Service*
("I can rely on my real estate salesperson to get the job done.")

CONFORMANCE—*Meet Standards for the Industry*
("My real estate salesperson satisfies the requirements that have been set.")

DURABILITY—*Service Life*
("I know that my relationship with my real estate salesperson is long lasting.")

SERVICEABILITY—*Ease of Handling Problems*
("If something goes wrong, I know that my real estate salesperson will correct the problem.")

AESTHETICS—*Experience of the Sense*
("I feel my real estate salesperson has done a fine job.")

PERCEIVED QUALITY—*Reputation*
("I perceive my real estate salesperson is of high quality and integrity.")

TIMELINESS—*Prompt Response*
("I receive the service in a timely manner.")

ACCURACY—*Exactness or Preciseness*
("This transaction is free from errors.")

Professional real estate salespersons must be of high quality and should know how their businesses are conducted and how they earn their living. Some real estate salespeople get confused on the difference between professional service and doing things for free.

> "The trouble with a great many of us in the business world is that we are thinking hardest of all about the

dollar we want to make. Now that is the wrong idea from the start. I'll tell you the man who has the idea of service in his business will never need to worry about profits. The money is bound to come. This idea of service in business is the biggest guarantee of success that any man can have."—Henry Ford

The best way to determine that our service is of the highest standard is to look at other professionals, such as those in the legal profession.

Attorney's Contingency

In the past, I was often accused of disliking buyers. While this is not true, I do believe that to avoid wasting time, some type of analysis needs to be done before agreeing to take on a client. Many other professions perform this same type of analysis, and we can take a lesson from them. For instance, my brother is an attorney and before he agrees to take a case on a contingency basis (where the attorney doesn't get paid if he doesn't win the case), he performs an analysis where the following must be true:

1. **The case is a sure win.**
   Easy enough, the facts are clear and we will win.

2. **The case has a sure-paying defendant.**
   For lawsuits, this means the defendant is capable of paying and will pay if challenged. Attorneys like insurance companies because they are sure-paying defendants.

3. **The case involves significant sums of money.**
   No attorney takes an insignificant case for little or no money.

I took this same technique, translated it to real estate language, and now use the analysis below when determining whether or not to take on a new client:

1. **The seller or buyer transaction is a sure win.**
   The seller is motivated to sell, and the buyer is motivated to buy.

2. **The seller or buyer is a sure-paying client.**
   In real estate, a sure-paying client is one who is financially qualified to buy or sell a property. Buyers must have the resources necessary to pay cash or get suitable financing. The salesperson must obtain this information before showing the buyer any house. Never show an unqualified buyer a house. It wastes your time and the buyer's time. Sellers must have the right to sell and the ability to pay. A seller who has to price a property out of the market in order to be able to pay the real estate salesperson is not a qualified seller.

3. **The seller or buyer transaction involves significant sums.**
   I think this is the one that bothers most salespeople. National sales trainer Tom Hopkins frequently says: "If you take time from my family, you will pay dearly for it." I like that! Stated simply, you need to get paid for your services. Make sure that you are being compensated for time spent away from evening meals, family events, and so on. I believe that your spouse should make the decision to give your money away. My wife is not that close to my clients, and she likes for me to get paid. She would not like it if I missed time with my family and yet came home with no money, and she is completely justified in feeling this way. I have seen countless salespeople work hard for a sale that nets them a couple hundred dollars or worse—nothing. Unfortunately, many salespeople are of the belief that "If I help them now, maybe they will remember me."

Everyone is a potential client of yours; why spend time with those who will not or cannot pay you? Check the section of this book on alternate fee arrangements for other ways to get paid and still help people. Now let's consider another question that my brother, the attorney, must ask when determining whether to take a case:

If you have a really nice person that does not meet all three contingency criteria, would you still work for them? The answer is "Yes," *IF:*

> The client is willing to pay for my services by the hour.

So in real estate, if the client was willing to pay by the hour or maybe a flat fee, I should work with them; however, I need to determine how much I am worth.

What you do or how you do it is of little concern to customers if they refuse to work with you. Our job is not to just sell property, but to get the customer to buy that property *through* us. The first thing we must do to get them to buy through us is to build rapport and learn their wants and needs.

A Little TLC

One of the most important aspects of relating and selling to people is TLC. In real estate sales, the letters mean:

T—Trust
L—Like
C—Close

A potential client must *Trust* you and *Like* you, before you can ever *Close*. I find that far too often clients are resistant to do business with you because you have rushed into the sale without getting to know them. People want to do business with people they like and trust. For example, I was talking with a single, elderly lady about the sale of her home. I was energetic and enthusiastic. I talked fast. I moved quickly. But I failed to recognize her needs. I asked her to market her home through me. She told me she wanted to talk it over with her son before she made a decision, and she would let me know the next day. Then I understood. I closed my marketing materials and sat back in my chair. I said, "Tell me about your son." And she did—for nearly an hour and a half. Afterward she said, "Okay, I will go ahead and market my home with you." What changed? I did. I stopped doing what I wanted and did what she wanted. I showed her I cared. She now liked and trusted me. As life improvement expert Zig Ziglar always says, "People don't care what you know until they know you care."

A salesperson came into my office one day to complain that a customer would not sign a required agency disclosure form. He said he had arranged to show a vacant house to a single woman and after taking her through it, she refused to sign the document. The next day he showed her another vacant house, and she still refused to sign the document. What was he to do?

Let's take a look at this from the buyer's side. A man whom she did not know met her at a vacant house and asked her to sign a document. She has no TLC for the salesperson. I told him that he should have her come to the office, perform a wants-and-needs analysis, and then discuss the disclosure form with her. The next day he came into my office with a smile on his face; his client had signed the document and agreed to buy a property through him within the week. What had changed? He did. He built "like and trust" before he closed for her signature.

Here is another way to build "like and trust": Make sure you know and use your customer's name over and over. Calling a customer "dude" over and over will not build rapport.

Institutes, Societies, and Designations

Being a professional entails more than the way one dresses and speaks; it also includes taking an active role. Being active does not just involve securing clients; being active in your professional community enables you to network with other real estate salespeople.

It opens a door of opportunity for sharing or for possibly taking a leadership role. The real estate industry has many societies and associations that offer courses or training that come with a designation to make you stand out among your peers. A designation is a nomination, appointment, or a distinguishing name or title. The following is a list of several professional organizations and some of the designations they offer.

Institutes and Societies	Designations
Commercial and Investment Real Estate Institute (CIREI)	Certified Commercial Investment Member (CCIM) Eight-hour exam
Counselors of Real Estate (CRE)	Counselor of Real Estate (CRE)
Institute of Real Estate Management (IREM)	Certified Property Manager (CPM) Accredited Management Organization (AMO) Accredited Residential Manager (ARM)
National Association of REALTORS® (NAR)	Graduate, REALTORS® Institute (GRI) Residential Accredited Appraiser (RAA) General Accredited Appraiser (GAA)
Real Estate Buyer's Agent Council (REBAC)	Accredited Buyer Representative (ABR) Accredited Buyer Representative Manager (ABRM)
REALTORS® Land Institute (RLI)	Accredited Land Consultant (ALC)
REALTORS® National Marketing Institute (RNMI)	Certified Real Estate Brokerage Manager (CRB) Certified Residential Specialist (CRS)
Society of Industrial and Office REALTORS® (SIOR)	Specialization in industrial and office real estate
Women's Council of REALTORS® (WCR)	Leadership Training Graduate (LTG) Referral and Relocation Certification (RRC)

Fair Housing

A professional real estate salesperson is not only ethical but is also a person who handles his or her business in the correct manner. No professional real estate salesperson would even consider violating anyone's rights to buy, sell, rent, or lease real property based on personal bias.

The earliest law protecting individuals in the lease or purchase of real property was adopted in 1866. The Civil Rights Act of 1866 prohibited discrimination based on race or color. Notice that the first Civil

Rights Act was written in 1866, not in 1968, the year most people associate with racial discrimination and race wars. The 1866 law required an aggrieved person to seek a civil suit in federal court. Not many people had the money to do this, so this law had no "teeth."

The law was revised in 1968 and added the classes of religion and national origin. The law also gave the right for investigation and prosecution to the Department of Housing and Urban Development (HUD). HUD has lots of money and can pursue an alleged violator without a financial challenge.

Title VIII of the Civil Rights Act is also known as the Fair Housing Act (of 1968).

The Civil Right Act of 1968 prohibited the following forms of discrimination:

1. Refusal to sell or rent a dwelling to any person because of his or her race, color, religion, or national origin.

2. Discrimination against a person in the terms, conditions, or privileges of the sale or rental of a dwelling. Setting more restrictive standards, such as a higher income or having inconsistent policies used to discriminate.

3. Advertising the sale or rental of a dwelling, indicating discrimination based on race, color, religion, or national origin, such as skin color.

4. Coercing, threatening, intimidating, or interfering with a person's enjoyment or exercise of housing rights based on discriminatory reasons or retaliating against a person or organization that aids or encourages the exercise or enjoyment of fair housing rights.

5. Falsely denying that a rental unit is available.

6. Refusing to accommodate the needs of handicapped tenants, such as not allowing a guide dog for the visually impaired.

Jones v. Alfred H. Mayer Co., *392 U.S. 409 (1968) is a U. S. Supreme Court case that held that Congress could regulate the sale of private property in order to prevent racial discrimination.*

An amendment in 1974 made a person's sex a protected class as well. Sex refers to a person's gender—being male or female. In 1988, familial status and handicap persons were added. Familial status refers to the relationship of people in a family (children and parents), and handicap persons are those with physical conditions that impair them, including those with AIDS and mental disorders. Under this law, a handicapped person may make minor modifications to allow safe access and use of a property as long as they return the property to its prior condition.

U.S. Code, Title 42, Chapter 21, Subchapter I, *(1982) All citizens of the United States shall have the same right, in every State and Territory, as is enjoyed by white citizens thereof to inherit, purchase, lease, sell, hold, and convey real and personal property.*

An alleged violation of the Civil Rights Act must be filed within one year of the action. A person has two years to file a federal civil court action. Civil penalties are $10,000 for the first violation and $50,000 for any subsequent violation. Damages claimed could include humiliation, pain, anger, embarrassment, emotional distress, and other relief. If the victim wins a federal civil court lawsuit, the law may also allow the victim to receive punitive damages into the millions of dollars. *Herron v. Blackwell*, 908 F.2d 864, 870 (1990)

Ethics

People hear the term "ethics" and cheer. There is the belief that if everyone had more ethics, the world would be a better place. Ethics is very different. Ethics is not for everyone else. Ethics is for the individual. Ethics is the way you behave in relation to others. Ethics is doing the right thing even if it is the difficult thing.

Definition

Ethics comes from the Greek words "ethickos" and "ethos," meaning moral character. Ethics in real estate is the way we treat others. It is the way we conduct ourselves in private and in social groups. Ethics has been a source of interest since early Greek times and will continue to be of interest for eternity.—*Stanford Encyclopedia of Philosophy*

NAR Code of Ethics

The National Association of REALTORS® (NAR) was founded as the National Association of Real Estate Exchanges (NAREE) on May 12, 1908. Its mission was "to unite the real estate men of America for the purpose of effectively exerting a combined influence upon matters affecting real estate interests." These were lofty words, given the state of affairs at the time. Real estate salespeople were writing contracts on sheets of paper and hiding property defects. As a group, they were considered unscrupulous. To combat that image and improve the reputation of the real estate professionals in the economy, in 1913 the NAREE adopted a code of ethics with the Golden Rule (do unto others as you would have them do unto you) as its theme. A requisite for membership in the NAR, this code sets the standards in writing by which its members abide. In 1916, the organization's name was changed to The National Association of Real Estate Boards (NAR) and the term "REALTOR®," identifying real estate agents as members of the NAR and subscribers to its code of ethics, was first used. Only real estate salespeople who belong to the NAR can use the REALTORS® designation. The NAR maintains a membership of over one million. To learn more, visit the NAR website at *http://www.realtor.org*.

Personal Code of Ethics

A personal code of ethics is simply what you would do if no one was watching. It is the way you behave when you are alone. People have an inherent knowledge of right and wrong. Personal ethics is how we act with that knowledge. Ethics is returning money to a cashier if you are given too much change. Ethics is returning a lost wallet with all the cash money intact. Ethics is being honest in your dealings with others. Ethics is always doing those things that you know are right.

I purchased an entrance mat from a distributor at a real estate conference. I paid for it and I took it. About 6 weeks later, I was shipped another one. I laughed and started putting it back in the box. My administrative assistant said, "What are you doing? We need one for the back door." Without hesitation I finished boxing it up, and it was shipped back the next day. My personal ethics would not allow me to take advantage of another person's mistake. I never thought about it until now, but can you imagine the precedent I would have set if I had kept it? No one could trust me to make the right decisions. You never know who is watching, maybe no one, maybe your boss. Consider what you would do in the following situations:

1. A buyer gives you $600 dollars for earnest money, thinking he only gave you $500.
    A. Return the extra $100.
    B. Buy yourself lunch with it; you deserve it.
    C. Keep the extra $100; if the buyers are that stupid, they didn't want it.

2. While showing a property, you break a valuable vase.
    A. Clean up the mess and call the listing salesperson immediately.
    B. Run—they will never know it was you.
    C. Break the back window and steal some stuff; the sellers will think they were robbed.

3. A seller's water well will not pass a water test.
    A. Disclose this issue to the buyer, and try to work out a solution even if it means losing the sale.

B. Get water from a different well and pass it off as the seller's well. You can later claim something just went wrong with the water, but it was fine during inspection; meanwhile, you have put a down payment on that new car you want with the handsome commission you made on the sale.

C. Forge false documents that indicate the well has no problem, so the seller can sell the property and you can get paid. Remember your duty is to represent the seller's best interest.

The answers to all of the above scenarios are "A." While not all personal ethics questions are that simple, don't let a hectic schedule or desperation lead you astray. I once saw a sign in a store that read, "You can take anything that God does not see you take." That is ethics. The following situations are a little more challenging:

1. A buyer calls your office and asks for Colleen, who is out of the office. You are on phone duty and respond to the caller by saying, "Colleen is not in; may I take a message?" The buyer then tells you that she received a flyer from Colleen and would like to buy a house.
   A. Put the caller on hold and check your office policy manual on how to proceed.
   B. Help the caller yourself.
   C. Take a message for Colleen.

2. You are representing a buyer, and you notice a small crack in the bedroom wall of the house you are showing. The buyers are obviously interested in the house.
   A. Disclose the crack and recommend further inspections.
   B. Don't say anything. You are not a structural engineer.
   C. Let the buyer beware. It is not your job to discover structural defects.

3. You hear a real estate agent in your office tell a buyer that a property is not in a flood plain. You know this agent is a good

friend, and you know he has seen and understood a report stating that the house is in a flood plain.
A. Discuss this with your broker.
B. Address this issue immediately before it is too late.
C. Keep quiet to save your friendship.

These are not as easy as the first set of situations, but again all the best answers are "A." Personal ethics will give you the true meaning of success. Having all of the money in the world yet not believing in yourself is not worth it. You always know yourself.

In developing moral character, consider the following:

- Practice being a mentor; treat everyone with love and respect.

- Practice moral discipline; use rules and moral reasoning.

- Practice moral reflection; read and discuss issues.

- Practice conflict resolution; solve conflicts fairly and without force.

Chapter Summary

This chapter deals with the way we feel about real estate. Real estate can be a mean business if our attitude is not correct. We must believe in ourselves because others might not. We sell ourselves, not houses, in the real estate business. A buyer will buy a property with or without us, but it is our job is to have that buyer buy through us. To accomplish this goal, we must believe that we are the best real estate people for the client. To that end, we must provide the best, most professional service to fulfill their needs.

Ethics is how we respond when no one else is looking. It is our innermost being and our integrity. It is what sets us apart from unscrupulous salespeople. It is how we want to be treated. Stay ethical and you can sleep at night.

Summary Questions

1. What is the mark used to denote a real estate salesperson affiliated with the National Association of REALTORS®?
   a. Realator
   b. NAR
   c. Agent
   d. REALTOR®

2. What is wrong with the following affirmation? "Every day I will try to better myself in some way."
   a. "Try" is an excuse for failure.
   b. "Will" is future tense, and affirmations must be in present tense.
   c. "Some way" is not exact enough to be an effective affirmation.
   d. All of the above.

3. Which of the following best describes the word "work"?
   a. Doing something when you would rather be doing something else
   b. What you have to do to get a paycheck
   c. Real estate
   d. An alien from Ork

4. Ethics comes from the Greek words "ethickos" and "ethos," meaning what?
   a. "Thick" and "ethics"
   b. "Moral" and "character"
   c. "Strong" and "ethics"
   d. "Silent" and "truth"

5. The NAR preamble is measured by what rule?
   a. 80/20 Rule
   b. Ethics Rule
   c. Rule of Thumb
   d. Golden Rule

6. Kimberly, a real estate licensed salesperson, fails to log in a customer's call per the established office procedure. The customer calls back on licensee Brittany's opportunity time but doesn't mention Kimberly's name. Brittany establishes a relationship with the caller and eventually sells him a house. When Kimberly finds out about the sale, she demands at least part of the commission as procuring cause. In this case, the broker should:
   a. Tell Kimberly to get a life.
   b. Tell Brittany to split the commission with Kimberly.
   c. Pay Kimberly out of the brokerage commission to avoid an in-office dispute.
   d. Refer Kimberly to the policy manual and advise her to follow office procedure.

7. You have given your current broker two weeks' notice that you will be transferring your license to a competing broker. On your last day of opportunity time, you get an incoming call from a buyer interested in purchasing a million-dollar property. What is the best course of action?
   a. Assist the buyer and ask your current broker to assign another salesperson after you leave.
   b. Assist the buyer and ask him to follow you to your new broker when you leave.
   c. Assist the buyer and ask your new broker for guidance.
   d. Assist the buyer with your current broker's permission and guidance.

8. You have written an offer from a customer for your sellers for $270,000. You could get both sides of the commission. Just when you are about to leave the office, the telephone rings with another competing agent who has an offer for your seller's house for full price at $275,000. What is the best course of action?
   a. Ignore the second offer because it is not in writing yet.
   b. Pretend you never received the agent's call. It is that agent's word against yours.

c. Present your first offer and tell the seller another offer may be coming in.
   d. Call your buyers and tell them they need to up their offer by $5,100 because you need to be higher than the other offer.

9. You have a commission dispute with another agent from a competing real estate company. What should you do?
   a. Call for a duel at ten paces with single-shot pistols in the parking lot of the local association of REALTORS®.
   b. Sue the other agent in a court of law.
   c. Consult your broker.
   d. File a grievance with the real estate commission.

10. Which of the following is not an unethical practice?
    a. Selling your own real property.
    b. Failing to remove the real estate yard sign after it has expired.
    c. Calling sellers from MLS data to see if they will change real estate companies before their exclusive listing has expired.
    d. Using imaginary houses to fill up advertising space.

Chapter 2

Characteristics of Successful Salespeople and Time Management

Chapter Overview

The purpose of this chapter is to review the traits of successful salespeople. We will look at everything from goal setting to what to wear and what to drive. We will discuss what to do with your money once you have earned it, we will explore time-management techniques, and we will learn the basics of planning out your day, your week, and even an entire year. Once you see what other successful salespeople do, you can do the same things and will be more likely to achieve the same results.

Key Terms

Budget:
An itemized summary of estimated expenditures for a given period.

Business Plan:
A proposal that requires a concerted effort.

Convention:
A formal meeting of members of an industry.

Financial Planning:
The management of money, banking, investments, and credit.

Goal:
The purpose toward which an endeavor is directed, an objective.

Investing:
To commit money or capital to gain a financial return.

Seminar:
A small group of students in study under the guidance of a professor for the purpose of exchanging ideas.

Time Management:
> The managing of one's time. Analysis of the operations required to create a service with the aim of increasing efficiency.

Characteristics of Successful Salespeople

Introduction

The characteristics of successful real estate salespeople can be categorized in three groups:

1. Eighty percent of real estate salespeople aren't sure they're going to make it in the business and are just "giving real estate a try." The first thing I do when I acquire an office is to interview each salesperson. I remember one particular woman who came into my office for an interview and casually plopped down in a chair. She started by exclaiming, "I've heard about you. You want people here that are serious about the real estate industry. Well, I am not sure I want to work that hard. I just want to *try* the business to see if I like it. So I don't think I will work out here." I agreed, stood up, and motioned her to the door. She looked at me like I was rude. Can you imagine talking to your new broker like that? I guess she wanted me to beg her to stay. The word "try" is not allowed in my office. The word breeds failure. When you do something, you *do it*. If you try something, you can always say, "Well, I tried it and it did not work out." Notice the blame is somewhere else. Instead, say this: "I took action, and the action I took failed." This is much better because you can always change your actions; don't blame yourself—just modify your actions. If you do the things you need to do consistently, you will not fail.

There was once a company vice president who made a mistake that cost a million dollars. When he faced the president the next day, he said, "You don't have to fire me, I will quit." The president responded,

"Fire you, heck I just gave you a million-dollar lesson!" The president knew this vice president would never make that mistake again. It is not bad to fail, but it is bad to fail and not learn from it.

If you are not sure real estate is for you, I understand. Do it right though, and give it your all. That is the only way you will really know. I have seen so many new salespeople who get into the business and wait for it to come to them. It doesn't work that way. You must get out there and work. I once worked for a real estate company where seven of the salespeople were driving brand new Cadillacs. The problem, however, was that no one in that office was making any money, and the company eventually went out of business.

2. The top 15 percent of real estate salespeople make 80 percent of the money. These salespeople are totally committed and are confident they will reach their goals. They are working and making money, but they lack the passion necessary for long-term success. They tend to burn out because they see the work as just a job, and eventually they lose their desire.

Are you a good real estate salesperson or a *great* real estate salesperson?

> The "GREAT" ones follow this formula:
>
> **G**—Get Off Your Assets and do something! Activity breeds success and doing something is always better than doing nothing.
>
> **R**—Respect. Earn respect.
>
> **E**—Ethics. Follow an ethical path.
>
> **A**—Accept the leadership role. You must be perceived as the leader.
>
> **T**—Trust. The ultimate goal is to have a trustworthy relationship.

3. The top 5 percent of real estate salespeople are highly skilled, totally committed, and have an overwhelming love for the real estate industry. These are the "winners." Here are some of the characteristics of the top 5 percent:

- They have something to prove. They want to prove they can be a success. That is why brokers are careful in firing salespeople. The person fired may become determined to prove the previous broker wrong, and that motivates him or her to succeed.

- They have an overwhelming desire to achieve, and they refuse to accept mediocrity. They will never accept second place.

- They love people and use money instead of using people and loving money.

- They operate like a business. They have a business plan even though they are salespeople. They work according to their plan and if the plan fails, they modify it until they achieve success.

- They pay attention to details, yet they don't get bogged down with small, unimportant stuff. They are organized, and they track their business numbers. Persistence is the most essential ingredient for a successful career in real estate, with organization being next. The salesperson who believes he or she can get organized later will never see later.

- They strive to keep balance in their lives, to reach goals in all areas: financial, emotional, physical, and spiritual. Take time to be at your son's ball game, at evening meals, at school events, and sometimes just hanging out. The real estate business allows you to work around your own schedule. I remember going to my daughter Brittany's school and spending the day with her. I sat in those little bitty chairs just to be by her. She would beam happiness to all the other students. It meant so much to me. No amount of money is worth what that time was to me. One of Brittany's teachers told me it was great to have me in class because so many of the children don't ever get to see their dads. Strive to keep balance because that is the only way to "true" success.

- They deliver a proven sales strategy with a non–sales-type personality. They are professional salespeople as well as ordinary people.

- They realize real estate is nothing but a big numbers game, and they must play the percentages.

- They have learned to love the word "No," and they know how to set goals. So let's learn about goals now.

Goals

A goal is defined as the purpose toward which an endeavor is directed, an objective. It is the objective that drives us to succeed. Without proper goals, we are directionless.

> *"Winning is a habit, so is losing. Which habit are you forming daily?"*
>
> —Dirk Zeller

Make a decision about what you truly want. Once you do, you can stay away from things that prevent you from setting goals. So many people don't know what they want. They meander through life and end up somewhere they never intended to be. If they had only asked themselves this question, "What do I truly want?" they could have designed their life to achieve it. If you follow your current direction, where will *you* be in a year? In five years? In ten? And is that where you really want to be? Be honest with yourself. What if you got on a ship sailing to Europe and asked the captain, "Got everything planned out to get us there?" And the captain said "Oh, no, I am just gonna head that-a-way and see where it takes us." How fast would you get off that ship? Don't run your life like that captain.

Goal setting requires five important items:

1. **The goal must be attainable and realistic.**
   If your goal is to be 7′4″ tall but you are 5′9″ and have stopped growing, you will not reach your goal. If your goal

is an annual income of $100,000 and the most you have ever made in real estate is $28,000, your goal may not be attainable. The problem is that if you have any doubts about your goal's viability, you won't work toward it. The goal will not motivate you. If you set more realistic goals and achieve them, then set a higher goal next time. On the other hand, a goal should also stretch you. Setting a goal of $28,500 for next year when you made $28,000 this year is not reaching far enough.

When Douglas MacArthur entered the U.S. Military Academy at West Point, he announced two goals: to lead his class and to one day become chief of staff. Leading his class was a short-term goal; becoming chief of staff was his ultimate vision—what he thought, at the time, would be the greatest achievement for a West Point cadet.

In his four years at West Point, MacArthur met his short-term goal by setting scholastic records. He later won fame as a front-line general in World War I, and in 1930, he met his long-term goal when President Herbert Hoover appointed him army chief of staff.

MacArthur went on to become the Supreme Allied Commander in the Southwest Pacific in World War II. He headed the occupation government in Japan and later led U.S. forces successfully against the Communists in Korea.

Set goals that stretch you, just as MacArthur did.

2. **The goal must be measurable.**
   How do you know when you have met your goal if you cannot measure it? When I ask real estate salespeople about their goals, I hear things like, "I want to be happy." How do you know you are not happy now? You may want to help the American Cancer Society (ACS) so your goal could be for every $10,000 earned you donate $100. Now your goal is to earn $10,000 so you can make your first donation.

3. **The goal must be flexible.**
   In real estate opportunities come up all the time. If it is not in your goal plan to go on a listing appointment and a seller calls you, change your plans. Do not step over a dollar to pick up a penny.

4. **The goal must have a specific time frame.**
   Goals without a specific time frame will never become more than a dream. I will have earned $100,000 through real estate sales within the next twelve months is a specific goal with a specific time frame.

5. **The goal must be in writing.**
   Your goal should not only be in writing; you need to review it at least twice a day. I always ask new recruits to show me their written goals. Time after time I get blank looks or they tell me they keep their goals in their heads. If your goals are not written down, they will stay in your head and never develop. Writing them down clarifies them and helps you commit to seeing them through.

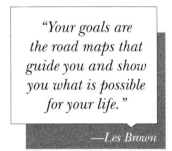

"Your goals are the road maps that guide you and show you what is possible for your life."

—Les Brown

Steps for Successful Goal Setting and Achievement

Goal setting is an extremely powerful technique for accomplishment, but effective goal setting requires more than just writing a list of dreams and filing it away. The following is a step-by-step process to develop goals.

1. **Create a well-formed goal declaration.**
   The goal declaration forms the basis for the entire goal-setting process, so pay careful attention to formulating a clear and accurate goal declaration.

The goal should be

- Specific enough so that you know exactly what you are striving for.

- Measurable so you know exactly what is to be accomplished.

- Scheduled so you know when to reach it.

- Action-oriented, declaring positive activity that will produce results.

- Realistic in that it is practical and can be achieved given a limited availability of resources.

- Tangible, meaning concrete and not vague.

The goal declaration "Increase listings 25 percent by the end of the fiscal year without increasing advertising spending" is an example that follows these rules.

2. **Break down goals into manageable steps.**
   Once you have a well-formed goal declaration, you need some direction to achieve this goal. While the goal "Increase listings 25 percent by the end of the fiscal year without increasing advertising spending" is a great goal declaration, this is a monumental task without being broken down into smaller detailed steps. The creation of goal steps gives you an action plan that when completed will lead to goal achievement. Steps also allow for tracking your progress toward the goal. Goal steps should be positive and not used to list obstacles that must be overcome. Otherwise, you may end up focusing on the negative, and negativity can kill motivation. There is power in positive thinking.

3. **Stay motivated and committed.**
   Motivation and commitment are what make us strive for achievement. They give us the push, desire, and resolve to

complete all of the other steps in the goal process. This motivation can be obtained by developing a personal statement that creates a high level of emotion and energy that guarantees achievement. Zig Ziglar says that as a child he was kicked out of his local country club pool because he was not a member. In response he made a goal of one day having a pool that is one foot bigger than that country club pool. The motivation of being asked to leave the pool provided the necessary fuel for him to achieve this goal. Commitment creates more accountability and is what sets us on a direct course to reach our goals. Failure to attain a goal may create costly negative consequences. Making a commitment is like having invested your savings in your new business. If the business fails, you will lose your savings. Motivation and commitment are specific to your situation and life, and only you can form statements that will ensure you reach your goal. I am committed to this goal of donating $100 to ACS for every $10,000 I earn because my sister died at an early age from cancer. This is a very serious, meaningful and motivating commitment statement.

4. **Set reminders and keep on track.**
   Reaching goals requires persistence and regular attention. You need some sort of system to keep you reminded and accountable. Use a combination of reminder e-mails, calendars, and reports to keep organized and on track. Sharing your goals with others who can help and support you is a highly effective way to increase your chances for success. If some accountability system is not used, then you are likely to lose sight of your goal and fail.

5. **Review and reassess frequently.**
   When you first sit down to define your goals, it can seem like a difficult task. However, over time it begins to get much easier. Patience is required. Goal setting is an ongoing process that is accomplished over time. Any goal program that defines goals and then ignores them will fail. All goals due in the next year should be reviewed weekly, if not daily. Frequent review forces you to make big decisions and determine priorities in life.

Keep an eye out for goals that are not being achieved on time or goals for which you keep extending the deadline.

Additional Goal-Setting Tips

- Determine the value of your time. How much are you actually worth to your clients? Anyone can make more money if he or she trades more time for it. Calculate your net earnings for the past year and divide that by the number of hours you worked. Be sure to add in all the time you spent driving around and doing odd jobs. You may be shocked at how low your "hourly wage" is.

- Develop a philosophy. Set guidelines for doing business and clearly define your world of business. For example, determine the type of sellers and buyers you want to work with, including their price ranges. When a buyer or seller is out of step with your philosophy, refer him or her to somebody else. However, before you profile a customer, do so only as a marketing technique; be sure that you are in compliance with Fair Housing law, which prohibits target marketing based on race, color, religion, sex, handicap, familial status, or national origin.

- Don't hurt your chances for success because of the little things, such as how you dress.

Dress for Success

It is said that you should dress so as not to be noticed. Perhaps a better way to say that is do not let your clothes speak for you. You have heard "Dress to Impress," but be wise: What you perceive as impressive may not be impressive to your customer. I've always worn ties to work. But when I purchased a real estate office outside of the city, all of the real estate salespeople in that office begged me not to wear a tie. It made them feel uncomfortable.

What you like might not be what someone else likes. Don't wear a $600 pair of dress shoes to show a cow pasture. Don't let your perfume arrive before you do. Don't let your hairstyle give the impression that you are a freak. Consider the following two points:

> **You only have four seconds to set a good impression.**
>
> **The customer is always right.**

I can remember a time when I went up against another real estate salesperson on a listing appointment. The other salesperson had already had their time with the seller, and now it was my turn. I covered my services and explained why this seller (single male) should list with me. When I was finished, I looked at the seller and said, "Put me to work for you." The seller agreed. After he signed the listing agreement, I asked why he decided to list with me and not the other salesperson. He told me that the other salesperson looked like the devil, and he didn't trust him. The seller was right; he did look like the devil. He had a flat top haircut that wasn't that flat because it stood up on the sides (looked like devil horns), and he had a scruffy goatee. The other salesperson asked me why I got the listing over him, so I told him. He did not like what I had to say. He said, "The way I look is up to me." That may be true, but it was costing him a lot of money. For the next several months, this salesperson struggled financially. He finally shaved his beard and restyled his hair. He is now one of the top producers in the area. Is your appearance costing you money? When you are at home, dress for home; but when you are working, dress for work. I have seen real estate salespeople show up at work in shorts and ratty t-shirts. They usually explain that they aren't really working; they just needed to do something on the computer. They don't consider that the rest of staff there is working, and there are clients are in the office. It's important to have respect for those around you at all times.

Dressing for success includes dressing in career apparel. Career apparel can be as simple as wearing a nametag to dressing in embroidered shirts and jackets. You should never be a "secret agent." Secret agents are real estate agents dressed in such good disguises that no one would know they sell real estate. Wear your nametag everywhere. I was once paying for groceries and a manager walked up to me and asked me if I sold real estate. I said, "I sure do." You never know when a small thing may lead to big results.

Drive for Success

Driving for success does not mean driving the latest, biggest, most expensive car on the road. It does mean keeping what you have in the best condition. Keep the exterior of your car clean and waxed and the interior vacuumed and neat. Fix minor dings or nicks. If your car is not brand-new, understand that people don't care what you drive as long as they know you care. When I first entered the real estate business, I drove an old beat-up, two-door Mustang. I loved the car and I kept that car clean and neat, but it wasn't the best car for real estate. Let me tell one story about that Mustang. I remember going to a particular listing appointment and parking down the street so that the seller would not see my car. When I was finished with my listing presentation, I asked the seller to list with me, and the seller agreed. Out of curiosity, I asked the seller why he listed with me and not my competition. The seller told me that the first salesperson he spoke with arrived in a brand-new Cadillac and proceeded to tell the seller what to do. The second one was driving a brand-new Lincoln Continental and also told the seller what to do. I drove up in a beat-up Mustang and parked it down the street. The seller said, "I saw you park down the street in that *car* and figured you must be hungry!" I don't believe the Mustang got me that listing; I got it because out of all three real estate salespersons, I was the only one who took the time with the seller and showed him I cared. But the Mustang did not eliminate me either. I now drive a better car, by choice, because I have earned it. Don't sweat the small stuff. If you want a newer or better car, then budget for it and when you have earned it, buy it.

Read for Success

It is amazing to me the number of people who never read. Reading is how you stay informed and current. It helps you start conversations and keeps you relevant. You should read at least two books per month to stay ahead of the game. You should also read as many real estate trade publications you can get your hands on every month. However, do not read during hours when you should be making money; set aside time at night or during off hours to read. For example, I do a lot of my reading when I am on the stationary bike. Regardless, do not take this advice lightly; your competition is reading and will leave you behind.

Listen for Success

It is said that you can get the equivalent of a college education in ten years by listening to educational material in your car and I firmly believe this. By taking advantage of the time I have spent in my car over the years, I am now comfortable with the sales and objection-handling techniques that I have learned from listening to such material. I see other real estate salespeople in their cars, singing along to their favorite songs, but then in sales situations they do not know what to say. You may know all the words to your favorite songs, but is anyone paying you to memorize those lyrics? How much more valuable would it be to learn how to further your career than to be able to sing to every song that you hear on the radio?

Seminars and Classes

The real estate industry offers numerous seminars and classes that deal with real estate and making money. A seminar is made up of a small group of students in study under the guidance of a professor or leader for the purpose of exchanging ideas. You should take advantage of as many of these as you can, as long as they are worthwhile and don't infringe on hours when you should be making money. Be smart and selective. Seminars tend to fire you up and get you on the right course. Real estate classes will give you added insight into the real estate industry. Most of the seminars are free because the speakers are trying to sell you their products. The only question is, should you buy the material? The answer depends on you. Will you use it? If not, don't waste your money on something that will only gather dust.

Conventions

A convention is a formal meeting of members of an industry. Real estate conventions are events where real estate salespeople get together to share, learn, and receive awards. Most large real estate organizations, such as the National Association of REALTORS®, have annual conventions. They are generally in different locations. These meetings are rewarding and valuable if you go to develop referrals. There is no better place to ask for referral business than at a convention. One real estate salesperson from California may meet a real estate salesperson from New York. Now they can pass referrals back and forth. If you do go, do so with the right attitude, press some palms, ask for referrals, and learn something new. This will make going worth it.

Ask Questions

The best way to receive knowledge is to ask questions. Too many people are afraid to ask questions because they do not want to look dumb. It is even more dumb not to ask. If someone does not want to help you, you do not want to learn from that person anyway.

Safety in Real Estate

The real estate profession is quite safe. As is true in any profession, bad things can happen and risks exist; however, such things rarely occur in the real estate profession. It is more likely that an individual will be mugged while shopping in a mall than while selling real estate. However, it has happened, and efforts should be taken to prevent any such instances.

The salesperson should never be left alone with a client, especially at the first meeting. This seems logical but is quite often overlooked. Consider this example. A salesperson takes a call from a buyer in the office; the conversation goes as follows:

Buyer:
"I would like you to meet me at the vacant house on Elm Street."

Salesperson:
"Sure, I'd love to!"

Almost every salesperson makes this mistake, and it opens the door for trouble. While we will learn more about the proper way to answer the office phone and how to handle calls like the above later in the book, let's go ahead and briefly review some techniques now. First of all, never agree to meet a buyer client, especially someone you have never met, by yourself. Seller clients don't present the same risk; the salesperson will go to their home, and the chances of anything bad happening are greatly reduced because of this. Trouble tends to occur out of the view of others; those who want to cause trouble do not want to be seen. Therefore, the salesperson should always try to arrange a meeting with the buyer at the real estate office. If the buyer is not local, the salesperson should meet him or her in a public place, such as a restaurant, before showing the property. If the buyer is reluctant to meet in a public place, this is a red flag. It only takes one time for the unthinkable to happen, and no sale is worth risking your safety.

Some offices recommend making a copy of a buyer's driver's license. This is probably a smart thing to do; however, if this is done, it MUST be done for ALL buyers. Otherwise you risk violating Fair Housing laws.

Here are some other tips for safety's sake:

- Keep your car's gas tank at least half full.

- Have your mobile phone with you at all times.

- Notify others of your whereabouts.

- Dress with personal safety in mind.

Business Plan

The professional real estate salesperson should have a detailed business plan for a real estate career. By definition, a business plan is a proposal requiring concerted effort. A well-written plan establishes goals and outlines how to accomplish them. You should be able to use your plan to track your progress and determine whether or not things are on track. The plan can then be broken down into yearly, monthly, and daily events. Each event should lead you closer to your goals.

Each daily event should be put into a daily planner or calendar, an essential tool that you should use, update, and refer to on a continual basis. Consider using your mobile phone's planner; you will always have it with you, and you can sync your planner with other calendars so your assistant will know your schedule.

Financial Planning

The real estate business is tough unless you have taken time to do some type of financial planning. A financial plan is the management of money, banking, investments, and credit. The average real estate salesperson receives large sums of money at different times per month. This makes any planning difficult.

Your plan should include a budget and some type of investment portfolio. It should also allow you to track statistics and do tax planning. All of these are addressed in the following sections.

Budget

Real estate salespeople must have a budget, or they will find themselves frequently without money. A budget is an itemized summary of estimated expenditures for a given period. I suggest that you place all of the money you earn from real estate into an account and then pay yourself a regular fixed salary out of that account. If you have money left after you withdraw your salary, you should invest

Some real estate salespeople will receive a commission check for several thousand dollars and use that money for a down payment on a car. This creates two problems: First, a new car payment increases your monthly expenses, and second, all of the commission is used up in one transaction.

The fluctuation in income is what I call the rollercoaster effect of real estate. One minute you are making money, and the next minute you are broke and have no listings. The only way to level out the income stream is to budget, and all money should go into that budget. I have seen a multitude of good real estate salespeople quit because they didn't have the discipline to budget their income.

How To Set Up a Personal Budget

- Start with a budget worksheet. There are a hundreds of budgeting apps for your smart phone and your computer. Look for one you understand and will use. Some of the apps take way too much time to learn and can be cumbersome to use. Budgeting should not be a hassle and if it is, you will never do it.

- Review your expenses from the last two to three months. Add and delete categories from the worksheet or app to fit your expenditures.

- Think about your hobbies, entertainment, and habits. Be sure to add categories for these expenses.

- Go through your pay stubs and bank deposits to calculate your average monthly gross pay.

- Add in any interest income, dividends, bonuses, or other miscellaneous income.

- For each expense category, determine a budget amount that realistically reflects your actual expenses while setting targeted spending levels that will enable you to save money.

- Once you're comfortable with your expense categories and budgeted amounts, enter expenditures from the last month.

- Track your cash expenditures throughout the month; total and categorize these at the end of each month.

- Subtotal the income and expense categories.

- Subtract the total expenses from the total income to arrive at your net income.

- If your expenses are greater than your income, your net income number will be negative. You will need to work on changing your spending habits in order to improve your financial situation.

- If you have a positive net income, transfer most of it to a savings or investment account at the end of each month. Extra cash left in a regular banking account has a way of getting spent.

- After you've tracked your actual spending for a month or two, analyze the results to identify where you can comfortably make cuts.

- Once the budgeting process is in place, take an in-depth look at your largest spending categories, brainstorm about ways to reduce spending in specific categories, and set realistic goals.

- Update your budget and expenses monthly.

Budgeting Tips

- Don't try to fit your expenses into somebody else's budget categories. Tailor the categories to fit your own situation.

- Make your categories detailed enough to provide useful information, but not so detailed that you become bogged down in minutia.

- Think of your budget as a tool to help you get out of debt and save money, not as a financial diet.

Tracking

Real estate salespeople should track their statistics to determine their current status. The items that should be tracked include:

- **Number of sales**—Are you increasing the number of people you are helping?

- **Dollar amount per sale**—Are you increasing your average sale? The higher the price range, the more money you make.

- **Time on the market**—How long does it take for you to sell a listing? What can you do to sell the properties faster?

- **Number of appointments per week**—How many face-to-face appointments do you have per week? How can you get more?

- **Number of prospecting contacts per week**—How can you get more?

- **Ratio of appointments to sellers (buyers)**—How many sellers (buyers) are you getting from your appointments? How can you improve that ratio?

- **Ratio of sellers (buyers) to solds**—How many of your sellers (buyers) are actually selling (buying)? How can you improve that ratio?

- **Ratio of number of hours spent in the business to your income**—How many hours does it take to make money? How can you improve that ratio?

- **Number of outgoing referrals sent to real estate salespeople in other areas of the country**—How many referrals do you send? How can you improve that number?

These statistics will show you where you stand in the real estate business and the areas in which you need to improve.

Taxes

This is a tough subject, but if you do not pay your taxes, the IRS gets really mad. One of the drawbacks of the real estate industry is that taxes are not normally withheld from commission paychecks. This means that you are responsible for paying taxes to the IRS on any money you make that year, which can be a substantial sum (actually you must pay quarterly to avoid a penalty). The best advice I can give you is to set up an account specifically earmarked for taxes and then deposit from each commission check the appropriate percentage to cover your taxes for that check. It is important that you keep this money separate and use it only to pay taxes. All other information on taxes should be attained from a tax authority.

Investing

Investing is committing money or capital to gain a financial return. Just the mention of the term "investing" strikes fear into the average person because people associate investments with risk. Most people do not like to take risks. However, to be a profitable investor, you must assume some risk. Each investment has a relationship between the risk and the return, so you will need to determine your risk tolerance.

The key to any successful investment is time. The more lead-time on an investment, the more money it will likely make. If you wait to invest until you need money, it will be too late. As mentioned earlier, paying yourself first means setting aside an amount for investments before paying your bills. Things might be tight at first, but eventually, you will have your bills paid off, and in the years to come, you will find that you are financially secure.

Savings

Saving is not really investing; it is providing a safety net. You should have enough in your savings account to cover your living expenses for six months. Invest this "safety" money in a secure mutual fund and don't touch it.

Stock Market

Many fortunes have been made and lost in the stock market. You should invest in companies you believe have a marketable product or service. As the company you invest in does better, you do better. The two main ways to make money in the stock market are by capital appreciation (the stock value goes up) and income (through dividends or sharing of the profit with investors). The drawback of the stock market is the time it takes to really follow the market—the time it takes to study trends, information, terminology, and the actual trading action. You can hire a professional investor, but the expense will limit your profit. In addition, you have no control in the company you're investing in. The company may look good on the outside, but on the inside, the managers may be embezzling money. If the company goes bankrupt, you'll lose your investment.

Real Estate

Real estate has consistently been the best investment in the long run. Everyone wants real estate. I have always said you can make a very good living selling real estate; you can also become wealthy investing in real estate. The two main ways to invest in real estate are capital appreciation (the investment property is worth more than you paid and every month you pay down on the note, assuming you are amortizing your note) and income (the investment property with positive cash flow). You can invest in residential real estate, commercial, industrial, agricultural, or any number of other types of real estate. The most popular way to invest is to buy an undervalued, small, single-family property that is in need of repair. Buy it, fix it up, and sell it for a profit. Some investors buy property and rent it for income and long-term capital appreciation. The reason I like real estate investing better than the stock market is because I have control. I get to make the decision on which property to buy and when to sell. I don't have to trust others with my nest egg.

Retirement

The real estate industry typically does not provide any retirement, so it is important that you do this on your own. There is nothing worse than having to stay in a job or profession you don't enjoy simply because you failed to invest in your future.

Personal Assistant

Investing in a personal assistant is very wise and essential for reaching your full potential. An assistant can help you with everyday office work and miscellaneous tasks, such as marketing, promotions, and follow-up. Paying someone $10 per hour to take on these important but time-consuming responsibilities will give you more time to spend on sales prospects. Depending on the type of work you expect from your assistant, he or she may need to be licensed, and you should check with your state for guidelines. However, don't hire an assistant so that you can goof off. Having an assistant only makes sense if you are putting that time gained to use out in the field. Keep in mind: If you don't have an assistant, you are an assistant.

Time Management

Have you ever had too many things to do and no time to do them? If so, you may have a time-management problem. Time management is the managing of one's time. It has also been defined as the analysis of the operations required to create a service with the aim of increasing efficiency. Time management can be misconstrued to be cumbersome, but it should not be. Time management is doing what you are currently doing but doing it better.

How you allocate your time is completely up to you. It is not something your broker, spouse, significant other, or especially your clients decide for you. Too many times in the real estate business, a client needs us immediately, or at least they believe they do. In turn, we jump. We drop whatever important business we are doing to meet them, show them a property, or straighten a crooked yard sign. Don't take this the wrong way; I am not suggesting you ignore your clients. However, I am saying that you need to be the one who controls your time. Imagine you are planning to fly to Vegas. You want to leave at 3:00 p.m. today, so you call the airlines and request that the airplane be fueled and ready for take-off at exactly 3:00 p.m. The customer service representative informs you that the next flight is not scheduled for departure until 5:15 p.m. What do you think your chances are of convincing the airline to change its schedule? Pretty slim, right? And why is that? It is because this is a *professional* airline you are dealing with. We call ourselves professional, yet we are quick to change our schedule and meet a client on command. What are we saying to the client? "Call me anytime, I have nothing to do."

Time Planning

The first step to planning your day is to determine what you need to accomplish and then put those items on a list. Next you must set priorities and stick to them; put your most important task first (and make sure that is the first thing you do before anything else on your list). Then move on to the next important, and so on.

The to-do list should be written and flexible, yet thorough. If you can get several items on the list done in one day, determine which item is your least favorite or most difficult. Perform that task first or during the time of day when you are most productive. For example, if you have a closing coming up, you should have a checklist to make sure you accomplish everything necessary. The checklist will include items on it that are fun and easy to do and things that are difficult to do. Don't put off the difficult things till the end; tackle those upfront and then you can enjoy doing the fun things after the hard part is done.

Here are some additional time-management hints:

- Create a time log (task analysis). Go through your day, hour by hour, and document everything you do. Don't put it off till the end of the day; you will forget small items that may be big time wasters.

- Review the time log and determine which processes and/or services can be streamlined or eliminated without affecting your bottom line.

- Implement new ideas and services that will help reduce the amount of time you spend on each client. [For example, a new computer software program can help you complete a CMA faster.]

- Determine tasks that, at a reasonable cost, can be delegated to the homeowner, lender, title company, or the other agent.

- Schedule your days, weeks, and months, and then stick to your schedule.

- Separate personal and professional time. Work at work and play at play.

    Waste time honestly. In all the offices I've worked in, there have been "nesters." These are real estate salespeople who have built themselves a nice "nest" at their desk. They have family pictures, old sales awards, novelty items, and the like. They are comfortable at their desks and wouldn't leave for anything, including a prospect. They now are wasting time. They could sit for hours remembering the "good ol' days." If you're going to waste time, don't act like you're working, waste it honestly. Go to your car and just sit. Stay there until you realize you are wasting time. You may get some strange looks when you come back in the office, but at least you are wasting time honestly. Now get back to "real" work. I might not sit in my car (especially in Texas in August), but I have left the office for a while to get my head straight.

- Sometimes the business has to wait. A family commitment should not be interrupted by business. Tell the potential client that you have appointment prior commitment that cannot be broken, even if that commitment is your child's soccer game. Most clients will reschedule. If they refuse, question whether they are the type of people you want to work with and consider referring them to another real estate salesperson who would accommodate them.

- Sometimes the family has to wait. If you have already made an important appointment with a client, your family may have to wait.

- Get help if you need it. Talk to your broker, title company, or your real estate commission when you need help.

- Establish family goals. Be careful here though. I once decided to involve my family when setting a financial goal for myself. I asked Brittany (my daughter who was 5 or 6 at the time) what she wanted if I accomplished my goal. Without hesitation she said she wanted to go to Disney World. I said, "Okay!" Well, a few weeks went by, and I came home exhausted one night after working late. When I walked in the house, Brittany demanded that I go back out and work because she wanted to go to Disney World!

- Do things you hate most early in the morning. It makes the rest of the day better.

- Use a communication log for your client files. Record your calls, texts, and emails by making a notes and placing them in the files. You could even make notes right on a file's inside cover. I know a real estate salesperson who does this. She records the date and anything that she and her client discuss, no matter how trivial the communication. Once, she was involved in a lawsuit with a former client who accused her of saying things she did not say. Because she had recorded in writing all of her conversations with that client (and she was able to prove that this was her standard operating procedure with all clients) and her client had no such recordings, the suit was dropped.

- Set aside some alone time. Work only five and a half days per week. This will lessen the chance of burnout. If all you do is work, then you are sending a signal that you cannot complete the work you need to in the time given.

- As mentioned earlier, if you don't have an assistant, you are an assistant! If you cannot afford an assistant, perhaps you can share time with another real estate salesperson who also needs an assistant. You can also hire a temporary assistant.

- Handle paperwork only once. Do it, delay it or discard it. It is easy to become a pack rat in the real estate industry. I once bought a real estate company and after the transaction closed, I began to "explore" my purchase. In the attic I found boxes of real estate files dating back 15 years. There were so many boxes I think they might have been weighing down the support structure of the building. I began shredding the information and placed the boxes outside to be picked up on trash day. My salespeople expressed concern that those files might be important someday, even though they hadn't been used or opened in over 10 years. So I told them, "Great, you can take home as many boxes as you want, but they must be taken home." No one took any boxes. They were fine with cluttering up the office, but not their homes.

- Look for good mortgage and title companies, and then let them do their jobs. Make sure they know your expectations of them from the beginning:

    – Have them pick up contracts.

    – Don't courier papers for them.

    – Give them contact numbers for everyone involved in the process.

- Give the title company complete papers, including the listing agreement.

- Use the Internet and e-mail for negotiating and prospecting.

- If you must do busy work, combine the activities.

  - Put up a sign, riders, flyer tube, and a lockbox at the same time. Keep one of each item in your car if you are allowed.

  - Do some prospecting while cleaning your car and filling it up with gas.

- Start the day early.

- Always have an educational book in your car to read if something comes up and you have to wait.

- Pay someone to do for you the things that are not enjoyable and take up your personal time, such as mowing the grass, washing the car, or cleaning the house. Some people like doing yard work. It is a form of relaxation. For me it is unnecessary work, and I delegate it to others.

- Learn to say "No." We want to be nice, so we say "yes" to things we do not have time to do. This puts us under more time pressure and can lead to burnout.

  - Refuse to do the other agent's jobs.

  - Delegate meeting with inspectors and appraisers to someone else, such as your assistant. You are not required to meet with them.

- Promise a little, deliver a lot. It is a simple time-management philosophy.

- At the end of each day, review what happened that day. Then look to tomorrow and plan what should be done. I call this review/preview. Review the day by writing down all of your thoughts about the day's business. This is your business journal. Include things like a conversation with a potential client. How did it go? How did you happen to meet this potential client, etc.? Do not include things such as Mary making you mad because she took the last jelly donut at the morning office meeting. Then preview what things need to be done tomorrow and itemize and prioritize the list.

Allocating Time to Build Your Business

To find the number of hours you have available for building your business:

_____ Hours sleeping

_____ Hours with family and friends

_____ Hours eating

_____ Hours driving

Total time _____ Hours committed to personal life

Subtract

from 24 _____ Hours available for work

Divide

by 2 _____ Hours for building your business

Why is time planning important? Time is money. Time planning prevents future problems.

Twelve Words to Live By:

I must do the most productive thing possible at every given moment.

Create the following "tickler files" on your computer for both buyers and sellers:

1. **For Sale By Owner (FSBO) or Specialized Area Leads**—Whether you specialize in FSBOs, expired listings, certain types of professions, and so on, keep contact names in your database.

2. **General Database File**—Use this file to store information on everyone you know, including friends, relatives, and social contacts—constantly update it when you meet new people.

3. **Past Buyers and Sellers**—Keep in touch with all your previous clients. Then, when they have real estate needs, you'll be the one they think of. You'll build repeat business this way. If you keep thorough records on previous transactions, you'll be prepared to handle their needs efficiently at any time.

4. **Expense File and Tax Records**—Keep all receipts and business expenses. All of these files should be on your computer in an information management software system. If you don't have one, budget to get one.

Invest time in high-payoff activities. How much is your time worth? Once you know this, make sure you're investing your time wisely. Decide what activities give you the highest payoff in your business, and then have the self-discipline to focus on these activities every day. Ask yourself if you are doing the most important thing you can at any given moment. If your answer is no, then stop doing what you're doing and do what is most important. Identify your top three income-producing activities and how you spend your time each day. Then shift your resources to where you get the highest return. As a salesperson, your job is to outthink your competition. Then outwork them, if you desire.

Qualify the potential client. This is crucial to success. The goal in qualifying is to eliminate customers who aren't truly motivated. They will waste your time and eventually drive you out of business, both emotionally and financially.

Create strong systems and delegate. Develop systems that create the results you desire without your involvement. You need systems for listings, escrows, buyers, sellers, leads, other agents, presentations, negotiating, and following up on leads.

Chapter Summary

If it is your goal to be successful in the real estate business, you first need to determine your definition of success. One person may want to be the top producer of the world; another may want less in money but more in time with his or her family. Both goals are possible in the real estate industry if you act professional and are determined.

Time management allows you to solve your problems more efficiently and can be a huge stress reducer. Daily planners will help guide you in setting and keeping a schedule that is doable. Listing and prioritizing your tasks for the day will also help.

Summary Questions

1. How many days should you work per week?
   a. 8
   b. 5 1/2
   c. 3
   d. 5

2. What is "nesting"?
   a. When agents keep personal items, books, and files all around them, and spend the day at their desk instead of leaving the office to go prospecting.
   b. The actual day a buyer moves into his or her new "nest."
   c. A type of knitting that agents give to buyers as house warming gifts.
   d. When an agent gets listings only from friends and family.

3. Goals must be
   a. attainable and realistic.
   b. completed within six months.
   c. rigid.
   d. oral.

4. Which of the following is a characteristic of the top 5 percent of professional real estate salespeople?
   a. Loves people and uses money
   b. Chooses work over family
   c. Overspends to create motivation
   d. Loves money and uses people

5. Choose the best "dress for success" statement:
   a. Do not have your hair in spikes longer than six inches.
   b. When the paint on the wall curls up, it is time to take a shower.
   c. Picking your nose is a good "ice breaker."
   d. Do not allow your appearance to speak for you.

6. Persistence is the most essential ingredient for a successful career in real estate. What is the next most important ingredient?
   a. Financial resources
   b. People skills
   c. Organizational skills
   d. Passion for showing houses

7. Which of the following is a simple time-management philosophy?
   a. Do everyone else's work and they will owe you later.
   b. Sleep late, go to bed early.
   c. Do personal work at the office.
   d. Promise a little, deliver a lot.

8. What should you do to avoid being a "secret agent"?
   a. Don't be seen at the office.
   b. Wear a nametag.
   c. Make calls from your home.
   d. Take a place of service with your local association of REALTORS®.

9. What determines how successful you will become?
   a. The car you drive
   b. The clothes you wear
   c. The way you sell yourself
   d. The friends you have in the business

10. Which of the following investments give you the most control?
    a. Real estate
    b. Stock Market
    c. Savings
    d. Precious metals

Chapter 3

Technology for
The Real Estate Professional

Chapter Overview

This chapter covers the effects of technology on real estate. It includes information on smartphones, personal computers, laptop computers virtual tours, handheld computers, contact management, websites, and digital cameras. Other information covered includes using email as a marketing tool and using the Internet to increase your income.

Key Terms

Social Media:
Social media is the social interaction among people in which they create, share, or exchange information and ideas in virtual communities, websites, applications and networks.

Database:
A database is an organized collection of data that enables the user to analyze and perform functions with the data.

Application:
An application is a software program that carries out a set of instructions.

Merge Code:
A merge code is a special instruction inserted into a document that brings into the document information from a particular field in each record selected for the mailing or e-mail.

Tablet:
A tablet is a mobile computer with features such as cameras, microphones, and touchscreen.

Spam:
Spam is the use of e-mail to send unsolicited messages.

Introduction

Technology can help you do your business better, faster, and more efficiently. Technology feeds the constant demand for more and meaningful information. The technology field is constantly changing and as a professional real estate salesperson, you should be able to keep up with it; otherwise, you may be left behind.

Social Networking (Social Media)

Social media is the social interaction among people in which they create, share, or exchange information and ideas in virtual communities, websites, applications, and networks. Social media can allow you to connect with your friends, family, friends of all of your friends, and even your real estate clients. Social media can build trust and knowledge in your career. Social media can even help your business through word-of-mouth marketing, but this must be achieved through others. However, social media cannot in itself make you money.

Facebook

Facebook is probably the best place to start with social networking. It is free for personal use, easy to use, and a popular way to get in touch with old friends and make new ones.

To begin using Facebook in your real estate career, you should set up a Facebook page separate from your personal account, as using your personal account for business lacks professionalism. If you have never used Facebook at all, you will need to set up a personal account first and then set up your real estate Facebook page. Once you have your page established, you need to make it fun and exciting.

Don't just talk about new listings and how well you are doing; you will lose followers that way. Instead, post interesting things about your neighborhood or maybe your marketing area. You could post information about events in the community or the benefits of living in your market area. If your area is holding a food drive, make sure you post that information. Post pictures of the local fireworks show and the local high school football team. Just be cautious of only showing things about real estate; that is the fastest way to be unfriended. Be imaginative and never violate the social media rule of 80/20: 80 percent of the content on your personal page should be about things of interest to all people and 20 percent can be real-estate related. Any more, and bye, bye friend. Whatever you do, don't ask for business on your page—that will come with patience.

My wife posts things on her personal page that she finds humorous. She posted a picture of a house that had been spray painted. She posted a picture of a square hole in the floor of a master bedroom (people enjoyed speculating what the hole was used for). She posted a picture of a house where each room was a different color (including the carpet). Because she has made this fun, she gets lots of comments and "likes." Find something that people will want to see, and your name will be in front of them—that's the goal of social networking.

Facebook allows all types of media, so mix it up by adding content through pictures and videos on both your personal and business pages. See how many people you can get to repost what is on your page. If you are going to show a new listing, do it as a contest. Offer a simple prize for the person who can most closely guess the actual selling price once the house closes. You may get a group of followers from the contestants hoping to win. Everyone loves to win!

LinkedIn

You should set up a LinkedIn account if you do not have one. LinkedIn connects business people with business people. Suppose I needed a car repair. I could go on LinkedIn and find a person whom several of my LinkedIn friends have recommended. Make sure your

LinkedIn business page contains all your contact information and that the information is current and correct. Then start connecting with your friends, family, and clients. You can even ask for referrals through the site.

Twitter

Twitter is a challenge because your tweet must be 140 characters (or less). However, Twitter can engage your followers and strengthen your relationships. You should have a Twitter account if nothing more than to understand it better. Some people are on Twitter all day long.

You could tweet interesting tidbits from your local area. Post questions to your followers, such as "What is the most stressful thing about moving?" And then add hashtags (#) for answers. Hashtags get your tweets seen by more than just your followers. Use relevant and specific hashtags to get found by those looking for your subject matter. You can dream up any question as long as it is controversial or thought provoking.

Always tweet when you are participating in charity events. This shows you are involved in the community and you believe in giving back. Many people consider the level of involvement a real estate salesperson has in the community when deciding who to use when buying and/or selling a home.

You can send tweets to specific people as well. Consider sending a tweet to congratulate someone who just received a promotion or to thank someone for helping you. This personal touch can be incredibly powerful.

Instagram

Instagram is a quick and easy way to share photos of your life with friends and business associates. It requires a simple download and is free to use. With this app you can take a picture of something you are enjoying, such as an event, a food, or simply a friend, and then quickly share that photo or video with your friends. You can even choose a filter to modify the picture to show it in its best light. The app allows you to take and send pictures as they are happening.

Instagram allows users to share posts on a variety of social-networking platforms, such as Facebook, Twitter, Tumblr, and Flickr. Instagram does have a couple restrictions: Photos are confined to a square shape, and the maximum duration for Instagram videos is 15 seconds.

Instagram gives real estate professionals the opportunity to take photos related to their profession, add a caption, and involve their friends, family, and business contacts in their career.

Tumblr

With Tumblr, you can post text, photos, quotes, links, music, and videos from your smart phone, desktop, email, or wherever you happen to be. Tumblr allows others to view your posts and then share your content with others.

Flickr

Flickr is the third most popular photo-sharing app, and each has their own viewers and ways to share photos. Most good apps have the ability to share with other apps so that an individual does not need to post on each.

YouTube

YouTube gives you the opportunity to make videos of what you do and share them with others. You don't need a lot of expensive video equipment or a studio to make a video. All you need is a simple digital video camera, and you are in business. Most smartphones can take digital videos. You could make videos of all of your listings to serve as virtual tours. You could make videos of helpful real estate hints, post them on social media sites, and include them on your personal website. If you produce meaningful, interesting videos, people will seek you out and suddenly you are the real estate expert. Everyone wants to do business with the real estate expert.

Personal Website

Personal websites promote the real estate salesperson and not his or her office. Should a real estate professional have a website? The answer is yes, but it should not be used for marketing or sales. To be honest, the main reason to have a website is to make sure you appear current and relevant. Don't spend a ton of money or time building your website or expect it to be a moneymaker. As of the date of this printing, there are 593 million sites that relate to real estate. If your site is number 265,982,243, what are the chances that a new prospect will see it?

Develop your website to be useful and informative, and then "personally" drive people to it. The URL for your site should be on every piece of marketing material you develop, and you should encourage people to view the site for more information about your listings and specific services you offer. You can even set up an area that is specific to each client with a passcode for correspondence about their specific sale.

It is most important that the site be simple and easy to navigate. Do not get carried away with all the bells and whistles—those are expensive and don't add anything but confusion to your site.

Blog

Blogs are a great way to demonstrate your knowledge and expertise about the real estate profession. You can use blogs to post news about the local market, interest rates, or trends in the industry. Blogs allow you to post more information than other media types.

Database

A database is an organized collection of data that enables the user to analyze and perform functions with the data. A database is the best way to keep up with your prospect leads. The best type of database is a contact manager software program designed to store all the information about your clients, your current listings, and sales. The contact manager also makes it easy for you to retrieve and manipulate all of this information and to do mail-outs to your entire client base.

> *"Past Trend: More and more mail-outs and see what sticks."*
>
> *"Future Trend: Less number of contacts, more often."*
>
> —*Rolf Anderson, National Real Estate Speaker*

As far as a time saver, a database is a must. It allows you to input timestamps on leads, which will notify you when to call a client. Further, you can make call notes that become a permanent part of that person's record. This is extremely valuable if there is a conflict at some point. You can input duties to be performed on your listings and closings and have each item on the list automatically appear on your daily calendar. You can have the contact manager notify you of reminders such as when it's time to install a sign or a lock box or to send mail-outs.

You can also use the database to target buyers or sellers. For example, you can select a group of people who might be interested in a particular new listing, then call or email them with a picture of the listing. The contact manager can also prepare a variety of reports, including contact, listing, and closing reports, which will come in handy during tax time.

Be careful about letting others manage your client base, though; this is your career.

Database Records

Information is stored in your contact manager database through the use of data records. Each record contains individual fields or input areas that contain specific information related to a person or property. You can search the database using a person's first name, property address, number of bedrooms, or any criteria you have entered into a field and instantly find information based on what you have entered.

The ability to search your database will help you market more directly. Say you find an article about area grade schools; you can search the database for potential buyers with children and email them the article.

While talking to someone on the phone, if you hear a dog bark, ask for the dog's name and enter it into your database. The next time you talk to that person, you can ask about the dog. Follow the same procedure if, for example, the caller says she has to hang up to get to her daughter's soccer game. Record the information in your database for future use. Most contact managers allow you to assign a contact type or category to your records. The contact type is your connection to that person or some way to identify the contact. You can enter how you came in contact with the person, such as call-in-buyer, referral, or For Sale by Owner, or according to hobbies, employment, or address. If you take a new listing, you can email it to all of your clients you think might be interested (buyer type). Once you create the group in the database, you can work with just that group.

Applications (apps) for your smartphone or tablet abound for this type of contact management. An application is a software program that carries out a set of instructions. Each one of these apps specializes in different areas, so choose the one that best fits your style of business. We could analyze these apps, but they change daily and the Internet continually updates the latest application trends.

Personalized Mailings

Using your real estate contact manager program gives your mass mailings and emails a greater impact than other types of communication. With the contact manager you can use the "merge codes" to personalize each of the letters, cards, or emails you send to a group. A merge code is a special instruction inserted into a document that brings into the document information from a particular field in each record selected for the mailing or email. For example:

> Dear <First Name>:
>
> **Just wanted to thank you for being a client of mine and remind you that tax season is approaching. If you need help filing for your homestead tax exemptions, please let me know.**

All of the finished letters will have the first name from your chosen database field in the proper place.

Reminders

Another fun feature of contact management software is the ability to set reminders for specific events. You can set a reminder for a client's birthday, anniversary of a home sale, or any other important date. If you send a birthday card, use this script in the body of the card:

> *"You're not getting older, you're building equity!!!"*

A good way to learn someone's birthday is to ask, "What month and day were you born?" Ask slowly, and never ask for the year. People will respond to you much better than if you simply ask for their birth date. You can set the reminder to alert you on an annual basis. (Smart real estate salespersons can also use this function to remind them of their *OWN* wedding anniversary.)

Notes

An interactive contact manager allows you to take notes regarding a person, listing, or closing and to attach the notes as a permanent part of the individual's record. You can print these notes at any time. These notes form an important part of your business "paper trail" for each transaction.

Reports

The contact manager software can produce a variety of reports for your use. You can print the latest activity for a listing and mail it to the seller as a progress report. You can print a report detailing the year's expenses for tax purposes. Several reports are generic to most software. Some software programs will allow you to integrate the local MLS data for custom listing presentation reports.

Computers

When you mention the word "technology," most people think about computers. Virtually every facet of our lives has some computerized component. The appliances in our homes have microprocessors built into them, as do our televisions. Even our cars have computers. But the computer that everyone thinks of first is typically the personal computer (PC).

Personal Computers

A PC is a general-purpose tool built around a microprocessor. It has lots of different parts, such as memory, a hard disk, and a modem, that work together. "General purpose" means you can do many different things with a PC. You can use it to type documents, send email, browse the Web, and play games.

How Computers Help in Real Estate

Your computer allows you access to email and to get the word out to the folks who count! Ten percent of the agents in your area probably sell 90 percent of the homes. Compile an email list of these sales associates so that you can get the word out when you have a listing. Get the sales associates' permission to add them to your email list, and then email them photos of the listing. If you have an open house, email these people in advance or, better yet, invite them to view the virtual tour of the home on your website.

Laptop Computers

Today's laptops have just as much, or more, computing power as desktop computers, without taking up as much space. You can take a laptop with you for computing or making presentations. Perhaps you prefer working comfortably by the pool instead of sitting at a desk. If this is the case, a laptop is for you.

Most laptops are so light and easy to use that almost every real estate professional has one. I have three laptops that I can set up and use at any time. One can be used to read and send email, another is being used to write this book, and a third is used for my research. The laptop I am writing on is my main laptop. It can be converted into a tablet by swinging the screen to the back and closing it. The screen is fully touch sensitive, and I can alternate between touching the screen or using a Bluetooth-enabled mouse. Important data are synced on all three laptops so that if one goes down, I can use any of the others without any delay.

Smartphones

Smartphones are revolutionizing the way we live and do business. With their built-in, high-resolution digital cameras, they have virtually replaced the freestanding digital camera. The screen resolution is so high on most phones, people can even use them to watch movies or their favorite television shows. You may not use, or see the need for, all of this technology on a phone, but if you are in real estate, you must have a phone, even if its features are limited.

However, there are advantages to having one of the more technologically advanced types. As mentioned above, the built-in digital camera is extremely helpful if you need to take some quick photos but do not have your digital camera with you. Most smartphones also have very good built-in GPS and client-management systems.

Apps are the best way to customize your smartphone to the way you work. Specialty real estate apps include mortgage calculators, business card scanners, levels, school districts, and floor plans, just to name a few. Most apps are free or can be downloaded for a nominal charge. However, don't just get an app because everybody else has it. Select your apps wisely because they do take up space on your phone. If you find you are not using an app, delete it. If you find that you want it later, you will still have it on your backup.

High-end smartphones have processors as powerful as ultra light laptops. These phones can dock to become full personal computers that allow fewer devices to be used.

Apps for Improving a Real Estate Professional

Before the Internet, life for a real estate salesperson was good. Buyers had to come to us to know what was available in inventory. Sellers had to come to us because we had all the buyers.

Those days are over. Buyers now have just as much or more information about available properties than we do. Sellers can market their properties through their own websites and create interest without an agent.

REALTORS have one advantage and that is we ARE better at selling real estate than ALL others. However, we must understand technology in order to compete.

Technology can be overwhelming. You may say to yourself "I will never catch up!" or "My daughter knows more than I ever will!" We need to learn to use the technology that is already on the market. We must learn to use the applications for ourselves and our business.

The following sections review some apps (tablet and smartphone applications) that may be of value to you as a real estate professional. There is a vast number of apps available, all of which meet different needs, serve different purposes, and offer various features. If you have a specific function or action, there probably is an app for that. Apps are added, discontinued, and updated/revised daily, so be sure to verify the information given.

Financial Planning Apps

The life of a real estate professional is busy. Between driving the kids to soccer practice, completing a CMA for the next listing appointment, and spending quality time with your family, managing your finances is probably the last thing on your mind. But don't worry, we've got a host of investing, banking, and retirement apps that make financial planning fun and easy.

StockTwits—FREE
REALTORS® make large sums of money all at one time and if some of that money is not invested, it will somehow disappear. You need your own retirement money, and you might consider investing in the stock market. Twitter has become a hot place for business news, and StockTwits is the place to connect for investment advice. You can find out which stocks are being tweeted about the most and are trending worldwide. You can connect with other traders and join in the conversation. You can even track your top stocks, which is quick and painless. Searching for stocks by stock symbol is easy and you will receive real-time stock prices instantly. StockTwits also adds a "Heat Tracker" that shows potential investors which stocks are "green" for buy and "red" for sell or don't buy.

RetirePlan—$4.99

Retirement planning is very important; RetirePlan can help. In just seconds, you can enter your projected real estate income and current financial status. Then the app will give you a financial plan for the future. This app has a ton of variables but allows you to enter as much or as little information as desired. The most valuable feature is that the app will answer questions regarding retirement, such as:

- When can I retire from selling real estate?

- How much do I need to save every year to continue my current life style?

- How much money will I get every year in my retirement?

- How long will my money hold out in my retirement?

You can add a spouse, figure out how much needs to be saved to send a child to college, or plan an automobile purchase or European vacation. If you are not on the right track, RetirePlan will indicate how much more money you will need to produce to meet your retirement goal.

Time Management and Organization Apps

Time management and organizational skills are critical to success in real estate. A real estate professional who does not have these skills has no direction appears scattered and confused, and wastes valuable time throughout the day. No matter how organized you think you are there is always room for improvement.

Things—$9.99

Considered a top task-management app, Things is easy-to-use and effective at helping you manage your time and stay organized. Sort your tasks between your Today list and other dates and then check them off as you complete the tasks. You can organize your tasks by various categories, including listings, sales, and marketing, as well as by tags to assign priorities and personal workflow. Add to-do's and store them in the Things cloud. Enter new ideas and sales tips as you get them.

Toodledo — $2.99

Toodledo is a mobile to-do list. The app filters and prioritizes your most important real estate tasks, creates an automatic smart list, analyzes your tasks to configure the best use of your time, and generates "alarms" for tasks that are due soon. Toodledo features two panes. The left pane tracks your task lists. The right pane displays individual tasks. Tapping the items in the left pane expands those items for further inspection. You can even upload and attach real estate files to your tasks, create subtasks, and share your tasks, such as marketing or office work, with your assistant.

With Toodledo you can:

- Track the priority, start date, due date, time, length, or status of a task.

- Assign the task to a folder, context, or goal.

- Flag the task with a visual star or tag it with keywords and notes.

- Get audible popup alarms.

- Create tasks that repeat on a schedule of your choosing.

- Start and stop timers to keep track of time spent on projects.

- View your tasks on a map and get proximity alerts when you are near a location where you have things to do.

- Quickly find important tasks with the "Hotlist." This smart to-do list is automatically filled with important tasks based on a mathematical formula.

DocWallet—Free

DocWallet is a personal document lock box on your tablet. All data is encrypted and securely stored. Whether for everyday use or for business, your confidential documents are clearly organized and securely stored in DocWallet. Bank and tax documents, real estate contracts and insurance policies, certificates and diplomas, wills and powers of attorney, photos and diaries, and medical records and results are all secured with DocWallet. Other features of this app are as follows:

- Securely synchronize your folders and documents.

- Read, save, and manage, as well as annotate, Adobe PDF documents.

- Use multiple formats such as Word, Excel, PowerPoint, photos, and more.

Find My iPhone—Free

This app allows you to pinpoint the exact location of your iPhone, iPod, or iPad (there is Find My Phone! for Android users) by accessing an app on a different device. You can tell the iCloud to play a sound on your lost device so you can locate it if it is nearby. You must have the location services turned to the "on" position on your devices or the iCloud won't be able to locate them. To do this, go to **SETTINGS** > **ICLOUD**, then toggle **FIND MY IPHONE** to **ON**. Keep in mind that the lost device must be on in order for this to work. If the battery dies while you are trying to locate your device, the app will not be able to find it for you.

OmniFocus 2—$19.99

This multifunctional app can help with time management and organizational functions for your real estate business. One of the features is the ability to organize your tasks by different contexts, such as by closing date instead of calendar date. You can plan out your day using a map mode to save time. You could pick up a yard sign, get a document signed, and place a lockbox all with the help of this app. The app allows you to break up large tasks or projects into smaller steps that you can track and check off individually. You can attach pictures of rooms and even include audio commentary of the property and notes; you can capture your thoughts and turn them into actionable to-do items or use them for marketing.

OmniFocus works in both portrait and landscape view with navigation on the left pane and data manipulation on a larger right pane. The left pane includes the New Task icon button, the Inbox icon button, and several additional navigation icons.

OmniFocus includes several ways to add new tasks to your list. The easiest is the Quick Entry window accessed with the icon at the upper-left corner of the left pane. The Quick Entry button allows you to add new tasks without leaving your current context or project. This is great for the little things pop up while you are working on other real estate tasks.

The dates pane lets you set start and due dates for new and existing tasks. Tapping the Date field opens the date picker. The Dates pane also has buttons to quickly move a task forward a day, week, or month. Start dates are useful with OmniFocus. Setting future start dates for tasks lets you push those tasks out of view until you need to see them. For example, if you are not going to get a listing until next month, set the start date for next month. Between now and then, the task will not clutter up your list.

Tapping Repeat allows you to set actions that recur. OmniFocus lets you set a repeating task on a set schedule, such as every five days after completion of a task. For example, you may only need to wash your car every two weeks but you may need to attend an office meeting every seven days regardless of completion.

The Notes pane gives you the useful functionality of adding detailed notes to a task. You can also use this field to paste a website link or portions of an email that you want to reference with the task. The Attachments pane lets you add photos and voice notes to your actions.

OmniFocus lets you set flags. To display flagged tasks, tap Flagged in the left pane. Flags are a good way to filter your real estate tasks and view just those critical items that must get done today.

The Forecast view breaks down tasks that are starting and due over the next seven days. Tapping on Tomorrow, for example, gives you a list of all tasks that are due or starting tomorrow, along with a timeline of your calendar events for the day. With OmniFocus's Forecast view, you can see at a glance that next Thursday you have a closing and a listing appointment and can plan accordingly.

eWallet—$9.99

eWallet is an app that organizes and keeps track of all your passwords. Protect all your passwords like MLS passwords, lockbox codes, online banking, personal identification (PIN) numbers, and email passwords. The app even has a built-in password generator to help you create super strong passwords.

eWallet protects your information completely with:

- Secure storage for passwords, usernames, and PINS

- Secure storage for bank and credit card info

- Time-out locks to keep your info safe

- iCloud interface to share your wallets between your devices

Clinometer—$1.99

Clinometer is an app that measures slopes precisely. It can be used for something as simple as aligning a frame or for something more sophisticated, such as measuring an arbitrary slope exactly. It works by using all edges of the device, as well as the camera, to measure the slope. It is a great tool to have on a listing, for example, to help sellers understand that there may be a slope in the floor, which could indicate foundation problems.

Scanner Pro — $2.99

Scanner Pro transforms your smartphone and tablet into portable scanners. It allows you to scan receipts, whiteboards, paper notes, real estate contracts, or any multipage document. Scanned documents can be emailed, printed, or uploaded to Dropbox, Google Drive, or Evernote.

Additional features of Scanner Pro are as follows:

- Scan receipts to keep track of travel expenses.

- Convert paper notes and sketches to digital copies.

- Sign with a pen and scan a real estate contract to email it back.

- Save interesting articles on real estate or pages from a book for further reading.

MagicPlan — Free

MagicPlan creates indoor maps. It measures a room and draws a floor plan just by taking pictures. Simply add objects, annotations, and attributes to create an indoor map. This is perfect for listing appointments, and you don't need to move furniture or other objects.

ShowHome — Free

ShowHome is the simplest way to quickly and elegantly receive feedback on real estate listings from your client while on a home showing.

Designed for the real estate professional, ShowHome lets you instantly pull in listings from your Point2 account (need to register) to provide your clients with information about a property. It also offers the ability to take notes as you tour your listings.

The ShowHome app

- Provides the whole picture; you can page through photo galleries of properties.

- Allows for instant feedback. You can add detailed notes and purchase offer information for each listing to keep a record of your client's thoughts.

- Gives you the ability to rate the experience. You can add ratings in real-time to each listing in order to get a better sense of what your clients are looking for.

- Makes you the local expert. You can instantly access neighborhood, school zone, tax, and crime information to anticipate your client's questions.

- Provides a paper copy. Send a PDF of all property information and notes taken during showings to your clients with just one touch.

Other Helpful Apps

Mortgage Calculator—Free
You can help your clients calculate mortgage payments with the Mortgage Calculator. Finding out when a client's mortgage will be paid off is simple. Just enter the property value, down payment, mortgage amount, and loan terms to see useful amortization tables and charts. This mortgage calculator will also determine which loan should be paid off first in order for a client to qualify for a home loan.

Secrets of Success—$0.99
You can learn valuable tips from the top business motivation pros with this app that helps remind you why you got into real estate in the first place. Leadership tips appear right on your smartphone or tablet with video clips to demonstrate the principles. Get a Daily Dose of Confidence from this app that can help you list that tough seller.

Here are some features of this app:

- Ninety video clips to show you exactly how to react in every situation

- Time-tested worry principles that help you manage and overcome stressful situations

- Valuable tips on how to motivate and engage yourself and your team

Inspirational Quotes — Free

It is best to begin your real estate day with an inspirational quote and there is no better place to find one than the Inspirational Quotes app. The thought-provoking quotes in this app encourage you to keep driving on, to make those calls to sellers whose houses haven't sold yet, or simply to help you live life to the fullest. Inspirational Quotes also offers the capability to share via Facebook or email so you can share with other people who may need encouragement, motivation, and inspiration.

"Property Search" Websites and Apps

The public now has the ability to search websites for information on buying a house. These sites contain multiple images of and information about each property. The potential buyer can apply for a loan, get payment numbers, add specific property search criteria, and save that criteria for later viewing. Each website also has an app so that the potential buyer can search for a property anywhere, anytime. Owners who want to sell frequently can actually place their listing on the website without the use of a Realtor. These sites have been around for years, and we will examine the most popular three:

The National Association of REALTORS® (NAR) has a website at www.realtor.com. If you Google "Find a home," it will be the first non-paid site offered. NAR was intuitive enough to foresee the power of the Internet for marketing real estate.

They developed this site many years ago, and they keep it relevant and up to date. All the public data that REALTORS® enter into their local Multiple Listing Service (MLS) is downloaded daily to the NAR website. This is the most current, relevant information offered.

Potential buyers have the ability to search for dream properties on the first page. Special sections focus on new homes, foreclosures, and specific communities that may be of interest to the potential buyer. The user can view property records and determine the value of a property for their own personal information and use. The site even gives the user the ability to look at rentals if that is of interest. The user can also check mortgage rates and use the mortgage calculator to find the best payment range.

Every real estate professional should be familiar with this website. Realtor.com offers real estate professionals access to the site for free, but for marketing purposes the professional could enhance (for a fee) their presence on the site. Your potential clients are using it; often they know more about a single property than you do because they have done their research on realtor.com.

Another popular website is Zillow (www.zillow.com). Zillow is a for-profit property search website. Like realtor.com, Zillow offers those that visit their site the ability to search for property with a multitude of variables. They offer specialty areas for foreclosures and new homes. Zillow also offers a For Sale by Owner section as well as a section for open houses, coming soon, and rentals.

The mortgage section allows the user to get pre-approved and check rates. Zillow offers several calculators, including mortgage, affordability, and refinance. The mortgage section includes a section on mortgage education.

The site sells access to these potential clients to real estate professionals. The real estate professional can answer questions and give advice, which increases their credibility.

The last site we will cover is Trulia (www.trulia.com). Trulia looks remarkably similar to Zillow. There are sections for buying, selling, rentals, information on mortgages, and how to find an agent. The user can also bookmark homes to review later. Trulia includes a section for real estate professionals to submit homes they have listed and advertise to potential clients. It does not cost anything to submit a listing, but additional marketing beyond that does involve a cost. Trulia offers real estate professionals a directory, the ability to send sellers a "Client Listing Report," and a section where they can answer real estate questions from buyers and sellers.

There are other sites like homefinder.com that may make an impact on property search websites, and as a real estate professional, you should always be on the lookout for the latest in consumer searches. The Internet is a viable source of potential clients, so don't miss the opportunity for this kind of exposure. Additionally, be sure to download the corresponding apps offered for instant access to these websites.

Hardware Devices

The real estate professional should consider purchasing any or all of the following devices that could help his or her career gain new heights. The devices can be purchased at local electronics stores and at a reasonable price. Technology has made these devices small enough that the real estate professional can take each to a listing presentation.

Digital Projectors

Digital projectors are a great way to do a listing presentation at a house. The projectors are small (no bigger than a sandwich), they connect in a matter of seconds, and they project on a nearby wall. The sellers will feel that they are a part of a VERY professional presentation.

Tablet Presentations

A tablet is a mobile computer with features such as a camera, microphone, and touchscreen. A tablet is a great tool for a presentation. You can move the slides by using your smartphone and an app. Some listing professionals even carry with them more than one tablet and give the other to the sellers for them to view.

Digital Cameras in Real Estate

One of the best aspects of a digital camera is adding photographs directly into your laptop listing presentation. Can you imagine the seller's excitement when viewing a professional image of his or her home on the listing presentation you are giving? All you need is the seller's authorization to get started.

You can take panoramic shots of a property for a wide-angle view. Some cameras allow you to take multiple photos and then put them together (stitching) into one final image that is actually wider than a computer screen. The client can then pan across to see the full image.

Digital cameras can be used to engage prospects who seem interested in the home. If you have someone who expresses interest in a home, offer to let him or her use your digital camera to take photos. Email them the photos so that they are in their inbox when they get home.

Other Useful Tools

Mobile Video

Reading is not as popular as it was in the past. People love videos, and real estate professionals are in a prime position to capitalize on this trend. Use full-motion video and auto-created animations for listings. Viewers can listen to the audio and/or watch the videos you create. Take advantage of the unique role that video plays in marketing. Unlike a virtual tour, a video can showcase a lifestyle or a community. Video is more enjoyable than text and can give just as much, or even more, information.

Technology in the Home

Most houses now are computer equipped. Many houses have security systems that you can view from your smartphone. If you forget to shut off the coffee pot, you can shut it down from your computer at work. Turn on lights, view your living room or change the thermostat, all from your car, if you need to.

Thanks to Internet-to-TV devices such as Apple TV and Google TV, programs that were once confined to laptop screens and iPods can now be enjoyed on the big screen in the comfort of your living room.

Websites — Online leads

Occasionally, you may get leads from a website. However, you need to be aware of a few simple truths about online leads:

Response Time
You must act quickly with online leads. With today's technology, lead time cannot be more than a few minutes. The contact success rate declines rapidly the longer the customer waits. Most potential clients will be off to another real estate advertisement within five minutes.

Repeated Attempts
An online lead needs to be contacted five or more times before the lead is considered dead.

Use e-Alerts
An e-Alert notifies the prospect of additional properties that fulfill their needs. These leads will likely visit your website repeatedly to get additional information.

Cloud Computing

Cloud computing reduces expensive infrastructure and will help power that hub, allowing you to work remotely and better serve consumers with valuable data at your fingertips. The cloud is a virtual way to store information over a network, usually the Internet. If you have too much data on your smartphone or tablet and you are getting error messages, send your music and photos to the cloud.

Responsible Use of Technology

Technology gives greater access to people and places, and with greater access comes greater power. Greater powers brings with it responsibility. No one likes junk mail—whether in print or electronic form. Ask for clients' permission before adding their email addresses to your contact list; otherwise, they may consider your message unwanted or what is known as "spam." Spam is the use of email to send unsolicited messages. Ask for the seller's permission (preferably in writing) before taking a digital picture of his or her house and putting it on your website. Otherwise they may feel like their privacy has been violated, and that's no way to build client trust.

Chapter Summary

For more direct and updated information on the latest trends in technology and products, use the Internet. If you do not know how to use the Internet, you need to learn. Technology should support you, not the other way around. Do not buy the latest gadget just to have it, and don't buy a product unless it will work for you. Be tech smart.

Summary Questions

1. What is the best way to track your leads?
   a. Don't have any leads; then you won't have to worry about it.
   b. Write them on pieces of paper.
   c. Enter them into a computer database.
   d. File them in your memory.

2. What is the purpose of real estate contact management software?
   a. To organize data on all of your people, listings, and closings
   b. To teach management skills to brokers
   c. To confuse real estate salespeople
   d. To run an office from home

3. Examples of searches in a typical database include which of the following?
   a. High-priority prospects
   b. Buyers looking for a house in a certain price range
   c. Buyers looking for a house in a certain neighborhood
   d. Members in your sphere of influence

4. Which of the following about social media is true?
   a. Real estate salespeople will fail without social media.
   b. Social media is the way to wealth in real estate.
   c. Social media can allow you to connect with people.
   d. A real estate professional must spend at least two hours a day updating social media sites.

5. What is the 80/20 rule of social networking?
   a. Eighty percent of people spend only 20 minutes a day on social media sites.
   b. Eighty social media contacts will get you 20 clients.
   c. Every $20 spent on social media should return you $80.
   d. Eighty percent of your content should be of interest to all people, and 20 percent should be real-estate related.

6. What is the main purpose of a personal website?
   a. Promoting the real estate salesperson
   b. Promoting the real estate sales office
   c. Generating leads
   d. Feeding the salesperson's ego

7. Why might someone create a blog?
   a. It is a great way to write about your knowledge.
   b. It is a great way to prove your expertise.
   c. It allows you to post more information than most other types of media.
   d. All of the above are reasons for creating a blog.

8. What are applications (referring to technology)?
   a. They are the requirements to obtain a real estate license.
   b. They are software programs that carry out a set of instructions.
   c. They are agreements between a broker and a salesperson.
   d. They are where data is stored on the Internet.

9. What are the advantages of a laptop computer?
   a. Lightweight
   b. Easy to use
   c. Versatile
   d. All of the above

10. What is the main purpose of cloud computing?
    a. To clear up title
    b. To reduce expensive infrastructure
    c. To produce more rain in West Texas
    d. To celebrate the achievements of Bob Cloud, the inventor of the modern-day computer

Chapter 4

Psychology
of Marketing

Chapter Overview

Marketing is offering something for sale and hoping someone will buy it. This chapter focuses on the psychology of marketing in real estate sales. You will learn how to determine a person's needs and how the individual processes those needs.

Key Terms

Marketing Philosophy:
Marketing philosophy is focusing the business on identifying and understanding the customer's preferences in terms of needs and wants and delivering them more effectively and efficiently than competitors.

Customer Satisfaction:
Customer satisfaction is the ability to create a sales situation that meets or exceeds the anticipated results from the customer's perspective.

Behavior:
The actions or reactions of persons or things in response to external or internal stimuli.

Ego:
The division of the psyche that is conscious; most immediately controls thought and behavior.

Introduction

Marketing has changed drastically in the last few years. We now must analyze not only the service we provide, but we also must analyze the client. The real estate business is made up of many different aspects, but the main thing you are selling is you. A buyer will buy with or without you. Your job is to have the buyer purchase that house through you. The same applies to sellers.

The following are some tips for strengthening yourself as a salesperson.

- Get tough with yourself. Real estate success demands hard work and long hours. Make a commitment to yourself to succeed; it's not as difficult as it may seem once you make a firm, unalterable decision to do it. You must learn to schedule your time and discipline yourself.

- Don't fear the competition, because the only true competition you have is yourself. When I teach students, they often ask me if I hold back on sharing the really good information. The answer is no. The only competition I have is myself. Real estate isn't a "limited pie" business. There is enough business for all of us. If I ever need more money, all I have to do is work harder. I don't fear competition, I don't fear the economy, and I don't fear the end of humankind. I know the only thing I can control is myself and if I do that then I win.

- You need to abandon your old ways and be open to new things. The real estate profession doesn't run on the typical corporate time clock. In this industry, your most productive work hours will be when others are off work. Don't expect success if you pack up your computer at 4:55 p.m. each day. You have to devote more time to real estate than you've ever devoted to any other job you've had. You're working for yourself! You may find yourself working weekends and even a holiday or two. Those are the times when clients are available for previewing prospective homes to purchase.

- Get yourself in the right frame of mind to succeed. You must develop and maintain a good attitude, or you won't survive. Attitude is infectious. If you have a poor outlook, it will destroy your best efforts. Top producers are enthusiastic about their careers!

- Look for and experiment with procedures that produce results. Once you find something that works, use it over and over again, until you become so good at your career no one will be able to compete with you. Don't give up on real estate if you do not make a sale in the first month. If you combine perseverance with singleness of purpose and you continue learning, you cannot fail. I am frequently asked for one word that describes success in the real estate business. That word is persistence.

- The one overriding factor to your success is confidence. You're a licensed professional in the business of selling homes. View every listing as a contest, one in which you, the listing agent, will be victorious, because you can anticipate the owners' moves before they make them and you know what to do to counter each objection. As a professional, everything is in your favor. You know what you're talking about, and you have a broad perspective of the market. If you don't know the answer to something when asked, go out and find it. I find that the number one reason new real estate salespeople fail is they are fearful of being asked a question they cannot answer.

> **Hint: Doing something is better than doing nothing.**

- Always be proud of yourself. Think of what you have done to get where you are right now.

    - You made the initial decision to get into real estate and you did it. Many people think about changing careers, but most never get beyond dreaming.

    - You studied hard, took the licensing exam, and passed it (or if you haven't, you will).

    - You survived office training.

    - You bought this book and are reading it.

    - You are in the real estate business for yourself.

    - You are demonstrating courage by calling a potential client.

- You are prepared for the call because of the knowledge and information that you have gained.

- Be proud of yourself and your accomplishments. You can only sell what you believe in, so believe in yourself. If you are experienced in the real estate industry, you should be proud that you are continuing your education to make yourself the best you can be!

- You have to like competition to do well in real estate. Make a firm commitment to out-list everyone! It's part of getting tough with yourself, and there's no reason you can't. Perseverance alone will eliminate most of your competition.

- Last but not least, you must generate enthusiasm. People like to do business with enthusiastic people. I once went on a field training exercise with a new real estate salesperson to his first listing appointment. While I was thinking about the weather, that I needed to wash the car, and whether the Dallas Cowboys would win the football game on Sunday, the new salesperson was literally shaking from his enthusiasm. I miss that.

Do you want to beat the top listing salespeople of the industry? Then be more enthusiastic. A thorough professional licensee who knows the real estate business and is excited about how it benefits his or her clients is the person people want to work with.

Marketing Philosophy

The purpose of marketing is to gain a balance between creating more value for real estate clients and customers and making profits for the real estate professional. To achieve this balance, many real estate professionals have adopted a marketing philosophy.

A marketing philosophy can be defined as focusing the salesperson on identifying and understanding the customers' preferences in terms of needs and wants and delivering them more effectively and efficiently than competitors.

Adopting a sound marketing philosophy means delivering greater levels of customer satisfaction, profitability, and sustainability. Customer satisfaction is the ability to create a sales situation that meets or exceeds the anticipated results from the customer's perspective.

Because customer satisfaction is the key to the salesperson's business, it is critical that the salesperson understand the customer. Marketing research techniques have been developed just for that purpose. A real estate professional can stay close to their customers by simply talking with them. The professional could use surveys, focus groups, or third-party research studies. Whatever the method, the end result is to know the customers so the salesperson can better serve them and not lose sight of their needs and wants.

The idea of keeping close to customers seems simple. In reality, however, it is very easy to forget the customer's needs and wants. Sometimes the real estate salesperson is so involved with his or her service that their own desires and wants begin to dominate, even though they have adopted a marketing philosophy.

Here are seven steps to create a great marketing philosophy:

1. **Customer-orientation:**
   All of the salesperson's activities should be directed to create and satisfy the real estate customer. Emphasis on the needs and wants of consumers keeps the salesperson on the right track. All marketing decisions should be made on the basis of their impact on the customer. The consumer becomes the guide of the salesperson's business.

2. **Marketing Research:**
   Under the marketing philosophy, knowledge and understanding of customer's needs, wants, and desires is vital. A regular

and systematic marketing research program is required to keep abreast of the market. In addition, innovation and creativity are necessary to match the real estate service requirements of customers.

3. **Complete a wants and needs analysis**

    The following are some questions that the wants and needs analysis must address:

    (a) What business are we really in?

    (b) Who are our customers?

    (c) What do the customers want?

    (d) How do we find customers?

    (e) How can we communicate most effectively with our customers?

4. **Marketing Planning:**

    The marketing philosophy calls for a goal-oriented approach to marketing. The overall objective of the real estate professional should be earning an income through satisfaction of customers. On the basis of this goal, the objectives and policies of marketing should be defined precisely. Marketing planning helps to inject the philosophy of consumer orientation into the salesperson's business and serves as a guide to the salesperson's efforts.

5. **Critical Budgeting**

    The real estate professional should create a budget through critical analysis of his or her current position with the wants and needs of the customer. It is of no use to promise a service and then not have the capital to see it through. Critical budgeting should be rigid. Budgets should not change often.

6. **Integrated Marketing:**
   Once the salesperson's goals are formulated, it becomes necessary to harmonize the salesperson's goals with the goals of the individuals working with the salesperson. The activities and operation of various areas should be properly coordinated to achieve the defined objectives. The listing team should work with the closing team, the listing team should work with the selling team, and so on, to accomplish the desired goals through the satisfaction of customers.

7. **Customer Satisfaction:**
   The aim should be to maximize a healthy income over the long run through the satisfaction of customers wants.

   Satisfying customer needs and business goals may involve conflicts that sometimes cannot be resolved. Salespeople who adopt a marketing philosophy will do everything in their power to meet the needs of their customers, but they must also make an income. Sometimes the wants of the customers may include a low commission or expenses that are not feasible for the salesperson if the salesperson is to make an income. Consequently, the salesperson must strive for a compromise between what the consumer wants and what is practical for the salesperson to provide.

   Today, the marketing philosophy stands as a formula for doing business, and many believe it is a prescription for success. It aims to satisfy customers by guiding the real estate professional to meet the customers' needs and wants while meeting the business's goals.

The six dominant buying motives are:

Pride of Ownership. Is the clout of that neighborhood important to your client? Why does someone purchase a nicer version of anything? The pride factor may be overt or subtle. Pride is a good thing, but it can become manipulative.

Desire for Gain. Does your client want a home that should increase in value? Most of our prospects will cite this as their primary motive whether they measure the financial gain directly or indirectly. If investing in real estate, then the expectation is to generate a return on the money invested.

Fear of Loss. The fear of loss is a greater motivator than the desire for gain. Once prospects find their perfect house, they may begin to wonder, "What about the houses that we have not seen? Maybe one of those is better…." Buying insurance is an example of spending to avoid a loss.

Love. Your client wants to be in a specific school system; she can't imagine her daughter going anywhere else. Love is an intense emotion. One person may describe love one way and another person may describe love quite differently. But all people seek love.

Need. Your client is a painter, so she needs a studio. Need is the lack of something necessary. It is more than a want. If the property does not fill the needs of the prospect, the prospect won't buy. If the property does not fill the wants of the prospect, the prospect may still buy.

Security. A person cannot live in constant fear. Smoke alarms or a security fence are good examples of purchasing for security. Security also involves the location of the property.

People buy emotionally, not logically. They will have different motives, and more than one motive may apply to the same kind of purchase. In general, people don't readily admit to, and may not even be aware of, their buying motives. People feel too exposed admitting to their vanities or fears, so they tend to hide the real reasons behind their purchases.

You should ask questions of your prospect and determine their main buying motive. Once the motive is discovered, you would be wise to focus on the motive that is most important to your prospect.

Be aware that more than one buying motive may apply, so keep asking questions to clarify the prospect's position.

Another motivation is ego—satisfaction of emotion. Ego is defined as the division of the psyche that is conscious, that most immediately controls thought and behavior. Behavior is defined as the actions or reactions of persons or things in response to external or internal stimuli. You might ask: "How important is security to you?" and you would find out how the person feels about security and protection. Then, as your presentation unfolds, you can emphasize the areas that are important to your prospect.

Chapter Summary

In this chapter we studied the average consumer's buying motives. Each marketing effort should be targeted to the specific group you are trying to reach.

Summary Questions

1. Which of the following is a sound real estate philosophy?
    a. Don't fear competition.
    b. Don't pay your taxes.
    c. Don't put your family above business.
    d. Don't listen to your broker.

2. What one word separates success from failure in the real estate industry?
    a. Organization
    b. Communication
    c. Persistence
    d. Experience

3. Of which of the following should a person be proud?
    a. Passing the state real estate exam
    b. Making a first sale

c. Being named top producer of the office
d. All of the above

4. Which of the following is untrue about enthusiasm?
   a. People like doing business with enthusiastic people.
   b. You cannot generate enthusiasm; it must come naturally.
   c. Enthusiasm makes people interesting.
   d. All of the above are untrue about enthusiasm.

5. What is the purpose of marketing?
   a. To gain a balance between creating more value and making a profit
   b. To outspend your competition
   c. To create a false image
   d. To become the top producer of the office

6. Focusing the business on identifying and understanding the customers' preferences in terms of needs and wants and delivering them more effectively and efficiently than competitors is known as what?
   a. Marketing philosophy
   b. Marketing strategy
   c. Marketing plan
   d. Marketing budget

7. Which of the following is good way to find out what a customer wants?
   a. Talking with them
   b. Surveys
   c. Focus groups
   d. All of the above

8. Which of the following is not a key step in developing a marketing philosophy?
   a. Customer orientation
   b. Marketing research
   c. Customer avoidance
   d. Integrated marketing

9. Which of the following is not a dominant buying motive listed in this book?
   a. Pride of ownership
   b. Desire for gain
   c. Physical effectiveness
   d. Fear of loss

10. Which of the following is not a dominant buying motive listed in this book?
    a. Love
    b. Need
    c. Security
    d. Hunger

Chapter 5

Marketing
Strategy

Chapter Overview

The main objective of this chapter is to gain an understanding of how marketing and advertising affect real estate. You will understand marketing strategies, learn how to write an effective real estate ad, and learn how to avoid the pitfalls of the legal aspects of advertising and marketing.

Key Terms

Marketing:
Marketing is the overall concept of offering a property for sale to the general public.

Marketing Strategy:
A marketing strategy is the overall marketing direction. All marketing efforts must be in line with the marketing strategy.

Marketing Plan:
A marketing plan organizes the marketing strategy.

Marketing Budget:
A marketing budget takes into consideration the current financial situation and then plans out all expenditures.

Marketing Project:
A marketing project is a specific marketing idea that is in the marketing plan and aligns with the marketing strategy. There is enough capital in the marketing budget to make it happen.

Marketing Campaign:
A marketing campaign puts a series of marketing projects together to be completed in a period of time to accomplish the marketing plan in fulfillment of the marketing strategy.

Name Recognition Advertising:
Name recognition advertising is the type of advertising that gets your name and what you do in front of people.

Prospect Generating Advertising:
Prospect generating advertising is designed to entice customers to contact the advertiser.

AIDA:
AIDA is the advertising acronym that stands for Attention, Interest, Desire, and Action.

KISS:
Kiss is the acronym for Keep It Simple and Short.

Networking:
Networking is the process of meeting people for the purpose of spreading business contacts.

Public Relations:
Public relations are getting the media to notice you in a positive light.

Introduction

Marketing is the overall concept of offering a property for sale to the general public. Good marketing reaches more people than if nothing is done. However, poor marketing reaches no one and is a waste of money. The more people who know a property is available, the better chance the property has of selling for the most money in the fastest amount of time. Marketing does not sell an overpriced property, but it will help sell properties that are priced correctly. Advertising is just one aspect of marketing, but it is probably the most recognizable.

Personal Marketing Strategies

A marketing strategy is your overall marketing direction. It should guide you in your decision making for spending money and time. Your marketing strategy should include projections for what you want to accomplish through marketing. It should be written out in detail but contain very little in numbers and finite dates. Those items will be included in your marketing plan. The following are specific steps to develop an overall personal marketing strategy:

- **Understand Your Business**—You must know your business both legally and ethically prior to developing a marketing strategy, or your strategy will ultimately fail. You must understand not only the products (real property) and services you are selling, but the environment in which you are conducting business. You must have the financial knowledge, business understanding, and comprehension of the legal landscape in order to handle a variety of multi-faceted, complex, and multi-party interactions both efficiently and effectively.

- **Promote the perception of ability**—Your perception of ability is only as strong as your worst critic's opinion of you. You should focus on providing awesome service and then ask for referrals. In addition to working hard and establishing a solid reputation, you can leverage your perception through public relations efforts, whether it be speaking at a real estate industry event or writing a column for a local business journal. You should strive to be a current, integrated force in your local market who is well-versed in the needs of your respective buyers and sellers. This overall effort of providing awesome service should be in each of your marketing strategies.

- **Cultivate the right relationships**—Whether your goal as a real estate professional is to sell more properties, represent more buyers, gain additional market share, or be a resource to the community at large, make sure you're spending time formulating the types of relationships that lend themselves to accomplishing such objectives. Real estate relationships are key to success; without relationships with motivated buyers and sellers of real estate, the best marketing strategies will suffer.

- **Decision Making**—You must make decisions when developing a personal marketing strategy that direct your entire marketing direction. The decisions made should include who, what, when, where, and how the marketing is going to take shape. This decision-making step should be conducted with concentrated thought over several days if not weeks. This strategy will be the basis of all of your marketing efforts. You may even want include your entire team when working on this segment. If you do not have a team, then consult with your broker.

The marketing strategy does not need to be lengthy, but it must be thorough. Writing an effective marketing strategy takes practice; the following is an example:

> *The real estate business of Dan Hamilton will center upon the residential real estate market in Colleen, TX (Laudan Subdivision).*

This marketing strategy is short but thorough. It identifies the real estate business name (Dan Hamilton). It identifies the type of real estate business (residential). It describes where the business will be directing its marketing efforts (Colleen, TX in the Laudan Subdivision). Notice that the marketing strategy is very specific to only one subdivision. If a marketing strategy covers too large geographic area, it cannot be marketed correctly, and the marketing efforts may get thwarted. Keep marketing strategies specific enough to be carried out without being burdensome. Any actual marketing ideas will be spelled out in the marketing plan. The reason this is so important is because from now on all marketing must follow the strategy. If someone wants to give you a great deal on a marketing idea in Smithfield Subdivision, your answer is "No" because it is not in the Laudan

Subdivision and hence not in your marketing strategy. This does not limit you from working other areas; it only limits your marketing to a specific area. Concentrated marketing is the key.

> *Dan Hamilton will concentrate his residential real estate career on first-time homebuyers in Amber, TX.*

This one is short but includes an entire town. Dan Hamilton is narrowing the marketing to first-time homebuyers only (no sellers are targeted). Developing a marketing strategy is not a goal-setting exercise. Do not include details such as "Dan Hamilton wants to make $100,000 from these marketing efforts" or "Dan Hamilton will capture 5 percent of the local market."

> *Dan Hamilton is in the business of residential real estate. He will direct his marketing efforts to the Mansfield, Texas, area. His marketing segment will be homeowners with properties that exceed $500,000.*

This marketing strategy is longer but still basically covers the same information. All specific dates should be in the marketing plan.

The marketing strategy must be through because it must be followed when developing a marketing plan.

Personal Marketing Plan

The marketing plan should organize your marketing strategy. A complete stranger should be able to pick up your marketing plan and understand all aspects of it.

Detail each step of the plan with exacting standards. (Analyze each step to determine its purpose and whether it aligns with the overall marketing strategy. If it does not, delete it or rework it until it fits with the plan.) Include beginning and ending dates with each step, as well as costs and contact people. If you are directly involved in any step, your time needs to be analyzed.

Also include all types of promotion, marketing, and advertising in your marketing plan. These may be planned promotional events, direct-mail campaigns, or advertising on the Internet. If you do advertise, you will need to separate name-recognition advertising from prospect-generating advertising. Finally, compare the entire marketing plan to what your competition is doing.

Expenses of a personal marketing plan would include those incurred for advertising, printing, marketing, mail-outs, and postage. Anything for the business that takes money away from you should be considered an expense.

Any expenses that are projected to be incurred must be analyzed and debated. Expenses can get out of hand quickly. A marketing budget should be set for each marketing project and strictly adhered to. You should also consider the time that would be involved in creating a marketing plan. Time is a valuable asset. If the project involves too much money or time, it should be revised or eliminated.

Personal Marketing Budget

A marketing budget takes into consideration the current financial situation and then plans out all expenditures. The marketing budget must be completed prior to the execution of the marketing plan. If the marketing plan calls for a marketing project that cannot be completed with the current funds available, then the entire marketing effort is wasted. Suppose a marketing idea is estimated to cost $25,000, but you have only $10,000 in the budget; the marketing idea will need to be terminated. Do not spend money you do not have; it puts entirely too much pressure on you to get results.

Personal Marketing Project

A marketing project is a specific marketing idea that is in the marketing plan and aligns with the marketing strategy. There should be enough capital in the marketing budget to make it happen. These are the minor projects that lead to completion of the marketing plan and fulfillment of the marketing strategy. Such projects could include advertising in the local newspaper, developing a website, and sending "Just Sold" cards to a neighborhood. All of these minor projects should contribute to the marketing effort and result in increased sales.

The type of advertising, whether name-recognition or prospect-generating, should be evaluated in the marketing plan and then carried out to accomplish the marketing strategy.

Personal Marketing Campaign

The purpose of a marketing campaign is to put together a series of marketing projects that are then completed in a certain period of time to accomplish the marketing plan in fulfillment of the marketing strategy.

Name-Recognition vs. Prospect-Generating Advertising

Name recognition advertising gets your name and what you do out in front of people. The purpose of prospect-generating advertising, on the other hand, is to get a prospective client to contact you. These two efforts are often confused.

Name-recognition advertising is critical in making your job easier, but it takes a long time to work and it can be expensive. Most national real estate companies spend millions of dollars per year on name-recognition advertising. Some examples include advertising on television, radio, Internet, bus stop benches, airplane trailer banners, personal brochures, shopping cart cards, name badges, career apparel, and car signs.

Prospect-generating advertising is designed to entice customers to contact the advertiser, either by phone or through the Internet. Ads on the Internet showing houses for sale make the phone ring. Other examples of prospect-generating advertising include listing yourself in telephone directories, sending out direct mail, installing "for sale" signs in yards, and passing out business cards. If you are on a limited budget, consider putting your efforts into prospect-generating advertising; let your company worry about name-recognition advertising.

Determining which type of advertising is right for you will be part of your marketing strategy.

Writing Effective Advertising

Before preparing ad copy—either for print or online—analyze the property and identify its features and benefits. Decide who your target buyer might be.

In addition to your personal appeal, which is critical to the success of your ad, every classified ad should carry the reader through four selling steps: Attention, Interest, Desire, and Action, or AIDA, as they are known throughout the advertising community.

1. **ATTRACT ATTENTION.** You need to catch prospects' attention within the first few words of your ad or you will lose them

forever. A catchy headline may do the trick. In fact, the headline is probably the most important part of your ad. Other tips for attracting attention are as follows:

- Use sincerity, not clichés.

- Include the price. People shop by price. If you feel including price is a problem, try running the ad without it. Always document your results to determine the best use of your money.

- Occasionally ask questions in your ad. People have a natural tendency to be attracted to questions.

2. **AROUSE INTEREST.** Once you have a reader's attention, use the interest stage to pull him or her in further. Otherwise, the prospect will stop reading and move on to the next ad. On the Internet, this time span is very short; you can lose a prospect in three seconds. Create interest and desire by highlighting features on lower-priced properties and by selling benefits and emotions on higher-priced properties.

3. **CREATE DESIRE.** In real estate, the desire is to have the property. Writing skill at this stage is necessary to create the right atmosphere for the prospect. If space is available, list the property's most desirable features so the prospects will able to picture themselves living in that house. Anything less and you will not receive a phone call.

4. **CALL FOR ACTION.** To get the sale, you must ask for the sale. Ads are written and sold exactly the same way. In your ad, you must ask for the contact.

    - Research has found that you will receive a greater response if you close the ad with a request to contact, using your full name. Be active. Tell your readers to "Call now!" or "Email now!"

- Research has found that by using the word "please," the close is softened and greater response occurs. So please call for action in your ads.

If your ad copy tells all the essential facts clearly, holds the reader's attention from start to finish, and makes a specific call to action, it will be successful. Use the following checklist when writing your ads:

1. Organize all the facts from the viewpoint of the reader, not your own. Buyers are looking for pictures of houses, not information about you.

2. Appeal to emotions; for example, love of comfort, status, family responsibility, and so on. The higher the price, the more emotional the buy and, hence, the more emotions you want to place in the ad; the lower the price, the more practical the buy and, therefore, the more features you want to list in the ad.

> *Buyers are looking for real estate houses, not real estate salespeople.*
>
> —*Luella Blaylock, Manager, Real Estate Office*

3. Keep It Simple and Short (KISS). Avoid long-winded sentences; however, do not abbreviate or use real estate jargon. If it is important enough include it in the ad, it is important enough to spell it out. There was a time when I was in the market for a small pickup truck. When looking through some newspaper ads, I noticed that some included "OBO" at the end. Because I didn't know what those letters stood for, I never called on those ads; I didn't want to be embarrassed by my lack of knowledge. Eventually, I learned that the meaning of the abbreviation is "Or Best Offer," but in the meantime, I probably missed out on an incredible deal. My point is, don't eliminate your potential client by using cute abbreviations. A potential buyer might not know their meaning. Sometimes we get so close to real estate that we forget what it is like to be a consumer. Try creating the ad from your prospect's direction.

4. Use meaningful words that stir emotion. Make the readers "smell" the steaks "sizzling" on the grill or feel the "cool" water across their skin when they jump into their new swimming pool.

5. Inspire confidence. Don't use over-exaggerated descriptions that are not believable.

6. Avoid clichés and overused words, such as "super," "great," "Mrs. Clean lives here," "Gingerbread house," and so on.

7. Sellers buy people, and buyers buy houses.

8. Differentiate your marketing. Advertise for three different markets:

    a. buyers and sellers

    b. other real estate salespeople

    c. self-promotion (normally to get listings, except for buyers brokers).

9. People first select housing by price, then they eliminate properties by comparing features and benefits.

10. Describe the most saleable feature in the headline. If the house is located in the most desirable part of town, say so. If it is a bargain, say so.

11. Stick to the truth. Misleading advertising is illegal and unethical.

12. Finish with a call to action: "Call today" or "Call now." Follow this with a phone number that is answered during the day.

13. Remember: The average person retains 1 percent of what he or she sees each day.

14. Marketing campaigns involving advertising should appear no less than weekly for a minimum of three months.

15. Consider these additional points:

- Do people like your ad?

- Is your ad memorable?

- Does your ad give you personality?

- Does your ad provide a simple message?

R. J. Wrigley commented on advertising:

> *"Tell them quick and tell them often. You must have a good product in the first place and something that people want, for it is easier to row downstream than up. Explain to folks plainly and sincerely what you have to sell, do it in as few words as possible, and keep everlastingly coming at them."*

Fair Housing Law Guidelines

Fair housing laws were passed to ensure that everyone has the same right to buy and rent real property. The law does not look at your intent. Do your actions indicate a discriminatory behavior?

Race, Color, and National Origin

When running either a print or online real estate advertisement, you cannot indicate preference to any group of people based on their race, color, or national origin. Advertisements that indicate a "type" of person that the particular property would suit (based on any protected class) would be a violation of Fair Housing guidelines. Phrases such as "master bedroom," "rare find," or "desirable neighborhood" are not in violation.

Religion

Advertisements should not reference or indicate a preference for any religion. The ad cannot direct members of that protected class toward or away from a piece of property. An advertisement that reads "down the street from a Catholic Church" could be a violation.

Sex (Gender)

Advertisements cannot indicate a preference for or exclusion of persons based on their gender. Advertisements that offer a multi-unit apartment for lease for "women only" could violate the law.

Handicap

Real estate advertisements should not show bias against a person with a handicap. Describing a property's amenities, such as "great for lovers of tennis" would not violate the act.

Familial Status

Familial status refers to the members of a family, especially those members under the age of 18. Advertisements may not state a preference or exclusion, based on the number or ages of children, or state a preference for adults, couples, or singles.

Ads that Comply with REG Z

The Truth-in-Lending Act (REG Z) was enacted in 1969 to "assure the meaningful disclosure of credit terms so that the consumer will be able to compare more readily the various credit terms available to him to avoid the uniformed use of credit." The Act refers to the fact that advertisers must tell the public all details of financing if certain "trigger" words are used. For fixed-rate loans if you advertise any of the following loan terms, you must also advertise the rest of the terms:

    I. Annual percentage rate

    II. Simple interest rate

    III. Down payment

    IV. Monthly payment

    V. Loan term (length)

Additional Marketing Ideas

Advertising is a great marketing tool, but there are many others. Let's explore some additional ideas that could fit into your marketing plan.

Business Cards

This is still the backbone of business communication. Order your business cards as soon as possible and reorder before you run out. It still amazes me when I ask a "professional" real estate salesperson for their business card and he or she tells me, "I just ran out," "I left them in my car," or "Give me yours and I will email you." You should never run out and should have them with you at all times. Give them to everyone!

You can be creative when laying out your business card, but be sure it includes your picture and contact information. Don't make it so cluttered that the important information is hard to find. I have seen business cards that have the salesperson's office number, home number, cell phone number, voice mail number, a web address, and e-mail address. Remember: Keep it simple. List your primary contact information on the card, and the rest can be provided to the customer at a later time.

Use your business card at all times. Give one to everyone you meet. Set a goal for the number of cards you want to pass out each day. Mine is 15, which doesn't sound like much until you factor in that you must give the card only to those you have not given one to in the past. You start dreaming of people to give cards to . . . neighbors, relatives, and so on. I even gave one to a policeman who was writing me a speeding ticket. Another rule I've made for myself is that if anyone takes my money, they take my business card. This means every time I eat lunch, the waiter gets my business card. When I go grocery shopping, the checker gets my card. When I mail my monthly bills, I include a business card in each envelope. Why? I once filled up my car with gas and when I paid, I handed the clerk my business card. He ended up buying a house through me. I gave him $43 for gas, and he gave me $4,300 for a real estate sale.

When you hold an open house, make up business cards specifically for that open house. Do a business card with your standard information on one side and a photo and information about the home on the other side. You could also put financing information for buying that particular home on the reverse side.

Personal Brochures

Personal brochures are usually tri-fold type letters that introduce yourself and your accomplishments. Use these sparingly. Their cost prohibits mass mail-outs. Instead, send them to any appointments you may have and leave them with anyone you talk to about real estate. The difference between a brochure and a business card is that everyone gets your business card and only serious prospects get your personal brochure.

You can create a personal brochure using your computer, if you have that capability. Be sure that if you do it yourself, you do it well. A cheap brochure means a cheap real estate salesperson. There are companies that will create personal brochures for you, but the cost is high.

Networking

Networking is the process of meeting people for the purpose of spreading business contacts. If you are in real estate and you meet someone who sells new cars, you should put that person in your network. If you sell someone a house and he mentions that he will buy a new car, refer that person to your new contact and vice versa. Sphere of influence (SOI) is a valuable marketing technique where certain groups sponsor events whose only purpose is to meet people. This is not "network marketing" where people try to sell you something, and it is also not a dating service—stick to business.

Public Relations

Public relations are getting the media to notice you in a positive light. Your objective is to get media attention at least once a month. When a newspaper writes an article on one of your achievements, it becomes truth to the reader. If you pay for an ad, on the other hand, the consumer discounts that because it was paid for.

Submit weekly press releases to the newspaper. The worst that could happen is the article is not used. Newspaper people need to fill in sections of their papers with stories. If you have stories handy for them, they might use them to complete the newspaper.

The stories you submit can be on virtually any subject. For instance, I once submitted a story on how our real estate office rescued a kitten that was trapped. No kidding, it made the front-page news complete with pictures. It sounds silly, but we got many calls thanking us for our kindness and concern. Here are some other suggestions for PR stories:

- New associate in the office

- Top listing salesperson

- Top selling salesperson

- High-dollar listing

- Any charity event

- Any award or recognition received

You never know what will be used or rejected; your job is to submit.

Look for blogs on the Internet that are related to real estate. Make short, straightforward, and appropriate comments on them. Some real estate home search sites allow users to post questions. Be a frequent visitor to these sites and answer any of the questions you can. It will give you credibility and build your status with potential clients on these websites.

Chapter Summary

Marketing is in almost every area of real estate. A marketing strategy is the overall marketing direction a real estate professional wishes to take. The marketing plan spells out the steps needed to complete the marketing strategy. Marketing projects are smaller, individual actions taken to complete the marketing plan. The marketing strategy puts marketing projects together to form a timeline of action, and the marketing budget plans out the costs of each item on the marketing plan.

Advertising is a big part of any successful marketing plan. Advertisements should be written using the AIDA formula and must comply with the Fair Housing Act.

Marketing can be fun and rewarding if done correctly.

Summary Questions

1. What do the letters AIDA stand for in the advertising community?
   a. Alternate Institutional Diversified Advertising
   b. Absolute, Individual, Demand, Actual
   c. Attention, Interest, Desire, Action
   d. AIDS Association

2. When you write an ad, what should you do?
   a. Change the ad layout and words each time it is run.
   b. Experiment with features of the ad.
   c. Document the calls received with each change.
   d. All of the above.

3. What is the overall marketing direction called?
   a. Marketing strategy
   b. Marketing plan
   c. Marketing project
   d. Marketing campaign

4. What organizes the marketing strategy?
   a. Marketing strategy
   b. Marketing plan
   c. Marketing project
   d. Marketing campaign

5. Which of the following is a specific marketing idea that is in the marketing plan and aligns with the marketing strategy and there is enough capital in the marketing budget to make it happen?
   a. Marketing strategy
   b. Marketing plan
   c. Marketing project
   d. Marketing campaign

6. Which of the following puts a series of marketing projects together to be completed in a period of time to accomplish the marketing plan in fulfillment of the marketing strategy.
   a. Marketing strategy
   b. Marketing plan
   c. Marketing project
   d. Marketing campaign

7. What type of advertising gets people to know your name?
   a. Name-recognition
   b. Prospect-generating
   c. Local area
   d. National area

8. What type of advertising gets prospects to make contact with you?
   a. Name-recognition
   b. Prospect-generating
   c. Local area
   d. National area

9. What does KISS stand for when referring to writing advertising?
   a. Kontrol Internet Social media Sensorship
   b. Keep It Simple and Short
   c. Keep Investing in Short Sales
   d. None of the above

10. What protected class is defined as "Under the age of 18 living with parent or guardian"?
    a. Race
    b. Color
    c. National Origin
    d. Familial Status

Chapter 6

Law of Agency and Alternative Representative Agreements

Chapter Overview

This chapter is an introduction to real estate agency law. While you may obtain further details from other sources, our objective is to keep agency law in the forefront of your mind during your real estate career.

In this chapter you will learn about representative agreements that are not used regularly in the real estate industry. Whether you actually use these agreements is not as important as is the knowledge of their existence.

Key Terms

Agency:
A business or person authorized to act for others.

Care:
The duty of care requires the broker to display reasonable care for his or her clients.

Obedience:
The duty of obedience requires the broker to follow the lawful instructions of his or her client.

Loyalty:
The agent must put the client's interest above his or her own.

Accountability:
The agent is accountable for his or her client's money.

Notice:
The duty of notice requires the broker to be informed about the real estate industry and communicate related information to his or her client.

Law of Agency

Introduction

Agency law is common law, meaning it applies to everyone. We tend to look at agency law only from the aspects of real estate. Sometimes we get more insight by looking at law from the lawyer's point of view. Attorneys know who their clients are. Both parties know whom they're working with. The attorneys spend a great deal of effort making sure their clients know about how they are being represented. We in real estate should do the same. We should disclose to interested parties our agency relationships.

Agency Relationships

An agency relationship exists when one person or business acts on behalf of another person or business. In real estate, an agency relationship typically involves a broker who acts on behalf of a seller. The broker is the agent, and the seller is the principal.

The purpose of the arrangement is for the broker to find a buyer and arrange the sale of the property on behalf of the seller. A similar arrangement exists when a broker acts on behalf of a landlord to find a tenant. The broker can also act on behalf of a buyer. In this respect, the broker finds a house for the buyer. This is called a "buyer's brokerage."

Brokers who help tenants find space or housing are called "tenant reps" in commercial situations, "apartment locators" for finding apartments, and a buyer's broker when finding houses for tenants. Tenant reps are common in major cities for leasing larger commercial spaces of around 10,000 square feet or more.

Only brokers (and attorneys) are paid commission directly by the seller, buyer, or principal. Salespeople are not required to become brokers. In practice, a real estate firm is often set up as a corporation, which holds a broker's license in its own name, and the corporation, as a broker, sponsors and holds the licenses of its salespeople.

Duties Brokers Owe to Clients

There are certain duties a broker owes to a client, including the duty of reasonable care, the duty of obedience, the duty of loyalty, the duty of accounting, and the duty of notice. These duties are obligations of the broker, and failure to fulfill any of them can lead to the loss of commission or worse. Key distinctions between duties given to a client versus those given to a customer are advice, opinions, and advocacy. These are general categories with specific duties that include care, obedience, loyalty, accountability, and notice. These five duties form the acronym COLAN.

Care
The duty of reasonable care requires the broker to display reasonable care for his or her clients. This includes but is not limited to:

- Keeping the property secure.

- Keeping the seller from legal harm.

- Pricing the property correctly.

- Filling in the purchase agreement correctly.

Obedience
The duty of obedience requires the broker to follow the lawful instructions of his or her client. This means that if the client directs the broker in a certain direction the broker must follow the client's wishes. The only exception to the duty of obedience is when the client directs the broker to do something that would violate a law.

Loyalty, Fiduciary

The words "loyalty" and "fiduciary" are sometimes used interchangeably. "Fiduciary" loosely translates as "putting the clients' wishes above your own." The salesperson must act in the client's interest even if it would jeopardize a commission. If a seller rejects a risky offer and you insist the seller take it so you will get your commission, this is a violation.

Accountability

You are accountable for your client's money that is involved in the real estate transaction. This includes any earnest money.

Notice

The duty of notice requires the broker to be informed about the real estate industry and communicate related information to his or her client. It requires the broker to tell the client anything that a reasonable person would find of interest. This includes any negotiating position, environmental concerns, or market analysis.

Office Policies on Agency Relationships

Most real estate commissions require each brokerage company to have a written office policy on how they will deal with agency questions. The following sections discuss typical office policies.

Seller Only

In the "seller only" office the real estate broker and the salespeople represent the seller only. Under no circumstance would the broker represent the buyer. A real estate salesperson can work *with* a buyer but cannot work *for* a buyer. The salesperson must treat a customer with honesty, integrity, and expertise.

Buyer Only

In a "buyer only" office, the broker and salespeople only represent buyers, never sellers. A real estate salesperson must follow all applicable laws (agency and state licensing laws) and must follow the lawful direction of the buyer.

Seller Only with Buyer Representation

In a "seller only with buyer representation" office policy, the broker and salespeople represent the seller only; however, if the buyer does not want a listing held by the broker, the salesperson might show the buyer other property and represent the buyer. Because it is not an in-house transaction, the salesperson is not obligated to represent the seller. If the buyer wants to buy an in-house property, the seller must be represented.

Buyer Only with Seller Representation

In this type of office the broker and salespeople all represent the buyer. If a seller wants to market his or her house, the listing agent is required to represent the buyer. In other words, if a buyer comes in the office to see the seller's property but decides against buying it, the agency may represent that buyer and show him or her other properties. If a buyer not represented by this company wants to buy the seller's house, this company now can represent the seller.

Intermediary

Under the "intermediary" office policy the broker may act as an agent for both the buyer and the seller, but with reduced representation to both while negotiating a transaction between the parties. With the intermediary policy, one agent in an office can represent a buyer and another agent in the office can represent a seller; the broker becomes the intermediary. The intermediary status has a few rules:

- The intermediary may not disclose that the seller will accept a price less than the asking price, unless authorized in writing to do so by the seller.

- The intermediary may not disclose that the buyer will pay a price greater than the price submitted in a written offer, unless authorized in writing to do so by the buyer.

- The intermediary may not disclose confidential information, unless one of the following conditions exist:

    - The intermediary is authorized in writing to disclose the information.

    - The intermediary is required to do so by the Texas Real Estate License Act.

    - The intermediary is required to do so by court order.

    - The information materially relates to the condition of the property.

- The intermediary must treat all parties honestly.

- The intermediary may not violate the Real Estate License Act.

- The intermediary may appoint associated licensees to communicate with and carry out instructions of the respective parties, but this requires written consent and notification of the appointments by all parties. The appointed licensees are not subject to the duty of impartiality.

Alternative Representative Agreements

In most real estate representative agreements, real estate salespeople are paid by commission. There are a few alternative representative agreements and working arrangements that should be considered as well. Take a look at each on its own merit, and don't dismiss them without seeing the possibilities. The future of big time real estate income hinges on the real estate broker being open-minded about alternative working arrangements. If you are not the broker, consult with your broker before attempting any of these arrangements. These arrangements are legal, but your broker must approve any income and all actions.

Dual Agency

If a broker represents a seller, it is the broker's duty to meet the seller's objective. Generally, the seller wants to get the most money for the property, but sometimes achieving a quick sale is more important. If a broker represents a buyer, the broker's duty is to meet the buyer's objective. When a broker represents the seller and the buyer in the same transaction, it is called dual agency. The broker must disclose this relationship and get approval from both principals before moving forward with the transaction. This type of agency is rarely used in today's market because of the inherent conflict of interest.

Non-Agency

A non-agency relationship is one that allows a real estate broker or salesperson to work with a buyer or seller, providing administration-level assistance, but not offer any representation. Some other terms that are synonymous with non-agency are consultant, counselor, facilitator, and transactional broker.

Not many customers want to pay a real estate professional if that person is not representing them. Why pay for non-agency when you can get full representation for the same money? Non-agency works in situations where you are to perform limited service, such as a fee-for-service type transaction (discussed later).

I was a non-agent once. I received a call from a "For Sale by Owner" seller who disclosed that she had found a buyer. She asked if I would do the paperwork for a percent of the transaction. I agreed to do so and met the buyer and seller at the seller's house. I brought out the purchase agreement, gathered a few details, and within 20 minutes, I was out the door with signatures on the agreement and $800 for my time. In this case I represented neither party and only did the paperwork. The reason I could not represent the seller is because that representation meant more than I had agreed to do.

Fee for Service

A fee-for-service type listing is one in which the seller picks from a smorgasbord of services and only pays for the ones he or she uses. This arrangement works well for sellers who believe they can sell their homes on their own, like "For Sale by Owners," and new home construction (builders). This allows sellers to get what they need without having to pay for those things they can do themselves. Several companies' entire businesses are set up under these terms. The services may even be bundled together and offered as packages.

Bonuses

Bonuses, in which the seller agrees to pay a little extra to a co-operating broker for bringing in a buyer, are not new in the real estate business. These are called "bonuses to the selling agent." The name is somewhat misleading, as all monies paid must go through the selling broker, not the agent. In my experience, these can generate a few more showings, but I would rather see the seller price the property correctly in the first place. That way no bonus is needed. A properly priced property will sell without any further incentives.

That said, I have seen some great bonuses, the highest being a $20,000 bonus on a $180,000 sale. Other bonuses I have seen include vacations, cash, and the most unusual: a brand new, cherry-red Lamborghini plus a $135,000 commission ($4.5 million sale).

Transaction Fees

Transaction fees are charged by a broker for expenses incurred in a real estate transaction. The fee usually amounts to a few hundred dollars paid at closing, although some brokers will bill the real estate salespeople if they do not charge the fee. It is somewhat like an origination fee charged by mortgage companies for processing mortgage loans. Real estate salespeople demanding a higher split while wanting the broker to pay more for more and better services are squeezing real estate brokerage firms' profit margins. As a result, transaction fees are higher to offset those costs. Some brokers and state agencies feel that these fees could be more than the client agreed to pay and are therefore unconscionable. I would recommend seeking legal counsel before taking on the practice of transaction fees.

Trades

Trades take place when you perform real estate services and, in return, receive something other than money. This type of transaction doesn't happen often, but twice in my career I have traded for services. Once, I took part of my commission as a timeshare on a lake and another time I traded for legal advice. No trade can be made unless all parties are aware of the cost of the trade and the trade is approved by your broker.

Tote a Note

Occasionally a seller will not have enough equity to pay the entire commission owed on a transaction. Instead of giving away your commission to make the deal work, tote a note. Have the title attorney (most will do this for little or no cost) draw up a promissory note to you for the amount owed.

For example, say a seller agrees to pay the listing broker 6 percent of the sales price to sell his house. The listing broker finds a buyer, but at the closing the seller is short $500 for the broker fee. The broker may choose to take a promissory note for the $500. The terms of a note are negotiable, but mine are simple: Pay $100 per month until the total amount without interest is paid.

If a seller chooses not to pay me, I won't do a thing. The notes are a promise, nothing more. I have taken notes three times: one was for $700 of which I received $500; another was for $1,500 of which I received $600; and the third note was for $500 of which I received nothing. Ultimately, you deserve your money because you have done your job. Taking a note is one way that could help your bottom line.

Rebates

A rebate is money returned that has already been paid. I will give a rebate on the listing commission to a seller who guarantees to buy his or her next house through me. There are a couple of criteria before I agree to a rebate. First, the next house the seller buys must be significantly higher in value than the one he or she is selling; and second, the seller pays me *all* of my commission from the listing sale. When the seller buys a new property through me, then I will rebate the money. This helps keep the seller honest. It ensures that the only way the seller gets the rebate from me is upon closing of the second house. Some real estate brokers will reduce their listing commission to get the buy side without using a rebate. The problem with that, however, is there is no incentive for the buyer to remain loyal.

Hourly Fees

Here is a novel idea: Charge by the hour. It is interesting that when I ask a class of students for the amount a real estate salesperson is worth per hour, I hear anywhere from $10 to $30. How cheap are we? If I were to work for someone on an hourly basis, I would require over $200 per hour. Here's why: I have to support a family and myself. Real estate salespeople do a lot of work that isn't actually billable.

Now, I don't believe we should gouge the consumer for our benefits, but we do have to make a living. I also know the consumer might not be too happy paying the salesperson $200 per hour. That's why commissions are the most popular method of payment. The consumer likes paying us only when we perform, and we make the money we need to survive.

Let's look into hourly fees in more detail because they can make sense in some situations. If a seller wants you to help on an open house but can handle most of the rest of a sale, charging by the hour for the open house makes sense. If a buyer can find a home himself but needs you to help with the contract, charging by the hour for contract writing makes sense. If a builder wants you to be on-site for a new construction property, charging by the hour makes sense. So don't dismiss hourly fees outright without thinking it through first. The best way to ensure you are paid your hourly fee is to charge a retainer fee.

Retainer Fee

A retainer fee is generally thought of as an attorney's fee. It is paid in advance of services rendered, ensuring that the payment is received. In real estate, a buyer pays this fee before the salesperson shows the buyer a house.

Flat Fees

Flat fees are charged in advance. For example, a real estate broker may agree to sell a property for a flat fee of $3,000 regardless of the amount the property actually sells for. A flat fee makes sense if the property is not worth much or if a variable commission would be too confusing.

I once agreed to sell a tract of land for a commission. Out of desperation the seller kept reducing the listing price. By the time the lot was sold, the commission was so low that I lost money. In this case, it would have been smart to charge a flat fee.

Chapter Summary

Be alert to all of the ways a real estate broker can be paid. If you are apprehensive or confused by these alternatives, seek out more information to determine what is best for you and your client.

Agency law can be very complex, and this introduction is in no way intended to be complete. If you feel you need more information about agency law, seek council from your broker and refer to the back of the book for additional information. Real estate salespeople must be confident of the people they represent. Salespeople must disclose all of their relationships to their clients. Salespeople must give their clients all of the duties, which include care, obedience, loyalty, accounting, and notice.

Summary Questions

1. What type of agency exists when a broker represents two principals in one transaction?
   a. No agency
   b. Double agency
   c. Dual agency
   d. This type of agency is illegal.

2. A seller agreed to pay a flat fee of $2,000 to a broker on a property that was worth $40,000. The seller took 8 percent less than the sales price. If the seller has $4,900 in additional closing costs, what is the broker's commission?
   a. $1,840
   b. $1,600
   c. $1,355
   d. $2,000

3. A real estate buyer's broker hired to locate a property for a buyer must comply with all of the following except
   a. lawful instructions of the buyer.
   b. lawful instructions of the seller.

c. law of agency.
   d. state licensing law.

4. Which of the following are key distinctions between the duties given to clients versus customers?
   a. Advice, opinions, and advocacy are given to clients, not customers.
   b. More advice and opinions are offered to customers.
   c. Customers get advice and opinions for free, while clients must pay.
   d. Clients must have a contract to receive services, while customers do not.

5. A real estate broker, acting as an agent for another in a transaction, has a primary duty to
   a. get the transaction closed successfully.
   b. help the parties reach a mutually beneficial agreement.
   c. treat all parties impartially.
   d. represent the interests of his or her client.

6. Which of the following is the responsibility of a buyer's agent?
   a. Provide advice on how much money to offer on a property
   b. Disclose any latent structure defects
   c. Show the buyer suitable property
   d. All the above

7. If you work for the seller, your relationship with a buyer customer is best characterized as
   a. a fiduciary relationship.
   b. a common law representation relationship.
   c. a caveat emptor relationship.
   d. a relationship of honesty, integrity, and expertise.

8. Which of the following best describes a fee-for-service type arrangement?
   a. It is a smorgasbord of services, and the customer only pays for the ones he or she uses.

b. A service is performed, and then the customer is billed for it at market rates.
   c. Services are rendered, and a commission is charged for the services.
   d. None of the above are correct.

9. What are the fees charged by a broker for expenses incurred in a real estate transaction?
   a. Fee for service
   b. Transaction fees
   c. Incurred fees
   d. Fees for expenses

10. What is the term for "money returned that has already been paid"?
    a. Commission
    b. Fee
    c. Rebate
    d. Retainer

Chapter 7

Prospecting for
Seller Apointments

Chapter Overview

In this chapter you will discover ways to get business. We will look at many of the opportunities that can lead you to potential clients and how to convert those opportunities into money. This is an exciting chapter that you will want to review over and over.

Key Terms

Fair deal:
An exchange of one thing for another at equal prices or for accurate fees.

Prospecting:
Searching for a potential customer or client; something expected, a possibility.

Clear-Cut Listing Appointment:
A listing appointment that has all the essential elements to get a listing.

Active Prospecting:
Actively pursuing real estate business.

Re-Active Prospecting:
Marketing yourself and the company and waiting for real estate business to come to you.

Introduction

Prospecting is the key to success in the real estate business, but one of the most dangerous aspects of this business is the free business. I once employed a brand-new real estate salesperson who, in her first two months, had over eight sales. She made nearly $80,000 in 60 days, which for someone brand new to the real estate business, is incredible. Unfortunately, it was also the worst thing for her career. All of this business came from her family and friends, who had waited for her to get her license so they could buy and sell their properties through her. She did not have to prospect for the business; it was given to her. This salesperson has since left the real estate industry. Do not ignore free business, but more importantly, don't forget that you must learn to earn.

> **An appointment a day keeps the creditors away.**

I have another real estate salesperson who works for me and has a different situation. She knows practically everyone in our small town. She makes her money on referrals and word of mouth, and she doesn't have to prospect for business. So what if there were a sudden change in her situation? What if she has to move? What if the economy in our small town dries up? The town is, in fact, changing. New people who she doesn't know are moving in, and her business is moving out. She's not prepared to go anywhere else and make money in real estate because, unfortunately, she doesn't know how to prospect.

What real estate activities will help bring you long-term career success? There are several: good evaluation skills, closing skills, listing presentation skills, referral activities, and so on. At the forefront of all these skills and activities is prospecting. According to *Merriam-Webster Dictionary*, the word *prospect* means "a possibility; an anticipation." The infinitive *to prospect* means "to explore, to search." In the real estate profession, *prospecting* means exploring and searching for a possible buyer or seller of real estate. You become a prospector, combing your territory for customers and clients, just as prospectors in the "old days" panned the rivers and streams in search of gold.

Your willingness to prospect consistently has a great deal to do with how successful you will become. In addition to seeking out current business, prospecting is a means of building a network of clients and customers to ensure future business. For this reason, prospecting is perhaps the most important part of the real estate business.

Here are a few "truths" about prospecting:

1. Prospecting should be *listing-based*. The real estate salesperson that lists is the one that lasts. If you have no listings you have no income.

2. Prospecting should be based on your real estate *goals*.

3. Prospecting methods should be *varied*. Try different things and new ideas.

A salesperson's primary focus should be salable, exclusive-right-to-sell listings.

1. Salable listings attract buyers.

2. Salable listings attract sellers.

3. A signed listing represents the seller's commitment to work with you.

4. Salable listings allow you to control your time.

5. Salable listings allow you to control your income.

6. Salable listings are like gold.

If you are going to be active and you do not have a lot of friends and family to "give" you business, you need to have listings. I knew a real estate salesperson who invested an incredible amount of time and money on specialized training courses that focused on attaining salable listings. After going through all of that, he walked into my office one day and announced, "I have a great idea: I am going to concentrate on buyers." His business lasted only a month; he had to quit and find a job where he could actually make money. All that training and advice, yet he paid attention to none of it. Don't ignore buyers, but remember to concentrate on listings.

Clear-Cut Listing Appointment

A clear-cut listing appointment is one that has all the essential elements to get a listing if you want it. Most real estate salespeople have so few listing appointments that when they actually get one, their attitude is to get the listing at all cost. However, a successful real estate salesperson will have enough listing appointments that his or her attitude can be, "Do I want it?" This allows the salesperson to be objective. If the seller is reasonable, the salesperson can take the listing. If not, the salesperson can walk away. This is truly the definition of a clear-cut listing appointment. If you go out to a client's property and you do not have a clear-cut listing appointment, you are *playing* real estate. There is nothing wrong with playing real estate, but it doesn't pay much. A clear-cut listing appointment is as follows:

- **Both**—Both or all of the people involved in making the decision to sell a property are present at the listing appointment. Do not go on an appointment unless all of these parties are there. If a husband and his wife are selling the property together, they both must be there. If the property for sale is an estate, the heirs must be there. (It is even better if one heir has power-of-attorney for all other heirs. That way you only have to deal with one person.) Regardless of how good your presentation is, if one of the sellers is not present at the listing appointment, you will not get the listing. Consider the following hypothetical conversation at a property where one of the necessary parties is not present:

    Salesperson:
    "Put me to work for you."

    Seller:
    "Sounds good. Just let me talk with my spouse, and we will probably list with you."

    Salesperson:
    "Forget him and list with me now!"

- Unfortunately, the chances of getting this listing just dropped to around 20 percent, and you have wasted valuable time.

Let's consider another example. How do you get a clear-cut appointment when you are talking to the client on the telephone? Ask for it.

> **Salesperson:**
> "Are you the only one making the decision on the property?"
>
> **Seller:**
> "No, my husband will be involved too, but I will decide who to list with because he is so busy."
>
> **Salesperson:**
> "Understood, will your husband be with us tomorrow night?"
>
> **Seller:**
> "No."
>
> **Salesperson:**
> "When would be a better time so everybody will be there?"
>
> **Seller:**
> "My husband is busy until the weekend."
>
> **Salesperson:**
> "Is Saturday or Sunday better?"
>
> **Seller:**
> "Sunday afternoon."

- Remember, you cannot win if only part of the selling party is at the listing appointment.

One additional point should be noted here: Technology has risen to the point that some real estate salespeople prefer to do all of a transaction without actually meeting anyone. The salesperson sends a listing agreement and sales information to a potential client. The salesperson asks the client to read everything and email a signed listing agreement, pictures of the house, and any additional information back to the real estate salesperson. This may work under certain circumstances, such as the following:

- if the seller is a close friend or relative.
- if the seller is a real estate investor because he or she is not emotionally invested in this type of sale.
- if the seller is not talking to any other real estate salesperson.

- Don't forget: Real estate is a relationship business. It can be difficult to build relationships working only online. Listings are important enough that you should really take the time to go out and visit the seller in person.

- **Two Hours**—You must set aside at least two hours for a listing appointment. A good listing presentation should take from 20 to 90 minutes, and the remaining time can be used to answer the sellers' questions. Be sure your sellers are aware of the amount of time you will need beforehand as well. What you don't want to happen is to be moving along in your presentation when the seller suddenly looks at his watch and says he needs to pick up his daughter from band practice. Not only do you risk losing the listing, but again, you have wasted valuable time. Again, whether you are setting the appointment over the phone or in person, make sure the client knows when you plan to arrive and how much time you will need. The following example is a good way to make sure conflicts will not arise during your appointment:

    Salesperson:
    "Great, Mrs. Seller, I look forward to meeting with you and your husband tomorrow at 7 p.m. In the event that something comes up and I am running a little bit late, how does the rest of the evening look to you?"

    Seller:
    "Oh, we will be home the rest of the evening."

- Now, what time do you show up? On time!

- **Competitive Market Analysis (CMA)**—Before the listing appointment, you should do a Competitive (Comparative) Market Analysis on the house. You can accomplish this by preparing and then asking the seller a list of questions regarding the house. Not only does this provide valuable information that you will need, but it also allows you to demonstrate your professionalism and concern for the seller.

- **Why**—It is important to find out why the seller wants to sell. Is it because of a transfer, and does that affect his timeline? Is it because it is spring, and he feels this is the best time to sell? Answers to these types of questions can give insight into what is motivating the seller, if the seller is willing to negotiate, and so on.

- **Price**—How do you find out what the seller wants for his house? You ask! You must know the price the seller wants for his or her house prior to the listing appointment. Unfortunately, getting the "real" price is not as easy as it may seem, and most sellers will want to set a price that is much higher than what their property is worth. Consider the following dialog:

    Salesperson:
    "Mr. Seller, how much do you want for your property?"

    Seller:
    "You are the professional, you tell me."

    Salesperson:
    "How much do you owe on your property?"

    Seller:
    "I don't owe anything."

    Salesperson:
    "After all your expenses resulting from the sale have been paid, how much money do you want in your pocket?"

Seller:
"As much as I can get!"

Salesperson:
"Would you be happy to get $230,000?"

Seller:
"No, I need at least $250,000!"

Let's look at the first part of this dialog. Asking how much the seller wants for the property will get this conversation started. The seller may come back with a number that is not even close to what the property is worth or what ultimately will be the asking price. This is not the time to challenge the seller's number; this can be addressed during the listing appointment. The most important objective at this point is just to have a number to work from.

The next part of the script above is what I refer to as the "net" script. This is where you learn how much the seller owes on the property and how much he or she wants to make. Then you can back into the price.

If that doesn't work you move to the "shock" script, where as you see above, you give the seller a ridiculously low figure and out of shock, the seller tells you what he or she wants.

Note that not all techniques work all the time, but it has been my experience that by using these three scripts I am always able to get a price from the seller.

One last point: Sellers may tell you that they don't know what their property should sell for, but don't let them fool you. Most of the time, they know! If they don't have an exact figure in mind, they at least have a ballpark idea, and that is the number you need to get from them.

Here is an example of how important it is to get the price before you go to a listing appointment. I once worked with an associate who was on "opportunity time" (opportunity time is when a real estate salesperson answers the telephone at the real estate office and if a lead comes in that salesperson would get the lead). He received a call from someone wanting to sell her house. After making the appointment, he hung up the phone and did a little dance, singing, "I got a listing appointment! I got a listing appointment!" This was his first listing appointment in five months, and he was obviously excited. The appointment was scheduled for the following week, and he spent the better part of that time doing a Comparative Market Analysis. Note that this activity is something that can be done in seven minutes. Rather than working, he was *playing* real estate. On the morning following the appointment, he arrived at the office and silently sat at his desk. It was obvious that he did not get the listing.

At our weekly sales meeting, I asked my associate to tell us how his listing appointment went. His response was: "The sellers were stupid." However, the actual issue was that he never took the time to find out how the sellers wanted to price their property. Instead, he insulted them, and they refused to do business with him. So why didn't he get the listing? He wasn't prepared. He did not spend the time leading up to the listing appointment getting prepared for the appointment.

The clear-cut listing appointment is your best opportunity to get the listing if you want it. If you fail to get all five aspects of the clear-cut appointment, you will struggle in your career.

Active Versus Re-Active

There are basically two types of real estate salespersons: active and re-active. Active prospecting is proactively seeking real estate business and bringing it back to the company. Re-active prospecting is marketing yourself and the company and then waiting for real estate business to come to you.

Which is better? It depends on you.

Some people are good at cold prospecting, whereas others are good at building relationships. To be successful in the real estate business, you must determine which category you fall into.

I have seen new real estate salespeople get into the business and begin to call for prospective real estate business. They hate it, and it shows. They do not get the results and soon quit. It doesn't have to be this way. Cold calling is a great way to make money, but it isn't your only option.

The advantage of being active is that business and money come fast—fast for real estate, that is. The active salesperson gets business by making telephone calls, knocking on doors, calling on For Sale By Owners, and numerous other means. This salesperson is constantly on the lookout for business; it takes every part of the day, and there is not a lot of time for socialization. As a result, active salespeople tend to not be good at long-term relationships. They have neither the time nor need to build those types of relationships. They may miss out on business because they do not follow up on the business they do have as well as they should. They work long, stressful hours because they are continuously seeking out new business. They have not constructed a business plan that returns leads to them.

Life for the re-active salesperson, on the other hand, is not as stressful. People call re-active people for the purpose of doing business with them, and a lot of their business comes from referrals from friends and past clients. The re-active salesperson can make a lot of money.

The disadvantage of being re-active is that it takes a long time to make any significant money. The re-active salesperson must prepare mail-outs, run advertisements, and press palms until a prospect needs and asks for his or her service.

Types of Active Marketing

While the following prospecting ideas are mainly for active real estate salespeople, they can be just as useful and productive for re-active real estate people.

Telemarketing

Telemarketing (sometimes called cold, warm, or gold calling) is the random calling to homeowners to determine if there is any interest in selling their homes. The advantages of telemarketing are as follows:

- Prospects are easy to find. All you provide is effort.

- More contacts with less time.

- Can call in any weather.

- Unlimited market.

- No competition from other real estate salespeople.

- Sellers unaware you are new.

- Perfect for practicing both telephone and listing techniques.

- Establishes your ability to get listings for the rest of your career.

- Basis of all real estate sales.

- Confidence-boosting.

There are certain categories of owners:

1. Not interested: No prospect—don't waste your time.

2. Not interested now but maybe in less than two years: Lead prospect—maintain contact.

3. Interested soon, but not now: Possible prospect—need to create an urgency.

4. Interested now: Grand prospect.

Keep in mind that only 1 out of 100 calls turns out to be a grand or possible prospect. Four out of 100 calls are lead prospects.

Telemarketing in today's market is difficult not because of the "Do Not Call" rules, which you must follow, but because most homeowners no longer have land lines. It is and always will be just ONE method of obtaining real estate clients.

Marketing Door to Door

Marketing door to door is also called door knocking. Some salespeople prefer marketing door to door because they are able to meet potential sellers face to face.

Let's review some important terms involving door-to-door marketing:

- Territory canvassing: This involves getting out in a neighborhood you are interested in working and knocking on doors for leads.

- The warm canvass door: This type of marketing is when you are in an area outside of your target neighborhood, but you are going to spend a day trying to gauge real estate needs.

Basics of Marketing Door to Door
1. After you ring the bell, back up a minimum of two feet.

2. Don't stare at the door; look up the street.

3. Don't turn toward the homeowner until he or she acknowledges you.

4. Face the owner with a genuine smile. (Be sure to be wearing your real estate name tag.)

5. Open the conversation with the following:

"Good afternoon. My name is Dan Hamilton, and I represent Acme Realty. There has been a tremendous amount of real estate activity in this area, and I am wondering if you've thought of making a move in the near future? Do you know of anyone in the neighborhood who might be interested in moving? Thank you so much for your time. I'm curious. If I find a home today, do you know any friends or relatives who might be interested in living here? Thank you again. By the way, when do you think you will be moving? I'd like to keep in touch. Would you like an evaluation of your equity position in the next few months? It's just a document telling what the homes in this area are worth."

This type of approach can lead to a discussion, during which you could learn more about the community and its residents. If you have impressed your new acquaintance with a pleasant manner and real estate knowledge, he may remember you in the event he should need the services of a good active salesperson. He may even tell you about a neighbor who intends to sell later. If there is no answer at the door, leave a door hanger with your contact information. Be sure you have checked beforehand, though, to make sure that soliciting is allowed in the area.

For Sale by Owners

The For Sale by Owner (FSBO) is a homeowner who believes in selling his or her house without a real estate broker; after all, who wouldn't want to save thousands of dollars if they could? A salesperson's job is to prove his or her worth; if you do your job right, the letters FSBO could change into the "Fastest Source of Business Opportunity!"

One advantage of the FSBO is that the person is obviously interested in selling. FSBOs believe they can sell their property themselves, and telling them they can't only angers them. Most FSBOs overprice their properties, which creates fewer showings and lessens the chances of a sale. Eventually FSBOs get the idea that they need help. We need to be in the forefront of their minds when they finally realize they need us.

Mike Ferry, a national real estate trainer, tells of a time in his personal office when he was frustrated that none of his real estate salespeople were calling FSBOs. He started one of his weekly sales meeting by pinning a FSBO newspaper ad attached to a hundred dollar bill on a corkboard.

He then turned to his real estate salespeople said, "Whoever lists this property gets the $100. I don't care if you list it for only a day. I don't care if you list it with no commission to be paid. I don't care if you list it overpriced. I just want you to list it. So the first one of you to do that gets $100!"

After a few days, Mike began to feel bad about what he had done to that FSBO. All his salespeople must be hammering the seller. Mike decided to call him and apologize. "Mr. FSBO, this is Mike Ferry with Mike Ferry Real Estate. I am sure you have heard from my company?" The response from the FSBO: "Nope." No one had called the FSBO. When Mike asked his salespeople why, they all thought that everyone else had already called.

In my market area there are over 6,000 licensed real estate salespeople. Only about 20–25 real estate salespeople call consistently. You have no competition.

Keys to Working FSBOs

1. To be successful in getting the listing, it is essential that you meet these people face to face.

2. Be professional.

3. Committed to this program for at least 12 weeks.

4. Follow up.

5. Follow up.

6. Follow up.

You must get in the door honestly, which means calling or stopping by. Some real estate salespeople make a big deal of showing the house to a potential "buyer" to impress the seller. The buyer turns out to be a friend of the salesperson and isn't in the market to buy a house. That is dishonest, and the only thing we ultimately sell is our self. If we don't believe in ourselves, how will others believe in us?

If you can't commit at least 12 weeks to this program, don't start. You will waste your time. Remember: The majority of FSBOs believe they can sell their property themselves. You must be willing to wait it out while the FSBO tries to sell and then comes to the realization that they can't. Waiting twelve weeks is a commitment on your part, and most likely the FSBO will change his mind in that amount of time.

Calling on a FSBO Ad

Salesperson:
"Hi, I am calling about the home for sale. Are you the owner? Would you consider working with Real Estate in any way? My name is Dan Hamilton with Acme Realty. I will be in your area later this week and was wondering if you would mind if I stopped by to take a quick look at your place?"

This script will get you into the homes of six of every ten FSBOs you call. Let's analyze the dialog. Nothing in the first three lines indicates that you are a licensed real estate salesperson. This is acceptable because the conversation has not become substantial. Be careful: Don't let the FSBO speak. He might end up giving substantial information. So immediately after your first sentence, ask the question, "Are you the owner?" You want to be sure you are talking with the owner and not a friend or someone else who may be helping the owner. The last line, "Would you work with Real Estate in any way?" is a purposefully confusing and rhetorical. You are trying to get the FSBO's attention. Most real estate salespeople will make a big announcement that they are in real estate, and the FSBO is likely to reject that salesperson immediately. This script allows you time to make an impression. Your response will be the same no matter how the FSBO responds. The final question is actually meant to solicit a "no" response. Read it again: "I was wondering if you would mind?" If the owner says "no," it means he or she doesn't mind letting you look at the property. Emphasize that you'll only be taking a quick look. These scripts are proven; don't vary them until you have called 100 FSBOs.

If the owner resists, try this:

Salesperson:
"Is it the fee that is keeping you from listing your property with a professional real estate salesperson?"

If they respond, "No," probe further. If they respond, "Yes," continue:

Salesperson:
"Well, if I have a buyer that I have been unable to help, could I send them directly to you?"

Whatever the answer:

Salesperson:
"I'm sure you have had buyers in your home who decided not to buy it, right? You see, those are still potential buyers to me. If you give me a list of those buyers, I would be happy to send you a buyer who I couldn't help. Now doesn't that sound fair?"

"It only makes sense for me to see the house so I will know which of my buyers might be interested in your home. I'm available tonight or would tomorrow be better for you?"

This script will get you in nine out of every ten FSBOs you call.

Alternate Response:

> "I show a lot of homes in your neighborhood and like to be familiar with everything that's for sale. It's good business for both you and me when I drive by your home with a client and say, 'That home has three bedrooms, two baths, and a lovely kitchen area. It is selling for $400,000.' My clients may wish to see your home."

Once you have the FSBO appointment, you should send a reminder card.

Door Knocking for FSBOs

Salesperson:
"Hi, my name is Dan Hamilton with Acme Realty, and I am doing a quick survey of why people try to sell their homes by themselves. Do you have a second?"

First visit or door knocking questions:

1. Why did you decide to sell your home yourself without a broker?

2. If you were to hire a broker, what would you look for?

3. If you don't sell the house yourself, will you stay here or will you hire a broker?

4. When will you make that decision?

5. What methods of marketing are you currently using?

6. Have you heard of Acme Realty's 21-point marketing plan?

Additional FSBO Hints

1. FSBOs have lists of buyers that have seen their houses and have not bought. Remember, we make money with buyers *and* sellers. If you get those lists, you can begin working with those buyers.

2. FSBOs may list their houses with agents who offer a variety of options for purchase. For example, the listing company may offer certain real estate services for set fees. The seller could choose the services needed without actually listing the property for sale. In this type of situation, all fees should be negotiable and paid in advance. I know of an agent in Las Vegas who made over $1,000,000 in one year by exchanging services for FSBOs in exchange for their buyer lists.

3. Follow up, follow up, follow up.

4. If you meet resistance when requesting to see the FSBO house, find out if you can help the FSBO find a new home. Call the FSBO as your company's Referral Specialist and attain a referral to another area.

5. FSBOs should be *one* area of your business. Don't devote all your time to them.

6. Mean FSBOs are the best FSBOs.

FSBO Stop-By Appointment

When a FSBO agrees to show you his or her property, you should do the following:

1. As soon as you hang up with the seller, put a reminder note in the mail. If you have their email address, send this by email. Be sure to include the date of the appointment and one of your business cards. Also include an agency disclosure form if one is required by local laws.

2. Take only a notebook and a pen or a tablet to the appointment. You agreed to a stop-by appointment. You should keep your briefcase and any necessary listing material in your car. If the seller wants you to list his house, you will be prepared.

3. Once you're inside the property, say the following: "Show me around and just treat me as if I am a buyer."

4. If the homeowner says something about the house, write it down. If it is important enough for him to say it, is important enough to write down. Take pictures (with the seller's permission) from your tablet.

5. When finished, leave the property. Do not ask a lot of questions. Do not offer any services. Do not even offer a business card. Be professional.

I have seen salespeople walk into FSBO houses and immediately begin to sell. Many times, the FSBO has already prepared a response to this. The FSBO may express something such as how real estate people don't do anything except take his or her money. These accusations may continue so that by the time the FSBO is finished, the real estate salesperson is leaving the house with his or her tails between their legs. You want the seller to believe you have something to offer. Every other real estate salesperson the FSBO has invited in has tried to sell. If you don't follow this same pattern, you leave the seller with the thought that you are different and may have some special qualities. I was calling FSBOs one day and set an appointment with one. I found out later that a new real estate salesperson in my office had an appointment with the same FSBO that day. I asked the other salesperson if we could go together so I could teach him some techniques for handling FSBOs. I told the new salesperson that we would not be saying much to the seller, that they would be doing most of the talking.

When we got to the house, I could sense that the seller saw us as typical salespeople, ready to take his money. We said very little, but I could tell the seller was expecting the same speech that he has heard from every other real estate salesperson: "Here's what we can do for you . . . ." When the house tour was over, I simply said "Thanks." As I walked by the new salesperson, I could tell he was horrified and curious as to how I could go to a potential client's house and not offer services or even my card. This salesperson whipped out his business card and quickly added, "If we can be of any help . . . ." Before the salesperson could finish his sentence, the seller laid into him. By the time we got outside, the seller was yelling at us. I expected it, and I wasn't disappointed. The new salesperson was shocked and never called on an FSBO again.

Here's the analysis of what happened. The FSBO believes he can sell the house himself. The salesperson comes in and tells the FSBO he needs help. This irritates the FSBO and challenges his integrity. It's no surprise that the FSBO now wants to fight. As far as the business card goes, you can mail it to the FSBO with a thank you, *after* the tour!

FSBO Follow-Up Facts

Put each FSBO lead in your database, and follow up weekly. Tracking FSBOs is of the utmost importance. They will not list with the first real estate salesperson who contacts them; they will list with the last real estate salesperson who contacts them, and that must be you. How do you ensure that you are the last? Follow up weekly with each FSBO you are tracking, and do it on the same day and time each week. This way the FSBO will know when you are going to call.

I called a FSBO and he quickly informed me that he did not need a real estate salesperson. I persisted (remember: the mean ones are the best ones) and made an offer he could not refuse. Finally, he told me to be at his house at 2:00 p.m. on Thursday. He would not be there, but his wife would. (It is okay to meet with only one person when you're only stopping by.) I was on time and as soon as the wife saw my nametag, she ranted and raved about how she and her husband did not need a real estate salesperson. I told her I understood but that her husband had told me to stop by. She then threw the door open, told me to look around, and walked off into another room. I quickly got the message, tossed my business card on the coffee table, and walked out. When I got back to the office, I deleted the contact from my database. The next day I got a call from a person who said he had decided to list his house with me. I told him I'd love to market his house and then realized that this was the FSBO from the day before. I "un-deleted" the FSBO's contact information on my computer, listed the property that day, and later sold it.

Why did those angry and bitter FSBOs list their property with me? Because I was the last to contact them. They were so mean that all of the other real estate salespeople had deleted them from their databases early on. The difference was that I timed it right before they conceded to needing professional real estate help.

The FSBO must be called every week. You should call either Sunday night or Monday. If you call on Friday, they have no interest because *this* weekend is the weekend they will sell their house. If you call Sunday night or Monday, they are less hopeful and more willing to talk. Also, you want to call at the same time each time you call. You never know when the sellers will decide they need you, and chances are they didn't keep anything you gave them. Here is a typical conversation:

FSBO #1:
"It doesn't look like we can sell it ourselves."

FSBO #2:
"True."

FSBO #1:
"Who should we call?"

FSBO #2:
"I don't know."

FSBO #1:
"How about the guy that keeps calling?"

FSBO #2:
"Fine."

FSBO #1:
"Did you keep his card?"

FSBO #2:
"Nope."

FSBO #1:
"Oh well, it doesn't matter. He will call tonight at 6:15."

The salesperson can offer the FSBO a "fair deal." The real salesperson wants an appointment to market the house. The FSBO might need any number of services, and the salesperson finds services that will trigger the FSBO to act. The services the salesperson offers may include MLS, yard "For Sale" sign, and any number of other services. What you offer as a "fair deal" is not as important as just offering something. You should develop a list of fair deals for yourself and post them in an area where you can review them when calling FSBOs.

Offering a Fair Deal

Salesperson:
"Mr. or Mrs. FSBO, it is a proven fact that buyers tend to believe that the price you are asking is more realistic if it is backed by written data. Do you have some evidence proving your home is priced right?"

FSBO:
"Well, no."

Salesperson:
"If you'd like, I can prepare a written report on the fair market value of your house and provide that for you to use. Are you available today or would tomorrow be better?"

Several things are happening here, so let us examine them separately. First, notice the fair deal of offering a Competitive (Comparative) Market Analysis (CMA) in exchange for an appointment. (Remember: A fair deal is an exchange of one thing for another at equal prices or for accurate fees.) The FSBO wants something from the real estate salesperson (in this case the CMA), and the salesperson wants a listing appointment.

Second, if the sellers don't need the CMA, end the conversation with an acknowledgement and a goodbye. Never say, "I'll call you next week," because their natural response will be to tell you not to call. If they specifically tell you not to call, you cannot do so (national "do not call" rules), and you have lost a prospect. If you just say goodbye, you can call again next week. Third, notice the close, ". . . today or would tomorrow be better?" Offering a choice to the FSBO reduces the chances of the seller responding "No." Finally, if the FSBO says something like, "Just mail it to me" or "I can drop by your office and pick it up," you must say: "I appreciate what you are saying, but the only thing worse than not having the information is to have it and not to be able to explain it correctly. I need to meet with you to explain it. It has been good talking with you. Do you have any other questions? Thanks, then. Goodbye." Never give a fair deal away because then it wouldn't be "fair." Before you do any work for anyone, you must secure an appointment. I see so many real estate salespeople do this or that for a FSBO and get nothing in return. My services are worth compensation and are not to be given away. If the FSBO is not interested in your fair deal, simply respond by saying, "Great, it was nice talking with you. Bye."

FSBO Food for Thought

Call until you find a FSBO you can work with. If you only work one FSBO a week for 50 weeks (two-week vacation), you could work with 50 FSBOs in a year. If 70 percent of those eventually list with someone in real estate, that would equal 35 listings. If you list half of those, that would be 17 extra listings per year, when they sell. If you average $8,500 per sale (I randomly came up with that amount), you will earn an extra $150,000 per year. This does not include sales from any other sources.

Expired Listings

The expired listing can be another excellent source of prospects. Expireds are sellers who listed their home with the wrong real estate salesperson (the right real estate salesperson would have been you!), and the home did not sell. The other salesperson has done all the work; all you need to do is come in and clean up the mess. The advantage of working on an expired listing is that you know the owners were once interested in selling and were okay with paying a commission.

Your first task in contacting an expired listing is to determine whether the owners are still interested in selling; if so, you need to arrange an appointment to discuss the advantages of listing with you.

You should prepare a long list of questions to ask when initially talking with the owners in order to get an appointment; they will typically want to get off the phone quickly. Ask them why they think their home didn't sell, how they felt about the listing price, why they want to sell, and what they will do if their home doesn't sell. Keep them on the phone as long as possible to build rapport.

Some Important Preliminaries
1. Learn and follow your local Board of REALTORS® regulations for contacting expired listings.

2. Do not criticize your competition.

Categories of Expireds
I will break into specific categories the different types of expireds so we can understand them and better prepare for how we should approach them.

1. **Motivated owners**—There are several categories of motivated owners who have become expireds. These owners are still motivated to sell but have different outlooks on their situation.
    a. An expired will relist with the current office. The real estate salesperson is a personal friend or they have some other relationship. This expired is probably not a prospect of yours, but contacting him or her might be worth a shot. Sometimes a seller may tell you over the telephone that he or she will list with a competitor, but if you can get in front

of them, you have a chance. A typical conversation may go something like this:

Salesperson:
"Have you already signed papers to relist the property?"

Expired:
"No, we are scheduled to sign them tonight."

Salesperson:
"How long was it listed the last time?"

Expired:
"Six months."

Salesperson:
"And you don't feel that was long enough to sell the property?"

Expired:
PAUSE

Salesperson:
"Doesn't it make sense to talk with at least one other broker to see what other services are offered? I am available at 3:00 p.m.? Or would 5:00 p.m. be better?"

b. *Interview alternative offices and current office.* An alternative office is one that is not the previous listing office. Good prospect, but you must overcome the seller's loyalty to the current office. This means that you have a good chance at getting a listing appointment, but if you cannot demonstrate a reason for the seller to select you over the previous company, it might be hard to get them to change. The expired believes that if all companies are the same, they might as well stick with the one they know.

c. *Interview alternative offices, but not the current office.* This is a major prospect. They will list with a real estate company but not with the previous one. The reason might be that they were so disappointed in the previous real estate company that they will not list with them again. This seller must be convinced that you will not be like the last one. A guarantee of service is powerful with these sellers.

2. **Non-motivated owners**
   a. *The seller's property is overpriced.* The expired may be a good prospect if you can suggest a more realistic price. These sellers believe that their home is better than anyone else's. You might be able to get a listing appointment, but do not overprice it again. Walk away if you cannot get the sellers to adjust their price.
   b. *The seller is waiting for (something).* This seller may be a good prospect if you can overcome the waiting. The sellers may be waiting on a child to graduate from high school in four months. They are not motivated because they have a long time before they need to be out. You must create some urgency for them to get realistic.
   c. *The seller hates real estate agents.* This is rare; the anger is not personal, and this is a good prospect if the anger can be overcome. It is very hard to talk with this type of seller. The key is to show concern by asking a series of questions without telling about yourself or your company. Once you are at the appointment, you can tell the sellers about those things.
   d. *The seller doesn't need an agent (currently a FSBO).* This is a good prospect, but you will need to show the value of your services. This is where offering a "fee for service" program may work well. When you are out on the appointment, you should treat these sellers as FSBOs and expireds.

Expect 5 out of 100 expireds you talk with to list with you, which is much better than telemarketing.

Expireds Procedure

Pull up the expired list from the MLS computer, and look up the owners from the cross directory on the Internet. Call every expired owner (be aware of the national "do not call" rules) in the MLS twice a day until you talk with them.

> **Salesperson:**
> "Mr./Mrs./Ms. …"
>
> **Expired:**
> "Yes."
>
> **Salesperson:**
> "This is Dan Hamilton with Acme Realty. I am calling about the property at 1604 Montgomery Street."
>
> **Expired:**
> "Yes."
>
> **Salesperson:**
> "Is that property still for sale?"
>
> **Expired:**
> "No."
>
> **Salesperson:**
> "Well, I'd like to stop by and take a quick look at the place. While I'm there, I'd like to explain why your property did not sell the last time. So if you do decide to put it back on the market, the same mistakes won't be repeated."

Leave the following message if you get an answering machine:

> "This is Dan Hamilton with Acme Realty. I am calling about the property at 1604 Montgomery Street, which was taken off the market today. I'd like to meet with you to become your new real estate agent. We offer several different programs, especially in your price range and in your area. So, if you still want to sell your property, please give me a call at _____."

The follow-up procedure on expireds is simple: Call twice a day until you actually reach the owner. Call first thing in the morning before he or she leaves for work and at night right before dinnertime. I once called an expired for three weeks until I got an answer. The owner had been away on a European vacation and did not know the property was off the market. It was an easy listing; I had no competition.

Because most people no longer have land lines and use only their cell phones, getting phone numbers is somewhat difficult. If you cannot find a home number, drive out to the property and knock on the door. It may be a hassle, but it also may be worth thousands of dollars to you!

Real Estate Waif

American Heritage Dictionary defines a *waif* as "something found and unclaimed." Real estate waifs are former real estate buyers who have been abandoned by their salespeople. Some real estate salespeople get a sale and then never follow up with their clients. Other real estate salespeople get a sale and then get out of the real estate business.

The best way to prospect for real estate waifs is to ask your broker or manager if you can go through old real estate sales files. When you find a real estate waif (or several, if you are smart), call them (following the national "do not call" rules), and use the following script:

> "Mr. or Ms._____, my name is Dan Hamilton with Acme Realty. I noticed that you purchased a home through our company a number of years ago. I am just wondering how you are enjoying the home and if you've considered moving again?"

Whatever the homeowner's response, you now have a warm prospect. These owners generally have a favorable outlook on your company and now you. They are also a great source of referrals. If their experience was not good and you can make things better, you can become their hero. Sometimes people just want someone to listen, as they feel they have been abandoned.

Generally people move every five to seven years. The files you have on these buyers will tell you how long they've lived in their houses. You can contact them with your marketing approach within six months or so of the time that they should, by national averages, begin thinking about moving again. In other words, you can get to them before they get the "itch" to move.

If someone has lived in his or her home quite a bit longer than the national average, contact that person and say: "Are you aware of your equity position? You have been in your house longer than the national average. Maybe we should investigate the possibilities of what your house could do for you."

If you stay in touch with these real estate waifs, you will have a huge source of future business. It is important not to let former clients become waifs; make contact with them at least twice a year.

Obituaries

You won't find much information about prospecting obituaries in most real estate marketing books. I've never done it because I choose not to. (Remember, you have choices in this business.)

I do know of one real estate salesperson who prospected obituaries. From the obituary section of the paper, he would take down all the necessary information. Then he would send flowers along with his business card. After a couple of days, he would make a follow-up call to the homeowner to learn the status of the property. He found that most widowers no longer wanted to live in the home. Almost all were receptive and appreciated the flowers. He had to deal with relatives frequently, but he gained four to six sales per year from prospecting using obituaries. (I don't have a script for this kind of prospecting. You are on your own here.)

On a happier note, you can also use this strategy to find potential buyers and sellers from the newspaper sections, the Internet, and social networks for "Job Promotions," "Weddings," and "Baby

Announcements." All of these might indicate a desire for new real estate.

Garage Sales

Garage sales are another way to find potential real estate sellers. Now these are fun! I love going to garage sales; I enjoy combining fun things with real estate. Here is a good script to use to get a conversation started:

> **Salesperson:**
> "Are you just clearing out some things, or are you thinking about selling the house?"

I found out that frequently this is a seller's first step in preparing to put a house on the market.

Every Thursday night, I check the newspaper and the Internet (there are also Apps for this) for "Garage Sales." Then I map out a route. I spend the first part of Friday mornings calling expireds, and then I leave on my garage sale tour. Waiting to leave till 9 a.m. allows for the early rush to pass so the homeowner will have more time to talk with you. On the way I study the market, looking for FSBO signs, unkempt properties for investment, and other real estate signs in the area. I drive with my car signs on the door. I dress professionally and always wear my name badge so there is no mistaking who I am and what I'm doing there. I mill around, looking at stuff until I get near the owner. At that point, I casually recite the script above. If the owner is interested, I get his or her name and telephone number and call after the sale. Getting this information is important, as you should not expect the owner to call you. Follow these steps at every garage sale you go to. Most likely, everyone will be in a good mood and will enjoy talking with you even if they are not interested in selling. If they indicate that they have considered selling, you should spend time talking about the market, sales in the area, or about their kids. The more bonding you can do here, the greater the results later. I may end up spending $6 for a garage sale trinket, but there are times I have often gotten $6,000 in return!

My wife has started this same routine. She goes to garage sales every Friday and Saturday to be sure she visits as many as she can. Sometimes she will find herself at an owner's second garage sale. She knows them from their first garage sale, and they immediately have a connection. She is attentive, but she is also demonstrating that she is active in the market. Her last three transactions have been because she made contact at a garage sale—and the best part is, it's fun!

Re-Active

In this section we will discuss the re-active side of the real estate business.

Sphere of Influence Marketing

Sphere of influence (SOI) marketing is one of the most powerful tools you will use during your real estate marketing career. It is the key to unlocking many gateways along your journey to financial freedom and is one of the most significant topics discussed in this book.

Sphere of influence (sometimes called center of influence) is the group of people that know you by name. It can include your mother, your dentist, the people you grew up with, your friends, people you work with, or people you've simply come in contact with at work or school. These people want to see you do well and will help you if they can. This category of marketing is the easiest and the most effective, because these people like and trust you already. They have the potential to be your best contacts if you will simply use them as resources. Creating a personal database of these resources can be the key to unlocking your successful future.

Start by making a list of as many people as possible. Don't get hung up on a specific number, but imagine that you are getting paid $100 per name. As time goes by, you will constantly add to this list through referrals, new contacts, old acquaintances, and so on.

The following categories should help "jog" your memory. Think about each specific description and who you might know within each one. It's very important not to prejudge anyone while compiling this list. Don't consider their potential interest or whether or not you'd consider working with them. This exercise is meant to get names out of your brain and onto paper.

1. Members of your own family
   a. Father, mother
   b. In-laws
   c. Children, children's children
   d. Brothers, sisters
   e. Aunts, uncles
   f. Nieces, nephews, and cousins

2. Your closest friends and those with whom you associate most
   a. Friends, neighbors
   b. People you work with now and in the past
   c. Members of your church or Sunday school class

3. People you know in organizations or clubs
   a. Civic groups, Rotary, Lions, Jaycees, and so on

4. People you do business with (who you buy from)
   a. Doctors, lawyers, barbers, merchants, grocers
   b. Gas station, laundry, postman, insurance salesperson
   c. Beautician, jewelers, favorite restaurant personnel

My brother is an attorney. He had a partner who became a friend of mine. We played softball together and went out to lunch frequently. He bought a house, but he didn't buy it through me. When I asked him why he did not buy though me, he said that he didn't know I sold in his area. I know if he had known, he would have bought through me. I took it for granted that he knew I could sell anywhere. Don't make the same mistake. Every person you know should be on your SOI list, and you should keep up with them.

I inadvertently prospected my daughter. When she was in second grade, her teacher asked her what her daddy did for a living. She told the teacher that her daddy put up signs and lock boxes. That's all she ever saw me do because I would take her with me. The teacher translated those activities and was interested in real estate. She contacted me.

Most people have over 120 people in their sphere of influence. Your challenge is to remember all of your SOI names and contact them. Also note that each of the 120 people on your list has a list of 120 people that they know, and so on and so on. Get it? The members on your SOI list will not mind you calling them. In fact they will expect it. Patrick Wyatt, manager of a Century 21, Judge Fite office, had a salesperson who ended all telephone calls with a request for real estate business. He found his leads and income increased dramatically. One person said, "I was wondering when you would ask me." You see these people want your help; they expect to be asked.

Prospecting is not limited to the areas we have mentioned. It is an 18-hour-a-day job. (You can sleep for six hours a day and then need to get back to prospecting!) A top salesperson is in love with this profession and eats, drinks, breathes, and lives real estate every waking moment. To be successful, between 70 and 90 percent of your time and energy should be spent pursuing real estate business. Wherever you go and whomever you meet along the way, you should always turn the conversation toward real estate. Everyone will know you are in the business, and you need to go out of your way to meet more people and extend your sphere of influence.

Geographic Marketing

Geographic marketing or "neighborhood servicing" is a planned prospecting campaign within a defined market group that delivers a specific message about you and your company. The objective of geographic marketing is to have homeowners think of *you* when they decide to sell their property.

Geographic marketing is a long-range activity. Major studies conducted in real estate markets show that the average geographic marketing area will require two years of work before the rewards are substantial. Be careful, though; this should only be a part of your prospecting, not your *only* form of prospecting. Do not get caught up in geographic marketing and forget your other prospecting methods. Remember, geographic marketing can take a while to develop.

Geographical marketing is cultivating people who you do not necessarily know but are living in a neighborhood where you are an expert. As the expert you should know as much about that area as possible, including the nearest schools, shopping, recreation, and people. You need to know all of the houses that are for sale, sold, expired, or pending. You need to know all the FSBOs as well. You may want to schedule neighborhood events, send e-newsletters, or plan other activities that will get your name out there. You should be a member of the neighborhood watch program, the homeowners association, and the city council. You need to be seen as the expert.

Geographic marketing differs from telemarketing in the following ways:

1. Geographic marketing is confined to a specific area or group.

2. Geographic marketing involves *repeated* contacts.

3. Geographic marketing has *long-range* results.

4. Geographic marketing is specifically intended to create "top of mind" awareness and to build personal relationships.

5. In addition to the obvious prospecting reasons for geographic marketing, another purpose is to compile neighborhood data to help provide your office with complete area coverage.

The most successful real estate salespeople are those who have learned the secret of being "a big frog in a small pond." In other words they know that it is difficult to be known throughout a large community, but comparatively easy to be well known by a small segment of that community. They also know that a small segment of the community is all that is necessary to produce a sufficient number of listings and sales to achieve the income they desire.

Choosing an Area

When developing a geographic marketing area, you must spend time and effort upfront in selecting your area. You need to focus on where you enjoy selling and where you feel a degree of personal identification. All of the homes in your geographic marketing area should be comparable to one another. A homogeneous neighborhood will produce far better results than a heterogeneous one. Age is no factor, as long as all homes are of approximately the same age and will sell for approximately the same amount of money. To start, your area should contain a maximum of 100 single-family homes. The reason for this is that a person just beginning geographic marketing does not have the skills or systems in place for handling more than 100 homes. Once you have mastered those, you can always add more.

You should drive around the area you are considering and look for real estate signs. Focus on signs from different companies, not one specific real estate salesperson. If you find that this particular area seems to deal with one company and one salesperson, you will need to find another area. This company and salesperson obviously dominates this specific geographic market. Over time you could break into that area, but why would you want to spend that much time and money when you can find another area without that competition? Remember, this is about money, not ego.

The area you choose should have some activity, but not too much or too little. In other words, make sure there are a few sales annually each year. You do not want to market to an area that rarely has sales. There are some neighborhoods where people live for years before selling. This is one of those areas you do not want to market to. You also want to be sure that the area does not have too many sales. Too many sales could mean a lot of listings but not necessarily a lot of sales—again, not an ideal situation. You want an area with enough sales to earn you some money.

Finally, you might be wondering if you should choose the area in which you live currently. That is up to you. One of the pros of being in your own neighborhood is that you should already be the expert in that area. Also, the things you do in the neighborhood directly benefit you. You may already know many of your neighbors and hopefully have good relationships with them. A con of working your neighborhood is that the sellers you list know where you live. They will come and find you, whether it's first thing in the morning, at dinnertime, or when you are getting ready for bed. Most of the time they just want to see how things are going, but they will show up at all hour of the day. You also need to consider that if you fail to actually sell a listing in that area, your neighbors will talk. You could damage your reputation in the entire area, and you may lose acquaintances.

After you have chosen an area, you need to get as much information as you can. You will need tax records for each property. You will need to preview all listed property, and you will need to knock on every door in your marketing area until you've spoken with every homeowner. Make note of everything you can find out about the owners for future use. As you obtain additional information on a family, the names of the children, in-laws living with them, leases, sales, photograph of the house, and so on, add those contacts to your data page.

Back at the office, transfer this information to the database on your computer. Organize the data in a fashion that will be useful, such as by street address. Then, whenever you make a contact, you can record that information in their section. Always review each page before ringing a doorbell to be certain you have all necessary facts. Over time, you will get to know everyone and every property.

You will eventually get the reputation as the real estate professional in this area, and people will automatically call you when they have a real estate need. People will begin listing their property with you, and you will begin selling those houses. The money will start coming in and will continue to do so as long as you continue marketing yourself in that area.

You should get 60 percent or more of the listings in your marketing area in the beginning and as much as 90 percent once it is fully developed. Out of the 100 houses in your marketing area, you can expect five to move in any given year. If you get 60 percent of those, you should get 3 listings. Now this may not seem like a lot, but it is only the beginning. Keep adding houses to your marketing area, and this will end up being a significant part of your business. And, it's fun!

Become the Expert

So let's review the actual steps, outlined below, that you will need to take to become the expert and make money with geographic marketing:

1. Choose an area.
    a. Analyze the number of listings and the number of sales in the area.
    b. Eliminate areas with established competition.
    c. Select no more than 100 homes.

2. Do research.
    a. Pull tax records on each property in your marketing area.
    b. Put all the information into your computer.

3. Knock on every door in the neighborhood.
    a. Use the script.
    b. Repeat at least once per year.

In addition, you should mail-out, email, or call everyone in your farm area monthly. Be sure to preview all listed properties and FSBO's in your area, and hold an annual event in the area.

Meet the Owners

Face to face is how you should meet the owners in your marketing area. (This is why I suggested starting with no more than 100 houses.) You should prepare for your first walk-thru by having your information ready. It is best if you have a tablet for going door to door. You can plan your visits anytime you choose. On one visit, you may want to go on a weekday morning, and then the next time, choose a time during the weekend. You should have your car signs on your car every time you are in your marketing area, and you should be dressed in your best career apparel, including your business nametag. Wear comfortable shoes, but not tennis shoes.

Drive to your area and park on public property, such as on the street. Walk to the first house (be respectful and use the walkways; never cross through someone's yard). Walk confidently up to the door and knock or ring the doorbell. When the door is answered, begin by introducing yourself.

> **Salesperson:**
> "Hi, my name is Dan Hamilton with Acme and I am the real estate expert in this area. I would like to know if you would participate in a quick survey."

You've introduced yourself and told them what company you are with. Then you tell them about a survey because you want to give them a reason for why you are there. The word "quick" tells them that you won't be taking up too much of their time.

> **Owner:**
> "Okay."

> **Salesperson:**
> "Have you thought about selling this house either now or in the near future?"

The very first question is to gauge how they feel about actually selling their house. Expect a "No" on this one because they may not be comfortable with you yet.

> **Owner:**
> "No"

> **Salesperson:**
> "How long have you lived here?"

This question lightens things up a bit. It is an easy question to answer, and it provides you with a great deal of information. It is impossible to tell how long these owners have been in the property by the tax records alone. Most people want to move every five to seven years. If these owners have lived there that long, they might be considering a move in the not-so-distant future.

Owner:
"About four years."

Salesperson:
"Why did you choose this area?"

Notice this owner said "About four years." Keep up with this one; they might be getting the itch to move. This question is also easy to answer and gives you a great deal of information. It gives you a feel for why others might want to live in the area. Having this knowledge makes you better at talking with both buyers who are interested in living in the area and sellers who already live in the area—in other words, it makes you the expert!

Owner:
"Well, we liked the neighborhood. This area has a lot of trees, and all the houses have side- or rear-entry garages. It seemed—and is—very quiet."

Salesperson:
"Great. If you were going to move, where would you move to?"

Look at all that valuable information you have received from this owner. This question is basically another way of asking if they have ever thought of selling.

Owner:
"Probably Granbury."

Salesperson:
"Interesting, and when would that be?"

Obviously, they have discussed it because they have a place in mind. Again, this is a good lead; you should pay special attention to them. With your next question, you are now reinforcing their thoughts about moving.

Owner:
"Oh, not for another year or so."

Salesperson:
"Thanks, would you like me to update you with the results of the survey?"

Now you have your time frame. You should be in touch monthly, but stop by again in six to twelve months. The last question again establishes your reason for being there and sets up another reason to stop by—to deliver the results of the survey.

Once you have completed the entire round of owners, compile your list of survey answers to present back to the everyone. You have gained some rich information. The owner might move in a year. Always cut in half what the owner tells you because it is better to be early than late. Mature trees are a selling point in the area. And you have a reason to come back, to bring the results. If a person is rude and tells you to leave, mark them on your tablet. If they continue to hassle you, delete them from your data bank because you do not have to work with everybody. However, this is your marketing area so be patient. They may soften up once they get to know you. That is the beauty of geographic marketing, and that is how relationships are built.

Remember to keep all of your notes and put them in the database for that specific neighborhood. Organize the information you have gained in a way that is interesting for the residents in the neighborhood. Make it sound like a story instead of dry data. If you do this on your computer, you can then mail it, email it, or pass it out door to door. Remember that knocking on doors is the most effective means of communication. In your geographic marketing area, you must do the difficult things first to reap the rewards later.

Monthly Follow-Up

After this first stop-by, you need to start a follow-up campaign of contacting the owners in your marketing area at least once per month. It can be via telephone, email, or another stop-by.

The first system you should design is for monthly contacts. The more automated you make your monthly follow-up, the easier and larger your farm area can be. You need to have email addresses for *all* of your owners, and then you can email them something every month. There are several creative ways you can get these addresses. You may want hold a contest in your marketing area for a giveaway. On the registration card for the giveaway, the contestants must include their email address. Be sure, though, that you are aware of and send emails out in accordance with anti-spam laws. The giveaway can be as simple as a dinner for two or a small television. Never be tempted to sell or let others use your list of emails. It is bad business and possibly illegal. No amount of money is worth the harm this will cause.

The purpose of your contact can be things of local interest, for example, the area high school sports schedule or a list of upcoming charity events.

Once you know your area well enough, you will begin to hear of personal stories such as kids' graduation, births, weddings, and other events that can be included in your mailings. However, be sure to get permission before using this information. The more personal you can make the emails, the better chance they will be read.

What you send them is not as important as sending them something. Real estate office manager John Lundquist suggests sending "something that is Evidence of Production." Possible mailings include area statistics, notices of houses that have just sold, and upcoming buyer/seller seminars. Be sure to put your contact information on the email and answer any replies promptly.

You can also contact owners in your marketing area by telephone. Again, be sure you are in compliance with the national do-not-call laws. Also, take note that you can quickly overuse this method. If you call an owner every month and ask if they have thought of selling, you will be asked to "NEVER CALL AGAIN!" That response is *not* what you are looking for. If you decide to call, you need to have a legitimate reason. You could call if there is a change in the start time for registration of classes for the high school. If you know birthdays, you can call for those. The two positive things about calling are that it is fast—it takes no time to call—and you can hear "sell signs" over the telephone.

The stop-by is a quick visit with one specific homeowner for a specific reason. Personal contact is always the best contact, but it is not feasible to personally talk to each owner in your marketing area every month. If you have that kind of time, you are spending *way* too much time on your area. You should have enough time in your schedule to be able to knock on every door about once per year. This does not mean to avoid your marketing area. You should be seen, but not actually knocking on doors. The top advantages of a stop-by are that they are quick, and because they are face to face, you can "read" the owners body language.

On this personal visit (stop-by) you should leave owners with something to remember you by. Some possible leave-behinds include key chains, candy, mouse pads, a binder of house papers, a CD case, or golf balls. Make sure whatever you leave has your name on it so the homeowner will be reminded of you whenever they see or use the object. You may also leave something as simple as a flyer on the front door. Here are some other informational ideas to use as reasons for contacting homeowners:

- New real estate sales in the area

- Recipes the homeowners may be interested in trying

- Upcoming events in the area

- Services you provide

- Upcoming community council meetings

- Real estate news

- PTA activities of the month

- News of sports activities

- Service club news of community interest

- National holidays

A monthly e-newsletter allows you to have an instant welcome into the house, but it can be time consuming to produce. I have seen real estate salespeople spend weeks each month doing an e-newsletter. I wouldn't suggest taking the time to do this. However, there are some companies that publish e-newsletter templates. You just need to add your picture and whatever facts you want to include and then email it out.

Mail-outs are expensive, but they do save you time. You can mail out any of the items discussed in the email section, plus you can include items of value. You can mail out refrigerator magnets, ice scrapers, or a calendar with your contact information. People love to get gifts in the mail, and no matter how simple, the owner will tend to keep them.

No matter which type of follow-up you choose to use, you should vary the delivery. Continually sending out emails will soon lose its luster. Add in some variety: One month use email, the next month, mail the owners something.

Over Time

After several months, the people in your geographic marketing area will begin to recognize you as their resident real estate guy or gal. After a few months, they will know your name and will associate you with the company you work for. Then they will receive the news that they are being transferred in their job. But now they know you, know what you do, and whom you are with. They believe you understand them and the area. It only makes sense to call you. This will be a common theme as you start to dominate that area.

However, no matter how successful you are in your geographic marketing area, if you neglect it, you will lose it to your competition. Never believe you are the only one contacting your owners.

Conclusion

Geographic marketing is a great supplement to your real estate business. When a person calls you to sell their home and you know the entire family, their likes and dislikes, and their birthdays, you are not only the logical choice; you are the *only* choice. This is when the business gets fun. Do not expect this to happen overnight, but be patient and persistent.

Multiple Geographic Marketing

When you have the geographic marketing systems in place and you find you want to expand your territory, you can add more streets. You can also begin multiple geographic marketing (MGM). Here you select areas that are not adjacent, but may be miles apart. Look for different areas of houses and different price ranges to identify sellers in one of your marketing areas who are ready to move up to a different marketing area you control.

Business Marketing

Business marketing is effective, but time intensive. Unlike SOI and geographic marketing, business marketing is cultivating "business" people who you may not know but who are working in your area. As the expert in the area, you should know as much about them as possible.

Business marketing can be successful because most people are at work during the day. When a famous bank robber was asked why he robbed banks, he simply replied, "That is where the money is." And that is why we market for prospects where the prospects are—at their place of business.

When approaching businesses, you don't want to look like a salesperson. You are not there to solicit sales; you are there only to introduce yourself. So don't wear your nametag or career apparel. Just carry a small note pad and pen or a smartphone, but keep it in your pocket. Walk into the office and introduce yourself to the receptionist. The receptionist is a very important player in this because that is the person who knows everything about the company.

Salesperson:
"Cindy?" [If you saw it on her name plate, if not just say good morning]

Receptionist:
"Yes."

Salesperson:
"My name is Dan Hamilton with Acme Realty. I'll be working in the area and just wanted to stop by and introduce myself to you.

Receptionist:
"Okay."

Gauge the temperament of the receptionist and depending on what you perceive, either continue with small talk or excuse yourself and leave.

Salesperson:
"I see that you are busy; it has been nice meeting you."

Either ask for a name or ask to take a business card if one is displayed. Do not ask for any business; it is not the time yet. When you step out of the door, you should record the receptionist's name, the name of the business, the address, and any other information you gathered while talking with the receptionist. Then move on and do the same thing at the next 10 to 12 businesses that constitute your business marketing area. Like geographic marketing, do not overextend yourself; keep the area small and grow it as your systems get better.

After you have been through your business marketing area once, return each month on the same day and time, such as the first Tuesday of each month at 9:15 a.m. so everyone knows your schedule. With each visit, try to find out more information. Don't expect the receptionist to remember your name and don't offer any services or ask for business. Continue this at each business for about six months and then bring in a gift. I usually bring donuts with my business card, printed as a sticker, stuck on both the outside and on the inside of the box. It is okay if a dozen donuts is not enough to feed the whole company; you are simply prospecting the receptionist. You will find that, on your day to bring donuts, some employees will be hanging around waiting for you. By the way, if you negotiate with the donut shop, you can probably cut yourself a deal.

Eventually, the receptionist may tell you that she heard Bob from the accounting department is being transferred and will need to sell his house and buy a new one in Seattle. You have now started to harvest this business. Be sure to update the receptionist on the referral and bring her a gift after closing.

How about this bonanza? The company needs to relocate its entire operation. If you are the person who has been there, you get the business of multiple executives.

I find that as long as you keep your visits brief and don't try selling anything, no one gets mad. I also find that it is at least six months before the receptionist knows your name and what you do. Again, business marketing should be a part of your business, not your entire business. And it is kind of fun.

Non-Occupant Owners (NOO)

Non-occupant owners (NOO) are the owners of real estate who are leasing the properties to renters. Some of these owners are "don't wanters," meaning they own property but don't want it. Some are so desperate to get out from under the burden of the property they become very willing to negotiate. I have said that selling real estate can provide you with a good living but to become wealthy, you must buy it. Prospecting the NOO is a great way for you to look for investment-grade property.

The six types of NOOs include:

1. **Not interested in selling.** These owners aren't worth your valuable time. Move on.

2. **Interested but has no equity.** These owners may be good prospects if they can sell and have money to pay closing costs.

3. **Interested and has a lot of equity.** Maybe this seller will offer owner financing. If so, you may want to buy the property as an investment. If not, list it and sell it.

4. **Interested but doesn't want to sell at the investment level.** List this property for sale on the open market and make the commission.

5. **An investor in real estate.** Keep these owners on a list for future prospecting. Almost all legitimate investors are looking for their next deal.

6. **A true "don't wanter."** These are the properties you want to buy for yourself. You must disclose all of the relevant information and work this with the guidance of your broker. If you don't have the money, work out a venture with an investor on your investor list.

You can find NOOs by pulling tax records of the street you are interested in prospecting. Most computers in a real estate office have an online tax database. If not, you must go to the courthouse to search the records. Once you find the tax records, look for any property where the mailing address of the owner is not the same as the address of the subject property. This indicates the owner may not be the resident. Then send the owner the following letter:

> **Mr. or Mrs. Owner,**
>
> **My name is Dan Hamilton with Acme Realty. I am wondering if you would consider selling the property at 1520 Westcreek to a prospect of mine.**
>
> **If so, please call me at 817-555-1212 as soon as possible. Thanks.**

The letter is short and simple. The prospect you speak of is yourself. Remember, you should want to buy property if the owner is a "don't wanter," and you can't know that until they call.

The form letter can be created on your computer. Just substitute the owner's name and the subject property address, print it out, and mail it in a plain white envelope. If you use a business envelope, it may not be opened. You are not violating the Deceptive Trade Practices Act because you address yourself as a licensed real estate professional in the body of the letter. You should also address the envelope by hand, instead of using labels. Out of 100 of these letters sent, you can expect the following results:

- 70% No response, not interested
- 15% Not interested, just curious
- 10% Investors
- 3%   Interested, but has no equity
- 1%   Interested, but not at investment level

One in every 500 are "don't wanters."

Floor Time

Floor time in a real estate office is sometimes called opportunity time or floor duty. Floor time means taking calls that come into the real estate office. Some offices have receptionists who screen the calls and pass prospects to the floor salesperson. Other offices require the floor salesperson to field and handle original calls.

Real estate companies rarely use floor time anymore because it is not productive for the salesperson. Most unsolicited leads now come from the company website versus any other type of advertising. These Internet leads can quickly be sent to the real estate professional by phone and text. No longer does the salesperson need to be at the office.

Property Knowledge

Property knowledge is the knowledge of the property in the salesperson's market area. The only way to gain that knowledge is to view property and show it to potential buyers. If you want to preview property (previewing property is viewing property only for the knowledge), do it sparingly and only as a break. Your time is better spent prospecting.

Market Specialization

Specializing in one market means concentrating on one main area. It does not eliminate other areas; it just centers your thinking and action. The more focused your career, the better your results. Here are a few specializations that might be of interest.

Third-Party Referral Companies

In this segment of the real estate business, third-party companies buy or control the selling of the houses for corporate moves. These corporations pay a great deal of money to the third-party companies who assign the actual sale of the properties to local real estate companies and their salespeople. The paperwork required by the referral companies is intensive, but the income is too. This is big business. Sometimes the transfer can involve hundreds of moves. Most of this business is already assigned to large, well-connected real estate organizations. Occasionally, the referral is only for a few top executives, and that business could be handled by one or a few salespeople. It is not easy business, but it would not hurt to talk with your broker or manager about getting involved in this business.

Hints for Getting Referral Company Business
Corporate calling involves finding the correct people to call. Make a list of companies in your market along with any state or federal agencies, universities, hospitals, community colleges, and school districts.

Check with the local Chamber of Commerce, search online, do research at the library, visit the economic development council and planning committees, and come up with names, addresses, phone numbers, and emails of the people who handle personnel for these companies.

Once you locate the correct people, it's time to call them. There are two types of calls. The corporate fact-finding call is simply to find out information. You need to find out who the correct person is that you should contact. Once you contact that person, find out if they have any plans for referral. The more information you can obtain, the more versed you will be when it comes time to ask for business.

With second type of call, you will actually ask for the business or at least set up an appointment to discuss the possibility of referral business. The latter would be used with smaller operations.

Once you get an appointment, treat it as business and not casual real estate. These are professional business people, and you must act accordingly. Ask for one transaction and then if you are great, you will get more.

Lastly, get educated. Go to a referral class, and get your referral specialist designation. Then make sure the referral directors are aware of your credentials.

Niche Markets

You can market your services directly to a niche market, which is a group made up of specific types of people, including any of the following:

- Doctors
- Lawyers
- Business owners
- Teachers
- Bankers
- First-time homebuyers
- Police officers
- Low-income homebuyers
- Professional athletes
- Seniors
- Military personnel

With niche marketing you should develop a program that is customized for that market you will be working. Doctors may want a program that lets them preview all properties online so they aren't wasting their time looking at house after house. The city may provide special financing programs that benefit teachers and police officers. First-time homebuyers need lots of attention; if you are going to take this as your niche segment, you had better have the patience.

Once you develop a customized package for your niche, you will need to set up a marketing strategy to reach that segment. After you close your first niche buyer or seller, you must ask them for referrals from other people in their niche. If you choose military personnel as your niche and sell one a house, ask the seller or buyer if they can get you on the base to do a "How to buy a house if you are in the military" class or at least pass out marketing material.

Niche marketing develops over time. I know one guy who decided that condo homeowners would be his niche at a time when condos weren't selling. He persisted and became known as the Condo King.

Builders

The builder market is unique because builders typically think they can sell a new home without the assistance of a real estate salesperson. Review the FSBO section of this book for a refresher on why this doesn't work. In fact, builders are quite similar to FSBOs. The difference is that builders can give you several properties per year.

Hints to Getting Builder Business

To get builder business, you must be noticed. About the only way to get noticed by a builder is to sell at least one if not several of their homes. Without selling one of their homes, how can you convince any builder that you would be great at marketing? Builders have buyers who you may be able to gain access to. Suppose a buyer shows up at a builder's spec (built to show work; speculation) house and does not like the builder's style. This buyer would be great for you because you can show them any property. If you could get access to these buyers, you could make a fortune. But first you have to get noticed and then ask for the buyers.

There are several other ways for you to gain access to builders and their buyers. For example, you can hold open houses for them and provide free advertising. You could offer a fee for service type of arrangement. The builders would not have to pay a commission but would pay for certain aspects of the selling process. The more ways you can work with this market, the better the chance that you will get noticed. Builders are in the business of building, and you are in the business of selling. It is your job to be sure this arrangement occurs.

Real Estate Owned Property

Real Estate Owned (REO) property is owned by banks and lending institutions. They acquired these houses through foreclosure. The banks do not want to hold these properties, so they are great opportunities for the knowledgeable real estate professional. Sometimes they make great investment properties if the bank is willing to finance them. If the bank is really desperate to sell the REO, it might even finance with no money down. Real estate professionals should approach getting REO listings the same way they approach the referral business.

Investors

A majority of investors are willing to pay a commission to real estate professionals for the right services. Be careful of these buyers, though, because they can eat up your time and you will get very little in return. You may spend time researching properties and presenting them to your investor just to have the investor give you an offer so low that the seller rejects it. Your time has now been wasted. This could happen many times before a seller ever accepts an investor offer. My question is, "If the investment was such a good deal, why did you not buy it?"

If you insist on working with investors, you need to set up some rules:

- The investor must sign a buyer's representation agreement with you. You could limit the area shown to your specific expertise, but you must get this. If the investor is not willing to commit to you in writing, then you should find other business.

- They must put up a significant amount of earnest money at a title company prior to showing a property. This ensures that the investor is serious.

- They must show proof of funds. It is not acceptable if they say they will be getting financing. If that is the case, then they are not investors, and you need to have them qualified *prior* to showing any property. Trust is not acceptable at this point.

- Do *not* let them take more than six hours per week of your time.

- If the investor is willing to work under these conditions (and there should be no reason why they wouldn't), then it may be worth pursuing.

Seller Seminar

A seller's seminar is given by a professional real estate salesperson to help sellers sell their own houses. While you may point out the reasons sellers would have better luck using professional salespeople, the seminar must include good marketing tips that the sellers can use. It is possible to give good and helpful information and still get the sale for yourself.

Each time you hold a seminar, you will get better and learn more. You should hold the seminar at different times and on different days to get a feel for what works in your particular area. It is important that you have a participation form that attendees must fill out when they come in so you can get all of their information.

The seminar should have a workbook the seller can keep and use to take notes. The workbook should have an outline of the material covered. The book could be paid for with advertisements from local venders.

The class should cover the entire process of selling a house. It should begin with an overview, then cover specifics, and end with a summary and an offer of assistance. The materials should cover marketing, financing, titles, closings, costs, and all the forms necessary to sell a house. The subject matter should be heavily laden with legalities to scare the seller a bit. Make sure there are "gaps" in the presentation so the sellers will realize they need you to fill in those gaps.

The seminar should include a fee to be determined by you. People see value in a fee. If the seminar is free, the public will perceive that it is worth nothing, and who would want to waste their time for nothing? The prevailing thought will be that it must be some kind of gimmick. Having a fee not only creates a perception of value, but it also can offset the costs involved in giving the seminar. You can use it to pay for refreshments and printed materials. If you are afraid the fee will scare potential customers, offer free tickets through a local mortgage or title company. Have the company pay a portion of the ticket price for that advertisement.

Be cautious about inviting important people to speak at your seminar. If you turn this into a huge production and no sellers show up, you end up being humiliated. I was invited by a broker to speak at a seller seminar, and only one seller actually showed up. Now if you think about it, the broker had a legitimate, interested seller; however, because the broker had invited a title officer, a mortgage officer, and myself to speak, she was so embarrassed that she did not even try to get the seller committed. My point is that one good lead is better than no lead at all. I believe it is best to speak yourself because you become the expert. If you feel you cannot speak, invite only one speaker you can count on.

Be sure to ask the sellers for their business before you end the seminar. Don't make the seminar a waste of time by not asking for the business. Also ask for the buying business. Once a seller sells, he or she becomes a buyer. With all the help you have given them, they may feel obligated to buy through you. Take them up on it.

Community Involvement

Well-rounded real estate professionals should give back to their communities. Community involvement should not be contingent upon receiving business; it should be from the heart. If your intentions are not honorable, it will be sensed. Not only will you fail, but you will disgrace yourself for being disingenuous.

I know real estate salespeople who select their places of worship based on the number of licensed real estate salespeople in the congregation. They believe that if they have no competition, they can get all the business. I believe you will fail if you choose this approach.

Community involvement will get you business simply by osmosis. You do a good deed, and others will want to help you out. (On the other hand, if you do a good deed and *expect* a return, you will receive and deserve nothing.) I know of real estate salespeople who help out in their children's school. They take care of printing the bags that hold school-related information that students take home to their parents on a daily basis. The school benefits because it doesn't have to pay for the bags, and the real estate salespeople put their names on those bags that go home to hundreds of families.

You are the only one who limits your involvement in the community. Volunteers are needed in all types of charity work. I wouldn't advise prospecting your fellow volunteer, but you can wear your career apparel. One word of caution though: Don't get so involved in the community and real estate associations that you never have time to make money. Remember to keep a balance.

Association Meetings

The real estate industry offers several support groups and associations. Participation in these groups will not make you money, but the money you get might be easier and more rewarding.

Associations help negotiate for the benefit of all real estate professionals. They form lobbying groups and take up the rights for the industry. An association can help if there is a disagreement between to competing brokers. Associations also offer education. If you cannot donate your time, then donate your money and vice versa.

Chapter Summary

As you have seen, there are many ways to make money in the real estate business. You need to practice each of these prospecting techniques to find your favorites and the ones that are most comfortable for you. You should concentrate on those. Do not pass over any of these techniques without putting in an effort to master them. You can either be active or passive. Neither is worse than the other; the better one is the one that fits you best. Market yourself through calls and knocking on doors. Develop your contact list with your sphere of influence and the areas you choose to farm. Call on FSBOs. Get involved in your community. These may not all pay off immediately, but in the long term they might be extremely profitable.

Summary Questions

1. Which of the following is an "active" way to prospect?
   a. Call FSBOs.
   b. Offer assistance to the Welcome Wagon.
   c. Run a personal advertisement.
   d. Join a health club to meet new people.

2. How many weeks should you follow a FSBO system to be successful?
   a. 3
   b. 12
   c. 18
   d. 6

3. What critical goal must be achieved when initiating and then developing a relationship with a FSBO?
   a. Work up a net sheet.
   b. Get a face-to-face appointment.
   c. Develop a mail-out campaign.
   d. Do a market analysis to see if the seller is priced right.

4. How often should you prospect?
   a. 12 hours a week
   b. Daily
   c. Constantly
   d. Depends on your real estate goals

5. What should you do in your geographic marketing area?
   a. Inform the neighbors if minorities are moving in.
   b. Send out a minimum of 12 mailings per year.
   c. Take all of the available listings, even if they are overpriced.
   d. All of the above should be done.

6. How many homes should be in your original farm area?
   a. No more than 100
   b. 800–1,000

c. Less than 25
d. 1,500–2,200

7. What are abandoned clients in the real estate business called?
   a. Protected Sids
   b. Revisions
   c. Waifs
   d. TLCs

8. What is it called when a real estate salesperson specializes in one particular geographic area and becomes the expert on property values and sales activities?
   a. Geographic Marketing
   b. Generalizing
   c. Active prospecting
   d. Sublocation

9. Salable listings can be compared to
   a. a prison sentence.
   b. gold.
   c. a ride on a roller coaster.
   d. a yo-yo.

10. All of the following often result when FSBOs overprice their properties, except
    a. more agents contacting them.
    b. higher out-of-pocket expenses.
    c. fewer showings.
    d. property sells too fast.

Chapter 8

Seller Listing
Procedures

Chapter Overview

In this chapter you will learn about seller listing procedures—everything from taking a listing from a seller, to the entire marketing process, to closing. There are many steps involved, and you should check with your broker or manager on the exact procedures specific to your office.

Key Terms

Competitive Market Analysis (CMA):
A CMA shows sellers where their property would sell in the current marketplace compared to other properties that have actually sold.

Market Value:
Market value is determined by the amount a seller is willing to sell his or her property for and the amount a buyer is willing to pay with open market conditions, all information known, and both parties acting in their own best interests with neither party under duress.

Appraisal:
An appraisal is only *one* person's *opinion* of the property's value.

Seller Listing Packet:
A seller listing packet includes all of the documents needed to place a property on the market.

Wants and Needs Analysis:
A wants and needs analysis determines the reason the sellers "want" to sell and also why the sellers "need" to sell.

Office Tour:
An office tour allows real estate salespeople in a particular real estate office to go out and view (tour) the most recent listings the office has taken.

Introduction

No matter how good you are at prospecting, if you can't sell your inventory you cannot help your clients or yourself. If you do a few things right, you will be able to market and sell your properties successfully. One of the most important first steps is to prepare properly before an appointment.

Preparing for the Appointment

Don't wait until the last minute to prepare for a listing appointment. You need to have all of your "stuff" together. You should be mentally prepared for the worst and toughest sellers imaginable. If the sellers turn out to be nice people (and most do), you have it made. If the seller is some type of nasty, cruel troll, at least you are prepared.

In a real estate office I once owned, I hired a nice young man who was relatively new to the profession. One day as he was leaving the office dressed in a pair of jean shorts and a t-shirt, I asked him where he was going. He replied that he was going on a listing appointment. Admittedly, I was shocked, considering how he was dressed (he shouldn't have even been dressed like that just for a day in the office). When I probed further, I learned that a friend of his wanted him to list and sell his house. When I asked if he wanted me to go along, he responded that there was no need. His friend knew him, and the listing was a sure thing. I also learned that he hadn't done a CMA; he said that because they were best friends, they would just "talk" about it.

When he got back, I asked him how it went. He confessed that his friend wanted him to list the house, but his friend's wife "knew" the friend. She knew him as a wild party guy, not a professional real estate salesperson. The couple had decided to let him list the property if he showed up and acted professional. He didn't, and they ended up listing with someone else. No matter how hard I tried to help him and lead him in the right direction, it didn't matter.

I remember a couple who had a property on the market that did not sell. After calling them, I went out to their home to list the property. At the presentation, they agreed with everything I said. At times they even remarked, "What a nice guy! You would do that for us?" It was one of those times when everything seemed to work. I finally said, "Put me to work for you." They said they would, but they were going out of town for two weeks and would call me when they got back. I usually would have pressed the matter and had them list with me right then, but in this case, I was sure of my position.

Two weeks later I got a call from them saying they were ready. I was certain the listing was mine, considering how well our initial appointment went. As I was getting in my car to go to list the property, a little voice in my head said, "You need to be better prepared and take everything you might need to do a listing presentation." I thought, "Nah, the sellers like me, it's in the bag." But I heard the voice again, only this time it was louder. So I decided to get better prepared and brought everything with me. After exchanging pleasantries, I said, "I have filled out the agreement with the terms we already discussed. I just need your authorization, and we will make every effort to get you happily moved."

And that's when everything changed. Suddenly they were bombarding me with questions: "What is it exactly that you are promising to do for us? How much are you charging? How long is the listing for?" I staggered back and said, "Let me go to my car and get my things." I sat down and began the listing presentation over from the beginning. After all was said and done, they listed with me.

But what if I hadn't listened to that little voice and had shown up unprepared? I think we can guess.

Boy Scout Motto:
Be Prepared

Before you show up at a seller's front door, you need to know the market in that area. Market research will allow you to describe current market conditions so the sellers can set a competitive price and understand your marketing strategies. This phase involves completing a market evaluation.

Competitive Market Analysis (CMA)

A solid Competitive Market Analysis (CMA) will help you get your listings sold. It shows sellers where their property would sell in the current market place compared to other properties that have actually sold. The CMA determines the maximum price that justifies taking the listing.

Market evaluation data are records of listings and selling prices of comparable properties. These facts of record will help you evaluate a property and determine a salable price range.

A CMA is not market value or an appraisal. Market value is determined by the amount a seller is willing to sell his or her property for and the amount a buyer is willing to pay with open market conditions, all information known, and both parties acting in their own best interests with neither party under duress.

Some real estate salespeople and the general public believe that an appraisal is value or what the property is really worth. This is not correct; an appraisal is only *one* person's *opinion* of the property's value.

I had a listing appointment in which the seller wanted more money from the house than the market would bear. I could not convince the seller that the property should sell for $115,000 because the seller wanted $130,000. I suggested using a professional appraiser. When the appraisal came back at $115,000, the seller agreed to it, and we began marketing the house at that price. Within a few weeks, a buyer offered the seller $115,000, the seller accepted, and the closing took place a short time later.

A CMA is a tool, not a weapon. Some real estate salespeople use it to beat the sellers over their heads. They don't ask questions of the seller to determine needs. They don't use other techniques to help the sellers see value. All they do is wield the CMA like a battle axe, and the sellers tend to fight. Hint: Never fight with your clients; you might win the battle, but you could lose the war.

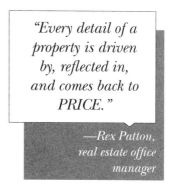

"Every detail of a property is driven by, reflected in, and comes back to PRICE."

—Rex Patton, real estate office manager

Types of Data for a CMA

There are three types of data that need to be included on a CMA.

1. **Actives**—This data includes properties that are currently on the market. The information gives you a look at your competition. If the sellers insist on pricing their houses for more, they will be priced out of the market. Actives are for reference only. Prices should be based on the prices of houses already sold.

2. **Solds**—This data includes properties that have actually sold. A ready, willing, and able buyer agreed to a price with the seller. We can use this price to determine a price for the subject property. Generally, the real estate salesperson should use three comparables for adequate evaluation.

3. **Expireds**—This data includes properties that were marketed but did not sell, typically because they were priced too high. This is valuable information for the seller. Do the sellers actually want to *sell* their properties, or do they just want to market them?

Good Comparables

It is best to drive around a neighborhood to see the area before doing a CMA. You are not doing the seller any favors if you present a CMA but don't know the area. You can learn the neighborhood quickly by looking at the statistics and driving around the neighborhood.

When running a CMA, a good comparable should include the following five considerations, which are listed in order of importance:

- **Area**—Where is the property located? If all of the comparables are in the same area, they typically have a similar build.

- **Square Footage**—If one house is 800 square feet and another house is 8,000 square feet, you cannot make any adjustments. The difference is not only in size but also in quality.

- **Age**—A property built 200 years ago is not the same as one built last year.

- **Amenities**—An amenity is anything that adds value.

- **Terms of Sale**—This includes creative financing, time on market, or any other nuances.

To run a CMA on your computer,

1. Pull up the tax records for the area.

2. Pull up the CMA program on your MLS.

3. Run the CMA by subdivision, then run it by map area.

If you come up with more than 20 comparables, you need to enter more criteria to reduce that number. You can do this by limiting the square footage, the age, or maybe including a special amenity like a swimming pool if one is available. Do not limit too much to start or you might not get a good comparable base.

Once you have narrowed the comparables to 20, stop and evaluate them. Look for the three best comparable properties using the above criteria. Once you have selected the three you will use, generate a full report on each of them, including the tax records.

A good, valuable comparable must be a property that sold within the last six months. Also, it should not be a distressed sale like a foreclosure unless the neighborhood has experienced several foreclosures and they now represent market value. Many sellers believe that the seller and the real estate salesperson set the sale price of a property. This is not true; the marketplace sets the price. Again, you need at least three good sold comparables for a worthy evaluation.

Outside factors, such as supply and demand, the local or national economy and seasonal variations, also play a part in determining a listing price. Consider these factors along with the information you collected for the comparables. Through experience, you will develop skills to incorporate all the variables involved.

Questions for the Seller

When talking with a seller on the telephone, there are a few questions you should ask before you go on the listing appointment; doing so will aid you in completing a CMA.

KEY QUESTION: Do you have a second to tell me a little bit about your home?

1. How many bedrooms and bathrooms do you have?

2. How many living areas are in the house?

3. Is there a garage? If so, how many cars does it hold?

4. What kitchen equipment do you have?

5. Is your patio covered?

6. Is there a fence? What is it made from, metal or wood?

7. Does the house have a security system or an intercom?

8. Do you have a swimming pool or a spa?

9. Does the house have central heat and central air?

10. What type of flooring is used in the house?

11. Is there a fireplace or a wet bar in the house?

12. What else can you tell me about your home?

FINANCIAL QUESTIONS

1. How much do you want to sell your house for?

2. What is the amount remaining on your house note?

Appraisals Are Getting Tougher

Appraisals are getting tougher, as demonstrated by the Federal Housing Administration's stringent property requirements, their review of completed appraisals, and the rapidly changing market values. Here are some hints about appraisals that will help you:

- **Like = Like.** The goal of any appraisal is to find comparable properties that are as similar as possible to the subject property. If there are no similar properties, the appraiser must go to other sales and start adjusting for the values. It is better to use a similar property than to adjust, because adjustment amounts are limited to no more than 10 percent of the value!

- **Current sales are required.** You can't use properties that were sold more than a year from the time of your listing. Six months is better. If there are no area sales in that time frame, explore other options.

- **Be aware of economic and functional obsolescence.** Economic obsolescence occurs when the market changes around a property (a house in the middle of an industrial district). Functional obsolescence occurs when the market demand makes features out of date (for example, a one-car garage vs. a two-car garage). These factors affect the approach the appraiser uses.

- **Property condition is critical, especially on FHA-priced properties.** Almost any FHA property will require some repairs, so prepare your seller for that. Keep in mind that lender-required repairs are always negotiable between buyer and seller.

Communicating the Results

When the time is right (one of the last steps in the listing procedure), you should communicate the results of the CMA. It is best to have the CMA on a computer-generated spreadsheet. You can buy electronic templates or software relatively inexpensively or you can just create your own. A spreadsheet looks professional and official.

Follow these steps when communicating the results of your CMA:

1. Explain how the CMA is organized.

2. Tell the sellers why each type of property in the CMA is important to the process.

3. Begin with recent sales, giving this section the most weight.

4. Describe each property thoroughly, comparing it to the sellers' homes.

5. Allow ample time for the sellers to digest the information.

6. Point out the range of values.

7. Present a net proceeds estimate based on the middle of your recommended range.

8. Remind sellers of their goals. Help the sellers to set the correct price.

Seller's Net Sheet

At this point in the presentation, you should present a seller's net sheet, including the amount of money the seller will walk away with after all expenses have been paid.

Seller Presentation

A seller presentation, also called a listing or marketing presentation, shows the seller the real estate salesperson's marketing plan for the seller's house. This presentation should be set up in a program like PowerPoint and should send a consistent message that keeps you from straying to areas that might be construed as violations of the federal Fair Housing laws. (Hopefully this is not a problem, but the material helps prevent any errors.) The main purposes of the presentation are as follows:

1. **Visually demonstrates the services offered.** Most people are visual in nature. Clients may gain a greater understanding of the plan by seeing it all laid out rather than just being told about it.

2. **Keeps the real estate salesperson from losing his or her train of thought.** One of the biggest fears of a new real estate salesperson is the listing appointment. It is easy to get distracted or lose track of where you are during the presentation.

   Most real estate companies provide a standard template of sorts that real estate salespeople can use when creating their presentations. The following should be included in this template:

   - Questions to keep people involved
   - Pictures for variety

- Bulleted statements, not complete sentences

- A walk-through of each segment of the presentation

Seller Listing Packet

A seller listing packet includes all of the documents needed to place a property on the market. Most real estate companies will make up listing packets for their salespeople. If the company does not do this, the real estate salesperson must. At the very least, a complete listing packet should include the following items:

- Seller's listing agreement

- Buyer's brokerage agreement

- Seller's property disclosure statement

- Agency disclosure form

- Multiple Listing Service input form

- Mortgage information letter

- Home warranty brochures

- Advertising submission form

- Yard sign call-up form

- Any additional forms required by law or your broker

Keep several of these packets in your briefcase and in your automobile. You never know when you might need a listing packet. I was with a new real estate salesperson on one of his first listing appointments. He was doing great. In fact, he was doing so good that when I looked at the sellers and asked, "Will you put us to work for you?" the sellers agreed. When I noted to my associate that it was time to present the listing packet, he gave me a look that told me he had forgotten it. Don't let this happen to you. The listing packet can also be documents on your computer that can be emailed directly to the seller in a group.

Tools to Bring

You never know what you might need to convince a seller to list with you. It's better to have too much than not enough. Keep what you're not expecting to need, such as the following, in your car:

- Listing packet
- Lock box
- Lock box key (if needed)
- Flashlight
- Note pads
- Writing utensils (more than one)
- Tape measure
- For Sale sign (if its size isn't a problem)
- Title insurance rate card

Arrival Time

Arrive on time to the listing appointment. Promptness shows the owner you will do what you say, and it shows you genuinely care.

On the other hand, do not show up early. I once made plans to meet an insurance salesperson at 7 p.m. At 6:50, the doorbell rang. It was the salesperson. I was not ready for the appointment, I was uncomfortable, and subsequently the salesperson did not make a sale.

It's ideal to arrive about 10 to 15 minutes early, but do not go to the door. Instead, drive around the neighborhood and look for other houses for sale. This helps you look like the expert if the seller asks about any of the other sales in the area, and you might even pick up a For Sale By Owner. You want to be early just in case of mishaps, like getting lost.

Park on the street in front of the house, if possible. It is best if you do not park in the driveway because someone might need to leave or park there. This way you won't have to get up from the presentation to move your car.

Another nice trick is to make an early trip to the property and take a picture of it. Get the picture printed at store that offers one-hour photo service. Place the photo in a folder with the property address and your name written on it. When the seller answers the door, hand them the picture and say, "Sometimes people do not have pictures of their home, and I thought it would be nice if you had one." It's simple but effective in breaking the ice. Newer technology, such as digital cameras and portable photo printers, make this something you can even do from your car.

Approach to the Door

When it is time for your appointment, either knock or ring the doorbell. The point is: Do something, don't just stand there. So which is better, knocking or ringing? Don't sweat the small stuff. Once somebody told me to give a hearty knock on the door. I hit the door so hard my knuckles started bleeding. By the time the owner got to the door, I needed a towel to clean up the blood. Now, I ring the doorbell.

Once you ring the doorbell (or knock), take a step or two back, allowing for a little space between you and the door. Look to the left.

Your name badge should be on your right lapel, so the owner can see it. If it calms you, you can even whistle softly.

Smile genuinely when the owner opens the door. Then offer to shake the owner's hand—it's what we do in Texas. Or do whatever seems comfortable to you. After you greet the owner, introduce yourself and say, "We have an appointment for 7 p.m." Look at your watch, and say, "It is exactly 7 p.m." This shows the owner you are prompt and you do what you say.

Entering the Home

As you enter the home, be sure to wipe your feet. You do not ever want to track anything into someone's house. Also, look for shoes piled around the door. If you see this, offer to take your shoes off as it may be their custom. Then pay the owner a compliment. The following are some tips for complimenting:

- Never compliment the house. Doing so may drive up their price.

- Never compliment if it makes you sound like a high-pressure salesperson.

- Never compliment the spouse on how great he or she looks because someone else might take offense to that.

So what can you compliment? How about the children? This is the best line if it presents itself: "Mr. and Mrs. Seller, I just wanted to say how polite your children were when I called to set this appointment. That demonstrates how well they are being raised." Smile and head for the kitchen table.

Meeting at the Kitchen Table

The first objective once you enter the sellers' house is to head to the kitchen table. This is where all domestic decisions are made. The living room is for entertaining, and you are not there to entertain or to be entertained. The kitchen table provides a surface where you can spread out your marketing materials, set up your laptop, and eventually get documents signed to start the marketing process. If you do not get to the kitchen table, you are already at a disadvantage to getting the listing.

The best way to get to the kitchen table is to lead. Once in the house and the compliment has been paid, head to the kitchen table. Don't hesitate. If the owner says the table is dirty, offer to help clean it off. No matter what, get to the kitchen table.

Once seated at the table, if the seller offers you something to drink, only take water, with ice if you prefer. It is also acceptable to ask the seller for a glass of water if one is not offered.

I arrived at one listing in the heat of the summer. It must have been 110 degrees in the shade. I was parched and asked the seller for some water. He held up a giant glass of iced tea and said, "My wife just finished brewing some iced tea. Would you like that instead?" The tea looked and sounded great, so I accepted a glass of it. In this case, unfortunately, looks were deceiving. The tea did not taste good at all. However, because I had accepted it and didn't want to offend the seller, I felt I had to drink it all. Now I only accept water; if it isn't pleasant tasting, no one is offended if I don't finish it.

Wants and Needs Analysis

The next step in the listing process is to discuss the agenda for meeting and conduct a wants and needs analysis. A wants and needs analysis determines the reason the sellers want to sell and determines why the sellers need to sell. A need is a stronger motivator than a want. The sellers will be curious about what will be discussed during the evening and will be more likely wait to ask questions if they know there is a process. The meeting should have the following track:

- **Ask questions.** Find out the seller's motivation for selling and what his or her goals are. This is where I determine if I even want the listing. You should follow this approach for every listing appointment. You're not going into an appointment to *get* the listing; you're going in to see if you *want* it. If you appear desperate, it will show. You will probably overprice the property and may take on a property that is in need of repair. If you go in with the attitude that you aren't sure if you want the listing, you will be much stronger.

- **Inspect the property.** Take a look at the property with the proper evaluation techniques.

- **Discuss your abilities to market the property.** List the reasons the seller should list with you.

- **Discuss your company's abilities to market the property.** List the reasons the seller should list with your company.

- **Discuss your personal marketing plan for the property.** Discuss the services you will provide if the property is listed with you.

- **Discuss how the property should be priced.** Discuss the best price for the seller.

- **Discuss the benefits for both parties of working together.**

Once you have gone over these items, ask the sellers if there is anything else they want to cover. If the sellers have questions, take them seriously and write them down. Regardless of how insignificant a question seems to you, if it is important enough for them to ask it, is important enough for you to write it down. The reason for writing the questions down is that you will be addressing them later; now is not the right time to do so. Let the sellers know that you will address all of their questions after the presentation. STAY ON TRACK!

Now it is time to ask the sellers a series of questions. Have a written list of questions where the seller can see them. Studies have proven that the salesperson who has a written list of questions is perceived to be more organized and professional. These questions should include the following:

1. Why are you moving?

2. When do you want or need to move?

3. How long have you lived in your present house?

4. What major improvements have you made to the house in the last year?

5. Who else are you talking with about the sale of your house?

6. Can you move without selling this house first?

7. Would you consider owner financing?

8. How much do you want to sell your house for? How did you arrive at your price?

9. Do you have any concerns about making a move?

10. Which of the following is most important to you: price, timing, or convenience?

11. What would it do to your plans if you couldn't sell?

12. What would it take for you to list with me tonight?

These questions should be asked exactly as written as all of them, including the order in which you ask them, will make a difference. The questions put the sellers through a process of evaluating selling their house, and you have time to decide if you want the listing. It is always better to walk away from a listing early in the process.

Let's analyze each of the questions listed previously.

Why are you moving? This is a simple question, but the answer gives insight into the seller's motivation. If the seller doesn't need to move but would if he or she could get the desired price, that seller is not motivated. If the seller has a job transfer and must be in another state, that seller is motivated. A motivated seller will be more realistic in selling the house. You should already know the answer to this question if you have a clear-cut listing appointment, but you should ask it again. There is a big difference between what people tell you over the telephone and what they tell you in person. Facial expressions and body language reveal a lot. This question and the next one will cause some tension for the sellers because they must now commit to a decision. Expect their hesitation.

When do you want or need to move? Again, the answer to this simple question gives insight into the seller's motivation. If the seller can move anytime within the next six years, he or she is not motivated. If the seller must move within the next 60 days, he or she is motivated.

How long have you lived in your present house? This question is designed to lighten the pressure the sellers may feel from the first two questions. It is easy to answer. The sellers know how long they have lived in their house. This question will tell you the seller's equity position. If the seller has recently purchased the house, he or she might not have enough equity to pay the closing costs. This may result in the seller demanding more for the house than it might be worth.

What major improvements have you made to the house in the last year? Keep in mind that some sellers believe that changing a light bulb is an improvement. Write down everything; do not challenge anything at this point. You are just gathering information. You can get into more details later. The answers you get to this question will also help identify any undisclosed features of the home you need to know about, which could make a difference in the value of the house. This question will put very little pressure on the seller.

Who else are you talking with about the sale of your house? As a real estate professional, you need to know about your competition, including their strengths and weaknesses. Do not discredit your competition;

however if you offer a service your competition doesn't, be sure to emphasize that. If the seller is not talking to anyone else, that is also good to know. This question could generate a lot of pressure if the seller is telling you a secret. Some sellers believe they can play one real estate salesperson against another to receive a better deal.

Can you move without selling this house first? The answer to this question should smoke out any potential problems the seller may have, including not having enough equity to sell. It also will tell you if the seller is already looking at other houses. You want to be the one to sell them their new home. If a seller does not need to sell first, gather information about their buying intent.

Would you consider owner financing? Owner financing is when the seller helps the buyer with all or part of the financing for the house. If the seller is willing to help, it will open up this house to more potential buyers. Most sellers cannot or will not consider owner financing, but you should still ask the question.

How much do you want to sell your house for? How did you arrive at your price? Pricing is usually one of the biggest objections a seller will have. Does it surprise anyone that the seller wants more than the house is worth? The answer to this question will help you determine how the seller got his or her price and whether or not it was based on fact or what just what the seller needs and/or wants. You also want to how the sellers arrived at their price. You want to know if you have other competition. "Another real estate agent told us what it's worth." You want to know if they have an appraisal. You want to know if they are guessing or maybe misinformation such asking a neighbor.

Do you have any concerns about making a move? Some sellers may have something that is holding them back from moving. It would be very disappointing if you put effort into selling a property and received a good offer only to have the seller decline because he or she doesn't want to sell before the end of the school year or the construction on his or her home won't be finished for another three months.

Which of the following is most important to you: price, timing, or convenience? These are the big three when it comes to the motivation of the seller. Will the seller be more motivated by the price received, the length of time it takes to sell the property, or simply the convenience of having the house sold so he or she can move on with life? The sellers will typically state that all are important, but you must isolate which is most pertinent. From there, focus your sales approach on proving you can get them what they need.

What would it do to your plans if you just couldn't sell? Some sellers don't believe they *have* to sell. This question makes them look ahead and maybe think more reasonably.

What would it take for you to list with me tonight? This is the most important question, and it must be asked. It may be intimidating for you because you are putting pressure on the seller. Don't mellow the question; ask it as it is written. You need to know upfront if the seller has any final objections to hiring you. It is easier to ask this question at the beginning of the presentation because it is not as threatening to the seller at this point. If you wait until the end of the presentation when you begin closing, the seller might clam up. It also gives you plenty of time to overcome the seller's final objections, if any.

In my career, I've learned that asking this question early in the process and receiving the seller's final objection gives me a chance to focus on these concerns during the rest of my listing presentation. For example, if the seller says, "Well, we would list it with you if you could get us our price," and I know the price is too high for that area, I can spend the rest of my listing presentation making the case for a lower price.

Property Viewing

The next step in the listing process is looking at the property. You should only proceed if the seller has answered the previous 12 questions to your satisfaction. Sometimes the seller is totally unrealistic on the price of his or her house. If you cannot overcome the objection and list the property at a reasonable price,

DO NOT TAKE THE LISTING. This is not the time for price objections. If the seller is a little off on pricing, you should wait until it's time to discuss pricing. It is only if the seller is completely unreasonable that you would end the presentation.

If you find the sellers are worth spending more time with, you should involve them when you inspect the property. They will then see the marketing of the property as a cooperative effort. During the tour you should make a note of all the seller's comments regarding the property. Again, if it is important enough for the seller to mention, it is important enough to write it down. Discuss and list the items that don't stay with the property. Note the condition of the property and understand the difference between *maintenance* items and *improvement* items. Maintenance items are things around the house that should be taken care of before selling. Improvement items are things the seller has added to the house, such as room additions, remodeling, and extensive landscaping. Some sellers believe the buyer should pay for fixing a broken door. The broken door is considered a maintenance item, not an improvement. These types of expenses should be absorbed by the seller.

You need to be able to look at real property through the eyes of several other individuals. The first should be the appraiser's eyes. What would an appraiser look for? Will the property hold market value? The next set of eyes is the property inspector's. What repairs should be done? Are there any hidden problems? The last set of eyes is the buyer's. Is the property in show condition? Are there things the seller can do to impress the buyer more?

Your property inspection will undoubtedly reveal minor items in need of repair and necessary cosmetic changes. Your recommendations might include the following:

- Removing clutter or excess furniture so rooms will appear larger

- Organizing closets and cabinets

- Touching up paint

- Landscaping

- Removing family pictures

During the walkthrough you should concentrate on building rapport with the seller. Make an effort to make small talk on subject matter that has nothing to do with real estate. If you see golf clubs and you are a golfer, ask the seller about golfing. If you see a piece of embroidery in the making, ask about it. Do not "ooh" and "aah" about the house while walking through, which is a common mistake when trying to build rapport. We want to make the seller think we like the property, but we are not going to buy the property. A seller's most frequent objection is pricing. Every "ooh" and "aah" raises the seller's expectations, and if you do this, it will be difficult to tell the seller his or her price is too high.

Laptop Presentations

If you have a laptop, you can customize the presentation for the seller or you can use generic listing presentation software. The presentation can have incredible graphics, voiceovers, and music. Some sellers are technologically sophisticated and expect a better presentation. You can burn the presentation to a CD and leave it with the seller to review. (Be careful never to leave anything with a seller that you don't want to end up in the hands of your competition. Weigh the pros and cons of leaving materials.)

Do not rely solely on technology, however. People need to feel they are doing business with a person, not a computer. Also, technology can fail; always have a hard copy backup of your presentation material in your car.

Discuss Personal Results
During this discussion you should share your personal results. These include the number of sales you have had in the last year, the clients you have helped to achieve their goals, and letters of

recommendation. (If you don't have letters of recommendation, GET THEM!) Discuss your personal successes as well, such as all of your real estate awards. Do not talk about your past career prior to getting into real estate, as your customers are only concerned about what you do now. If you are new to the business and don't have real estate successes, spend your time talking about your company. You can use the word "we" because it is your company, and your company's successes are also yours. Close this section out by asking the seller if he or she has any questions.

Discuss Company Results

In this section of the listing presentation, you should discuss the positive activities of your company. Refer to your listing material to make sure you stay on track. Discuss successes, including the number of sales and any recognition or awards. Form a list of a select group of house addresses and the length of time it took your company to sell each one. Select properties that took 60 days or less to sell. Use only the street name, not the street number, and avoid giving directions. All you want to do is impress the seller with the amount of houses you and your company sold within 60 days' time.

You should describe the team you have formed, including your broker, all the real estate salespeople in your office, and any affiliates such as appraisers, inspectors, mortgage officers, title officers, and structural engineers to name a few. This is a good time to promote anything your company does that the competition may not do. Think outside the box to develop this section to its fullest. Ask your broker and other salespeople in the office for their ideas.

During each section to follow, you should be asking a series of questions to get your point across. I hate the word "presentation" because it means I talk and you listen. It's important to get the clients involved; you need their input, and they feel better if you are concerned about their opinions. It has a much different effect when you ask, "What is most important to you?" than when you say "This is the most important thing you should be concerned about."

I once was told I should view a new real estate salesperson's listing presentation because it was so good. I was excited to take notes on such a good presentation. We sat down as if I was a seller, and the real estate salesperson began the presentation. Forty-five minutes later he was still going. I don't think he took a breath. He had no listing presentation manual, he never asked for my input, and I don't think he wanted me to talk at all. He focused a lot on the job he had prior to his real estate career. As a potential seller, I was not only turned off by his arrogance, but I was also offended by his lack of caring. I disengaged myself from the presentation and almost fell asleep. When he *finally* finished, he asked, "How was that?" "Great," I said and got up and left.

So why did I not help him? When the student is ready, the teacher will appear. If I had tried to help him, he would have been offended. He did not want any criticism; he wanted praise. Too bad, because that praise will not make him any money. It is interesting to note that the seller will do the same thing to you, except you will hear the words, "We'll call you." But they won't.

An involvement technique is when you let the seller finish your sentences for you. Do not labor at this as it should come naturally. For example, suppose you have a sentence that has an easily recognizable finish. Instead of finishing it yourself, pause briefly to allow the seller to finish it for you. If the seller does what he or she is supposed to do, affirm the response by saying, "Right" or "Exactly," and they will continue to do it.

Once you complete the discussion about company results, close this section out with the seller. Make sure to close every section to avoid objections from the seller later.

When I was a new to the real estate profession, I was afraid of objections. What if I could not handle the objection? How silly would I look? Because of my fear and lack of presentation skills, I received a lot of objections and was always stressed about listing appointments. I began closing each section by addressing questions as they came up; now I rarely receive objections late in the presentation. Try this:

Salesperson:
"Mr. and Mrs. Seller, do you have any questions about my company?"

Seller:
"No."

Salesperson:
"Do you believe my company can help you sell your house?"

Seller:
"Yes."

The key point here is that the seller must say yes. Do not settle for, "Well, I guess." If needed, ask again.

Discuss Specific Marketing

A professional real estate salesperson should have two marketing presentations. The first one should be a standard marketing presentation for use in any situation. The second should be a marketing presentation designed specifically for the current potential client.

Both presentations should follow the same format, spelling out the step-by-step process for selling the property. Be sure to include each activity and a schedule for completion. Some real estate salespeople often overlook this step, but don't make that mistake. Take time to mention even the little things, such as the following:

- Entry into the MLS

- Presentation to the office salespeople

- Office tour

- Advertising campaign

- Marketing flyers

- "For Sale" sign installation

- Lock box installation

- Presentation at the local Association of REALTORS®

The presentation (marketing plan) should be updated as the marketing time progresses. Send it to the seller so that he or she knows you are working. Finally, don't forget to close this section out.

Discuss Price

After the seller agrees to let you market the property, move to the last section of your presentation: pricing. Pricing tends to be the seller's biggest objection. You can't fault the sellers for wanting the most they can get for their property. You should already know what price the seller is looking for because you asked them while on the phone setting the appointment. If this is in line with your Comparative Market Analysis (CMA), your pricing discussion should be as follows:

> **Salesperson:**
> "Mr. and Mrs. Seller, if I believe I can get the price you are asking for, would you list with me right now?"

Right to the close, I like it! Too many times we "professional" salespeople get so enamored with our presentation that we forget our purpose of getting the listing. Don't sell with la–di–da when you can sell with LA. That simply means don't oversell, don't talk too much, and close early and often.

I once went on an appointment with a new real estate salesperson to help out. He was doing great and the seller, a single woman, was buying into everything he was saying. It was going so well that I could sense it was time to close. When the salesperson failed to do it, I stepped in and said, "Put us to work for you." The seller looked at us and said, "Yes."

Without hesitation, I began to get out the paperwork for her to authorize. The other salesperson looked a bit shocked and continued his presentation. I looked at him with distress in my eyes and tried, through body language, to let him know it was time to end the presentation. He did not. I assume he wanted to further impress the seller, his mentor, or himself.

Finally he mentioned holding an open house to get buyers in to see the property. Typical enough, and most sellers like that. This lady said, "You would do an open house on my property?" The salesperson smiled brightly and exclaimed, "Oh, yes!" The seller stood up (it's never a good sign if you're in a meeting and the boss stands up) and asked us to leave. I tried to do what I could to salvage the appointment by quickly asking, "What is it about an open house that is a problem?" She explained that she once listed a house, and the real estate salesperson held an open house. During the open house, someone stole a family heirloom. She was emphatic that she would not go through that again and promptly asked us to leave.

I pride myself in handling objections, but I had no chance; the seller had become emotional. The point here is do not oversell. Here are some words to live by:

Promise less and deliver more.

So back to pricing… if you feel the seller's asking price is higher than you can sell the property for, begin the pricing process with the following questions:

Salesperson:
"If the market won't give you the price you want, what will you do?"

Salesperson:
"How did you arrive at that price?"

Salesperson:
"If the property sells, what are your plans?"

Salesperson:
"If you can't sell the property, how will that change your plans?"

Even though you might have asked a question before, you can try asking it again to see if sellers are consistent in their answer. Continue probing until you find a crack in the seller's armor. Typically a motivated seller will truly want to sell; if you can find their true motivation, you can convince the seller of the correct price. One point here: I am making the assumption you are representing or will represent the seller. This is not meant to be manipulative because it *is* in the best interest of the seller to price a property correctly.

I have had unsuccessful real estate salespeople tell me that it is our duty to price the property at the price the seller wants and to do our best to sell it at that price. I disagree. We should meet the seller's goal and, in this case, that goal is to sell the house. And the only way to do that is to market the property at the correct price.

In my first two months in real estate, I took 14 listings. That is actually a very good number. For some, it takes an entire career to do this type of business, but I did it in two months. I was invited to have breakfast in Dallas with the owner and founder of our company, which employed 800 real estate salespeople. I felt good and thought, "This business is easy."

This business *is* easy if all you do is agree to list the properties at any price the sellers want (all overpriced). Out of the 14 overpriced listings I took, none were sold. Every day I got calls from sellers who were yelling at me, telling me I was worthless, and asking me to release the listings. I started thinking of another career until I came to the following conclusion:

> *"I would rather make a seller upset now and happy when the property sells than happy now and upset when the property doesn't sell."*

I REFUSE TO TAKE OVERPRICED LISTINGS.

It is tempting at this point in the pricing section for the real estate salesperson to use the CMA to get the seller to understand what the price should be. Remember, the seller is acting emotionally, and data (in this case the CMA) are logical pieces of information. So regardless of how good the CMA is, the seller won't see it. Instead, keep asking questions. Eventually, you can present the CMA, but again, it is a tool, not a weapon. Don't beat the seller over the head with it.

Close for the Seller Listing Agreement

Once you and the seller agree on a price, ask the seller for the listing. Do not make this difficult. New real estate salespeople tend to be frightened about closing the seller. If you have completed your presentation correctly, most of the time the close is a logical outcome. My general final "close" is as follows:

> **"Put me to work for you."**

Now did that really hurt? Closing does not need to hurt if you have done your job correctly. Many sales have been lost because we do not ask for the listing.

Types of Listings

Listing agreements obligate both brokers and sellers to perform. The five types of listing agreements include:

1. **Open**
   The open listing allows anyone to sell the property. Only the broker who actually sells the property deserves to be paid. If the seller sells the property, no commission is paid. This type of listing is totally nonexclusive. The seller can list with multiple brokers at one time.

2. **Exclusive Right to Sell (ERS)**
   With the Exclusive Right to Sell (ERS) listing, the broker that lists the property is the only broker to be paid. This type of listing is totally exclusive. Only one broker has the right to sell the property, and all other brokers must work through the listing broker. The listing broker pays all other brokers who sell the property. If the seller finds a buyer, the listing broker is still due a commission. According to most ERS listings, the seller does not even have the right to negotiate with buyers without the listing broker.

3. **Exclusive agency**
   The exclusive agency listing is similar to the ERS listing except in an agency listing, the seller could sell the property alone, without having to pay a commission.

4. **Net**
   A net listing is a listing in which the seller wants a net amount of money, including closing costs, and the broker can have any amount over the net amount.

5. **One-time**
   A one-time listing is a listing that is good for only one buyer for a set period of time for one property.

Finalization

The last and best thing left to do is to ask for the listing. Once the sellers accept your offer, they must sign the papers in the listing packet. Be sure to get the seller to give you a key to the property, including keys that open gates, screen doors, outbuildings, and any other locked rooms. Also, be sure to get the pass code to the security system if one is on the premises.

Here are some final points on listing presentations.

- Do not tell jokes during the presentations. What you think is funny may offend someone else.

- Do not talk to inattention. This simply means if the sellers are not listening, do not continue. I was on a listing presentation and a neighbor knocked on the door. When the neighbor heard I was there, he tried to excuse himself and the seller said, "No, come on in." Both the neighbor and seller sat in the living room, leaving me with his wife at the kitchen table. I asked the husband if he wanted to join us, and he said, "Just go on, I can hear you." That was not acceptable. I told them to call me when they were serious, and I left.

- Film yourself. Get a digital video camera and have a friend film your presentation. As a young real estate salesperson, I struggled with listing properties. I could get the appointments, I just couldn't get the sellers to sign the listings. And nothing I did seemed to work. To find out why, I asked my dad to video my presentation. Oh my! After watching that video (which I immediately deleted!); I realized that I wouldn't have listed with me either. I was trying to overcome my youth by acting professional, and all I accomplished was coming off as cold. I had this serious look, a scowl actually. Seeing myself on video allowed me to change my presentation for the better.

Post-Agreement Discussion

The post-agreement discussion occurs after a listing is signed. During this discussion, you should mention the following:

- **Open houses:** Open houses should occur only when needed and approved by you. Discuss this with the seller, who might feel you should hold an open house every weekend. You should also be honest and tell the seller if the house is not conducive to an open house. Consider saying something like "Mr. and Mrs. Seller, we have discussed open houses. I feel that this house is not well-suited for an open house because it is located so far off the main traffic ways and it will not draw enough good buyers. Never fear though: At open houses for other properties, we will move buyers here. The good thing is that while high traffic open houses draw a lot of people, those people tend to buy in more secluded areas such as this."

- **Pets:** Pets can be a problem. Some people like cats and dogs, and some do not. Pets must be put up in a bathroom, utility room, or outside when the house is being shown.

  Too many pets can also be a problem. I once was in a house that had 62 fish tanks. Fish tanks were everywhere—in the living room, in the kitchen, in the bedrooms, and even in the bathrooms. All I remember about the house was the fish tanks and that the house would not be salable until they were removed.

  There was another time when I was showing a property to a couple. They seemed to like it and wanted to go into the back yard. There was a sign on the door that said, "Beware of Dog," but when we looked out, we couldn't see a dog. I opened the door a crack and hollered, "Here dog!" I opened the door wider and stepped onto the patio. Still no dog. However, just as the buyers came out onto the patio, here came a huge Doberman Pincher from the side of the house, growling and baring his teeth. We all made it inside okay; unfortunately I accidentally hit one of the potential buyers in the back with my forearm as I ran over her to get inside. The couple never bought from me. A pet is not a real estate salesperson's friend.

- **Advertising:** Most real estate offices have an advertising policy to rotate listings if they are paying for advertising, meaning a listing might only be advertised once a month. However, they will typically keep all of their listings posted on the website all of the time. Some seller's expect their house to be advertised every day in a newspaper. Let's go over the realities of advertising and then discuss how you should approach this with the seller.

  Advertising's only purpose is to make the telephone at the real estate office ring with buyer and seller inquiries. It is not used to actually sell a specific property. Only about 2 percent of the time do advertising calls or Internet inquires result in the given property selling.

  All of this is great, but the sellers just don't care. They want you to advertise their property all the time. To demonstrate, pull up a page of listings from your website and show it to the seller. Then ask the sellers to find their house. Of course their house is not on that page. After a minute or so of them searching, point out a house and say, "There is your house." They will immediately say, "That is not." Then point at another house and say, "This is your house." Now the sellers will look at you strangely because that is not their house either. Then say, "Do you understand why I'm pointing out all these ads and claiming they are your house?" The sellers will stare blankly and shake their heads. Now explain to them that when your office advertises one of its properties, it is the same as advertising all of its properties. If call-in buyers do not like the house they call in on, you will convert them to your seller's house. This is the advantage of real estate because every week their house is either directly or indirectly advertised.

- **Security:** Warn the sellers never to show their property to anyone who isn't accompanied by a real estate salesperson. This is a breach of security and should not happen. Leave the sellers a stack of business cards, and tell them to call you if anyone approaches them about seeing the property.

- **Safety:** Look for things in the house that are not safe, such as exposed electrical wires, toys in walking paths, or dimly lit stairs.

- **Quick sale:** Prepare the sellers for a quick sale. If you don't and an offer comes in on their property the day after it is listed, they will believe their house is underpriced. They will reject the sale and you. Tell them that you will present all offers regardless of the price and terms and to be excited if they get an offer tomorrow.

- **Showing:** Tell the sellers that you are paid as a marketing specialist. Your job is not to sell the house but to get the house sold. If the house is being shown, that is good. If you personally are not showing the house, that is good. It is a sign that you are marketing the house properly. Some sellers believe the listing salesperson should show the property. We will, but our first job is to get the property sold no matter who shows it.

Convince the seller to leave during showings. If this is impossible, then instruct the seller to stay in one place during the showing and not wander around the house. Real estate salespeople say very little and let buyers discover the house on their own. You definitely don't want your seller to talk with the buyers at length. If a seller talks, the buyers cannot discover the home for themselves. Tell your seller to be invisible.

Prepare the seller that if a real estate salesperson is parked out front with a buyer (maybe they were just driving by), they may want to see the house without notice. It should not happen often, but they need to be prepared to show the house on a moment's notice. They should not refuse to show it.

- **Odors:** Odors must be addressed. If you smell pet odors, cigarette odors, or other types of smells, it is best to be upfront with the sellers and tell them they need to take care of it.

- **Cleaning:** If the house needs to be cleaned or is in need of repair, you need to tell the sellers. Create an itemized list of specific items that must be dealt with and give it to the sellers with a due date for completion. Then follow up to be sure it is done. No matter how difficult, the house must be in show condition at all times.

- **Stuff:** If the sellers have too much stuff, they need to get rid of it. I have had sellers take down pictures because potential buyers were spending too much time looking at pictures and not at the house.

I once set an appointment with an expired listing. The property was priced right but had not sold. When I entered the property, I soon found out why. The seller had three complete households of furniture in the property, including sets from both the seller's deceased mother and sister. We literally had to walk through a path that separated the furniture. My initial impression of the master bedroom was that it was small until I looked into the back corner of the roof and noticed it was actually quite large.

It appeared small because of the three beds in the room plus three dressers and end tables. Even sentimental things may need to be removed from the house while it is on the market. I was finally able to convince the seller to put all of the extra furniture. The property sold in less than two weeks.

- **Expensive items:** Expensive items, such as breakable vases or jewelry, should be removed from the house as well. My dad always said that we lock our doors not because we believe people are evil but to keep from tempting the good ones. The same story is relevant here.

  In that same vein, the sellers should not have money in plain sight. I had a new real estate salesperson call me and ask me to take a look at her new listing. She was concerned that the seller's house was vacant and they had left some baseball cards upstairs. I thought this new salesperson was overreacting, but I went to see anyway. Once upstairs, I understood her concern. There were two rooms that were adjacent to each other and about 400 square feet each. In each room were baseball cards stacked floor to ceiling on shelves. There were uncirculated, full sets of baseball cards from the 1940s to present day. There were 6-inch binders full of individual players' cards. I pulled out a binders on Nolan Ryan. Inside were rookie cards that could be worth thousands of dollars. I was literally frightened to be in the room. I called the seller directly and told her she had 48 hours to remove the cards. Can you imagine the liability on my part in showing such a property? I learned later that the seller's deceased husband had owned several card shops, although he collected more cards than he sold. The seller had no idea that the collection was valued at $3.2 million. Can you believe that? Three million dollars in baseball cards in a vacant house worth $100,000!

- **Miscellaneous points:** Instruct your sellers to avoid answering too many questions. They need to remember that we are the professional negotiators, not the sellers. The sellers could inadvertently cause liability for themselves. Tell the sellers you will call every week to give them an update. Finally, make sure the sellers know to tell you anytime they are going to be unavailable for any length of time. There is nothing more frustrating than a great offer that can't be presented because no one knows how to get ahold of the sellers.

Seller Servicing

Seller servicing is taking care of the listing after the listing agreement has been signed. The number one seller complaint is that their real estate salesperson listed the house and never did anything else. Sellers basically want to know their money is not being wasted. Generally, they are happy just hearing from their real estate salespeople.

Weekly Callbacks and Emails

Call the sellers weekly. They need assurance that you are still alive and actively marketing their properties. This is the most important aspect of seller servicing.

I had a listing that I called on every week for almost six months. When I went to see the sellers, they relisted with me because they felt I had done everything possible to get their house sold. I sold it within a month from the time I relisted it.

In a different situation I once failed to call my sellers for over a month because I was "busy." Sellers hate that. An offer on the property came in, and I went to meet with the sellers. They accepted the offer but made sure that I knew they were disappointed in me. They felt I had stolen their money because I had not done anything that warranted being paid a commission. I had actually done a lot to sell their home, but I did not convey that I was working. They called my broker, not to refuse to pay a commission but to make sure I didn't get any of it. Then they asked me not to show up at closing because they never wanted to see me again. Not good!

What is the difference? I did virtually the same for both sellers, but the sellers in the second example never knew what I was doing.

You can email the sellers information, but this should be in addition to the weekly calls. The timing of the calls should be the same time each week. If the seller has any questions, he or she should wait until the agreed-upon weekly time. This saves you from being interrupted by sellers calling for information mid-week.

Open House

The open house can be a very good source of obtaining buyers and sellers. Notice, I said "and sellers" (more on this later). It is also a good opportunity to prospect in the neighborhood. The open house is used by a select group of successful real estate salespeople, and for some, it is their main source of prospective buyers and sellers. These salespeople can be called "open house experts" due to the special way they hold an open house.

Other real estate salespeople consider the open house a waste of time. There is no greater waste of time than sitting at an open house with no activity.

One important reason to hold an open house is to get the names, addresses, and telephone numbers of motivated buyers who are in the market and are looking for a home in that area. Another important reason to hold an open house is to locate those owners in the area who are thinking of selling their home in the near future. Make a good impression on these owners, so that when the time comes to sell, they will remember you.

> Our main reason for holding open houses is to
> **MEET PROSPECTIVE BUYERS WHO 98 PERCENT OF THE TIME PURCHASE SOME OTHER HOUSE.**

The selection of properties for open house is very important. Your broker or manager can assist you in this selection and help you with procedures and recommendations to maximize the results of your open house.

The overall goal of an open house is to set a subsequent appointment.

The following procedures for open houses will help maximize your efforts.

The "Open House" Must Be Priced Right

It is a complete waste of time to hold open a house that is priced at more than 4 percent above its true market value. To do so will make a sale more difficult and will be harmful to your reputation, which in the long term is all you have. If you list a property for sale at $250,000 when it should be listed for $225,000 and then hold it open, several things happen. First, any potential buyers who come to the open house will think less of you and will not want to work with you. Their perception will be that you will show them other "overpriced houses." Second, you are wasting the sellers' time and yours. It is extremely difficult, if not impossible, to sell an overpriced property. The most important criterion for choosing an open house is to have that property priced at or below the market prices in the area.

Location Is Critical for the "Open House"

Hard-to-reach streets and/or dead ends usually make poor open houses. The best open houses are ones that are on highly traveled streets; ironically, these are typically also the most difficult to sell because of the high traffic.

Preferably a highly sought-after area, based on current and past activity, is best for open houses. If no sales have occurred, it might indicate a slow-selling area and a waste of your time.

Advertising the Open House

Advertising is an important factor in preparing to hold an open house. The newspaper ad, the Internet ad, and any other marketing pieces must be complete.

A "blind ad" is one in which some important detail has been omitted in the hope that the buyer, becoming interested in the rest of the ad, will be anxious to know that detail and will make a phone call to the office or come to the open house to find out. Your ad should be all-inclusive, giving the street address and town, the size of the house, kind of architecture, number of bedrooms and baths, and the price. A person reading your ad will decide if the house is as good as you say it is and if he or she should take a look at it.

The enticement of the open house to average buyers is that they don't have to go to a broker's office. They can simply drive by the property and, if they like the appearance of the house and the price is within their means, they can go in. They don't feel obligated to one real estate salesperson. Again, you can see why the price must be right. If the buyers don't like the appearance of the house in relation to the price quoted in the ad, they will simply drive by.

Naturally, you want as many prospects to show up during the open house as you can get through the door, and a good open house may bring in as many as 10 or 12. But if it brings in only one, it is still worth the cost, for it is one more than you would have had without it.

Directional Signs Are Necessary
Another method of advertising an open house is through the use of directional signs. These should be placed at every corner leading from a main street to the open house. Always check with local authorities on the use of temporary directional signs. Also ask the person who lives on the corner for permission to place your directional sign. Explain that you will place it between the curb and lawn, so as not to injure the grass, and that it will be removed by six o'clock. Almost always, the owner will grant your request. In fact, he or she will probably chat with you about real estate, at which time you should invite him or her to visit the open house.

One excellent method of calling attention to a directional sign is to accent it with open house flags. These flags will draw attention to your directional sign from five times farther away than will the directional sign by itself.

Always Schedule Two Open Houses

Every Tuesday you should select two market-value–priced homes to be held open the following Saturday and Sunday. The reason for selecting two homes is the possibility that between Tuesday and Saturday, a well-priced house will sell, wiping out any plans for an open house that weekend. If you select two and neither sells before the end of the week, you hold one open Saturday and the other on Sunday. If one is sold, you hold the other open both days.

The Owner Must Be Absent

Whenever possible, it is best to arrange to have the owners away during the open house period. This makes all the difference in the world. Buyers feel uncomfortable in the presence of owners. They will not relax, ask questions, or raise objections. They will not make an offer, either. In selling residential property especially, you must make the buyers comfortable. They should be able to sit down, feel at home, and enjoy their surroundings. They cannot and will not do this if the owners are present.

With the owners away, you can greet your buyers as they arrive by introducing yourself and remarking, "The owners have left for the day, won't you come in?" The buyer's reaction will be immediate. They will relax, inspect the premises, raise objections, mentally place their furniture, imagine living there, and get down to talking price and financing.

It is important, then, that the owners leave, preferably early in the day. You should tell your sellers, "If I do not sell your property before this coming weekend, I intend to hold an open house on Saturday, or perhaps both Saturday and Sunday. I would appreciate your arranging to be away from the house on those days from 1:00 to 5:00 p.m."

It is not difficult to induce the sellers to be away for the open house if there is a definite plan and you have attitude behind your approach. Holding this open house is not a rushed, last-minute arrangement but rather, in the hands of an expert, a well thought-out plan.

Preparation for the Open House

A. The day before the open house

1. Deliver open house invitations to neighbors and ask them and their friends to stop by.

2. Drive by all listings in the immediate area and go see any you aren't familiar with.

3. Check for recent area sales activity on the Multiple Listing Service.

4. Inform the sellers of the open house, and make sure they have plans to be away from the house.

5. Go door to door around the area on the morning of the open house to remind neighbors.

6. Have a back-up person at the office who can relieve you from the open house in case you need to show a potential buyer another property.

B. Preparing the property

1. Pick up the yard, any old newspapers, trash, and so on.

2. Arrange patio furniture.

3. Close the garage door.

4. Open the drapes.

5. Play soft music on the radio or use your own iPod or CD.

6. Generally tidy up house. (Ideally the seller should have already done this.)

7. Start a fire in the fireplace if there is one.

8. Warm a few drops of vanilla in the oven to give a nice quality to the property.

9. Turn on all the lights throughout the house.

10. Have copies of the listing available for additional information and for any other brokers who bring their buyers to the open house.

11. Place directional signs and flags around the area so drivers can see them and have time to turn.

C. Closing the open house

1. Turn out the lights.

2. Close the drapes.

3. Clean up coffee, refreshments, and so on.

4. Extinguish the fire in the fireplace.

5. Turn off the oven.

6. Lock up the house, including the garage.

7. Leave a thank-you note for sellers, including the day's results.

Buyers Who Are Sellers

Twenty-five to thirty percent of the people who inspect an open house are not buyers. They may look like buyers, talk like buyers, act like buyers, and ask all the questions buyers ask, but they are not buyers. They are sellers, and in most cases, they are only potential sellers.

These sellers may have received one of your invitations or saw your house with the flags and signs reading, "Open House on Sunday."

Now here is a house right in their own neighborhood. Wouldn't it be natural for them to go through the open house and act as a buyer to find out the asking price, make a comparison, and arrive at a tentative valuation of their own property? Such people are not buyer prospects; they are seller prospects.

At one time or another during a selling conversation, a successful salesperson will ask the following questions of every person to whom he or she shows the open house:

Salesperson:
"May I ask, do you presently rent or do you own the home you're living in?"

Homeowner:
"We own our home."

Salesperson:
"Do you intend to sell your property before you purchase the home you are looking for?"

Homeowner:
"Yes."

Salesperson:
"Do you presently have your home up for sale?"

Homeowner:
"No."

At this point the salesperson knows he or she has a seller instead of a buyer and should work toward a listing appointment. Consider using this script:

Salesperson:
"Why don't I drop over to see your property this evening and talk over the situation? At that time I can do a market analysis and we can find out if you have sufficient equity established to do the things you are looking forward to doing."

If the seller already has his or her home on the market, follow this script:

> **Salesperson:**
> "It is your house listed with a real estate broker?"
>
> **Homeowner:**
> "No."

At this point the salesperson knows he or she has a For Sale By Owner instead of a buyer and should work toward a listing appointment. Consider using this script:

> **Salesperson:**
> "I would be happy to call on you this evening to inspect your property. There is an excellent chance that, among the buyers I contact daily, I will find a suitable prospect for your house. Do you mind if I cooperate with you while you are attempting to sell your own home?"

If the seller has already listed with a real estate broker, then help the homeowner as best as you can, but do not try to interfere with another broker's listing.

Refreshments for the "Open House"

There are procedures for enhancing a cozy atmosphere. In the winter you can have coffee ready—freshly made, good, and hot. It is no chore to carry a little open-house kit with you, containing a coffee maker, coffee, little packages of sugar and cream, some disposable cups, and even some sugar cookies. Set this up in the kitchen and while you are talking with the buyers in the living room, you can offer them this extra bit of hospitality. It will have a mellowing effect, make them more responsive to your questions, and enable you to qualify them without seeming to be moving too fast.

In the summer you can vary the menu by serving lemonade or soda, perhaps outside on the patio or in the backyard if these are attractive areas. Though not as important as other items mentioned, such little hospitable touches will help the buyers relax, enjoy the scene, and experience the pleasure of living in the house. Be sure to clear the refreshments with the sellers.

Open-House Invitations and Door-to-Door Marketing
On the Wednesday morning before the open house, address 60 open-house invitations (30 for each of the two locations) to the neighbors surrounding the open house. Obtain the names and addresses for the neighbors from a cross directory or from a title company. The invitations need to be delivered on Thursday or Friday, at the latest. Mailing these 60 cards will produce little result, but as a basis for future personal meetings with these same neighbors, it is extremely effective. Such meetings are brought about by professional door-to-door marketing just prior to the time scheduled for the open house. Check with the local authorities for regulations concerning door-to-door marketing.

Door-to-door marketing plays a big part in the open-house technique. The people you will be calling on will have received a card inviting them to the open house. Now you are reinforcing this contact with a face-to-face invitation. By persuading some of these people to accept the invitation, you increase the sales potential for this house because neighbors sometimes buy open houses. They may buy as an investment, if the price and payments are right, and rent it out. They may also have friends or relatives who might be interested. If they like the house, they will call these friends and relatives and urge them to inspect it. Here is your script:

Salesperson:
"Good afternoon, I am Dan Hamilton from Acme Real Estate. Did you get my card about the open house we are holding today?"

Homeowner:
"Yes."

Salesperson:
"I wanted to make sure it had been delivered and to add my personal invitation to visit. It is a beautiful, realistically priced

home, and I am sure you would enjoy seeing it. The owners are away for the day so if you are free this afternoon, we would enjoy having you drop by. We'd also like to have your opinion on the price of this property in comparison with others in the neighborhood."

Bring the following items to your open house:

1. An adequate number of open house signs and open house flags.

2. A hammer or mallet to help place the signs in hard soil. Be sure to check your local ordinances governing the use and placement of signs; if you aren't certain, check with your broker or manager.

3. A computer printout of the most recent sales in the neighborhood to use as a reference.

4. A legal pad or pad of scratch paper.

5. Your smartphone so that you can use the calendar feature for setting appointments.

6. A portfolio of your successful closings and awards.

7. A tablet that has a financial qualifying application.

8. A blank purchase agreement. (It is rare for a house to sell at an open house, but it does happen.)

9. Several working pens.

10. Some work to do between visitors.

11. Your business cards.

12. A tablet that has a mortgage amortizing schedule application.

13. Feature sheets and cards (special features specific to the home).

14. A guest register.

Set up your laptop in a prominent location during the open house and have a virtual tour, complete with voice narration, running at all times. Have the volume up loud enough so that visitors can hear you narrating the tour.

Have alternative listings, including houses in other price ranges, ready to show as well. This can salvage a prospect who is not interested in the home you're holding open but may be interested in another property. Such tours don't take long to put together, and they can result in big commissions!

Have CDs containing virtual tours ready to give away. Include area tours, a tour of the listing you're holding open, a tour of local schools, and tours for specific subdivisions and condo projects for visitors who are not interested in that particular home. Make sure the disks have nice labels that feature your photo and contact information.

Multiple Open Houses

If you have multiple listings in one area, hold them open all at the same time. I know of one real estate salesperson whose main focus is holding open houses. She makes nearly a half million dollars a year for herself with four or five open houses in a particular area every Sunday. In several rooms of each house, she sets up boards on a-frame easels. The boards are full of details and professional photographs of each of her other open houses. Each board also includes the price of the house and maps. If a buyer is in a house that is too expensive, for example, he or she may look on a board and notice a beautiful home in his or her price range that is open down the street. (Guess where they go?) She also has two real estate salespeople at every house and two "rovers" in place for security and to handle rushes. If a buyer wants to look at a different property, one of the salespeople on hand can leave the open house and show that buyer another property.

If both salespeople need to leave, a rover will show up to supervise the open house. She never has trouble finding salespeople to help her because these open houses generate several qualified buyers.

If you don't have multiple listings in a certain area, you can form alliances with other real estate salespeople in your office. What about cooperating with competitive offices for the betterment of all?

Broker Open House
Broker open houses are for licensed real estate salespeople, not for the general public. They are designed to expose the property to real estate licensees, so they will be familiar with it in case they have a buyer who might be interested in this type of property. A broker open usually corresponds with area property tours and, like all open houses, the seller is not to be there.

While the listing salesperson should offer lunch during the broker open, some creative salespeople hold "progressive broker open houses." In the first house on the tour, visitors have a salad; in the second house, they have a main course; and in the third house, they have dessert. In each house, the visitors receive coupons. And if there is a fourth house on the tour, visitors holding all four coupons are eligible to participate in a prize drawing. You can arrange this progressive open house with real estate salespeople from different real estate companies as long as the listings are in the same area.

The typical meal is made up of deli sandwiches, cookies, and soft drinks. I have seen real estate salespeople do evening opens and serve alcohol, but I don't think that is appropriate.

Broker opens can be expensive, so don't hesitate to solicit the seller's help. I have had sellers offer to pay for everything and actually had it catered by a local barbeque restaurant. If you have talent for cooking, this might be your game. I knew a real estate salesperson who made the best chicken enchiladas. Real estate salespeople would drive 30 minutes just to go to her broker opens. It ended up being a great marketing tool for her.

Advertising

Advertising their property in print is one of the top expectations a seller has of his or her real estate salesperson. A real estate company usually advertises on a rotation basis. In a rotation, if the real estate company pays for a weekly advertisement that has twelve slots for listings and the company has 48 listings, your listing will be featured once a month.

Office Tour (Caravan)

An office tour gives real estate salespeople in a real estate office the opportunity to view (tour) the most recent listings the office has taken. Some refer to this as a jailbreak because the real estate salespeople almost run through the houses. The objective is to be familiar with the office inventory so if a buyer calls into the office, you will be more helpful. Most sellers appreciate an office tour to show support for their sale. You should use feedback cards or a feedback sheet that has questions you feel are important about your listing. Some questions may include pricing, appearance, and whether the property is salable. Communicate the information to the seller immediately so he or she can make any necessary changes.

Some real estate brokers are now using virtual tours of their properties instead of walking tours. This is an effective time- and money-saving technique. The listing agent puts together a couple of slides that feature the house, and the broker puts together a slide show of all the new listings. At an office meeting with all the salespeople from the office present, the broker starts the show and the listing agent gets to verbalize the aspects of the property. At the end of the tour, the group of real estate salespeople can ask questions. Once that presentation is over, they move on to the next group of slides.

Multiple Listing Service

The Multiple Listing Service (MLS) allows for worldwide property exposure. A buyer transferring from out of state can find houses on the MLS that are currently for sale in the specific area he or she is moving to. Some services are more protective and allow only real estate salespeople on the MLS site. A majority of real estate sales stems from the MLS.

When promoting your properties on the MLS, be sure to include as many pictures as allowed. Buyers want pictures. If the MLS allows video, then video the best aspects of the property. Be professional. If you have to redo, then redo. If you have to hire someone to take professional pictures and video, then do it. It represents you. Are you professional enough to take the pictures, or are you just wanting to save money?

Write any comments very carefully. Sometimes this is how a buyer decides which properties to see. Sell the house to them using words. Pique their interest. Use the AIDA formula mentioned previously.

Be sure the data is correct. Don't get in a hurry and leave information out or make something up that you plan to verify later. Review your listing information every other week, and if needed, rewrite the comments. Have others read your listing information and consider their suggestions.

Internet

For real estate salespeople, the Internet is an advertising medium, and that is about it. Do not think it is a savior to all your prospecting needs. Some real estate salespeople pay thousands of dollars per month for websites that no one sees. See Chapter 3 for a more thorough discussion of the Internet.

Yard "For Sale" Sign

There are basically two types of signs. The first is a post sign. It looks like a big upside down "L" with a sign panel hanging off the wood post. These are large signs and look very nice. The post sign has plenty of space for a "rider" on top or hanging from the sign. Riders are additional specific bits of information, such as the salesperson's name and contact information or describing the property as lakefront or qualifying for special financing. These additional tidbits of information help the potential buyers form a better opinion of the property. Be careful though. Post signs are big and bulky. Generally, they are placed by professional installers. If you install your own signs, be aware of and take care not to damage your seller's sprinkler system.

The second type of sign is the stake sign, which is usually made of metal and has stakes that anchor it into the ground. These signs are much cheaper than post signs and are easier to handle. However, they do not have the visibility of a post sign. Also, be careful when transporting these signs in your car. I have seen the stakes go right through seat cushions.

Some signs, such as a sign that indicates, "This house will be open on Sunday," are informational only. These signs can be constructed of foam board because they are only temporary.

Lock Box

A lock box is a security device that is placed on the seller's door. It has a key inside of it to allow access to the property. There are basically two types of lock boxes. The first is electronic and allows access through an electronic keypad or from a smartphone app such as the Supra eKEY. Without the proper codes, the lock box is inaccessible. This type of box also records, for security purposes, what keypad or smartphone opened the lock box. The second type of lock box is a dial-type combination lock that works like a padlock. It will open when the proper sequence of numbers is dialed into the lock box.

Some sellers are apprehensive to place a key outside their door. I once had a seller who refused to have a lock box on his door. I went to my car, retrieved a lock box, and brought it back inside with me. I handed it to the seller and told him if he could get the key out in less than a minute, I would give him $10. He struggled, pried, banged, and pounded the lock box for a while. I turned to his wife and casually asked her if she thought it would be faster just to break the window. She laughed, and he accepted the lockbox.

Price Reductions

If a property is not selling, a price adjustment may be necessary. Some real estate salespeople believe they will be perceived as having made a mistake if they told the seller to list their property at one price and then later have to suggest a reduction. This may be true, but I know I am not perfect. I have listed property at too high a price to sell. But making a mistake is not a problem if you learn from and correct it.

The best way to get a price reduction is to ask the seller. If the seller refuses or expresses misgivings, have your broker call them. The broker, as an authority figure, will be able to persuade the seller to drop the price. Over the years, whenever I had my broker call for a price reduction, the seller always came around.

Do not settle for a small price reduction. You need to be sure there is only one. I have seen a $450,000 listing that should be priced at $425,000 get an initial price reduction of only $5,000. That small of an amount makes no difference in this case. The real estate salesperson should have tried to get a $25,000 reduction. If you listed a property at the seller's price and it didn't sell, you need to put it at the right price. Note that this would be a non-issue of the property is priced right in the first place. Remember:

> *"I would rather make a seller mad today and happy when it sells, than happy today and mad when it expires."*

I work numerous expired listings. These are properties that have been marketed through a real estate salesperson and the property did not sell. Almost every time, it is simply because the property was overpriced, and the real estate salesperson was too apprehensive to ask for a price reduction. When the property is listed at a lower, more appropriate price, that is when it sells.

Property Brochures

A property brochure provides details of the property. It is a minimum of four pages and is usually printed in color on high-quality paper. The cost of a property brochure usually restricts its use to fine homes and estates. It should be filled with exciting photos of the property. It should place the buyer in the home and evoke a feeling of prestige. It should have minimal information and is not meant to be a tool to market the salesperson. All that is needed is the salesperson's contact information.

I know one real estate salesperson who only deals in elite executive homes. She publishes each property brochure with a blank page to hold a business card. She leaves the page blank so other salespeople have a place to print contact information and then pass out the brochures to their clients. She has figured out that if she puts her contact information there, the other salespeople do not pass out her brochures. She knows her job is to get the property sold, and the best way to do that is to cooperate with other salespeople.

Because of the cost, distribution of these brochures should be limited to potential buyers and real estate salespeople who work with this type of home. You will want to save a few to give to other potential sellers of high-end properties to show what you can do.

Property Profile Sheets

The property profile sheet is also called a property graphic. This single sheet of paper includes details and a picture of the property. The property profile sheet is much less expensive than property brochures and should be used on almost all your listings.

I print two kinds of property profile sheets that are essentially the same except that on one set, I use a color picture of the property and on the other set, I use black and white. I have the seller place some of the color sheets on their kitchen table, and the others are available for distribution at the real estate office. The set of black-and-white profile sheets are placed in an information tube or box attached to the real estate yard sign so that people can take one as they passed by the property. You want to be sure you are budgeting wisely and because the sheets out on the sign tend to disappear quickly, those need to be the cheapest in cost. You may even be able to arrange for the printing company you are using to send the sheets directly to the seller. The seller can then fill the tube or box as it empties. I've never had a seller object to this.

The property details on profile sheet include information about the number and sizes of rooms, all the best amenities, schools, taxes, and, most important, information about you and how to get in touch with you for a showing.

Staging the Property for Sale

Staging the property for sale means setting up the property to look its best. A listing's fiercest competition is new construction. Professionals decorate the interiors of model homes with the finest furniture and accessories. Your job is to compete with those model homes. The way to do this is room by room.

Walk through each room with the sellers, detailing the items to be removed, added, cleaned, or painted. Suggest things that will freshen the room, such as adding brighter light bulbs. Focus on the outside too. Be sure the sellers mow, edge, and landscape the yard.

These are things the seller must do. Some sellers are hesitant to do anything, while others are more than willing to do whatever it takes to sell. I guess Jerry Maguire was right when he said, "Help me help you!"

Residential Service Contracts

Residential service contracts (also called home warranties) are basic insurance policies that protect buyers for one year after the purchase of a home. The number one fear of any buyer is that he or she bought a lemon. The number one lawsuit results from a buyer feeling he or she was lied to about a property's condition. A residential service contract can remove a lot of problems. It covers most mechanical items in the home. Check each policy for terms, or better yet, provide the buyer with several and let them choose the residential service company.

From the sales side, if you get your sellers to agree to get a residential service contract, you can now market the home as covered. It may give the potential buyers a bit more security in believing that they are not buying a lemon. Most residential service companies will provide you with a sign rider notifying potential buyers the property is covered.

Association of REALTORS®

The Association of REALTORS® is a great way to promote your listings. Every time they have meetings, bring graphics on your properties and pass them out. Use your tablet to have a quick slide show of all of your properties; offer to send the slides to another salesperson if they would like to review it. One of the REALTORS® you talk to may have a waiting buyer, and you then make a sale.

Chapter Summary

With all the ways you can market a property, you can't do all of them for each one of your listings. You should develop a marketing plan and checklist and then work forward to market a property. Prepare for your listing appointments, and choose useful comparables in your CMA. Try to convince the sellers of the best market price for their homes, if necessary. Work open houses to the advantage of everyone. Always act professional, confident, and respectful.

Summary Questions

1. What or who covers mechanical breakdowns that might occur in heat/air, plumbing, electrical, and built-in appliances?
   a. Repair allowance
   b. Residential service company (home warranty)
   c. Hazard insurance
   d. Owner's title policy

2. What is the most critical factor in determining a good comparable for a CMA?
   a. Area or location
   b. Amenities in the home
   c. Square footage of the home
   d. Age of the home

3. A successful open house meets all of the following requirements except
   a. It should be priced above market.
   b. It should be easily accessible.
   c. It should be in good condition.
   d. It should be fairly new to the market.

4. Which of the following is not a recommendation in setting up an open house?
   a. Turn on every light in the house.
   b. Call friends over to increase the number of visitors.
   c. Create a pleasant smell throughout the house.
   d. Play soft music.

5. If an open house is slow, you should
   a. take a nap.
   b. use the seller's telephone to call friends long distance.
   c. rummage through the fridge to see if there is anything to eat.
   d. do client follow-up paperwork or computer work.

6. Which of the following is not a factor when setting up for a successful open house?
   a. Call the neighbors and invite them.
   b. Bring brochures about yourself.
   c. Put out one open house sign.
   d. Know all the properties for sale in the area.

7. What type of data should not be included on a CMA?
   a. Homes currently on the market
   b. Homes whose listings expired
   c. Homes that were foreclosed
   d. Homes that were sold

8. What is the minimum number of comparable sold properties that should be on a CMA?
   a. One
   b. Three
   c. Ten
   d. None

9. When should you arrive at the seller's front door for a listing appointment?
   a. You should show up on time.
   b. You should arrive 10 minutes late so you look extremely busy.
   c. You should show up early so you appear excited and enthusiastic.
   d. Timing is not important, show up whenever.

10. What is the main goal for the real estate salesperson when potential buyers arrive at an open house?
    a. To provide them with your promotional materials
    b. To schedule subsequent appointments
    c. To establish rapport
    d. To have them sign buyers agreements

Chapter 9

Prospecting for Buyers

Chapter Overview

In this chapter you will learn how to answer the real estate telephone and convert the call into a buyer prospect. This chapter will delve into the types of buyers in real estate and how knowing the types of buyers can add value to your service. You will discover the best ways to attract buyers through your specific efforts.

Key Terms

Floor Time:
Real estate position of answering the company telephone for business.

Non-Occupant Owner:
A non-occupant owner is one who has given up possession of a property but not ownership. A non-occupant is a property owner who does not live in the home that is listed on the tax record.

Telemarketing:
Telemarketing is randomly calling home renters or apartment renters to gauge their interest in buying a home.

Hot Buyers:
Hot buyers are ready, willing, and able to buy today.

Warm Buyers:
Warm buyers are potential buyers who want to buy, but something is keeping them from doing so.

Cold Buyers:
Cold buyers are potential buyers who have a specific need that can't be met at this time.

Introduction

Where do we find buyers? The same place we find sellers. What works for the seller will work for the buyer.

The following are additional ideas for generating buyers:

- Once the sellers' property sells, they become buyers.

- Wearing career apparel and a name badge can drum up business.

- Always ask for two leads at closing to get additional buyers.

- Prospect builders and their agents to get buyers they can't help.

- Prospect FSBOs as buyers.

- Prospect other agents, other property managers, and apartment locators and ask for buyers they can't help.

- Attend business luncheons and take advantage of business networking opportunities, asking those present if anyone they know wants to buy.

- Conduct buyer seminars.

- Make hotel/motel and postal worker contacts because they may know of people moving into the area.

- Contact people who know people and ask them if they know anyone wanting to buy.

- Meet new people. This is always a great way to get contacts for both buyer and seller leads.

- Prospect your sphere of influence. Ask them for potential buyers.

- Contact past customers and ask them for leads.

- Give away your business cards. Give to everyone for possible buyer business.

- Display car signs and sign riders. This is basic prospecting and it will yield buyers.

"FOR SALE" SIGNS

A large inventory of listings creates potential buyers.

ADVERTISING

Effective local ad campaigns can generate a great number of incoming buyer calls for the office.

OPEN HOUSES

Properly conducted open houses generate numerous prospective buyers.

REFERRALS

Personal and company referrals give you current and future buyers.

COLD CALLS

Making cold calls to apartments can locate first-time buyers. Expand prospecting activities to include buyers.

Most productive salespeople quickly develop a pool of prospects from which to draw. Buyer leads can come from anywhere and everywhere. It's mostly a matter of being alert and curious.

Active Prospecting Ideas for Buyers

To be active in prospecting means that the real estate salesperson goes out and brings the business into the real estate company by direct action of the salesperson.

Telemarketing

Telemarketing is randomly calling home renters or apartment renters to gauge their interest in buying a home. Before we begin telemarketing for buyers, we must know where potential buyers are located. We have listed several ways to find buyers. Let's now concentrate on renters who may be interested in buying.

The best places to find renters are apartment complexes. Multitudes of potential homebuyers in live in these concentrated areas. Like all telemarketing, you are randomly calling renters to determine if there is any interest in buying homes. As always, be aware of and abide by all national "do not call" laws. To get a buyer client, you will need to be persistent; keep calling until you get one who says, "Yes." Consider using the following basic script:

> **Salesperson:**
> "Mr. or Mrs. Renter?"
>
> **Renter:**
> "Yes?"
>
> **Salesperson:**
> "My name is Dan Hamilton with Acme Real Estate Company. I am wondering if you have considered buying a home either now or in the near future."

Telemarketing for buyers is very difficult because fewer and fewer people have land lines, and apartment dwellers frequently move.

Marketing Door to Door

Marketing door to door, which is more time consuming than telemarketing, involves knocking on doors in an area of single-family units known to be rentals. Note that trying to do this type of marketing in apartment complexes may result in you being thrown out by security. Most apartment complexes won't appreciate the efforts being made to take their renters from them. Apartment complexes are better suited to telemarketing than door-to-door marketing.

Reactive Prospecting for Buyers

With reactive prospecting, you make an initial effort to find buyers but then expect the client to come to you. Reactive prospecting may not be as cost-efficient or as effective as other methods of prospecting.

Non-Occupant Owners/Renters

One good way to find buyers is to examine the tax records and look for non-occupant owners. A non-occupant owner is one who has given up possession, but not ownership, of a property. A non-occupant is a property owner who does not live in the home that is listed on the tax record. For example, if the property address is on Main St. and the owner's address is on Brittany Lane, it is apparent that the owner does not live at that property. When you come across this type of situation, you should send the following letter to the property address, at the renter's attention:

> **Dear Property Occupant:**
>
> **Would you consider purchasing a home if the monthly payments were in line with what you currently are paying for rent? If you would like to learn more, please call me at:**

> Dan Hamilton
> Acme Real Estate Company
> P.O. Box 123
> Dallas, TX 77777
> 214-555-1212
>
> Thanks.

This letter should be on standard 8½" × 11" paper and should not be on letterhead. You should use a plain white envelope with a generic return address. In the body of the letter, you must identify yourself as a licensed real estate salesperson.

Personal Marketing

Personal marketing involves promoting yourself constantly. Do not be a secret agent. Secret agents are people who nobody knows are in real estate. They do not wear career apparel, they do not wear a name badge, and they never discuss real estate. They feel that would be uncouth. They also have no money.

To be a good personal marketer, consider having some of the following:

- **Personal brochure:** This brochure should convince a potential client to do business with you, and only you limit the complexity and cost of it. There are companies that will create these brochures for you, but it is expensive. The other option is for you to create the brochure yourself, but you will still be faced with the expense of printing. Because of the cost, these should only be given to truly potential clients.

- **Professional business cards:** Your business card has the potential to set you apart from the crowd. Your card should be multicolored and include a picture of you. Don't crowd the card with too many phone numbers, and do not include your home number.

Doing so not only reduces your professional image; it also will reduce the amount of time you will spend with your family. Think about it: Do you have your attorney's home number?

- **Personal advertising:** All of the advertising you create should promote you, not your real estate company. The company name will need to appear in the ad, and local laws and/or office policies will dictate the size of it relative to the entire ad, but remember: You need to promote yourself, and the company will promote the company.

- **Career apparel, name badge, car signs, and name riders:** You should always be on the lookout for ways to put your name in front of potential clients.

Floor Time (Opportunity Time)

Floor time is the time that a real estate professional spends answering the office telephone, greeting people who walk into the real estate company, and responding to any generic inquires on the company website. In order to generate business from this effort, you must

- Know all the properties that are being advertised.

- Preview all the listings in the office inventory.

- Obtain a list of alternative properties.

- Be serious about answering the phone or greeting a person.

- Smile and smile BIG. Imagine that the caller or walk-in has a check made out to you for $12,000, and all you have to do is get it. This should give you the incentive to pay attention.

Types of Buyers

Hot buyers are ready, willing, and able to buy today. They have the money, they are motivated, and they have a specific time frame.

A prime example of a hot buyer is one who just sold his or her house and has to move now.

Hot buyers can buy property today. They are being transferred from another state and are moving to your area. They want a home before the end of the month. They will be paying cash that they received from the sale of their previous home.

These buyers are HOT!!! Don't let them out of your sight. Pick them up at the airport when they arrive so they don't take a ride from a taxi driver who is a part-time real estate salesperson. Show them houses all day long, if necessary. Handcuff your ankles to theirs so they cannot look for houses in the middle of the night without you. Yes, I am that serious. I have said that you do not let real estate take time away from your family. The exception is when you're working with a hot buyer.

Warm buyers are potential buyers who want to buy, but something is keeping them from it. You have their name and number, and you have met with them, but one of the following may be holding them back:

- They have a house to sell.

- They are waiting for a credit problem to be cleared up.

- They are saving for a down payment.

- They are waiting for their income tax refund.

- They just haven't found the right house yet.

Warm buyers may seem very similar to the hot buyers, but they can eat up your time. Follow up with these buyers, but don't waste too much time on them. They are not ready yet; maybe the time is not right.

Cold buyers are potential buyers who have a specific need that can't be met at this time. Typically they are in no hurry. They may be shopping, and if the perfect house comes along, they'll make a move. You have a name and number but have not been able to get a face-to-face appointment. The best thing to do with these buyers is to refer them to real estate salespeople who have nothing to do but drive around cold buyers.

Focusing your time and energy on hot and warm buyers is more practical and makes economic sense. You can include in your client database buyers who are not ready to purchase, so when the time comes, you will have their information available.

Breakdown of property calls, walk-ins, and Internet leads:

60% are from cold buyers

35% are from warm buyers

5% are from hot buyers

Buyer Objectives

One of the keys for determining whether a lead is solid is to identify the potential buyer's objective. Most real estate salespeople believe that the buyers want to buy the advertised houses, so the salespeople try and sell them those houses. This is a critical mistake. Only 10 percent of buyers actually buy the actual house they called in about, 20 percent of buyers buy the house that they came into the office to inquire about, and 10 percent of buyers buy a house they found on the Internet; most of the time, the buyers end up purchasing a different house. Our job in the real estate industry is to sell the buyers houses, whether or not they buy the houses they inquired about. So what is the objective of the buyer if it is not to buy the advertised house?

The buyer's objective in responding to an ad (print or Internet) is to eliminate the ad. The problem with that strategy is that when the buyer eliminates the ad, he or she also eliminates the salesperson.

To prove my point, I wanted to buy a pick-up truck for hauling yard signs and doing other miscellaneous jobs that a car isn't well-suited for. I did not need the pick-up to look good. However, because I am not an auto mechanic, I needed it to run well. So I scoured the "Trucks for Sale" section of the newspaper. If I read an ad that could be eliminated, I would eliminate it. For example, if the ad read, "Needs some work," I would eliminate the ad. If an ad read, "Could be a steal with a little work," I would eliminate it. If I found an ad I could not eliminate, I would call and ask, "How does it run?" If the person gave me any answer other than "Perfect!" I would make an excuse and hang up. Why? Because I do not want to buy a truck that needs work.

The same goes for real estate. You might eliminate yourself by telling too much or being too specific about a property in an ad. The things we feel are important may not be important to the buyer.

Salesperson's Objective

Your objective is to get an appointment. It is not time to build rapport; that comes when you are face to face with a prospect. It is not time to describe a property, to overcome objections, or to sell you. It is only to get an appointment! And the only way to be sure you have a serious buyer is for that buyer to come into the office for the appointment.

Broker's Objective

The broker's objective is to make the telephones at the real estate office ring with buyers. It is to get potential buyers to come to the office. It is to get Internet buyers to reply. It is not to appease an overpriced seller or make a real estate salesperson feel good because his or her name was in the newspaper or featured on the company website. The only objective is to get buyers.

Don't Forget the Seller

A large percentage of inquires coming in to the real estate office is actually from people who need to sell their homes. They are inquiring to check out their competition. Finding out what other houses in the area are selling for and getting additional information that will help them sell their homes faster are their primary goals. Always ask the question, "Do you live in the area?" If they say "Yes," you are now working with a seller prospect.

Into the Office

If you are a professional and you believe in your company, then it will be easy to convince customers to come into the office. Getting the buyers into your office is your main goal and quite possibly your only goal. At the office you can conduct an interview with the buyer, which will give you a clear picture of the buyer's needs and wants. You can also determine the buyer's readiness, willingness, and ability to buy. The following are some reasons why you should meet prospective buyers at your office:

- Anyone who takes the time to meet you at your office is serious. Don't waste your time on people who are not serious.

- The office provides security. I don't believe that real estate is a dangerous business. However, it never hurts to take every precaution and stay alert. It is not wise for a lone real estate salesperson to meet a "buyer" at a vacant house. Be smart; meet them at your office instead. If a person's aim is to cause harm, they will refuse to come to the office. Meeting in the office also offers the buyer a greater sense of security.

- You have control. If you meet buyers at the property, on the other hand, they can leave anytime they feel like it. You cannot control the situation. You cannot look professional.

- Your broker or manager is available at the office to lend expertise if needed.

- You can make a presentation.

- You can financially qualify them.

- You can gather all the information you need.

- You do not lose business time. If the buyers are to meet you at your office and they don't show up, you can still be working. If you meet them at a property and they don't show up, you have wasted your time.

- It enables you to take advantage of the ready access to necessary files and other resources.

- It is easier and less threatening to the buyer.

- It allows you to build rapport. Experience shows that building rapport and uncovering the emotional issues involved helps build a foundation of trust and confidence.

The office has all the tools to get buyers the best house for the best price in the shortest amount of time. When someone calls in about an ad, the first thing you should do is start asking questions. Avoid questions about the property they called in about. Instead, start with the following questions:

- "How long have you been looking?"

- "How soon do you need a home?"

- "Are you working with any other brokers?"

   Then begin qualifying with questions like:
- "How much are you willing to invest to buy your home?"

   Use fair trades, such as:
- "I will be glad to work for you; all you have to do is meet with me."

   Finally, close for the appointment:
- "I am at the office now or would this weekend be better?"

Property Knowledge

Before taking floor time, you need to view each of the properties that are currently advertised. This might not be possible in all cases; however, you should make every effort to view properties on a daily basis. Don't let this replace prospecting; nothing replaces prospecting. Just take half an hour or so to view three or four properties. You can increase your productivity by making your visits brief and deciding which properties to view based on their proximity to each other. Over time you will get to know the inventory.

Sphere of Influence (SOI)

One of the best sources of buyer leads is your sphere of influence (SOI). Your SOI includes the people who know you and what you do. As was stated earlier, you need to put everyone who is in your SOI into a database and begin calling or emailing them and asking for business. Yes, I said ASK FOR BUSINESS! In essence, that is your main job as a salesperson. For a reminder of how to handle your SOI, refer back to Chapter 7.

Chapter Summary

After reading this chapter, you should know more about buyers and how to find and deal with them. You should also understand the differences and the similarities between buyers and sellers and how to prospect for both of them. Buyers need a real estate professional who cares for them and will spend the time necessary to see that all of their wants and needs are met. To fail with buyers means you are not willing to give them your best.

Summary Questions

1. What is the best way to ensure that you get a buyer lead from calling on apartments?
    a. Call 100 renters per day.
    b. Call for two hours straight in midmorning.

c. Call until you get a buyer.
d. Cold calling does not work.

2. Which of the following is true about buyers?
   a. More often than not, they have a house to sell first.
   b. They don't always feel loyal toward their real estate salespeople.
   c. They typically feel the best home for them is the one they have not seen.
   d. Each of the above statements is true about buyers.

3. Which of the following is not a good way to get buyers?
   a. Hold at least two open houses every weekend.
   b. Prospect the police officer as he puts you in jail.
   c. Wear your nametag everywhere.
   d. Call FSBOs offering referral services.

4. Working with buyers does not include which of the following?
   a. Meeting them at the office first.
   b. Showing no more than five homes at one time.
   c. Allowing children to abuse the sellers' personal property.
   d. Watching the buyers for emotional reactions to the properties.

5. How can an agent convert an ad call into an appointment?
   a. Describe his or her background and success record.
   b. Ask the caller to come into the office.
   c. Give a detailed description of the property's features.
   d. Emphasize the property's price.

6. What is the term for the people who know you and what you do?
   a. Your friends
   b. Your relatives
   c. Your past clients
   d. Your sphere of influence

7. Which of the following is not a benefit of meeting a buyer at the office?
   a. You lose control.
   b. You can make a presentation.
   c. Your broker is available.
   d. You have more security.

8. What is the objective of the buyer when they call into a real estate office?
   a. To buy the house they are calling about
   b. To complain that house prices are too high
   c. To eliminate the property
   d. To determine the racial make-up of the community

9. What type of buyer is motivated and has a specific time frame?
   a. Hot buyer
   b. Warm buyer
   c. Medium buyer
   d. Cold buyer

10. Which of the following is not what a successful marketer in real estate looks like?
    a. A successful marketer wears a nametag.
    b. A successful marketer wears career apparel.
    c. A successful marketer says "Yes" to everybody.
    d. A successful marketer has car signs on his or her vehicle.

Chapter 10

Buyer Listing
Procedures

Chapter Overview

We tend to treat buyers and sellers differently, and this should not be the case. Buyers and sellers should both be considered clients, and as such, you have the fiduciary responsibility of putting their interests above your own. Remember: Buyers expect and have the right to be treated in a fair and honest manner. In this chapter, we will discuss how to set up a buyer meeting at the office and complete that meeting for the benefit of both parties. We'll also explain the viewing of properties all the way to the purchase.

Key Terms

Wants and Needs Analysis:
A wants and needs analysis helps identify a potential client's buying wants (what they actually want) and needs (what is absolutely necessary to meet their needs).

Buyer Representation Packet:
The Buyer Representation Packet should include all the necessary paperwork to fully represent a buyer.

Hot Buttons:
Hot buttons are the things the buyers mentioned during the wants and needs analysis as their wants.

Buyer Signs:
Buyer signs are cues that indicate an interest in the property.

Introduction

Your duties as a buyer broker are the same as they are when you represent a seller.

A few misconceptions about buyer brokerage include the following:

- It is the buyer broker's job to get the buyer the best deal. When you deal with a seller, you know that full price is not always the best for the seller. Terms like "all cash," "delayed possession," or "seller financed" all make an impact on the seller's decision. The same applies to the buyer. The buyer might not need the best price if the seller finances the transaction. Also remember that the buyer buys emotionally, not logically, so do not assume your thinking is the best for the buyer.

- Buyers will not pay for a buyer broker. This thinking is based on cost, not value. If a buyer can understand the value given, the cost will not be the main factor. Also note that in reality the buyer will be paying the seller, who pays the listing broker, who pays the buyer broker.

- The buyer will not sign an exclusive buyer broker contract. This belief was held back in the 1930s, when all listings were open listings. At that time, real estate salespeople did not believe in their service. Eventually, attitudes changed and real estate salespeople would only take exclusive listings. Today, you never see a property with multiple "For Sale" signs in the yard. The same thing will happen with buyer brokerage as soon as the real estate salespeople begin to believe in their service.

I believe the key to dealing with any buyer is to treat that buyer just as though he or she were a seller. You would not throw the listing contract at the seller and demand they sign it. Do not do that with buyers either. Create a buyer presentation and give it to all buyers you work with.

Preparing for the Appointment

To prepare for an appointment with a buyer, get your head straight. Clear your schedule so you aren't interrupted. Make all of the calls you need to make before your appointment. Behave professionally, and mentally walk through the appointment before the appointment actually begins.

Buyer Presentation
Developing a buyer presentation is essential. The presentation helps you and the buyer through the home-buying process. It describes the services you offer and ends with an agreement to represent the buyer.

Buyer Representation Packet
The buyer representation packet should include all the necessary paperwork to fully represent a buyer.

Tools to Have
To be prepared for any contingency, you should have everything at your fingertips, such as a buyer representation agreement, a purchase contract, a calculator, and your buyer presentation on your tablet or computer. This is a perfect reason to get the buyer to meet you at your office because you should have access to everything you need at the office.

Appointment Time at Office
Working with buyers can be an emotionally satisfying experience, but it can quickly become frustrating if you haven't first interviewed your prospects and then followed time-proven procedures for showing property and closing for the buyers' agreement to purchase.

Your initial meeting should involve a balanced process of determining the buyer's readiness, willingness, and ability to complete a purchase; it's also an important time to establish rapport and build the trust and confidence necessary to earn the buyer's loyalty.

Meet at the Conference Table
Once the buyers arrive at your office, take them to the conference room. The conference room holds a certain power; it is where

business decisions are made. Taking them back to your desk is less professional, even if you have a nice work area. If your office does not have a conference room, you will have to make do, but avoid interruptions, forward your calls to another phone, and, if necessary, clean your desk of that cheeseburger from your lunch last week.

Discuss Agency Law

During your first interview with a buyer, you may be required by law (or local regulations) to review a proper agency disclosure concerning your legal obligations to sellers.

Wants and Needs Analysis

A wants and needs analysis helps identify a potential client's buying wants (what they actually want) and needs (what is absolutely necessary to meet their needs). Everyone benefits when you match a buyer's wants and needs to the specific properties available for sale.

The wants and needs analysis will give you the opportunity to understand your clients better and then serve them better by finding a property that meets their needs and fulfills some wants.

The best way to understand your buyer clients is to listen more and talk less. When you do speak, ask questions. The best questions are probing questions or questions that have purpose. When asking probing questions, the clients feel that you are truly interested in their best interest and begin to trust you. Probing questions also reveal the core of the buyers' wants and needs. An example of a probing question would be, "Will you describe what you feel is the perfect home for you?"

Once the buyer begins to describe the perfect home, you should continue asking probing questions. For example, if the buyer states that they need four bedrooms, you could ask, "and how many bathrooms?" Over the next few minutes, the buyers will give you a wish list (their wants) of amenities for their perfect home.

Now look at the list and probe more into each one. "You said you wanted four bedrooms but would three bedrooms and a study work?" If the answer is "Yes," then four bedrooms is a want, not a need. If the client responds, "No, we must have four bedrooms," then it is a need.

After you have asked your buyers what they want and then narrowed it to their needs, you have completed the analysis.

When you begin questioning buyers about the specific things they are searching for in a home, the questions are naturally of a practical nature. That information will help you narrow the selection of properties to show.

However, the decision to buy a particular house is often more emotional than practical. Getting a sense of their lifestyle gives you better insight into their emotional needs. Ask questions such as the following:

- "Will anyone else be living in your new home?"

- "How many bedrooms do you need?"

- "How will you use the third bedroom? Will it be a guest room or an office?"

- "Is a dining room important? Why?"

- "Are there any special features you must have in your home?"

- "How soon will you need possession?"

- "Must you sell your present home to buy another?"

- "Are you currently renting? If so, when does your lease expire?"

- "Are you familiar with today's procedures for buying a home?"

- "Have you seen any homes that you liked?"

- "Did you make any written offers?"

- "Are you working with any other real estate agents?"

- "Why are you moving?"

- "What do you like best about your present home?"

- "What do you like least about your present home?"

- "Do you have any special hobbies?"

If you take your clients on more than five showing appointments with no strong possibilities, perhaps you should sit down and reevaluate their wants and needs.

Discuss Company Results

During this stage of the buyer interview, you should discuss the results of your company. Have a detailed plan showing the features and benefits of doing business with you and your company. Include information on financial qualifying, client qualifying, product searches, market analyses, closing costs, and basic real estate buying information. Also include a section on past successes. Show pictures of happy buyers, recommendation letters, and ancillary businesses (like appraisers, repair and remodelers, inspectors, engineers, and mortgage officers to name a few). All of these can help the buyer.

Discuss Personal Results

The personal results section of the interview can be tricky if you have not been in business long. If you do not have past successes with buyers, leave this section out and spend more time discussing your company. Regardless of what you did in your previous career, do not talk about it. The buyers expect you to be an expert in real estate. If all you talk about is your past career, they will assume you are not an expert in real estate. You do not have to earn credibility; you are given it when the buyer first meets you. Your job is to keep that credibility.

Discuss Financial Qualifying

We will discuss buyer financial qualifying later in this book, but we will briefly touch on the sequence of events here.

After establishing rapport and talking in depth about the buyers' housing needs, begin to collect financial information to determine their financial ability to buy. Once you have information on the money available for a down payment, closing costs, and the affordable monthly payment, you can select the best properties to show. Explain the buying process and the costs involved in buying a house to help set aside any apprehension buyers may have. Being well-informed gives buyers the security to act when it's time for them to make a decision. The following are some questions you may want to ask:

- "How much of your savings do you plan to invest?"

- "What is your present income?"

- "Do you have any other income?"

- "What are your current monthly expenses?"

- "Are you a veteran?"

- "Can you afford what you want?"

- "Is anyone helping you with financing?"

Most buyers expect to be qualified, so don't be shy. Remember to qualify all the time. Ask direct questions since you want and need clear answers.

Solve problems immediately. Problems do not solve themselves or merely go away. It is much easier to resolve them at the beginning of a transaction than later.

Always qualify buyers financially before showing them houses. If you don't, you may be wasting their time and yours.

Close for the Buyer Listing Agreement

After discussing your commitment to the buyer, you can ask the buyer to let you be their initial contact for any property of interest. The following is a guideline of how your buyer appointment at the office should go:

1. When the buyers arrive at the office, always take them to the conference room.

2. Pay a compliment. Say something nice to the buyers.

3. Show how you work. Bring out your buyer presentation and begin your presentation.

4. Ask questions. Get the buyers involved by asking them questions.

5. Financially qualify the buyers. This is the time to find out if the buyers can actually buy what they want to buy.

6. Qualify the property. This is the time to do the wants and needs analysis.

7. Once you determine the types of properties the buyers are interested in, search the Multiple Listing Service website and find what matches their wants and needs. Print out, in full page format, all the matches. Then let them select three to five properties that they would like to see.

8. Show the properties. Once the buyers have selected the properties they want to see, map out a route and take them to see the properties.

9. After viewing each property, find out what the buyers liked and disliked before moving onto the next. After each property

is shown, you should ask the buyers to buy it. You never know unless you ask, "Do you want to buy this property?"

10. Continue the process until a property is selected. Once a property is selected, fill out the purchase agreement immediately. Do not waste time taking the buyers back to the office. When they are ready, you should be too.

The following are some examples of both emotional and practical qualifying questions.

- "How large is your family? What are the ages of your children?"

- "How long have you been looking for a home? Have you seen any homes that appeal to you? In which area is that home located? Tell me what you liked best about that home? Was there anything you disliked?"

- "What did you and your family like about your last home? Was there anything you disliked about your last home?"

- "How soon will you need to take possession of your new home?"

- "In which area do you prefer to live?"

- "What are your requirements for your next home?"

- "Do you own your present home or do you rent?"

- "Will you need to sell your present home before you buy?"

- "With whom are you associated, Mr. Client? Where do you work, Mrs. Client?"

- "Are you familiar with today's procedures in purchasing a home?"

- "Have you decided how you would like to finance your new home?"

- "Would you prefer a large down payment and smaller monthly payments or a small down payment and larger monthly payments?"

Working with buyers can be a rewarding experience. It is, however, more time consuming than working with sellers. Many sales associates rate buyers relative to their readiness, willingness, and ability to buy. If you have an abundance of listings, or listings that appeal to a certain type of buyer, you may want to direct your prospecting activities specifically toward the following:

- First-time buyers

    - Do not have to sell a current home before purchasing

    - Are often very motivated by the tax advantages

- Move-up-or-down buyers

    - Growing families

    - Families with children approaching adolescence

    - Upwardly mobile families

    - Empty nesters

    - People approaching retirement

- Investors

    - Many people who recognize the value of having real estate in their portfolios buy residential real estate as an investment. This can be a lucrative source of business for you.

Property Viewing

Just before you leave on your showing appointment, you should explain to the buyers the protocol for viewing properties:

- Explain that you have officially set these viewing appointments, and you must respect the sellers. This means that if you pull up in front of a house and the buyers hate the outside, you must still go through the house. First, the sellers have spent time cleaning the interior. If they see you stop for a moment and then drive off, they will be upset and most likely will tell others about it. I once heard another real estate salesperson complaining that his seller was upset that another broker had pulled up and then left. He went on to say that the broker could not do anything about it because his buyers refused to view a property. In other words, this salesperson had no control over the buyers. Make sure you have control of your buyers, and you set the rules beforehand.

- Tell the buyers that they need to stay together when viewing the property. Even if one person wants to stay in a room longer than the other, they should stay in the room until both are ready to move on. The reason for this is that you need to watch their behavior and be on the lookout for buying signs, which we will discuss later.

- If children will be on the tour, make sure the buyers are aware that they will need to keep the children from playing with toys while they are in the house.

- Reinforce your accessibility to any listing for showing.

Upon Arrival

If you have properly educated the buyers, the showing will go smoothly. Here are some principles for showing houses:

- Make your showing appointments for an approximate time. Arrange for sellers to be absent or inconspicuous.

- Start with homes at the lower end of the buyer's range and move up in value as you go.

- Do not show more than five properties without taking a break for review. Some buyers want to see every house on the market. However, everyone gets too tired to enjoy the later properties, and it is difficult to remember details of any single property. Stop at a fast food restaurant and buy them a drink. (Some agents offer to pay for lunch.) Review each property you have looked at and eliminate all but one. Then ask them to buy that home. If they want to see more properties, that is fine. But now you have helped them cut down the previous properties to one, so it will be easier to compare this with the new properties. The others they have seen can be forgotten.

- Make sure you have a keybox opener or all the necessary keys, if applicable.

- Have information about each property readily available.

- Be flexible.

- Point out neighborhood features, especially those that the buyers have identified as being important.

- Park across the street to provide a full view of the property. This will also ensure you don't block anyone else from using the driveway.

- Enter through the front door, even if it is not the most frequently used entrance. You should enter first and have the buyers follow.

- If the sellers are in the house when you enter, briefly introduce the buyers to the sellers. Then let the sellers know that if you need them, you will find them.

- Lead the buyers through the house. Turn on and off lights as you go.

- Unlock and lock each door.

- Watch for the buyers' responses, verbal and nonverbal.

- Show the buyers their hot buttons first, and be sure to return to those before leaving. Remember, hot buttons are the wants the buyers identified during their wants and needs analysis, such as a swimming pool they really want, but do not have to have.

- Give the buyers plenty of time in each room, and keep comments to a minimum to allow for "psychological ownership."

- Stand close to the wall to enhance room size.

- Ask questions to help the buyers visualize their furniture in the house.

- Don't sell the home, just reinforce positive comments.

- Advise the buyers to make notes about each property after inspecting it.

- Point out any defects you know about, but be sure to point out a positive feature at the same time. For instance, "There is a crack in the wall but the listing sales associate told me the sellers have had it inspected by a qualified engineer and are having it repaired. If this is the right house, we can get the documentation as part of the offer."

- When you are driving to a property, you may want to forewarn buyers about a particular problem or even overplay it so the problem doesn't seem as bad when they see it for themselves. Be sure to discuss problems when you are away from the sellers.

- Allow the buyers to discover the property on their own. Point out only those features they might miss.

- Explain features as benefits.

- Listen to the buyers' comments, both positive and negative. Ask additional questions to clarify needs.

- Make sure the home is secure before leaving.

Buyer Signs

While viewing the properties, you also should be aware of buyer signs or cues that indicate their interest in the property. Do this by listening to verbal signs, by watching nonverbal signs, and by asking questions.

Verbal buyer signs include the following:

- Asking specific questions, such as "Is this a Hamilton built home?"

- Noting minor concerns, such as "The taxes here are kind of high."

- Asking about personal property, such as "Will the seller leave the refrigerator?" Buyers won't express interest in a refrigerator if they don't like the house.

- Wanting to show the property to a friend or relative, such as "Could we bring my mother back to see this one?"

Nonverbal signs include the following:

- Lingering, taking their time, or wandering back into rooms they have already seen.

- Acting nervous and jittery, talking fast, eyes shifting.

- Imagining furniture in rooms; looking at one wall and then another.

- Touching each other, holding hands, putting their arms around each other.

- Touching things in the house, touching the walls for texture, touching the carpet, and opening cabinets.

After Viewing the Property

Spend some time with the buyers, asking some of the following questions to refine the list of properties you'll show them later:

- "What did you like best about this house?"

- "Would you consider this house as your next home?"

- "Why did you like the second house better than the first?"

Buyers don't always want what they think they want. Sometimes you need to stop, regroup, and clarify. If you've shown several homes and sense that nothing is clicking, probe beyond the buyers' stated likes and dislikes. Try to uncover additional information that will give insight into their emotional and psychological needs.

Remember to complete a competitive market analysis to show the buyers what the market indicates the price should be. The buyer cost sheet indicates the amount of money the buyer will need to bring to closing. The process for figuring a buyer cost sheet is the same as that for figuring the seller's cost sheet.

Finalization

The buyers should make the best offer they can. I have seen buyers try to steal a property by offering a low amount. This tends to set bad parameters for the transaction. The sellers now believe the buyers are trying to take advantage and the buyers believe the sellers are unreasonable. You should guide the buyers to offer the best price they can and then let the sellers respond to the best offer.

Chapter Summary

Working with buyers can be very rewarding. They want to know that you care about them and that they are worthy of your attention. If you do not show them the attention they feel they deserve, they will find someone who does. Build rapport at the first appointment and then do a wants and needs analysis. Revisit their wants and needs over time, if necessary. Also, financially assess your buyers before showing them any properties. Working with buyers can be a great source of income for the real estate professional who understands them.

Summary Questions

1. What is the maximum number of houses you should show a buyer before taking a break?
   a. Three
   b. Five
   c. Ten
   d. No maximum

2. What are the two separate qualifications for a buyer?
   a. Needs and financial
   b. RESPA and HUD
   c. Price and terms
   d. Timing and area

3. What should you do if a qualified buyer hasn't bought a home after three showing appointments?
   a. Direct the buyer to an area with like people.
   b. Increase the purchase price.
   c. Take the buyer on more showing appointments. Your broker thinks you're working.
   d. Reanalyze the buyer's wants and needs.

4. Which of the following is not a misconception of buyer brokerage?
   a. The buyer broker is to get the buyer the best deal.
   b. Buyers will not pay for a buyer broker.
   c. The buyer broker ultimately is paid through the agreement with the buyer.
   d. The buyer will not sign an exclusive buyer broker contract.

5. Which of the following actions describes the services the buyer broker performs?
   a. The closing
   b. The buyer presentation
   c. The option
   d. The contract

6. The initial meeting with a buyer should determine all of the following except
   a. the buyer's readiness.
   b. the buyer's willingness.
   c. the buyer's ability to pay.
   d. the buyer's race.

7. When a buyer is at the real estate office, what is the first room you take them to?
   a. The bathroom
   b. The conference room
   c. Your personal office or desk
   d. Your broker's office

8. What is the process called that determines a buyer's wants and needs?
   a. A buyer presentation
   b. A wants and needs analysis
   c. Making the sale
   d. Fiduciary

9. What type of question reveals the core of the buyer's wants and needs?
   a. "If then" question
   b. Closed question
   c. Probing question
   d. Closing question

10. Which of the following is NOT a secret to success when showing houses to buyers?
    a. Asking the buyer the following question after viewing each property: "Do you want to buy this house?"
    b. Keeping cash money in your pockets, around your desk, and in your car to look successful.
    c. Keeping your gas tank always half full or more.
    d. Meeting the buyers for the first time at the office.

Chapter 11

Objection Handling
Techniques

Chapter Overview

In this chapter, you will learn to classify objections posed by your clients and to identify the differences among stalls, conditions, and objections. This chapter will enable you to use a multitude of closing techniques. It will give you the ability and confidence to deal with a wide variety of common objections. This chapter combines both theoretical and practical information and is based on the principle of overcoming the cause of the objection rather than dealing with the symptom.

Key Terms

Benefit:
Benefits fulfill a need or satisfy a preference.

Condition:
One that is indispensable to the occurrence of another. A condition stops the transaction.

Feature:
A distinctive aspect, quality, or characteristic.

Objection:
A reason or cause for expressing opposition. It is the real reason clients believe they should not make a decision.

Stall:
To bring to a standstill. Prospects will stall when they want to delay a decision.

Introduction

A lot of this chapter deals with making money. I say this because the real estate professionals who know how to handle objections and close the sale make more of the money. They know their clients and always act in their clients' best interests. Professionals know their jobs are based on helping people make tough decisions. They must help the sellers price their houses right to get them sold. They do not want to overprice a house and jeopardize the sale even if the seller wants more money. The professional helps the buyer make a decision before taking a chance of losing the purchase.

Let me give you an example of a professional salesperson: my daughter, Brittany, at age four. At that time Brittany could talk, but reading had not yet come. We were driving down the road, and she spotted an ice cream sign.

"Daddy, if you were to get an ice cream, would you get chocolate or vanilla?"

Now for you professional salespeople, you recognize this as an alternate of choice close. Saying "No" is not an option here. This technique will be discussed later.

I decided to find out what my little girl was made of, so I said, "Well Brittany, if I were to get an ice cream, I would get vanilla."

And without hesitation, she said, "So will I."

This is an assumptive close.

Let's analyze. First, did she get the ice cream? Of course she got the ice cream. How did she know what to say? Most students I ask this of assume that I taught her the technique. (I never discuss techniques around my house. Home is for family, and business is for work; I try never to mix the two.) I believe the reason Brittany knew what to say is that she knows me better than anyone in the world. She knew that if she asked me to get her an ice cream, I could have said "No," and she knew she could not argue with me once I said "No." So in her little head, she wondered, "How would daddy respond best?"

Was Brittany's response manipulative? No, because she did me a favor. Notice how I said that: She did me a favor. What she did was allow me to make her happy, and I would do anything to make her smile. That's professionalism!

If you are having trouble getting the client to make a decision that is in his or her best interest, maybe you should spend more time getting to know the client and learning what works best when dealing with him or her.

Objection versus Rejection

An objection is a reason or cause for expressing opposition. It is important not to see the objection as a personal rejection. All of us fear rejection to varying degrees, and it is important to recognize that we may have a tendency to take an objection personally, especially if we've had a tough day. Begin thinking of objections as questions with emotional content. This will help you deal in a more positive way with the substance of the objection and the person objecting.

Whatever the case, don't worry. Most objections are not as serious or formidable as they seem. Often what appears to be an objection is merely a request for more information.

Objections can be helpful if they mean that your client

- Is interested in what you are saying.

- Is listening attentively enough to have objections.

- Is thinking through your solution.

- Is trying to resolve foreseeable difficulties.

- Wants more information about your proposed solution.

Remember, too, that the *absence* of objections can be a warning that your client may not be interested or is not listening.

Objection versus Question

The main distinction between an objection and a question is that a question requires only information. An objection has some emotional content and often indicates resistance to your proposal. In the latter case, you have to provide reassurance as well as information.

Types of Objections

All objections can be lumped into three categories—stalls, objections, and conditions. Of the three, you should be able to overcome all stalls and objections.

Definition of a Condition

A condition is one that stops the transaction. It cannot be overcome. If you run into a true condition you cannot go forward. This is important: You must believe there are no conditions. Most real estate people fail to close because they feel they have run into a condition when it is only an objection. Again, you must believe there are no conditions.

Which of the following are conditions?

- The buyer cannot get financing.

- The house has a foundation problem, and the sellers don't have the money to fix it.

- The seller wants more money than the property can get.

- The buyer's uncle must approve of the house because he is giving the buyers the money.

Out of the above list, only the last one is actually a condition. Let's analyze these in more detail.

- The buyer cannot get financing. *What if the seller financed? This is an objection.*

- The house has a foundation problem, and the sellers don't have the money to fix it. *What if the foundation company fixed the foundation but waited until closing to get paid? This is an objection.*

- The seller wants more money than the property can get. *There are several ways to approach this objection.*

- The buyer's uncle must approve of the house because he is giving the buyers the money. *This is a condition because the uncle is actually the decision maker. No matter how much the buyers want the house, the uncle could say "No."*

Conditions arise most commonly because you are not negotiating with the decision maker. That's why it's critical to talk with that person. In this case, have the uncle go on showings or put the money in the buyer's bank account so that they now have control.

Definition of a Stall

A stall happens when the prospects raise some type of objection because they want to hide, for whatever reason, the real reason they don't feel they should make a decision. Stalls sound legitimate, but make no mistake: The clients just feel nervous that they might have to make a decision. Here are some typical stalls:

- "We would like to think about it."

- "Can we call you tomorrow?"

- "If it is meant to be, it will happen."

- "We never make a decision until the next day."

- "We need to pray about it."

Let's first take a look at what might happen if the client waits. The seller might lose a sale because the buyer might find another property. The buyer might lose the property because another buyer purchases it while your buyer waits. You might argue that this is your client's decision. True, but you must help them make a decision now. If they lose the house, it will be "your" fault. You are the professional third-party negotiator, and your client is willing to pay you a great deal of money to help them make the right decision.

One further note: If it is not in your clients' best interest to accept the transaction, you must stop them. However; stalling is not in their best interest. The best way to handle a stall is to ask questions. These questions should be directive and closed-ended.

1. Agree with the client.

2. Direct the client to his or her final objection by asking minor questions.

3. Now that you know the client's final objection, you can handle a true objection.

The most common final objection is price for both the seller and buyer. So, direct them there by using closed-ended questions. For example, consider the following situation:

Buyer:
"We would like to think it over first."

Salesperson:
"I understand that this is a difficult decision. Let me ask, are you concerned about the size of the home?"

Buyer:
"No, the size is fine."

Salesperson:
"Is it the area where the home is located?"

Buyer:
"No, we like the area."

Salesperson:
"Is it me, do you like and trust me?"

Buyer:
"Of course, we like you." Big pause, then slowly . . .

Salesperson:
"Is it the price?"

Buyer:
"Well, you know, it is more than we wanted to spend."

Salesperson:
"I remember, but let me ask you, if we could agree upon a price, would you buy the property tonight?"

Buyer:
"Yes . . . yes, we would."

Notice the way the salesperson moved through a series of questions until discovering the final objection and then closed on that objection.

Here is a last resort if the questions don't work. Excuse yourself for a short period of time to give the clients some time alone. If you are at the office, tell the clients you will leave the room; if you are at their house, make a quick trip to the closest convenience store. This gives them time to discuss the situation with the knowledge that you will be back. Remember, this is a last resort.

Definition of an Objection
An objection is the real reason clients believe they should not make a decision today. However, if you can change this belief, they will proceed.

When I first began my career, I was so afraid of objection that it almost got the best of me. Now I silently beg the client to give me an objection I cannot handle. What is the difference? I spent a lot of time over the years studying how to handle objections. Studying gave me knowledge, and knowledge gave me confidence. You must make an effort to learn; it will not just come to you over time. However, don't study while you should be prospecting. Study only at times when it is not possible to be making money.

To handle objections you must ask lots of questions. Sound familiar? It should. It is the same thing I said about handling stalls. You have to learn how to ask probing questions, or questions that have a purpose. Once you excel at asking questions, you will excel at handling objections.

In the following sections, we will discuss seven steps for handling objections or addressing concerns. These techniques are almost foolproof and also work well in diffusing tense situations.

Step 1: Hear Them Out
When someone trusts you enough to tell you what's bothering him or her, be courteous and listen. Don't feel like you have to address every phrase they utter. Give them time; encourage them to tell you the whole story behind their concern. If you don't get the whole story, you won't know what to do or say to change their feelings. Don't interrupt either, because you may jump in and answer the wrong concern. This is important: While listening to your clients, take notes on everything they say. Doing so allows you time to analyze what they are saying, gives you notes to look back on at a later time, and most importantly, shows that you care about them.

Step 2: Feed It Back
By rephrasing their concerns, you are, in effect, asking for more information. Be certain the clients have said all they had to say so that no other concerns crop up after you've handled this one. In doing this, you're asking them to trust you. Clarify the concern by probing to learn why they feel that way. People sometimes need help expressing their feelings. It helps all parties understand the true nature of the concern. Begin your probing questions as follows.

- "If I understand . . .?"

- "Are you saying . . .?"

- "Will you tell me more . . .?"

- "Will you explain further . . .?"

- "What you are saying is . . .?"

When the concern is clear, move on to the next step.

Step 3: Question It
This is where subtlety and tact come into play. If the clients object to request to put up a yard sign, don't say, "What's wrong with it?" Instead, gently ask, "A yard sign makes you uncomfortable?" If it does, they'll tell you why. Maybe they don't want their neighbors to know they're selling. Probe further, "Why do you not want your neighbors to know you are selling?" If your questions are from your heart and the clients feel you care, you should be able to ask numerous questions without irritating them.

Step 4: Dignify It
Dignify the concern by identifying with it and validating the person's feelings. Noting that others in the same situation have had similar feelings warms the other person to your response.

- "I can appreciate that. Others have felt the same way . . ."

- "I understand how you feel . . ."

- "That's a reasonable point of view . . ."

- "That's a good question . . ."

Step 5: Discuss It
Once you're confident you fully understand their concern, you can discuss it by providing information that explains the advantages of your perspective and reassures the other party.

- "We have a large inventory of buyers at this time . . ."

- "Market data shows houses are selling in 90 days . . ."

- "I could help you with . . ."

Step 6: Confirm Your Answer
Once you've answered the objection, it's important that you confirm that your clients heard and accepted your answer. If you don't complete this step, they are likely to raise the same objection again. If they feel that your comment answered their concern, then you're one step closer to persuading them. If they are not satisfied with your answer, now is the time to know, not later when you're trying to get their final approval to go ahead. Confirm that the concern has been successfully addressed. Ask the clients if they believe the information you have just presented could make a difference in the situation at hand. Ask if they see the benefits. (Make sure there is no longer a concern.)

- "Will that be okay . . .?"

- "Does that sound like a service you could use . . .?"

- "Do you see the benefit of . . .?"

Step 7: Lead In
Lead into the next section. Don't just keep talking. Take a conscious, purposeful step back into your presentation. If it's appropriate, change the screen on your tablet or computer. Point to something other than whatever generated the objection. Take some sort of action that signals to the other person that you're forging ahead.

These seven steps, if you learn them and apply them properly, will take you a long way toward achieving your goal of selling others even when they raise objections or concerns.

Questioning Techniques

Why do we ask questions?

- To gain control

- To isolate areas of interest

- To get minor agreements

- To arouse emotions

- To isolate objections

- To answer objections

Questions can be placed in two major categories: the open-ended question and the closed-ended question.

The open-ended question solicits a discussion on the part of the receiver. The receiver can talk forever because of your question. The best open-ended questions paint a picture, and the receiver finishes that picture for you. Some examples include:

- "If money was no object, what would your dream home look like?"

- "What are your concerns about selling your house?"

- "Think back to your parents' home. Are there any features from that home that you want in your home?"

The closed-ended question is meant to solicit a "Yes" or "No" answer. It is used to direct the client and prevent the client from expanding on an answer. Some examples of closed-ended questions include:

- "Do you want to buy this home?"

- "Can you make a decision today?"

There's another reason we shoud ask questions instead of immediately responding with our own answers: A question engages the other person and helps create a more meaningful exchange and a better relationship. It shows we are interested in what that person has to say. You can't move forward in real estate sales with a reluctant prospect unless and until you manage to create a climate in which that person is talking with you, not just listening to you.

Objection-Handling Worksheets

Objection-handling worksheets are used to prepare for all anticipated objections during a sales presentation. Realize that while all objections cannot be overcome, good sales presentations help buyers and sellers move closer to problem resolution. The main key to handling objections successfully is to identify the specific nature of the objection, which can only be given by the buyer. Remember that any time an objection is resolved, the opportunity exists to move the buyer closer to purchase or problem resolution.

Here are the basic steps in developing an objection-handling worksheet:

1. List all potential objections that someone might have to buying your service.

2. List all the potential causes of those objections.

3. List potential questions to identify the cause for the individual's objection. You will need more than one question to match the style of the interaction. Phrase these in actual question format.

4. List objection-handling techniques for each cause. Phrase these using your actual wording.

Once you complete an objection-handling worksheet, you will find that you are prepared to handle almost any objection.

Features and Benefits

Professional salespeople know the difference between features and benefits. The features are the aspects of the service. The benefits fulfill a need or satisfy a preference. Many real estate salespeople never figure out the difference between features and benefits. They go through their entire career trying to sell the features of their service only to have the clients reply, "So what?"

I believe that selling is an art form. My family and I once went to Disney World. While there, we were offered free tickets if we listened to a presentation on timeshares in Orlando. My wife was not thrilled, but I love to get exposure to other salespeople. I find that I learn from the good ones and the bad ones.

When we arrived, a young salesman greeted us. He shook my hand, introduced himself to my wife, and then bent down and gave a great big smile to our daughter, Brittany. He then spent time making friends with Brittany. He knew that to score points with me, he should become friends with Brittany. If Brittany likes you, I like you. Selling is an art form, and it is beautiful to watch.

We sat down, and the salesman began asking us a lot of questions. Did you hear that? He asked questions. I wonder where I have heard that before? He learned a great deal about us that he would need later.

We then went to look at a timeshare unit. Of course, it was immaculate. It overlooked Disney World and two full-sized swimming pools. The interior was perfect, with fine dinnerware on the tables, designer comforters on the beds, and beautiful furniture, none of which would be there when we got there. I could see through the show because I was a professional salesperson myself, but I think I started losing my wife. She remembered that we were paying several hundred dollars a night for a cramped hotel room, and now she was looking at plush accommodations. Selling is an art form, and this guy had it down.

We went back to the conference room. The salesperson began asking more questions. Wait . . . you can ask MORE questions? Yes, you can! This is how he set me up. Remember, I am not interested, and I am a professional salesperson myself. And did he know I was in sales? Of course he did; he asked what my occupation was.

> **Salesperson:**
> "Dan, do you and Kimberly have money set aside for Brittany's college?" (I had given him permission to use my first name.)
>
> **Dan:**
> "Yes we do. We have a mutual fund." (He wasn't going to catch me not taking care of Brittany.)
>
> **Salesperson:**
> "Dan, do you and Kimberly have money set aside for your retirement?"
>
> **Dan:**
> "Yes we do. It also is in a mutual fund." (He wasn't going to catch me not providing for my family.)
>
> Long pause
>
> **Salesperson:**
> "Dan, do you have money set aside for time with your family?"

How good is that? He drew me in like a fish on a line. He asked questions; he even knew how I would answer. Then BAM, he hooked me. What could I say? I knew where he was going, but I could do nothing but stammer. I was not angry; I was flat-out amazed. Selling is an art form, and artists ask the right questions to get interest and will never alienate their clients by making them angry.

But I was not done yet. I had objections. Do you think he already knew what they were? A professional salesperson always knows the clients' objections before they even ask them. I am amazed when

I see a so-called professional salesperson look bewildered when I have an objection. How could they not be more prepared?

> **Dan:**
> "Sure, it sounds great, but what if we can't come down here the same time each year?"
>
> **Salesperson:**
> "Dan, that is an excellent question. If I could show you how you can come here anytime, would you buy today?"
>
> **Dan:**
> "Uh, no, but explain what you mean."
>
> **Salesperson:**
> "I would be happy to explain. Here at Acme Timeshares, we believe in you and care about you. We actually keep 15 units set aside for you whenever you want. Just call us a week in advance, and we will have one ready for you and your family. Isn't that a great feature? Can you see how that benefits you?"

Oops, he took care of my first objection well. Notice his questions. Notice his words. Selling is an art form.

> **Dan:**
> "Yeah, that is nice. But what if I get bored with Orlando? Have I just wasted my money?"
>
> **Salesperson:**
> "Dan, take a look at this."

He brought out a book that showed all of the destinations around the world that were part of this timeshare network. Within this network you could trade destinations with another member. You could go to their destination, and they could take your spot in Orlando. In the end, I did not buy a condo, but I did leave feeling that I had been in the presence of a true sales artist. I might not make a sale every time, but I do want the people to think good things about me. It is my life's work.

Closing Techniques

When I meet a person, my first goal is to get him or her to like me and trust me. If someone tells me something, I have a tendency to doubt them. But if they ask me something, that's different. Focus on asking, not telling. The following are techniques that can be used either by you or on you. Some of them are manipulative. To be manipulative, the technique benefits only you, not your client. Be sure your interest is always directed toward your client. If you choose not to use any of these, at least you will recognize them when they are used on you. These techniques are in no specific order.

Trial Close

The trial close is used to gauge the "temperature" of a buyer or seller. A trial close asks a question, and if the clients agree, they are interested. If their answer is negative, the clients are not ready to make a decision. The best trial closes are "tie-downs" and "if-then" closes.

The following is an example of a trial close: "When do you want to take possession of the house?" If the clients like the house, they will answer. If not, they will protest. Now you know whether or not to move to the final close.

The Tie-Down Close

A tie-down is a question at the end of a sentence that demands a "Yes" response. A trial close is used to see if the client has any interest. If the client responds with a "Yes," he or she might be interested. If the client is apathetic to your "tie-down," then this is not the right property for the client, and you must move on. For example:

- "A reputation for professionalism is important, *isn't it?*"

- "It would be convenient to move as a family, *wouldn't it?*"

- "Double moves are expensive, *aren't they?*"

- "As a specialist in this area, I can better serve you, *can't I?*"

- "You are interested in the home having complete exposure, *aren't you?*"

These questions are not necessarily designed to get an answer; just a nod of the head will do. You can use the tie-down in the beginning or middle of the sentence if you so desire.

- "*Wouldn't you agree,* this a peaceful neighborhood?"

- "A big back yard... *isn't it* exciting the activities that can be done there?"

Like all the techniques, this one can be overused, so be careful.

If–Then
The "if–then" close is one of my favorites. It is the perfect trial close. Consider the following question, which is worded exactly as the buyer says it:

> **Buyer:**
> "Will the sellers leave the refrigerator?"

A less-experienced or less-skilled real estate salesperson might respond to the buyers with the following: "They probably will," or "We can ask."

However, what I "hear" when the buyer asks the question above is the following:

> **Buyer:**
> "We really like this house. We want to buy it if you can close us. If not we *will buy* it through another real estate salesperson.

Oh by the way, if we could get the refrigerator that would be great!"

When you really analyze the question, you see what the buyer is actually asking, and you can respond more effectively, such as with the following:

> **Salesperson:**
> "Mr. & Mrs. Buyer, if I get the sellers to leave the refrigerator, then would you buy this house?"

Regardless of how the buyers respond, I now know a whole lot more than I did 10 seconds before I asked the question. Don't miss the opportunity to use a great close if it is handed to you. This is the difference between a professional real estate salesperson and "just another" salesperson. As with all techniques, don't overuse this one.

Alternate of Choice Close

An alternate of choice is a question with only two answers. Both are minor agreements leading toward major decisions. For example:

- "I have an opening now, or would later today be more convenient?"

- "I can be available at 2:00 p.m. or 4:00 p.m. Which time would better suit your schedule?"

- "I can clear my schedule for you on Saturday or Sunday. Which would you prefer?"

- "If everything goes according to your plan, about how soon would you like to move, 60 or 90 days?"

Assumptive Close

An assumptive close is a question that assumes the salesperson has made the sale. The client must stop the salesperson or the salesperson is moving forward for the final close. For example:

- "Laurie, what personal property do you want to leave?" Notice, the salesperson is expecting the seller to agree to a listing and is simply addressing the personal property to be left. If the seller does not agree, then identification of personal property to be left is irrelevant.

- "We have our preview of new property on Friday. Will you be home or shall I bring a key?" Notice that the salesperson is expecting the seller to agree to a listing and is simply addressing getting into the house. If the seller does not agree, there will be no preview.

Feedback Question Close

The feedback question close is taking a minor objection and warmly feeding it back to the client in the form of a question. For example:

Seller:
"I don't want to give out a key."

Salesperson:
"You don't want to give out a key? Will you elaborate on that?"

Seller:
"We don't want to tie the property up with a listing."

Salesperson:
"Oh, you don't want to tie the property up with a listing? Will you elaborate?"

Seller:
"Can you have the home sold in 60 days?"

Salesperson:
"Does 60 days suit your time schedule best?"

Seller:
"Will you put a sign on the property?"

Salesperson:
"Did you want a sign on the property?"

Seller:
"Will you call before coming over to show the home?"

Salesperson:
"Would you prefer that we call for an appointment before showing the home?"

Similar Situation Close

A similar situation close involves sharing a story about someone else who was in the same situation as your seller or buyer (make sure the story is true). Consider the following example:

Seller:
"We can always rent this home. We don't have to sell it."

Salesperson:
"That certainly is true. Renting a home is a good investment; however, it's a proven fact that few tenants take the pride in ownership that an owner does. In fact, it's feasible that any appreciation in value could be offset by what we call deferred maintenance. Have you ever rented or managed a home before? It can be a rude awakening. In fact, the other day I was listening to a program in which the instructor decided to rent his home. Unfortunately, he rented to people we call 'professional tenants.' He said that after receiving no rent for six months, he finally went through eviction proceedings. It cost him over $14,000 to repair and refurbish the home. This is the type of thing that bothers me about renting the home, and I would hate to see the same situation happen to you."

Reduce to the Ridiculous Close

There are all kinds of ways to describe the price of something. If you asked someone who builds airplanes what it costs to fly a 747 from coast to coast, he or she would not tell you it costs $150,000. They would tell you it is 22 cents per passenger mile.

You are working with a buyer who truly wants to buy a certain house but doesn't want to pay the extra $5,000 the seller wants. Consider the following script:

> **Salesperson:**
> "I know $5,000 seems like a lot of money, but tell me, how long do you plan on living in the home?"
>
> **Seller:**
> "The rest of our lives."
>
> **Salesperson:**
> "Well I appreciate that, but let's say you live there only for the duration of the loan, which is 30 years. If you break down that $5,000 per year, you're only looking at (enter numbers into your calculator or phone) $167 a year. If you look at that from the big picture, you get the home you want with the whirlpool tub in the master bedroom for the price of a hotel room. Let's see what that works out to be (enter numbers again): less than $14 per month. That's lunch money! Could the two of you miss one lunch during an entire month? If you could, you could get the home you really want.
>
> We looked at several houses and this is the only one that allows you room to put in that garden you always wanted. I wonder what that is per day (enter numbers in the calculator). Forty-six cents per day! That is less than you would pay for a cup of coffee.
>
> Let's get serious, you want this house. We are sure the seller will accept the offer if you raise your offer by $5,000.

As a matter of fact (rummage through your pocket for two quarters and toss them on the table), let me pay for your first day. All I need you to do is authorize this paperwork and I will do my best to get you into this home." (Hand the buyer your pen.)

Some explanation is necessary. First, not all techniques work all the time, but all of them work some of the time. Also note that the buyer wants this house. If you are pushing the buyer into a decision just to make a commission, you are being manipulative. We are professionals, not high-pressure salespeople. To use this technique properly, start big at an annual figure and work your way down to the daily amount.

I used this technique on an accountant once. After I finished, the accountant said, "Your numbers are all wrong. Financing $5,000 is a lot different, plus there are tax consequences and the time value of money to consider. But we want the house, so we will pay the $5,000." Now, I am not sure what happened, but the buyers got the house they wanted. Sometimes the buyers just need a moment to reflect.

Puppy Dog Close

This close is just like it sounds, and it came from pet shop owners. A family might walk into the pet shop and look at a cute puppy dog. The kids and wife fall in love with the puppy. The husband also falls in love with the puppy but is hesitant to buy the puppy. The pet shop owner says, "It's Friday, take the puppy home with you over the weekend, and if on Monday, you don't want it, just bring it on back." What happens? Of course the family never brings back the puppy.

This is a favorite technique of auto dealers. They offer to let you take the car for a test drive, hoping you will fall in love with it and won't be able to give it up.

So how can we use this in real estate?

This happened to me. I had a couple of "those" buyers. You know; the kind of couple that can't agree on the same house. He likes one house and she likes another. I was willing to stay with them because I knew they would buy and use me. We finally went through a house, and neither of them had anything negative to say. Still, they were not ready to make a decision. So I asked them to sit down in the living room. After about 20 minutes of silence, one of them said, "What do you think?" And the other replied, "Yeah, we should buy this one."

Good Guy–Bad Guy Close

Envision the following famous police integration: One bad cop beats up and threatens a perp until it gets out of hand and the good cop steps in and removes the bad cop. "Come on Joe, go get yourself some coffee." Joe steps out saying, "Okay, but I am not done with you yet!" The good cop says, "Man, you had better tell me what I want to hear before Joe gets back, 'cause I have never seen him that mad."

I have never attempted this close, but some friends of mine worked this one to perfection. They are a husband-and-wife real estate sales team. He is the bad guy and she is the good guy. He takes over the listing appointment and "tells" the sellers what is needed to get the house sold, including price. His information is correct, and some sellers agree and sign up. Other sellers hesitate, and he pounces on them. He begins to raise his voice and his gestures become forceful. Just about the time the sellers throw him out, his wife steps in and says, "Honey, stop, go to the car." To the sellers she says, "I am sorry for his behavior, but his point is valid. . . ." The sellers list with her at the correct price and terms.

The team has learned that some sellers need the real aggressive type while others prefer a softer approach. The team literally covers all territory.

Take Away Close

The take away close is most famously used by car salespeople. They ask you for your best offer, and whatever you say, they reply,

"What? I can't do that; I guess you will have to find a less-expensive car. Could I show you the . . . ?" But no other car will do for you, so you pay the greater amount.

My dad worked this technique against the same car dealers, and he is the most mild-mannered man you will ever meet. He never studied these techniques, he just knew them intuitively. I wanted a new car for college, and I found my dream: a brand new Ford Mustang. It was a beautiful car, and I was in love. I am glad my dad was there because I would have paid anything to get that car. (Salespeople are the easiest to sell). My dad made an offer that the salesperson refused. I was hysterical about losing the car, but my dad calmly said, "Okay, bye."

Then the salesperson said, "Wait a minute, let me check with my manager." He came back a few minutes later and asked my dad if he could give any more than what he had offered.

My dad said he could not and got up to leave. We got to the door of the office before the salesperson said, "Hold on, take a seat. Maybe we could do this. . . ."

A short time later, my dad was saying no again, and we got up to leave. This time we made it to the front door of the dealership. The next time we made it to the car, and the final time we were in my dad's car driving away from the dealership. The salesperson was running after us screaming, "You've got your deal! You've got your deal!" My dad had used the take away close to perfection!

Later I asked my dad how he knew he could get that price. He replied calmly, "They make more than one Mustang. Whatever they claimed was their best deal, I knew we could go elsewhere and get the same deal." What a concept! There's the advantage of a third-party negotiator.

You can use this technique in real estate too, but be very careful. This one is highly touchy. Sellers can and will feel you are manipulating them if you use this technique more than once. I went to an appointment for an expired listing in an area of town that had been declining for about five years. Prices were dropping so much that people owed more on their houses than they could sell them for. I wasn't real thrilled to go to this listing appointment because if the sellers were upside down, I knew I could not help them. The house had been priced at $174,000, so I figured (based on the CMA) that it should sell for about $160,000. At the appointment I asked these questions:

> **Salesperson:**
> "So how do you feel about the price?"
>
> **Seller:**
> "I don't agree with it."

(Great, I thought, now let's see if he lowers it by $14,000.)

> **Seller:**
> "We want to raise the price to $185,000!"
>
> **Salesperson:**
> "What? It did not sell at $174,000. What makes you think it will sell at $185,000?"
>
> **Seller:**
> "It's worth it, and we will wait till we get our price."
>
> **Salesperson:**
> "And I don't blame you." (I begin to gather my laptop and things together.) "I have just one question for you. What is the market doing in this area? Is it going up? Or is it going down?"

Notice I did not judge the area, I just asked a simple question. I continued packing my things.

I wasn't pretending to walk away in an effort to get them to change their mind; I was honestly leaving. I could not help them at that price.

At about this time, the wife looked to her husband, and the conversation took place as follows:

> **Seller (wife):**
> "I won't be here in a year." (Notice she didn't invite her husband to go with her.)
>
> **Seller (husband):**
> "But honey, we can't give the house away."
>
> **Seller (wife):**
> "I won't be here in a year."
>
> **Seller (husband, now looking at me):**
> "What will it take to sell?"
>
> **Salesperson:**
> "After looking at the CMA, I believe . . ." (The wife interrupts me.)
>
> **Seller (wife):**
> "Put it on the market for $148,000!"
>
> **Seller (husband):**
> "But . . ." (The wife interrupted with just a look and it was over.)

I listed the house at $148,000, and it sold in 10 days. The take away close worked so well here because I was prepared to leave. Don't try to fake this one; you will be caught. I later found out that the couple's son was being beat up every day at school, and parents will do whatever is necessary to protect their children.

Appeal to the Higher Authority

When you are asked to do something that you don't want to do, you may be tempted to blame it on someone else. For example, a seller may ask us to cut our commission. The standard reply is, "My broker won't let me." Isn't it annoying when someone says, "I'm sorry, we cannot do that because it is against company policy"? That is an example of appealing to the higher authority. You will be thought of as the higher authority in a transaction. Never use the words, "I have to ask my broker." Or "It is against the law for me to do that." Both are reckless uses of "appeal to the higher authority." You may get a seller who responds, "Well then, I guess I should be talking to your broker." You will no longer have any credibility.

Chapter Summary

The ability to handle objections will give you confidence in a sales situation and that, in turn, should make you more money. The fear of objections is a huge problem in the real estate industry. It will freeze potentially successful real estate salespersons into inaction, and that will lead them out of the business. Study this chapter over and over so that these techniques come naturally to you as soon as you are faced with an objection.

Summary Questions

1. An objection is a question that should be answered.
   a. True
   b. False

2. In what type of close do you ask, "When do you want to take possession of this home?"
   a. If–then
   b. Questioning
   c. Trial
   d. Puppy Dog

3. What must an agent do to handle an objection?
   a. Give lots of reasons.
   b. Ask a lot of questions.

c. Ignore the all objections.
   d. Take a lot of notes.

4. A "benefit" to a seller always answers what question?
   a. Will I make more money?
   b. Will it sell faster?
   c. So what?
   d. Will it be more convenient?

5. While listening to your clients, what is the most important thing you should do?
   a. Smoke a cigarette.
   b. Think of how to close them.
   c. Watch their body language.
   d. Take notes on everything they say.

6. "If I could get the sellers to leave the refrigerator, would you buy this house?" What is the name of this closing technique?
   a. Good guy, bad guy
   b. Puppy dog
   c. If-then
   d. Ben Franklin

7. "I cannot reduce my commission without my broker's approval." What is the name of this closing technique?
   a. Good guy, bad guy
   b. Tie-down
   c. Ben Franklin
   d. Appeal to the higher authority

8. What is the closing technique called that removes what the buyer wants?
   a. Wants and needs
   b. Take away
   c. Tie-down
   d. Appeal to the higher authority

9. What is the closing technique called where one person is nice and the other is mean?
   a. Appeal to the higher authority
   b. Ben Franklin
   c. Good guy, bad guy
   d. Puppy dog

10. Which of the following is a good way to prepare for all anticipated objections?
    a. Get a good night's sleep.
    b. Develop an objection-handling worksheet.
    c. At the presentation, do not allow the clients to ask questions.
    d. Ignore them.

Chapter 12

Client
Follow-Up

Chapter Overview

This chapter will teach you how to learn about your clients and their needs. You will learn that the "close" is just the beginning, and you will learn to keep in touch with past clients and turn them into future prospects. It is important to understand that a current client is so much better than a future client because a future client needs to be sold on your skills. The current client understands that you are qualified and will help them. You need to make all clients into future clients.

Key Terms

Event:
A social gathering or activity.

Internet:
A wide area network that connects thousands of separate networks and provides global communication.

E-Newsletters:
An e-newsletter is an informational letter sent to prospects, clients, and all others who might be worth getting business from.

Closing Gift:
A closing gift is something given to clients after closing with the purpose of reminding the client of the salesperson long after the sale.

Introduction

You must develop tracking techniques for your business. The best way to do this is with computer and client management software.

Client management software gives you the ability to track clients and respond to them in a timely manner. If a contact should be called in a week, flag them to be called four days out. For contacts that don't need follow-up for a year, have them flagged to be called in six months. Whatever the time frame clients give you for following up, divide the time in half and call them then. For example, if a client tells you he plans to put his house on the market in six months, follow up with him in three months You do not want to make a follow-up call to client who listed with another salesperson just last week.

Tracking Techniques

Track your entire current buyer and seller leads in the manner discussed above. Track active listings, pending listings, and any buyers working on financing. Do not let this information slip through your fingers. You should be calling people back every day.

Software

Client management software (also called Customer Relationship Management [CRM] software) not only records your client base but also notifies you when they should be called, tracks when special dates (birthdays) occur, and monitors your expenses for tax purposes. There are several good software products on the market, which we will discuss in the following sections.

Microsoft Outlook

Microsoft Outlook is a client management software that nearly everyone has on their computer. Microsoft Outlook is often viewed as an email organizer (and it is), but it can also be used as a simple client management tool. You can enter a new client into the contact section and include all of the important information. You can even flag the contact when they need to be contacted again.

You can categorize a certain group of contacts and contact them as a group. For example, do you want to send a group email to all of your For Sale By Owners? You can categorize each of them as a FSBO and then pull up only that group. You can create the FSBO category very simply by adding it to the current categories.

Salesforce

Salesforce is a popular client management software that will give you a complete view of your customers, including activity history, key contacts, customer communications, and real estate discussions. You can get contact information for each client, even their picture, their social interests, and other distant but important communication information.

You can tap into social networks with this software and discover what customers are saying about your services. You can also find out what real estate issues are troubling them and become their hero by solving those issues!

Act!

Act! claims to be the number one, best-selling contact management software. It is very popular and has been around for some time. With Act!, you can quickly tap into all relationship details, seamlessly interact with productivity and social tools, and leverage integrated e-marketing services.

Act! interfaces easily with current products such as Office, Google, Dropbox, and social networking sites. Integrated e-marketing services enable you to easily capture and segment your prospects and then design, send, and track email campaigns.

As with all client management software, it is a great place to have all of your clients' contact information. Act! also has a to-do list.

Top Producer

This is the best of the best for real estate professionals, and because of that, it doesn't come cheap. Top Producer is designed for real estate professionals for tracking their clients. You can set up FSBO campaigns, expired campaigns, buyer campaigns—the list is endless. The software also helps you track sales all the way through closing and even sets up accounts for tax purposes.

Top Producer has follow-up systems for all clients as well as contact information at your fingertips. Top Producer is Internet based so all your information is constantly with you via your tablet or smartphone. Top Producer is supported by many local associations and offers training courses to teach the finer points of this remarkable software.

Internet

The Internet is a wide area network that connects thousands of separate networks and provides global communication. The Internet is an inexpensive way to follow up with clients. With little to no money and the touch of a button, you can send mass email messages to all of your past clients, updating them on area market data. This is why you want to get the email addresses from all of your leads. You can have a website that your past clients can always tap into if they want information about real estate or want to leave you a message. The Internet is also the fastest way to stay in touch. (Why do you think people call mail from the post office "snail mail"?) Be sure to get permission from your client before sending them email and follow the national anti-spam laws. Include a good subject line so your clients won't mistake your email for unwanted advertising or spam. Finally, check your email at least twice a day.

E-Newsletters

An e-newsletter is an information letter sent to prospects, clients, and all others who might be worth getting business from. Sending out an e-newsletter is an easy way to keep in touch with your past and present clients. With the click of a button, your message is sent to as many people as you like. And, like email, the cost of sending out an e-newsletter is almost nil. You can even work from an e-newsletter design template so you're not faced with coming up with a new design each time you want to send the newsletter. That way, all you have to come do is write what you want to communicate. Again, it is so important to obtain email addresses from all of your contacts.

When you host an open house, have your notebook open to your e-newsletter. As your guests sign in, offer to email your monthly newsletter to them. You can also customize it with local market information so your clients know they are getting something that they can't get anywhere else. It's a great follow-up tool to capture uncommitted buyers.

Closing Gifts

Offer a closing gift to clients so they will remember you long after the closing. The gift should not be too expensive, but not cheap either. Avoid gifts that can be used up, such as gift baskets filled with fruit, or tickets to the opera, or anything else that will be forgotten when used. Also, don't give the gift of flowers or a plant or anything else that will die. When the gift dies, your contact information will die with it. Instead, gifts should be long lasting. For example:

- A brass door knocker with the owner's name and your name as "Presented by Dan Hamilton with Acme Real Estate." This will last for as long as the owners are in the home. Every time they enter the home through the front door, they will see your name. When it comes time to sell, they will remember you. Just a thought: You might even offer to put it up for them; otherwise, they may never get around to mounting it.

- A six-inch binder with sleeves to hold all of their important house documents. You can put this together easily for a few bucks. The sleeves should include things like:

    - Closing papers

    - Survey

- Appraisal
- Deed
- Tax records
- Purchase agreement
- Insurance papers
- HOA documents
- Information on you

- The exterior can be as fancy or as simple as you wish. Each involves cost. Some companies provide these already made up for you for a price. The owners will keep this book for as long as they own the house. They will refer to it when they need any of this information, and they will know how to contact you if their plans change.

- Offer to take digital photographs of the contents of their house for insurance purposes once the owners get settled. Put the photos on two compact disks (CD)—one for the owners and one for yourself (with their permission of course) in case theirs is destroyed. The CD case and disk face should include your contact information for future use by them. This is a thoughtful gift, and it is very inexpensive.

Whatever you do, do something. Don't let these buyers become real estate waifs.

Events

One way to thank your past clients is to have a year-end party or event. An event is any social gathering or activity. This is also a great time to see old faces and remind them you are still in the real estate business. You should invite ALL of your past clients because time heals all wounds. If the transaction went great, then they love you. If the transaction went bad, then they have forgiven you. The party can be expensive; however, it is well worth the money. Here are some suggestions:

- Have the party at a movie theater on a Saturday morning. It is relatively inexpensive and fun.

- Host a chili cook-off. This is inexpensive for you, considering the cooks bring the food. It also allows you a lot of time for building rapport.

- Offer some take-aways to remind them of you after the party.

- Provide snacks.

This is for fun; do not make it an advertisement. These people already know you; all you want is for them to remember you.

Chapter Summary

Whatever method you choose for following up with your past clients does not matter as much as the actual contact. Do not let your past clients become waifs, or abandoned clients, that some other real estate salesperson can take over. It is always better to retain clients than to scramble for new ones.

Summary Questions

1. What is probably the best and least expensive way to follow up with past clients?
   a. Let them call you when they are ready.
   b. Use the Internet.
   c. Send out direct mail weekly to your contacts.
   d. Make use of area billboards.

2. How often should you check your email?
   a. Weekly
   b. Hourly
   c. Daily
   d. Twice a day

3. Which of following is the best closing gift?
   a. A plant or tree
   b. Theatre tickets
   c. One-month membership to a health club
   d. A monogrammed door knocker

4. What skill must you employ when learning to read a potential buyer?
   a. Listening
   b. Speaking
   c. Writing
   d. Organizing

5. What is the best way to track your clients?
   a. Sending out note cards
   b. Using client management software on the computer
   c. Giving them good contact numbers and relying on them to contact you
   d. Closing all your transactions so no tracking is necessary

6. What should client management software do?
   a. Track your clients
   b. Track special dates
   c. Monitor expenses
   d. All of the above

7. What is an informational letter sent through the Internet called?
   a. Letter of recommendation
   b. Mortgage information letter
   c. E-newsletter
   d. Community newsletter

8. What are the two main rules on closing gifts?
   a. Buy gifts that are cute and cuddly.
   b. Buy gifts that don't rust or get ruined.
   c. Buy gifts that are reasonable and recognizable.
   d. Buy gifts that don't die or are consumed.

9. Which of the following is not recommended as an event?
   a. A beer bash
   b. A party at a movie theater
   c. A chili cook-off
   d. A Christmas party

10. Which of the following is NOT a benefit of holding a chili cook-off as an event?
    a. It is relatively inexpensive for you.
    b. It is a great time to get drunk with your clients.
    c. There is a lot of time for building rapport.
    d. The cooks bring the food.

Chapter 13

Contract
Writing

Chapter Overview

In this chapter you will study the elements that make up a valid contract. You will learn the most effective ways to write a contract on real estate and understand the laws involved in contract writing. A real estate contract is the fundamental document that is involved in a real estate transaction. The ability to "fill-in" that contract is critical to the success of any real estate professional. The best professionals are those who can write contracts.

Key Terms

Addendum:
Something added, especially a supplement to a contract.

Competent:
Legally qualified to perform an act.

Consideration:
Something in exchange for something.

Contract:
An agreement between two or more parties, especially one that is written and enforceable by law.

Mutual Assent:
Mutual assent is an agreement of the minds and occurs when all parties agree to all terms in the contract.

Introduction

The law of contracts is one of the most complex areas of common law. We will not get to that level of complexity in this chapter.

It is expected you have been or will be introduced to contract law in other courses. We will discuss writing contracts in a manner that will enhance your professional image.

Real estate contracts normally include listing agreements, earnest money contracts, leases, deeds, mortgages, liens, and partnership agreements. In this chapter, we will focus our discussion on the creation and construction of contracts.

Purchase Agreements

It is important that you have an understanding of some of the fundamental elements of contracts before discussing the specific requirements of real estate contracts. A contract can most simply be defined as an agreement between one or more parties with the following four requirements: competent parties, legal subject matter, consideration for the promises contained in the contract, and mutual assent.

Competent parties are those individuals who have the mental capacity to understand the agreement in which they are involved. Competent parties are legally qualified to perform an act and must be of legal age, which in most states is 18 years of age. If a party is not competent, the contract could be held as voidable by the incompetent party or by that party's guardian.

The contract must be legal. Any contract for an illegal purpose is considered void, as if the contract had never happened. I once knew a real estate salesperson who listed a house with the "seller." The next day a different man called her and asked about the sign she had put in "his" yard. After some investigating, it was discovered that the renter was trying to sell the property without the knowledge or consent of the actual owner. That contract would be held void because the legal owner of the property was not a party to the contract.

Consideration is something in exchange for something. There are two types of consideration: valuable and good. Valuable consideration is something of value. Generally this is hard currency (cash).

It can be an interest in a car, boat, or other things of value. Good consideration, on the other hand, is for "love and affection." Good consideration is when a father gives his daughter a house for her wedding present. Even though no valuable consideration changed hands, the courts would still consider it a valid contract because of the good consideration (a father's love) that was exchanged.

- Mutual assent is an agreement of the minds and occurs when all parties to a contract agree to all the terms in that contract. A purchase agreement (a contract) is the written form of mutual assent.

Contract Writing Hints

The following are a few hints on writing contracts:

1. Keep the contract neat. For best results, use a word processing program on your computer or tablet. I have seen contracts so sloppy that it jeopardized the validity of the contract and the professionalism of the real estate salesperson who wrote it. If you have to edit a contract by hand, be sure to get signatures on the revisions. You can print out a copy for your clients to have or you can email a copy to them. Always keep all versions of the contract on file.

2. Do not leave blanks in a contract even if you think something is unimportant. Completing the entire contract makes you look so much more professional. Use "N/A" (Not Applicable) as needed.

3. Use blue ink on originals to differentiate from copies.

4. Use full names when filling out a contract. This makes the contract clearer and helps the people at the title company with their research. Do not use Latin (such as: et ux, et vir, et al, femme sole, baron sole, and the like) in the contract for descriptions of persons or things.

5. Always double-check all the numbers and figures.

6. Always double-check that all the dates match and that you are not closing on unattainable dates (weekends, holidays).

7. Be sure to collect all personal checks necessary (earnest money, option).

8. Be sure your clients initial all pages and changes and sign the back.

9. Be sure your clients receive copies of everything they sign and provide them with the original as soon as possible.

10. Be sure all addendums necessary to the contract are with the contract.

11. Always double-check the legal description to be sure you wrote it correctly.

12. Explain the contract to your clients, but do not fabricate anything. I have heard real estate salespeople create answers to their clients' questions because they think they should know the correct answers. If you don't have an answer, say so, and then find the correct answer.

Do not assume the way something has always been done is the right way. Verify all of your information through some other reliable source. Ask yourself:

"Is this correct? How do I know?"

13. Do not make any promises regarding a contract. Let your clients know that the contract doesn't do anything but put in writing the desires of the parties to sell real property.

14. Do not get creative in writing contracts. "Creative" in this context means "practicing law." Only licensed attorneys may practice law.

15. Do not use the term "as-is." Instead use the term "no repairs."

16. Never use the word "sue"; you are not a judge.

17. If the contract has a "$" symbol before the blank, use a dollar amount. Do not get creative by using a percentage even if you are trying to avoid changes on counteroffers.

18. Do not accept poorly written contracts from other real estate salespeople. Doing so may put you at risk also. Instead, rewrite the incorrect portions with the approval of your client.

Addendums

An addendum is a document that is "added to" a contract. Addendums typically add information that is needed to clarify the contact itself. For example, an addendum is usually needed for financing because the paragraphs in the standard form need more information to be clear. Addendums are also known as riders or attachments.

Chapter Summary

As a real estate person, you do not have the authority to write contracts from scratch. You may only complete or fill in an approved contract by your state real estate commission through the direction of the parties involved. In this chapter you learned some effective ways to write contracts to be completely legal. Contract writing will be an essential function you will need to perform.

Summary Question

1. Which of the following is not an essential element of contract writing?
    a. Writing neatly
    b. Completing all blanks
    c. Including the clients' full names
    d. Including the clients' weight

2. Which of the following areas of common law is one of the most complex according to this book?
   a. Agency law
   b. Contract law
   c. Anti-trust law
   d. Fair Housing law

3. Which of the following is a contract?
   a. Mortgage
   b. Listing agreement
   c. Lease
   d. All of the above

4. Which of the following is not a requirement of a valid contract?
   a. Competent parties
   b. Earnest money
   c. Legal subject matter
   d. Mutual assent

5. What is the term for individuals who have the mental capacity to understand an agreement?
   a. Legal age
   b. Competent parties
   c. Mentally able
   d. Sound mind

6. What does a contract with a minor become?
   a. Void
   b. Voidable
   c. Enforceable
   d. Valid

7. What is something of value in a contract?
   a. Valuable consideration
   b. Good consideration
   c. Gratuitous consideration
   d. Adequate consideration

8. What is cash considered?
   a. King
   b. Non-refundable
   c. Valuable consideration
   d. None of the above

9. Which of the following is not a good idea when writing contracts?
   a. Keeping the contract neat
   b. Leaving blanks
   c. Using full names
   d. Giving originals to the principals

10. Which of the following is not a good idea when writing contracts?
    a. Double-checking the numbers
    b. Ensuring that all the personal checks are collected
    c. Ensuring that addendums are added after acceptance of the contract
    d. Double-checking the legal description

Chapter 14

Negotiating
and Closing

Chapter Overview

The objective of this chapter is to provide you with information about mortgage and title companies. You will learn to differentiate between mortgage brokers and mortgage bankers, and we will take you through the closing process.

This chapter will provide you with a basic knowledge of negotiation as well. You will learn certain words and how your clients perceive them. Finally, you will learn negotiating strategies, how to use them, and how they are used on you.

Key Terms

Mortgage Company:
A mortgage company provides the funds to allow a buyer to purchase a property.

Closing:
The action of the buyer and seller signing the closing papers.

Loan Processor:
The loan processor works from the borrower's loan application to obtain verifications of employment, bank balances, charge accounts, and note balances.

Nonverbal Communication:
Nonverbal communication consists of the communication two or more persons send and receive without the use of words.

Mortgage Banker:
A mortgage banker is a lender who actually funds the loan at the time of closing.

Mortgage Broker:
>A mortgage broker is a company that originates and processes loans and delivers them to another lender for funding.

Negotiating Introduction

Negotiating is an art. While it is defined as conferring with another in order to reach an agreement, it is still an art. The best artists are paid the best money. Negotiating does not mean one side wins and the other side loses. Rather, it means coming together to a reasonable conclusion. The best negotiating is accomplished when all sides feel they have achieved their goals.

Communication

An important part of negotiation is communication. If during a negotiation the other party does not understand your meaning, you may end up with the wrong solution or no solution at all.

Nonverbal Communication

According to psychologist Albert Mehrabian, 93 percent of all communication is nonverbal. Nonverbal communication consists of the communication two or more persons send and receive without the use of words. It is the way you hold your face; it is the way you hold your hands; it is the way you sit. All are examples of nonverbal communication. Paying close attention to the nonverbal communication of your clients provides insight to their wants and needs. If they tap their feet and stare into the distance, you are probably losing their attention. However, be careful of overanalyzing a person. Not everyone who scratches his or her nose is lying; maybe he or she just had an itch. You need to be able to recognize and understand nonverbal cues.

Verbal Communication

The basis of communication is the verbal interaction between people. For real estate salespeople, communication is the key to the business. If you cannot communicate effectively with clients, you either need to learn how to or you need to find another career. Some clients have a hard time articulating their wants and needs. Our job is to communicate with them by asking a series of questions to clarify their desires.

Listening

Many people assume that to be good in real estate sales you need to talk constantly. This couldn't be further from the truth. In fact, the most successful real estate salespeople are those who are active listeners. The best skill employed in learning "to read" a potential client is listening. By listening, you not only become more likable, you are also better able to hear the wants, needs, and objections of your potential clients. The problem is too many times we focus in on what we want to say without hearing what the potential client really wants. To persuade, influence, and motivate others to buy and sell real estate through us (and, hence, earn more money) is to become an active listener.

The Five Rules of Active Listening
1. **Limit your own talking.**
   The more you listen, the more opportunity you'll have to find out what the customer really wants. Spend half as much time talking and twice the time listening.

   Practice this when you are in a group. Don't talk; just listen. You will find that everyone likes you better, and you will find out a lot more information.

   Too many times we are so concerned about what we want to say that we don't hear the other person. Because we don't give total attention to our clients, we end up "selling" them on what we think is important and not what they really want. This frustrates the potential client, and in many cases, we lose the sale. You may hear the phrase, "We want to think about it." This simply tells you that you were not listening to your client.

2. **Don't interrupt.**
By interrupting the client, sensitivity, rapport, and commitment are all destroyed. If you continually interrupt your clients, you will eventually shut them down, and they will stop providing important information. Although at times it seems expedient to interrupt, this perceived lack of respect for your client causes the relationship to deteriorate and makes it harder to close the sale.

3. **Notice nonverbal communication.**
If you're talking to prospects and they start doing things such as crossing their arms, crossing their legs away from you, yawning, leaning back, looking bored, or avoiding eye contact, you need to "listen" to their body language as well as their words. If their body language is telling you to change your delivery—change it. Remember, this is for them, not you.

4. **Use an appropriate setting.**
To get others to listen to us and focus on the substance of our message, distractions must be minimized. Is your office too hot or cold? Is the telephone ringing all the time? Are you doing two things at once? Are there other people around? Do you have distracting habits like pen-tapping? Are you making direct eye contact or are your eyes wandering? Ask yourself: Do you like it when a "customer service representative" is talking to someone on the telephone when they are supposedly helping you? To make sure active listening takes place, you must alleviate all distractions and pay total attention to your client.

5. **Use lots of questions.**
Instead of talking, spend more time asking questions. The answers you get from these questions can help make clear what the client is thinking. It is also important to repeat what the client has told you so you can be sure he or she understands

and you are proceeding in the right direction. The amount of information you can gather by just asking questions is amazing. The only trick is to refrain from being sucked into the conversation and talking about yourself. Stay focused on the client, and you will do well.

To close more sales, we must determine the wants and needs of our clients first, and then work backward to determine the best services for them. The best way to do that is to listen intently.

Words Mean Things

Before negotiating, we need to be aware that some words have negative connotations, and we need to adjust our wording accordingly. We have all heard of buyer's remorse, which occurs when a buyer puts in an offer on a property and then backs out because he or she is apprehensive or regrets the decision. I believe some of that fear and doubt comes from the real estate salesperson. Be careful when using the following words:

Dangerous Words	Better Words
Contract	Paperwork, Agreement
Sign	Authorize, O.K.
Down payment	Initial payment
Monthly payment	Monthly investment
Sales price	Total investment
Terminates	Ends
Commission	Fee for service
"As-is"	"No repairs"
Et ux	And wife
Home if buyer	House if seller

Negotiating Strategies

You will use negotiation throughout your real estate career. Here we will primarily concentrate on the presentation of an offer because this is the most concentrated time for negotiating. I have seen transaction after transaction fail because the real estate salesperson did not negotiate properly.

The first thing you need to do before presenting an offer is prepare. Do not take this lightly. Preparation is necessary whether you're preparing for a listing presentation or an offer-to-purchase presentation. Doing so will give that extra ingredient for a successful presentation. Here are some basic steps to follow:

Step 1: Do not discuss any aspect of the offer over the telephone. You are representing your seller's best interest, and you cannot do a fair job explaining the offer unless you are face to face with the seller. This allows you to see the seller's face and gauge it for approval or disapproval. I know there will always be circumstances where you must present an offer over the telephone (the seller lives out of state), but do your best to avoid it.

If the offer is exactly what the seller wants, you may scan the contract into your computer and email it to the seller. Some types of software offer a secure document-signing feature and should be used. Just remember though: You do lose the ability to read the seller's face when you present a contract in this manner.

Most real estate regulatory bodies require you to present all offers to the seller. I will take it further. You should present all offers, regardless of the circumstances. How you present unreasonable offers, however, is up to you. If the seller's property is worth $180,000 and someone offers $60,000, there is nothing wrong with presenting that offer over the telephone. For example, "Mr. or Mrs. Seller, you have received an offer for $60,000, and I think you should reject it. What do you want to do?"

Step 2: Review the facts about the listing, including number of showings, days on the market, and feedback.

Step 3: Update the comparable sales in the area for any changes that may have occurred.

Step 4: Make up a new seller's net sheet.

Seller's Net Sheet

A seller's net sheet is a document that allows the seller to examine all the possible costs associated with selling a property. Most of the time sellers are more interested in what they walk away with from the sale than what the property actually sells for.

To effectively prepare an estimate, you will need the following information from the seller:

- Principal balance of the loan

- Monthly payment amount

- Yearly taxes

- Yearly hazard insurance premium

- The type of financing on the loan

- Closing costs they will pay on the buyer's behalf

- Any secondary liens on the property (swimming pool)

The following sources are available for this information:

- Seller's verbal estimate or answer

- Seller's monthly statement from the mortgage company

- Returned Mortgage Information Letter (MIL) from the mortgage company

- Tax records (MLS) or the actual taxing authorities (tax info only)

Preparing an estimate before going on the listing presentation is easy if you get the information before you meet with the sellers. They will rely on your expertise to estimate what the house will sell for, what type of financing will be used, and how fast the house will sell. As more information becomes available to you, you will need to adjust your estimate accordingly. For example, let's say the seller told you he owed about $85,000 on his house. You receive the Mortgage Information Letter from the lender, and it shows that the seller owes $88,000. When you receive a physical offer, you will need to prepare another estimate based on the terms of the offer. If anything changes between the time the contract is executed and the closing date, you will need to adjust the numbers again. Remember, the seller is holding you accountable.

If you have a tablet, there are numerous apps that will run a seller's net sheet for you instantly. Plug in the correct information, and you will get the correct seller's net. For record keeping, it would best to have a printout because a seller's memory (and yours for that matter) can change over time. The advantage of using a net sheet app on your tablet or phone is that if the seller wants to change anything, you can do it instantly.

Figuring a Seller's Net Sheet
Use the following data to construct a seller's net sheet.

The sale price of a property is $100,000. The owner's title insurance policy is $992, which is given on a title insurance rate card. (Generally, these rates are set by the state for all title insurance companies.) The escrow fee for the seller is $250. Recording fees are $50. The deed preparation fee is $75. The home warranty is $495. The real estate commission totals 7 percent of the sales price. There is a first mortgage payoff of $70,000. There is no second mortgage payoff. There will be a miscellaneous fee of $200 to cover any possible overages, but there should not be any additional expenses. (Note: These fees will be explained in later chapters.) Notice that all the fees are added together to get the seller's total cost of sale, which is then subtracted from the sales price to find the seller's net amount.

Description	Cost	Receives Fee
Sale price	$100,000	Seller
First mortgage payoff	$70,000	Previous lender
Second mortgage payoff	$0	Previous lender
Owner's Policy of Title Insurance	$992	Title company
Prepayment penalty	$0	Previous lender
Escrow fee	$250	Title company
Title attorney fee	$0	Title attorney
Lender attorney fee	$0	Lender attorney
Filing/recording fees	$50	County
Restrictions	N/A	Lender
Deed preparation	$75	Title company
Loan discount points paid by seller	$0	Lender
Underwriting fee	$0	Lender
Home warranty	$495	Warranty company
Photos/amortization schedules	N/A	Lender
Tax certificate	N/A	Title company
Tax service fee	N/A	Title company
Wood Insect Inspection (POC)	N/A	Inspector
Buyer costs paid by seller	$0	
Real Estate Commission	$7,000	Real estate broker
Courier/overnight delivery	N/A	Title and/or lender
Miscellaneous fees and expenses	$200	
Other expenses	$0	
Seller's settlement costs	$79,062	
Prorated interest (0–30 days)	N/A	Previous lender
Prorated taxes	$900	Tax authority
Other prorations	$0	
Prorations for seller	$900	Seller
Total cost to seller	$79,962	Seller
Estimated net to seller	$20,038	Seller

So let's get back to the steps in our negotiation process.

Step 5: What are the benefits of this offer?
    a. Closing date
    b. Possession date

c. Terms
   d. Qualified buyer

Step 6: What are the possible objections?
   a. Price
   b. Closing costs

Presenting offers is a very challenging aspect of our business, but following the procedures discussed below will increase your chances of being successful:

1. Humanize the buyer. Some sellers have lived in their home for years and have raised their families there. They want to feel confident that the buyers will take care of their "home." Your job here is to talk favorably about the buyers.

2. Present the terms and conditions of the agreement.
   a. Agree on minor items before moving on to major ones.
   b. Show the features of the contract, but sell the benefits.
   c. Continuously interject the seller's motivation for selling.

3. Present the net sheet and answer any questions the sellers have about it.

4. Overcome the objections by asking lots of questions.

5. Ask for the seller's approval.
   a. Acceptance
   b. Rejection

Notice the seller's only options are acceptance or rejection. Many real estate salespeople will tell the seller they can "accept, reject, or counter." If you give your seller this third option, this is all they will hear. Don't suggest it, at least at first. Just as a side note, a counteroffer is actually a rejection of the first offer and a putting forth of a new seller-originated offer. So in essence, a counter is a rejection.

If a buyer's offer is not in the best interest of the seller, you shouldn't pressure them to accept it. Negotiating a counteroffer, by following the steps below, may be necessary to save the sale.

Step 1: If the seller doesn't take the buyer's offer, start by reducing the net difference. Subtract all possible expenses the seller might incur if he or she waits for another offer. Always counter the sales price, not the terms of the contract. The reason for this is because if the buyer needs the seller to pay for a portion of the closing costs and the seller refuses, the buyer probably cannot buy the house. However, if the seller asks for more on the sales price, the buyer could do that, as long as the house will appraise for the additional price.

Step 2: Confirm that the seller's objection is the only thing standing in the way of the sale. This is known as isolating the objection. If you do not do this, the seller will keep coming up with new objections.

Step 3: Negotiate a counteroffer from the seller. What does the seller believe is a good offer?

Additional Negotiating Strategies

In the real estate business, negotiations between the actual buyers and sellers are rare because the communication is usually between the real estate salespeople. So let's take a look at it from that angle. The way you conduct yourself in a negotiation with another real estate salesperson can dramatically affect the outcome. Be sure that while negotiating, you clearly know who you represent and never violate his or her negotiating position. Here are a few suggestions for better negotiating:

> **Get the other side to commit first.**

Talented negotiators know that, for obvious reasons, they're usually better off if they can get the other side to commit to a position first:

- The first offer may be much better than you expected. With real estate negotiation the seller has made the offer first by committing to a list price. From then on, the negotiations move forward with the buyer (through his or her salesperson) making the next offer. If you are the listing agent, do not let a buyer's agent get you to budge from the list price without a formal written offer. Some buyers' agents might say, "My buyers feel the list price is too much. Will the sellers take less?" If you reveal to the buyer's agent the seller's lowest price, you are in violation of your agency duties to your seller. Similarly, if a listing agent wants to know your buyer's lowest price, you (representing the buyer) cannot disclose the information.

- It enables you to bracket the proposal. If the listing agent states a price first, you can bracket the proposal. You have your list price (highest price) and you have the offer (lowest price).

Be calm, not a know-it-all.

When you are negotiating, you're better off acting as if you know less, not more, than everyone else does.

The well-trained negotiator who understands the importance of acting calm retains these options:

- Requesting time to discuss the offer with his or her clients so that they can thoroughly think through the dangers of accepting or the opportunities that making additional demands might bring.

- Deferring a decision while he or she checks with the broker or manager.

- Asking for time to let legal experts review the proposal.

- Pleading for additional concessions.

- Taking time to think by reviewing notes about the negotiation.

> **Concentrate on the issues.**

Professional real estate salespeople know they should always concentrate on the issues and not be distracted by the actions of the other salespeople.

I have witnessed real estate salespersons get so frustrated with the other salesperson that they lose their cool and hurt their client's negotiating position.

Former Secretary of State Warren Christopher once said, "It's okay to get upset when you're negotiating, as long as you're in control, and you're doing it as a specific negotiating tactic." It's when you're upset and out of control that you always lose. To demonstrate how emotional negotiating can become, let's take a look at a situation in which I was involved. I had a listing with a seller who refused to accept a price less than $275,000. I agreed to take the listing, and we put the property on the market. A few weeks later, we got an offer of $262,000.

The seller countered at $275,000; however, because the buyer needed closing costs to be paid, the seller's net was only $258,000. The buyer refused the offer. A couple more weeks went by, and I received an offer for $273,000, which netted the seller $267,000, more than the seller would have received from his first counter. I figured this was a slam-dunk, so I called him into my office. Once in the conference room, I handed him the contract and said, "Congratulations." He looked down at the contract and saw the price of $273,000. He ripped the contract in half and actually threw it in my face, shouting, "I told you I would not accept a dime less than full price!" He left and took with him any chance of me making a commission on that listing.

So what did I do wrong? I did not prepare for the appointment. I expected him to accept the offer and when he didn't, I reacted. This mistake cost me several thousand dollars—not smart! Be prepared.

> **Always send a thank you to the other real estate salesperson.**

When you're through negotiating, you should always congratulate the other side. The best way to do this is to send the other salesperson a simple thank you card in the mail. This not only fosters goodwill, but it leaves no hard feelings if you happen to cross paths again.

The Closing

The closing is an action as well as a process. The action is when the buyer and seller sign the closing papers.

The closing process begins at the signing of the purchase agreement and goes through closing action. We will cover the basic process.

Mortgage Companies

Mortgage companies generally provide the funds that allow a buyer to purchase a property. The mortgage company takes a look at the buyer and determines his or her credit worthiness. The mortgage company can provide the buyer with prequalification or preapproval. A prequalification is the least of the two. With a prequalification the lender asks the borrower some financial questions and usually runs a preliminary credit check. If the numbers work out, the lender will give the dollar amount that a buyer qualifies for purchasing a property. The prequalification is not a guarantee of a loan. Several variables could prevent a buyer from getting a loan. A preapproval, on the other hand, is the lender's word that this buyer will be able to buy if the house they find meets the lender's approval. With a preapproval, the lender has run a full credit check, verified all work records, and checked previous residences for discrepancies. If a buyer has been preapproved, he or she has leverage with a seller because to the seller this is nearly the same as cash.

Almost all real estate transactions require funds from third-party lenders. The term *third-party* is used here because the seller is thought of as the party of the first part and the buyer as the party of the second part; therefore, the lender is the third party to the transaction.

A mortgage company employs loan officers to contact real estate agents and/or builders to present them with the benefits of doing business with their company. The loan officer takes a buyer through the loan process. They put all the paperwork together and handle all potential problems of the loan. These are the mortgage people with whom you will generally deal.

Ultimately, the borrower will make the decision regarding the lender he or she will use, but you can have considerable influence in the selection. When selecting a lender, the buyer should take into account not only the interest rate and loan charges, but it is also important for the borrower to "like" the mortgage officer.

A loan processor works from the borrower's loan application papers to obtain verifications of employment, bank balances, charge accounts, and note balances. The loan application is completed and signed at the initial meeting between the borrowers and the loan officer. All disclosures statements are signed at this time too.

Loan processing involves verification of employment, residence, and assets of the buyers. A full credit report will be obtained and an appraisal of the home will be made. All of the information necessary to meet the investor guidelines will be assembled and prepared for the underwriter's review.

Underwriters are employed by mortgage companies to make the final decision on each loan application the company is considering. The underwriter checks the work of the loan processor and the appraiser. The loan package is put together in a file and presented to the underwriter for review. The underwriter's job is to determine whether or not the loan package meets all investor guidelines. After the review process, the approval is issued.

Upon loan approval, closing documents are prepared for closing. The buyers *must* bring a *certified* check to the closing. The check must be made payable to the title company in the amount due or have the money wired to the title company directly from their bank account. Do not forget to tell the buyers they must have certified funds. The title officer cannot close if with a personal check unless the check is for less than $1,500. During closing, the principals sign all of the closing documents (and there are a lot of them), and then the title officer disburses all funds. This is when you get paid!

Mortgage Bankers

A mortgage banker is a lender who actually funds the loan at the time of closing. These companies are set up with underwriting, closing, funding, packaging, and selling of loans to the secondary market.

Mortgage Brokers

A mortgage broker is a company that originates and processes loans and delivers them to another lender for funding. There are many levels of service that mortgage brokers render to the consumer. Most brokerages are small operations that depend on the wholesale lender to help with processing, underwriting, and closing. Other mortgage brokers have good operations with adequate staff to give good service.

Title Companies

After the contract has been signed and the method of finance chosen, the title insurance company is retained to make sure that all the details come together and that the buyers receive insured title to their property.

The title company, working only from the contract and the lender's instructions, completes the entire transaction. Title insurers search and examine the title and inform the parties involved of title problems that may arise, such as liens or mortgages that were not properly satisfied. They also coordinate preparation of documents for the closing and secure a closing package from the mortgage company when a lender is involved. The services of a notary are included in the closing procedure, as well as recording the documents in the public records office and making sure all the expenses of the closing are paid.

A title company handles the funds for the closing or consummation of real estate transactions. A fee is charged for handling the funds and for the title insurance policy. The amount of premium paid is set by the State Board of Insurance and is dependent upon the price of the home. The title insurance policy protects the buyer from financial loss as a result of a title defect that existed when the property was purchased.

Closing Process

Once a loan has been approved, the mortgage company prepares a sheet of instructions for delivery to the title company, more specifically the title officer handling closing procedures. The closing instructions direct the title officer in how to handle the closing, what documents must be signed, and the correct legal name to be used. The instructions will include any special documents the mortgage company will need to finalize the loan and fund the transaction. Also, a truth-in-lending statement is prepared for the purchaser-borrower's signature at closing. The instruments and procedures may vary between title companies according to how their staff attorneys interpret state laws.

In most states, the closing is actually held at the title company. However, this is not a requirement. I have closed transactions at my real estate office, at the lender's office, and at the seller's house. If one of the parties is at a remote location, the documents will need to be sent by overnight courier and the closing could actually happen in different states.

At the actual closing, the buyer and seller execute all of the required documents, and the funds are distributed. The title company must pay all real estate fees to the correct persons. Here is a hint: If you want to be paid at closing, have your broker execute a "Commission Disbursement Authorization" form to the title company. This form gives permission to the title company to pay you at the closing table so you do not have to wait on your commission check. This is called table funding.

Chapter Summary

The type of information discussed in this chapter is covered throughout this book. Negotiating is a form of the objection-handling technique. It is used when dealing with clients. After reviewing all the material in this book, you will see that negotiating is a thread that flows throughout. Remember to listen to verbal and nonverbal (body language) communication and to always keep your cool.

Generally, real estate salespeople enjoy the closing action (usually when we are paid) but do not concentrate as much on the closing process. You should track the closing process with the mortgage company and the title company to be sure everything is flowing properly.

Summary Questions

1. At the time of origination, a mortgage creates a lien on the mortgaged property in states that subscribe to which of the following theories?
   a. Lien theory
   b. Title theory
   c. Intermediate theory
   d. Both A and B

2. What do buyers need to bring to the closing?
   a. Driver's license
   b. Verification of homeowner's insurance
   c. Certified funds for closing costs
   d. All of the above

3. What is a better word than "contract"?
   a. Agreement
   b. Form
   c. Binding document
   d. Legal document

4. Which of the following offers should be presented?
   a. An offer that you know won't fly because the buyer is in bankruptcy
   b. An offer for less than half of the sales price
   c. An offer presented orally
   d. Any offer received

5. The listing agent has an offer to present to the sellers; how should they respond?
   a. Accept the offer.
   b. Reject the offer.
   c. Counter the offer.
   d. Any of the above.

6. Which of the following is a lender who actually funds the loan?
   a. Lender
   b. FDIC
   c. Mortgage bankers
   d. Mortgage brokers

7. Which of the following originates and processes loans and delivers them to another lender for funding?
   a. HUD
   b. FDIC
   c. Mortgage bankers
   d. Mortgage brokers

8. What does loan processing involve?
   a. Verification of employment
   b. Verification of residence
   c. Determining the assets of the buyer
   d. All of the above

9. Who makes the final decision on each loan application a lender would consider?
   a. Loan processor
   b. Underwriter
   c. Loan officer
   d. President

10. Which of the following is important when choosing a lender?
    a. Interest rate charged
    b. The amount of loan fees
    c. The mortgage officer
    d. All of the above

Chapter 15

After Acceptance

Chapter Overview

In this chapter we will discuss what happens once an offer on a property is accepted—from the perspectives of both the seller's and the buyer's representatives.

Key Terms

Appraisal:
An appraisal is one person's opinion of value.

House Inspection:
A house inspection is a complete inspection of the house by a professional inspector.

Pest Inspection:
The purpose of a pest inspection is to look for problems related to insect infestation.

Radon:
Radon is a colorless, radioactive, inert gaseous element formed by the radioactive decay of radium.

Survey:
A survey is a graphic look at the property boundaries.

Introduction

Just because we have a buyer and a seller who agree on a sale doesn't mean our job as professional real estate salespeople is over. We must now take care of all the details to ensure that a successful closing takes place. Do not forget to follow up with your clients because this is a critical time for them and you.

Listing/Buyer Status Changes

As soon as possible, the listing salesperson should change the status of the listing in the Multiple Listing Service to pending (or whatever is applicable). The listing person then turns a copy of the contract and the earnest money check over to the title company and receipts the earnest money. The listing person takes a file to the appropriate person within the company for processing.

The buyer's salesperson should get a copy of the contract (may require an original) to the mortgage company, to their own company, and to the title company.

Both principals need to have an original contract in their hands.

Appraisal

An appraisal is one person's opinion of value. An appraisal is generally required when a property is sold, especially if a loan will be originated. Ordering an appraisal is not typically handled directly by the real estate salesperson; however, the salesperson needs to make sure it is ordered.

Inspections

Inspections of the house should be mandatory as they protect all parties involved in the transaction. There are many types of inspections. The inspections you use depend on the house and the buyer. Without exception, however, a general house inspection and a pest inspection should be performed.

House Inspection

A house inspection is a complete inspection of the house by a professional inspector. The inspector will look for signs of problems. For starters, the inspector should check all appliances, the electrical system, the plumbing system, the roof, the structure, the drainage, and the overall appearance of the house. The inspector is not responsible for commenting on subjective things like carpet color or outdated fixtures. These things are based on personal preferences. The inspector will not generally make direct statements like, "The house has foundation problems." It is more likely he or she will say, "There are signs of cracking, and I recommend a structural engineer report."

Some inspectors believe they should find something wrong with the house. I heard one inspector say that the toilet seat in the main bathroom was loose. It took longer to write that in the report than it did to tighten the wing nut under the seat. Here is a theory: Let the inspector find some issues, and he will be happy. In other words the seller does not need to fix every single problem before an inspector checks the property. Don't worry about fixing a cracked window. That is easy for an inspector to find; he will feel like he's done his job. And it is not an issue for a buyer when looking at the property; they probably would not even see it.

The house inspection benefits the buyer, seller, and agents. The house inspection aids in the disclosure of property defects. The number one lawsuit for real estate transactions is undisclosed property defects. The buyer should choose a licensed inspector.

You should not be the one to recommend an inspector, although you can provide a list of licensed inspectors from which the buyer could choose. The buyer should also be at the inspection. You may choose to attend as well. I believe that new real estate salespeople should be there to experience the inspection. If you do go to an inspection, do not comment on anything; you could become liable.

Buyers may want to save the expense of inspecting a property. Every reasonable effort should be made to convince the buyer to have the inspection. If the buyer refuses, a broker might consider asking the buyer to sign a waiver acknowledging that, against the broker's urging, the buyer chose not to have the inspection. The waiver also states that the broker is not a licensed inspector and has not made an inspection of the property.

Some purchase agreements give the buyer the right to have inspections, and the option paragraph allows for negotiation between the buyer and the seller on repairs. You should be aware that there are set timeframes in most real estate contracts for the buyer to get the inspections completed.

There is a difference between lender-required repairs and repairs on inspection reports. The lender-required repairs must be completed before closing or the lender will not make the loan. Any other repairs may be done or could have an allowance paid at closing if the lender agrees to allow it.

Pest Inspection

Pest inspections are designed to look for problems related to insect infestation. For the most part, these inspections are concerned with termites and carpenter ants, both of which destroy wood. Note that most mortgage companies want an original pest certificate before they will fund the money for the sale of the home to prove that pests are not present. This type of inspection is typically required by mortgage companies but is not a legal requirement. Make you specifically tell your buyer to get both a house inspection and a pest inspection. I once told my buyers to get "inspections," and they called a house inspector. At the closing, the title officer asked the buyer for the pest report. The buyers did not have one, and I was blamed for not being more specific. They were right. Most inspectors will do both; unfortunately, the inspector these buyers hired did not.

Septic System

Septic systems can cause major problems. Septic systems are an individual owner's method of waste disposal when there is no access to a city sewer system. Wastewater flows into the septic tank at one end and then out at the other end. The tank is usually buried in the back yard and empties into what is known as a drain field. Any solids remain in the tank and are broken down by bacteria. The water in the drain field is absorbed by the ground. As long as this system is working properly, septic systems are a viable means of waste disposal. Frequently, however, these systems must be pumped out because some of the material cannot be broken down and will fill up the tank. Also, roots from trees can cause severe damage to these types of waste disposal systems.

Most mortgage companies require a septic inspection to be sure they are working properly and have the needed capacity. These inspections can run several hundred dollars and could lead to additional repairs and expenses. Properties that typically have septics are more rural—where no public system is available.

Well Inspection
Water wells are driven down into the ground and are relatively safe from contamination. Water wells have been around for centuries and will be around for years to come. Like septic systems, wells are usually found in rural properties and often require an inspection to obtain a mortgage. The inspector will test the water to be sure it meets necessary standards.

Radon
Radon gas is a colorless, radioactive, inert gaseous element formed by the radioactive decay of radium. It seeps from the ground into a house. It comes from radioactive material underground, which is kind of scary. Radon is estimated to cause many thousands of deaths each year. Radon is second to only smoking as a leading cause of lung cancer. Testing is the only way to know if radon is present in a home. The proper inspector can check for high levels of radon gas in a house. Do not attempt to measure one of your listing's radon levels yourself by using a store-bought kit and don't allow the homeowners to do it either. By doing so, you and/or the homeowners assume liability.

If radon is in the home, there are radon reduction systems and they work very well. The proper system can reduce radon by 99%. Some builders have radon-resistant building methods. These should be considered and used in areas known for radon problems.

Environmental Assessment

Environmental assessments are usually carried out on commercial properties or large tracts of land. These assessments test the soil for contaminates and other hazards. The reports are designed to identify recognized environmental conditions and are site specific. They are also extremely expensive to conduct. If a buyer wants to have an environmental assessment prior to being obligated to purchase a home, then you should use an addendum that gives the buyer the right to get the report.

Structural Engineer's Report

A structural engineer's report comes from a structural engineer who looks at the structure, conducts a foundation analysis, examines the soil conditions, observes the internal support system, and other aspects of a property to determine the viability of the structure. The structural engineer will also conduct an elevation survey to measure the differential movement of the foundation. Most reports are for the substructure (usually includes the floor and the structure below it), not the superstructure (the area above the floor). Using an engineer to perform a structural analysis results in a valuable, unbiased report. If a foundation company is used, on the other hand, they have a vested interest in finding problems with the structure of the property, because most likely they will be the ones chosen to fix it—for a fee.

Survey

A survey is a graphic look at the property boundaries. Usually on lightly colored paper, it is a drawing of the property's boundaries, easements, exterior of any improvements, and location of fences.

Repairs

If repairs are required by the purchase agreement, be sure they are completed according to the agreement. Take your time when describing the repair. I know of one real estate salesperson who wrote in the repair amendment that the tree limbs needed to be cut back six feet from the house. The seller cut the limbs back and left them on the ground. The seller refused to clean up the mess and claimed he had cut the limbs according to the amendment. Guess who cleaned up the three truckloads of limbs? The salesperson who wrote the amendment had to haul them off.

Repairs are generally required to be completed by licensed repair people. If the sellers want to do the repairs themselves, they need to be warned of the liability they will incur if a problem arises as a result.

If you are representing the buyer, provide the listing salesperson an itemized list of repairs to be completed. And remember to follow up to be sure the repairs have been made. The best way to do that is to allow the buyer the opportunity for a final walk-through.

Final Walk-Through

The final walk-through allows the buyer the right to observe the property just prior to the closing. The buyer should check for any damage to the property that occurred since the agreement was consummated. This is not the time for the buyer to ask for more repairs or remodeling. Make sure your buyer is aware that the purpose of the final walk-though is to check for damage, not to add to what was already agreed upon.

Chapter Summary

Once a contract is accepted, your responsibilities continue. You must make sure all of the property inspections are ordered, the appraisal and survey are ordered, and your clients are satisfied with the transaction. Do not neglect your clients at this stage of the process; it is a great time to get referrals for business.

Summary Questions

1. What is a graphic look at the property's boundaries?
   a. Observation
   b. Survey
   c. Boundary analysis
   d. Appraisal

2. What is the colorless, radioactive, inert gaseous element formed by the radioactive decay of radium?
   a. Radiation
   b. Gas of decadence
   c. Radon
   d. Inertia gas

3. What allows the buyer the right to observe the property just prior to the closing?
   a. Standard language in the contract
   b. The title company's authorization
   c. The final walk-through
   d. Langeloea (latin for "culmination")

4. Who is generally required to complete all repairs (actual work)?
   a. Seller
   b. Uncle Bob
   c. Licensed repair people
   d. Buyer

5. What is not included on a survey?
   a. Property's boundaries
   b. Easements on the property
   c. Previous owner's names
   d. Location of fences

6. What will a structural engineer examine?
   a. The structure of the improvement
   b. The soil conditions
   c. The internal support system
   d. All of the above

7. What is the best aspect of a structural engineers report?
   a. It is unbiased.
   b. It is a seller's cost.
   c. It is mandatory.
   d. Any licensed engineer can complete a structural engineers report.

8. What assessment tests the soil for contaminates and other hazards?
   a. Post assessments
   b. Environmental assessments
   c. Health assessments
   d. Governmental assessments

9. How can a buyer be sure that the property does not have radon?
   a. Trust the sellers.
   b. Breathe; if there is radon present, the customer will become dizzy after a few minutes.
   c. Get an inspector to do an air quality test.
   d. Check the courthouse records.

10. What type of inspection tests for insect infestations?
    a. Termite inspections
    b. Roach inspections
    c. Carpenter ant inspections
    d. Pest inspections

Chapter 16

Financing

Chapter Overview

The objectives of this chapter are to introduce you to different types of financing and provide you with an understanding of the good faith estimate and qualification process. You should be familiar with creative financing options as well.

Key Terms

Conventional Financing:
Conventional financing is defined as any financing that is not government backed.

Creative Financing:
Creative financing refers to the sale of real estate with terms of financing that are different from those on new loans and that are established by current market forces.

Alienation Clause:
An alienation clause gives the lender the right to call the note due and payable if the property is sold in any way.

Balloon Note:
A balloon note is a note in which the final payment is larger than any of the previous payments.

Assumption:
An assumption occurs when the buyer takes over the current mortgage of the seller.

Buy-Down Mortgage:
A buy-down mortgage is a fixed-rate mortgage in which, for a fee, the interest rate is lowered for a period of time.

Introduction

I once heard the following: "If a buyer wants to buy and a seller wants to sell, financing should not get in the way." I agree with that. The more we understand about financing, the more people we can help. If a buyer has two of the following three things, he or she should be able to finance a property:

1. Good credit

2. Substantial, steady, and verifiable income for at least two years

3. Large reserves of cash on hand

Good credit is a start toward establishing someone to be worthy of a loan. But good credit must be matched up with one of the other two things to be adequate. With good credit and good income, a person can buy a property with little or no cash. If someone has good income, and plenty of cash, but terrible credit, he or she also can get a loan. (However, this is the most difficult route to take.) Last but not least, money talks; if the buyer has enough cash to put 25 percent or more down, he or she can finance the rest of the cost with poor credit and no job history. Of course, all of these situations still depend upon the specific lender.

Now let's take a more detailed look into the financing of real property.

Government Financing

"Government financing" is somewhat of a misnomer here because the federal government does not finance real estate purchases. The federal government actually insures the lender against losses due to default. Lenders are concerned about risk—will they get their money back? If the government insures the loan, the lender feels certain about loaning a person the money. However, one must qualify through the government entity that they are being insured by (FHA and VA are the most common).

Conventional Financing

Conventional financing is defined as any financing that is not government backed. Conventional financing is done through banks, mortgage companies, savings and loans, and any other primary lender. The lenders do not have the stringent guidelines that a government-insured loan normally has. Lenders are loaning their own money and will qualify a borrower using their own set of criteria. Typically FHA financing is easier on the borrower, and conventional financing is easier on the property. So if you had a borrower with credit problems, you might want to look to an FHA loan first. If the property is in disrepair, you might want to look at a conventional type of loan.

Fully Amortized Loan

Amortization is when a loan is paid down in small segments each month until the entire amount is paid off with the last payment. Each payment (to principal and interest) is for the same amount every month (except for the last payment, which may vary slightly as a result of any interest or principal differences), so the borrower can budget more effectively. The balance of the loan decreases with each payment and becomes zero at maturity. This is typically how most loans are structured.

For example, suppose a person borrows $100,000 from a lender. The interest on the loan is 10 percent for 30 years. The payment to principal and interest is $877. The breakdown of the first payment would consist of $833 going to interest and only $44 dollars going to principal. This would change each month, however, with more of the payment going to principal and less to interest over time. However, the payment would stay consistent at $877. (Some of the previous numbers were rounded for ease of explanation.)

Partially Amortized Loan

A partially amortized loan has equal payments of principal and interest like the fully amortized loan does. However, with the partially amortized loan, at some point there will be a balloon note, and the rest of the loan will be paid off.

Suppose a seller was financing the property for the buyer but only for five years. The note between the buyer and seller would amortize the note over 30 years, keeping the payments reasonable. After five years, however, the remaining balance would be due and payable by the buyer. Sounds bad, but after five years, the buyer should have established himself so that he could get a mortgage company to refinance the seller out.

Budget Mortgage

A budget mortgage is simply a mortgage where the loan payment includes the principal, the interest, the property taxes, and the property insurance. The taxes and insurance are prorated amounts for the year and are place in an escrow account. This means the payment includes PITI. At year end (or when the insurance is due), the lender pays those amounts from the escrow account, and the borrower doesn't need to worry about doing so. This is called a budget loan because it makes budgeting easier for the borrower.

Creative Financing

Creative financing refers to the sale of real estate with terms of financing that are different from those on new loans and that are established by current market forces.

Seller Financing

Some sellers want to finance their property for a buyer. The advantages include more potential buyers for the property, an income on the property, and lower closing costs. In addition the seller will not have to pay capital gains taxes at the closing. The advantages to the buyer include lower closing costs, minimal qualifications, and faster closing. You will see seller financing on property that is difficult to sell, such as raw land.

Adjustable-Rate Mortgage (ARM)

An ARM is a fully amortized loan with one key difference: The interest rate on the loan is tied to an index. That means that the interest rate, and hence the monthly loan payment, will fluctuate with the interest rate.

An ARM can be a good route to take for those sophisticated enough to understand this loan and who may be moving within a five-year period of time. However, some may have trouble with this type of loan, such as a borrower who is on a fixed income. When the interest rate adjusts up, the borrower no longer can afford to make the payments.

Package Mortgage

A package mortgage is one in which all of the personal property is included. These types of loans are rare though. Defining what exactly qualifies as actual personal property and therefore is eligible to be included in the sale can get tricky. For example, is furniture personal property? Probably. Are dishes personal property? Hmmm. Are pictures of the family personal property? Probably not. If this type of mortgage is being considered by one of your clients, you should use a bill of sale (transfers personal property rights), itemize all property that remains with the sale, and have all parties sign the bill of sale addenda. Most likely, you would see this type of transaction on something like a furnished condominium at the beach, in which case, nothing in question would even be in the condo when it was to be shown.

Just on a side note: Lenders do NOT like lending on personal property!

Blanket Mortgage
A blanket mortgage has more than one parcel of land pledged on the loan. A partial release clause allows individual parcels to be released from lien as the balance is paid down. This type of transaction is performed almost exclusively with builders and developers.

Reverse Annuity Mortgage (RAM)
A RAM is where the mortgagee (lender) pays the mortgagor (borrower) monthly payments that increase the loan amount every month. RAMs are for individuals 62 years of age or older. This type of "loan" allows the borrower to have more money to spend in their retirement and yet not move out of the house they love. The loan is repaid upon the death of the mortgagor or sale of the property or when the balance reaches the maximum limit.

Wrap-Around Loan
A wrap-around loan is a not an actual loan. This type of transaction usually involves a seller who has a current loan that does not have an alienation clause (an alienation clause gives the lender the right to call the note due and payable if the property is sold in any way). The seller "wraps" an additional loan around the existing loan. For example, a seller has a current loan on a property for $60,000 and a buyer is willing to pay $100,000 for the property but cannot qualify through normal financing channels. The seller would "wrap" a note for $40,000 around the current loan of $60,000 for a total of $100,000. The borrower would make the payments directly to the seller, and the seller would be responsible to the original lender to make the payments on the remaining $60,000. This type of financing should be done through attorneys who are familiar with wraps because of the unique way this transaction is formed.

Balloon Note
A balloon note is a note in which the final payment is larger than any of the previous payments. The basis of this type of loan

is to finance over a long term and get paid off in the short term. Let's take a closer look. Say a seller would not have an issue with financing a property for three years but not for 30. The buyer could not afford the payments to amortize (equal payments until the loan is paid off) the loan in three years. The balloon note would allow the seller to finance the loan over 30 years and have a balloon payment due for the remaining balance in three years. In three years, the buyer could refinance and pay off the seller.

Lease/Purchase
A lease/purchase is where a person agrees to lease a property for a few months and then purchase the property at the end of the lease. The buyer must buy at the end of the lease. The lease/purchase is usually for a buyer who has some problems being approved for a loan. While the buyer is leasing, he or she can also work on clearing up any outstanding problems with their credit and be ready to apply for a loan. The lease time gives the buyer time to save money for a down payment. It can also be arranged that a portion of the monthly rent payment be used for the down payment later.

Assumable Loans
When a buyer takes over the current mortgage of the seller, this is called an assumption. The new buyer "assumes" the same terms and payments to which the original lender agreed. Loan assumptions are very popular, especially if the interest rate on the current loan is less than current market rates.

Buy-Down Mortgage
A buy-down mortgage is a fixed-rate mortgage in which the seller prepays some of the loan interest to "buy down" the interest rate for the buyer-borrower for some period. This type of financing becomes more popular in periods of high interest rates.

Buyer Qualification

A competent mortgage officer generally qualifies the buyer. We will touch on buyer qualification here just in case you do not have a mortgage officer on hand.

Buyer qualification refers to the process of determining the risk of loss on a residential loan. If a lender is willing to loan money for real property, the risk level for the lender must be tolerable. Qualification is used to determine the ability of the buyer to make mortgage payments from his or her current income and still have enough for family expenses.

Lenders use an income ratio and a debt ratio to measure a buyer's ability to pay back a loan. The income ratio is traditionally recognized to be of the buyer's monthly income. The debt ratio is the relationship between the buyer's long-term debt and the monthly income. For example, consider the following:

> How much can a buyer earning $3,600 per month afford to pay on a loan with an income ratio of 25 percent?
>
> $3,600 × 25% (0.25) = $900 per month

Thus, the buyer can afford a $900 monthly payment.

Chapter Summary

Knowing the different ways to finance real estate is the key to your success in the real estate business. This chapter discussed several loan programs that may be of interest to one of your future buyers. A general understanding of all aspects of the real estate business is necessary; intimate knowledge of the details is for the experts. Hopefully, this chapter has given you some insight into the loan programs that are available, and you will be able to share that knowledge with your buyers when the time comes. Choosing a lender that understands the details of lending and knows a multitude of loan programs is best for you and your client.

Summary Questions

1. Dan and Kim wish to obtain a new loan. Their combined monthly income is $5,500. What is the monthly payment they can qualify for if the lender uses an income ratio of 28 percent?
   a. $1,450
   b. $5,500
   c. $1,540
   d. $2,800

2. Preston and Brittany have found a house that will have a monthly payment of $1,350. If the lender allows 27 percent to the income ratio, what is the required yearly income for the buyers?
   a. $36,450
   b. $60,000
   c. $13,500
   d. $64,800

3. Which of the following is not considered to be an important aspect when qualifying a buyer for a loan?
   a. Good credit
   b. Ethnicity and gender
   c. Personal income
   d. Cash on hand

4. Which of the following does the government actually do on a regular basis?
   a. Lend money to buy houses
   b. Qualify buyers
   c. Insure loans
   d. All of the above

5. Which type of financing is defined as "not government backed"?
   a. Conventional
   b. FHA
   c. VA
   d. HUD

6. What gives the lender the right to call the note due and payable if the property is sold in any way?
   a. Hazard clause
   b. Wrap clause
   c. Alienation clause
   d. Acceleration clause

7. Which type of note has a final payment that is larger than any of the previous payments?
   a. Inflation note
   b. Balloon note
   c. Yeast note
   d. Bomb note

8. What is it called when the buyer takes over the current mortgage of the seller?
   a. Wrap
   b. Switch
   c. Turn-around
   d. Assumption

9. Which type of note does the seller prepay some of the loan interest lower the interest rate for the buyer for some period of time?
   a. Prepayment penalty
   b. IR Drop
   c. Buy down
   d. LTR—Lower the Rate

10. The process of determining the risk of loss on a residential loan is referred to as which of the following?
    a. Wants and needs analysis
    b. Buyer qualification
    c. Refinancing
    d. Subjugation

Chapter 17

Referrals

Chapter Overview

In this chapter you will learn to identify the two types of referrals and to find and obtain referral business. Referrals are frequently overlooked by real estate salespeople because they are busy with their current clients. This referral business is easy, rewarding, and will keep a real estate professional in this business longer. This chapter also includes the scripts that will help you obtain referrals.

Key Terms

Referral:
A buyer or seller of real estate who is sent from one broker to another.

Incoming (Inbound) Referral:
Receiving a potential client from another salesperson for a real estate sale.

Outgoing (Outbound) Referral:
Sending a potential client to another salesperson for a real estate sale.

Qualified Referral:
A qualified referral has been contacted, wants to buy or sell, and wants (expects) to be referred.

Introduction

In addition to the business of listing and selling real estate, a sales associate has even more opportunities to make money by sending referrals to other real estate offices. As a source of both buyers and sellers, referrals are what every salesperson should seek, since a satisfied customer is an extension of you and your own sales effort.

In the real estate industry, "referral business" is the business generated by an individual, family, or company when they relocate to a different location. Generally, these people will sell their current residence and will look for a new one in the city where they are relocating. Both of these situations could generate a profitable commission. Real estate brokerages want referral business. When the broker begins to receive referral business (or even before then), they want to be sure their real estate salespeople can handle the business and outperform all other real estate companies. A referral is a buyer or seller of real estate who is sent from one broker to another. Referrals are the most overlooked potential sources of money in real estate. Real estate salespeople tend to concentrate on other areas and neglect the referrals. Even I have had sellers move to other cities, and I did not get the referral to that city because I forgot to ask.

There are two types of referrals: referrals sent (outgoing) and referrals received (incoming).

Incoming referral: *Receiving a potential client from another salesperson for a real estate sale.*

Outgoing referral: *Sending a potential client to another salesperson for a real estate sale.*

"Referrals sent" refers to potential clients sent from one salesperson to another for a real estate sale. The sending salesperson receives a portion of the commission back as a referral fee. The fees charged are negotiated between the brokers. "Referrals received" refers to those clients received by a salesperson from another salesperson for a real estate sale.

Recognizing Referral Opportunities

To recognize a referral opportunity, you must have referrals at the forefront of your mind. Some real estate salespeople never have any referrals to send out. The main reason for this is that they don't concentrate on referrals.

Buyer Referrals

A buyer referral is a potential homebuyer to whom the service has been explained and who has agreed to be contacted by the destination area broker. The minimum amount of information needed is as follows:

- Name, address, email address, and phone numbers (both home and cell) for the customer

- Destination city and state with a maximum of two to three separate geographic areas

- First home-finding trip to take place within a specified timeframe, preferably six months or less

- Reason for moving and their motivation

- Type of property or price range

Seller Referrals

A seller referral is a homeowner, interested in listing property, to whom the service has been explained and who has agreed to be contacted by the designated broker servicing the geographic location of the property.

- Property conforms to local zoning and standards

- Property not presently listed, or soon to expire

- Property deemed to be salable by the destination area broker

Rental Referrals

Rental referrals are those individuals who would rather rent than buy. Rental referrals do not have to be accepted by the destination broker. They are accepted at the discretion of the destination broker.

However, if a referred party is expecting to rent for a period of six months or less, courtesy and business opportunity would dictate providing assistance to that referral party.

If a rental referral purchases within 18 months of the initial contact by the destination broker, a referral fee is due and payable to the referring broker in accordance with the referral fee schedule in effect at the time of initiation.

Only the originating broker can "qualify the lead" and make this a real referral. It must be accepted, and it is best to have it in writing.

How to Cultivate Referrals

One of the most critical tools in the area of prospecting is referrals. New real estate salespeople are told over and over again to "get referrals, get referrals, get referrals." You make a sale and when it's completed, you must remember to get referrals! So how do you do this? You can't just ask your clients if they know anybody else who is interested in buying or selling real estate. They will look at you blankly and say, "I can't think of anybody." You have to learn how to prospect for referrals.

Ask your clients the following questions: "Are you involved in any type of group participating sports activity? Do you golf, bowl, or belong to any types of clubs?" These questions are more probing in nature and will lead your clients to share more information.

For example, if your client responds, "Yeah, I golf," then you can ask him if he golfs with anyone who might be interested in buying or selling real estate. You have given him something to visualize, which may help jar his memory. If he gives you a name, be sure to write it down.

You can break this prospecting into many areas, including church, parents, friends of your children, and so on.

Outgoing Referrals

Like listings, the outgoing referral is controllable and measurable. It gets your name out there and brings in new business.

Send only qualified referrals, such as the following:

- Customers who want to be referred

- Prospects whom you have personally contacted

- Prospects who are willing to buy or sell

- Prospects who expect a contact from the receiving office

- Prospects who are referred to a specific office

- Prospects who have no prior commitment to another real estate company

The destination office can then use this information to provide counseling, real estate assistance, and additional information to the person(s), whether a buyer or seller, being referred.

Your clients may not see how a friend or relative of theirs who lives in another city or state can provide you with referral business, unless that friend or relative is actually planning to move to your city. However, those contacts can bring valuable business your way. Maybe your client's Aunt Sally knows a person who is moving from her city to your city; in that case, you can get a referral for the sell side and another referral for the buy side. We fail to communicate that information to Aunt Sally.

I remember going to my first year-end real estate awards banquet. That year the top award went to the salesperson who had sent the most referrals over that year, which was 18—just over one per month. I thought: I can do that.

So I set a goal to send more referrals than any other real estate salesperson. I asked around and learned that the referral business is based on luck. If you had the right seller, you might get a referral when the seller moved. You could get lucky on a call-in buyer, but that's about it. I also found out that real estate salespeople love getting referrals (they will even get into confrontations over whose turn it is to receive a referral), but not many of them give referrals. I know of a company that spent hundreds of thousands of dollars to belong to a national referral service (they controlled corporate moves as well as individual moves and could give hundreds of referrals yearly). In order to stay in the network, the company was under pressure to give more referrals. Their incoming referrals were decreasing because they weren't sending any outgoing referrals.

I, being new to the real estate business, had a different idea. The system I describe above didn't seem to be working. Salespeople loved receiving referrals, but they didn't want to put the work into finding referrals to give. So I decided to work differently and go out and get referrals on my own. The question was, where would I find these referrals? I began to think about people who are moving and quickly came up with my answer: For Sale By Owners (FSBOs)! These people believe they can sell their houses themselves without using brokers. However, when they do sell, and some do, they still have to find another house.

I decided I wanted to become the referral specialist in my office. I went to my broker, she granted my request, and with the wave of her imaginary magic wand, she named me the official office referral specialist." Now that I had my title, I began calling FSBOs. Here is the script I typically used:

Salesperson:
"Hi, I am calling about the house for sale. Are you the owner?"

FSBO:
"Yes."

Salesperson:
"Well, my name is Dan Hamilton. I am the referral specialist with Acme Realty. Now, I am not calling about helping you sell your home. I'm calling to see if I can help you after you sell it. Are you planning to stay in the area or are you moving out of the city?"

The answer didn't matter; I was getting a referral. I spent an hour calling FSBOs and ended up with four outbound referrals, twice the goal I set for myself for the entire month. From then on, whenever I had time to spare, I would call for outbound referrals.

Once I was teaching a seminar in Lubbock, Texas. I had some downtime in my hotel room, so I picked up the local newspaper and began calling FSBOs. I ended up getting one FSBO who said she would be moving to Denver. I told her I would put her in touch with a real estate professional there. She responded, "Great, and could you have someone from Lubbock help me sell our house here?" Notice, I got two referrals from this one person; this is a good reason to call a FSBO and get listings in your area.

By the end of the year, I had sent 38 referrals, more than double what was sent by the top referral person the year before, and I had not worked that hard.

Some other good sources for outgoing referrals include the following:

1. Listings
2. Buyers
3. Relatives
4. Past clients
5. Attorneys
6. Spouse's company
7. Floor duty
8. Open house
9. Anywhere

You can ask the following questions:

- On an ad call
  - Are you moving here from out of town?

- Is your home for sale now?

- May I have a real estate office give you a call?

• Buyers

- Do you know of anyone else moving to town or being transferred?

• Sellers

- Do you know of someone in your company or neighborhood who is moving out of town?

Offer to provide information about the new area at no cost or obligation.

One of the best things about outbound referrals is that all you have to do is give them, and then you get money. If you are in some type of referral network, others in the network will follow the lead and make sure you get paid. You don't have to spend time tracking the progress of the transaction after you have made the referral. It is a great "fire and forget" weapon. For example, there were times when I would be working in the office and my broker would come up and hand me a check for between $200 and $1,000 on a referral I had sent several months ago.

For peace of mind, though, it is a good idea to track your referrals to make sure everything is being done to make the referral happy. This is not mandatory if you are dealing through a referral network, but it still is a good idea. There are at least five opportunities for you to stay in touch with an outbound referral:

1. Call the referred party the next day to make sure the receiving office made contact.

2. Call several days later to see if the referred buyer has received an information packet in the mail.

3. Call, if possible, during the buyer's home-finding trip to check progress.

4. Communicate with the receiving sales associate to convey the transferee's wants.

5. Check back in several weeks (and periodically, thereafter) to make sure no problems have arisen. It's important for you to remain in control of the referral.

Hopefully you've realized by now that outgoing referrals are fun and easy!

Incoming Referrals

The referral specialist is the real estate professional who handles incoming referrals properly and professionally. As a referral specialist, you will be able to handle a referral buyer or seller with the greatest of ease and ability. You should strive to become great at the referral business.

Characteristics of Great Referral Specialists

Let's first look at some of the characteristics of a great referral specialist. Notice that these characteristics can apply to outstanding people who work in any profession:

- **Emotionally stable**

  Great referral specialists must be able to tolerate frustration and stress. They cannot allow themselves the pleasure of getting personally involved in buyer and seller disputes. Overall, they must be well-adjusted and have the psychological maturity to deal with anything they are required to face.

- **Commanding**

  Great referral specialists are often times competitive and decisive, and they usually enjoy overcoming obstacles. Do not misunderstand: I am not saying these people are mean; I am saying that they are strong. Overall, they are assertive in their thinking style as well as their attitude in dealing with others. They believe in protecting their clients best interests at all times. Remember, the word is commanding, not demanding.

- **Enthusiastic**

   Great referral specialists are usually seen as active, expressive, and energetic. They are often very optimistic and open to change. Overall, they are quick, alert, and tend to be uninhibited.

- **Conscientious**

   Great referral specialists are often dominated by a sense of duty and tend to be very exacting in character. They usually have a very high standard of excellence and an inward desire to do their best. They see the big picture and operate on a higher plane. They also have a need for order and tend to be very self-disciplined. They understand that all of their actions are being watched and are constantly careful.

- **Socially bold**

   Great referral specialists tend to be spontaneous risk takers. They are usually socially aggressive and generally thick-skinned. They are good at building powerful relationships. Overall, they are responsive to others and tend to be high in emotional stamina.

- **Tough-minded**

   Great referral specialists are practical, logical, and to-the-point. They tend to be low in sentimental attachments and comfortable with criticism. They are usually insensitive to hardship and very poised overall.

- **Self-assured**

   Self-confidence and resiliency are common traits among great referral specialists. They tend to be free of guilt and have little or no need for approval. They are generally secure and are usually undeterred by prior mistakes or failures.

- **Composed**

   Great referral specialists are usually seen as controlled and very precise in their social interactions. Overall, they are very protective of their integrity and reputation and consequently tend to be socially aware and careful when making decisions or determining specific actions.

- **Highly energetic**

   Long hours and few days off are usually prerequisites for referral business, especially as more and more clients are received. The referral specialist should remain attentive and stay focused.

- **Intuitive**

   Great referral specialists have learned to listen to their intuition. While they have a great deal of information available to them, it still might not be enough. Having discernment in situations is invaluable, especially with interpersonal relationships.

- **Mature**

   To be a great referral specialist, personal power and recognition must be secondary to the wants and needs of clients. In other words, maturity is based on recognizing that more can be accomplished by helping others get what they want. As a matter of fact, a great referral specialist enjoys the successes of the people they call clients more than they enjoy their own successes.

- **Team oriented**

   Great Referral Specialists today put a strong emphasis on teamwork. In any real estate office working as a team and helping each other is a prerequisite. Real estate salespeople are independent contractors but they also want to feel part of something bigger and more important, so the Great Referral Specialists will get the other salespeople in their office involved in helping better serve the client.

- **Empathetic**

    A great referral specialist has empathy, but not sympathy, for their clients. In other words, a specialist should be able to know how someone feels without crying with them. Without empathy, you can't build trust. And without trust, you will never be able to get the best for your clients.

- **Charismatic**

    Great referral specialists who are charismatic are able to arouse strong emotions in their clients by defining a vision that unites and captivates them. Using this vision, the specialist motivates all those involved to reach a goal by tying that goal to substantial personal rewards and values.

Here are some additional characteristics of great referral specialists:

Persistent	Honest	Trustworthy
Patient	Good communicator	Opportunistic
Organized	Problem solver	Exudes integrity
Educator	Mentor	Mediator
Pleasant	Neat in appearance	Ethical
Tactful	Understanding	Motivating
Detail oriented	Great memory	Knowledgeable

The majority of the above characteristics are inherent in all of us to varying degrees. You need to work on developing or strengthening those you struggle with. For example, if you have always had a problem being honest, you won't suddenly become honest once you are a referral specialist. Can you further develop these traits and become the best referral specialist you can be?

Sequence of Events in Receiving a Referral

1. You receive initial information from referring source.

2. You contact the customer and qualify the referral.

3. If the referral cannot be qualified, you notify the referral source and give reasons why the referral does not qualify.

4. It is generally accepted procedure that you confirm the referral within 24 hours of receiving it.

5. Once the 24-hour rejection period has passed, the acceptance of the referral is assumed. You will owe the source of the referral a fee if the customer purchases or sells a home.

6. You should send monthly updates on the status of the referral until the file is closed.

Prior to Arrival

- You must be available to service the customer.

- If any situation occurs whereby the customer cannot be serviced, you must contact your referral source.

- Initial contact with the customer must be within 24 hours of confirming the referral.

- Always identify yourself as a licensed real estate salesperson and a referral specialist.

- Make sure the customer has your name, telephone number, email address, and company name.

- Verify all the information you have from the initial needs analysis. Send the relocation package and agree to research schools, churches, sports facilities, and so on.

- Confirm the date of the customer's home-finding trip.

- Prescreen all properties before the home-finding trip, make appointments for viewing, and plan an itinerary.

- Report all activity to the referral source on a weekly basis.

During the home-finding trip, make sure all of the following apply:

- Be prompt at meeting the customer.

- Make sure vehicle is clean and in good running condition.

- Counsel the customer in your office or at a convenient location.

- Explain agency representation laws.

- Have a map available that shows the location of schools, points of interest, and new job location if possible.

- Conduct an area tour prior to previewing homes.

- Know where you are going.

- Provide an information or MLS sheet for each home.

- Listen to what the customer is saying and include in the tour only those properties that most closely meet the customer's needs; be prepared to change.

- Adjust the itinerary if necessary.

- Review with the customer at the end of each day the properties viewed. Don't start the next day without having done this.

Be sure to take advantage of these follow-up opportunities:

- Keep in close contact with the customer.

- Send a thank you note with your business card enclosed after their home-finding trip. Contact the customer by telephone, email, or by mail every 10 days, or as agreed.

- Send information regarding recent sales and new listings that come on the market.

- Send local newspapers or website information, if feasible.

Home Purchase

Before showing a property, you should offer the customer the opportunity to be prequalified by a mortgage company. After the contract to purchase the home has been signed, the specialist should notify the referral source immediately. Provide them with the estimated closing date, financing being used, sale price, and commission.

Contact the customer two weeks after closing to see how they have settled into their new home and neighborhood. These customers could become a good source of referral business for you!

Chapter Summary

Referrals should be based on give and take; if you take a referral you should give a referral. If this would happen, a lot of real estate business would take place, and all of us would make more money. Don't forget, referrals are probably the most overlooked and easiest part of the real estate industry.

Summary Questions

1. What is one of the most overlooked sources for making money in real estate?
   a. Buyer brokerage
   b. Seller brokerage
   c. Referral business
   d. Door knocking

2. When one real estate professional gives another real estate professional the contact information of a potential buyer or seller for a fee, it is referred to as what?
   a. Gifting
   b. Passing on Business (POB)
   c. Doubling up
   d. Giving a referral

3. Receiving a potential client from another salesperson for a real estate sale is referred to as what?
   a. Incoming referral
   b. Outgoing referral
   c. Incoming ancillary business
   d. Outgoing ancillary business

4. Sending a potential client to another salesperson for a real estate sale is referred to as what?
   a. Incoming referral
   b. Outgoing referral
   c. Incoming ancillary business
   d. Outgoing ancillary business

Chapter 18

Deceptive Trade Practices Act
and the Consumer Protection Act

Chapter Overview

In this chapter you will learn about the Deceptive Trade Practices Act and how to avoid some pitfalls that can lead to trouble. We will review things you should and should not say and how to recognize and address problem areas. You need to be aware of all aspects of the Deceptive Trade Practices Act; this law can make you, the real estate professional, look guilty before you even have a chance to defend yourself.

Key Terms

Fraud:
A deception deliberately practiced in order to secure unfair or unlawful gain.

Misrepresentation:
Misrepresentation means giving an incorrect or misleading representation of something. It is a false statement.

Punitive:
Damages awarded by a court against a defendant as a deterrent or punishment to redress an egregious wrong perpetrated by the defendant.

Unconscionable:
Not restrained by conscience; beyond prudence or reason; excessive. It is taking advantage of the lack of knowledge, ability, experience, or capacity of a person to a grossly unfair degree.

Intent:
The person making the representation must have known the representation was incorrect yet continued in the misrepresentation.

Introduction

The Deceptive Trade Practices Act (DTPA) is probably the best protection for consumers in business transactions and nearly every state has a version of it. Real estate salespeople see many of its provisions as unfair because it makes them responsible for things that are not always under their control. Some states have limited or exempted real estate professionals' liability with regard to the act; however, clients do have a right to expect professionalism, knowledge, integrity, and honesty from their real estate salespeople.

The primary purpose of the DTPA is to protect consumers against false, misleading, and deceptive business practices. The DTPA is sometimes used to bring a suit against a real estate salesperson when property defects are discovered by a buyer that the real estate salesperson failed to disclose.

It is not unlawful to make representations in the real estate industry. However, if you make a representation, you had better be right. Sometimes we think that the consumer expects us to know everything, but in reality the consumer only expects us to know how to find out an answer. For example, if the consumer wants to know the boundary line of a particular lot, the consumer does not expect us to actually know, but he or she does expect us to find out.

The law provides for a consumer who prevails in a DTPA suit to receive actual damages. If it is found that the conduct of the defendant was committed knowingly (fraud), the award may be three times (treble) the amount of actual damages. These treble damages are called punitive (punishing) damages.

Punitive damages are damages awarded by a court against a defendant as a deterrent or punishment to redress an egregious wrong perpetrated by the defendant. Punitive damages have been awarded even though the buyers would have discovered the misrepresentations had they exercised reasonable diligence. Reasonable diligence applies to the actions of the buyer. Suppose there is a crack in the plasterboard of a wall caused from foundation problems that the seller is aware of; also suppose that with an ordinary inspection, the buyer should have seen the crack. The buyer could still seek damages if not disclosed because the buyer is not required to inspect the property; the sellers (and their agents) are required to disclose problems.

A consumer may maintain an action for damages based on breach of an express or implied warranty or for any unconscionable action. An unconscionable action is defined as an action that takes advantage of the lack of knowledge, ability, experience, or capacity of a person to a grossly unfair degree or one in which there is a gross disparity between the value received and the consideration paid. Those are a lot of fancy words, but basically it means that if you could do such a thing, you must not have a conscience.

Senate Bill 1353—Effective September 1, 2011—An act relating to certain claims against persons licensed as real estate brokers and salespersons.

BE IT ENACTED BY THE LEGISLATURE OF THE STATE OF TEXAS: SECTION 1. Section 17.49, Business & Commerce Code, is amended by adding Subsection (i) to read as follows:

(i) Nothing in this subchapter shall apply to a claim against a person licensed as a broker or salesperson under Chapter 1101, Occupations Code, arising from an act or omission by the person while acting as a broker or salesperson. This exemption does not apply to:

1. an express misrepresentation of a material fact that cannot be characterized as advice, judgment, or opinion;

2. a failure to disclose information in violation of Section 17.46(b)(24); or

3. an unconscionable action or course of action that cannot be characterized as advice, judgment, or opinion.

Misrepresentation

Misrepresentation is a false statement. Misrepresentation can occur by commission or omission. Commission refers to the making of a mistake or error, and omission is the leaving out of information. Generally, real estate salespeople have errors and omissions insurance to help protect them from these types of mistakes.

Misrepresentation can also involve fraud. Fraud is the intentional misleading of a person. Fraud is a deception deliberately practiced in order to secure unfair or unlawful gain. No insurance will cover fraud. Certain factors must be in place for fraud, including:

1. **Reliance** on the information. The consumer must have relied on the information given. Would an ordinary person have believed the representation?

2. **Intent** to fraud. The person making the representation must have known the representation was incorrect and continued in the misrepresentation.

3. **Damage** to the individual. The individual must have incurred some type of damage caused by the misrepresentation.

Note how these three words form the acronym RID, which provides an easy way to remember these factors.

A real estate professional is paid to put a buyer and seller together, not to make representations. I have seen more real estate salespeople get into trouble because they do not know when to keep quiet. For example, a buyer may ask the real estate salesperson what the square footage of the house is. For whatever reason, the salesperson thinks he or she should answer that question rather than the appraiser, whose job it is to provide this information. In these cases, it is wise to tell the buyer you will find out the answer and will let him or her know as soon as possible.

Two Questions

The DTPA is dependent on the answers to the following two questions:

1. Did you know there was a misrepresentation?

2. Should you have known there was a misrepresentation?

These questions are typically asked when determining if there has been an action for a DTPA violation. For example, a buyer purchases a property through a real estate salesperson and upon moving in, discovers foundation problems. Did the real estate salesperson know of the defect? If the answer is yes, meaning the salesperson did not disclose the defect, then he or she has violated the DTPA. If the answer is no, then the next question is asked: Should the salesperson have known of the defect? How the salesperson spoke and acted would have indicated if he or she was aware of the problem. This type of liability has been limited in recent years to the point that the real estate professional must have actually conducted fraud.

Three Defenses That Will "Probably" Work

The reason the word "probably" is inserted in the heading above is that most DTPA cases are settled without a ruling.

The following three defenses should be used, when possible, to protect you:

1. **Inspections by licensed inspectors:** It is the job of licensed inspectors to find out what is potentially wrong with a property. Once they give their professional opinions on an inspection report, they are liable for their opinion.

    If you or a buyer is unsure of the inspection report, consult the inspector. If you are at an inspection and your buyer looks at you and says, "What do you think?" you should smile and say, "Well, the inspector is here. Let's ask him." Don't ever try and correct an inspector—inspections are the inspector's job, let them do it. Every time you open your mouth you assume more liability. If you can't resist speaking, leave the premises or at least the room.

Inspectors probably won't say that the roof needs replacing. Instead they will note that there is evidence of roof damage, and they may recommend a professional roof inspection. The buyer is now on notice of possible problems. This is a disclosure to the buyer, and it limits the buyer's right to sue if there is roof damage.

2. **Written seller's disclosure statement:** A seller's disclosure statement is a document that describes the property in detail. It allows the seller to note anything on the property that is not functioning properly.

    The statement is not mandated, and most states only require that the seller disclose in writing. Some third-party referral companies use their own forms.

3. **Information given by the government that you have no reason to believe is false:** The government publishes such information as flood maps, zoning restrictions, and tax records, which usually include the year the house was built and square footage of a property. The real estate salesperson can generally rely on information to be correct. If he or she "knows" it is not accurate, the information cannot be used.

Notice: All the defenses mentioned here put the burden on someone else. Be the "source of the source" of the information. Let the experts do their jobs, while you concentrate on finding buyers and sellers. The word "misrepresentation" is interesting; if you don't make any representations, you won't make any misrepresentations.

Three Defenses That Will Not Work

The following three defenses under the DTPA will not work:

1. **Waiver:** A person's right to sue cannot be waived before the event happens.

2. **"As-Is":** Similar to a waiver, this phrase means the buyer is stating that he or she will not sue the seller even though the buyer is not fully aware of any problems the property could have. In the real estate industry, we need to be sure to use the words "no repairs."

3. **Caveat emptor (let the buyer beware).** Under DTPA, the buyer does not have to show due diligence. We must, therefore, disclose every material defect. While this tactic might have worked in the past, it no longer does.

Laundry List

The DTPA contains a list of deceptive trade practices that are prohibited. Several acts violate the DTPA, and as a result, consumers may sue. In some states, real estate licensees are exempt from these rules. There would be no violation for those licensees unless the action was intentional or negligent. The following are some select acts that could apply to real estate:

1. **Passing off goods or services as those of another.**
   It is forbidden to claim that goods or services are of one company when they are not. Say a buyer insists on a home built by Hamilton Builders. They really like the house you are showing them, but it is built by Henderson Brothers Builders. When they ask you, you say, "Of course, this home is a Hamilton-built home." You have violated DTPA because you misrepresented the builder in order to earn a commission.

2. **Causing confusion or misunderstanding as to the source, sponsorship, approval, or certification of goods or services.**
   This section furthers section (1) by the words "causing confusion." It is a violation to say you are a certified appraiser when all you have is a real estate license.

3. **Causing confusion or misunderstanding as to affiliation, connection, or association with, or certification by, another.**
   This section would prohibit you from claiming yourself as a REALTOR® when you are not a member. (To use the REALTOR® name, you must be a member of the National Association of Realtors®.)

4. **Using deceptive representatives or designations of geographic origin in connection with goods or services.**
   This section prohibits, for example, a person from claiming that the entryway tile is Italian marble when, in fact, it was mined at the local pit up on Highway 7.

5. **Representing goods or services that claim to have sponsorship, approval, characteristics, ingredients, uses, benefits, or quantities but do not; or a person claiming to have a sponsorship, approval, status, affiliation, or connection but does not.**
   This section is quite comprehensive. I own a property across the street from a very popular lake. My neighbors have a dock that is actually on the lake. If I was to tell a potential buyer they could use that dock, I would be representing that my property has benefits it does not have.

6. **Representing that goods are original or new if they are deteriorated, reconditioned, reclaimed, used, or second-hand.**
   This section prohibits a seller from claiming a roof is new when the roof is actually 15 years old.

7. **Representing that goods or services are of a particular standard, quality, or grade, or that goods are of a particular style or model, if they are of another.**

This section prohibits a seller from claiming appliances are of a designer name when they are not.

8. **Disparaging the goods, services, or business of another by false or misleading representations of facts.**
   This section prevents a real estate company from talking bad about a seller.

9. **Advertising goods or services with intent not to sell them as advertised.**
   I knew a real estate salesperson who needed one more house to fill out a full-page advertisement. He did not have any more listings, so he put his brother's house in that slot. He said he would just tell any callers that this particular house was off the market. The problem with this is that it is a direct violation of this section. Notice that it is a variant of the old "bait and switch."

10. **Advertising goods or services with intent not to supply a reasonable expectable public demand, unless the advertisement disclosed a limitation of quantity.**
    This section deals with the "rain check" you are offered at many retail stores. They advertise a television at an unbelievably low price but only have one in stock. This is illegal unless they offer the same price when their stock is replenished. An example of this type of violation in regard to real estate would be to offer an apartment for lease at a low rate. When the calls start coming in, you explain that you only have one property at that lease price, but you have several others at a higher price.

11. **Making false or misleading statements of fact concerning the reasons for, existence of, or amount of price reductions.**
    Some sellers try and mask the real reason for price reductions. For example, a seller may tell the buyer that the reason the price is so low is that they have been transferred; however, the truth is that the house has major foundation damage, and the seller hasn't disclosed that.

Chapter Summary

The DTPA is designed to prevent the sellers of products or services from misrepresenting any aspect of those products or services. This chapter points to the need for such an act. The purpose of the DTPA is to protect, not punish; however, if a violation occurs, the law can punish.

Summary Questions

1. All of the following defenses would probably work under the DTPA except:
   a. Inspections by licensed inspectors
   b. No intent
   c. Written sellers disclosure notice
   d. Any information given by the government

2. Which of the following is not one of the three defenses that will not work under the DTPA?
   a. A written waiver
   b. Agreement to an "as-is" contract
   c. Caveat emptor
   d. Did not know and should not have known

3. What are punitive damages?
   a. Damages that are small in nature but big in principle
   b. Damages that are punishing
   c. Damages that were caused by a pun or joke
   d. Damages that were fake or falsified

4. Which of the following is the nickname for the DTPA list of forbidden acts?
   a. Forbidden list
   b. Action list
   c. List of violations
   d. Laundry list

5. What are the two main questions asked in reference to determining a violation of the DTPA?
   a. What is the damage? How much is the damage?
   b. Are you licensed? Did you act in accordance with a license?
   c. Did you know? Should you have known?
   d. Was there a signed agreement? Was an attorney representing you?

6. What are the two types of misrepresentation if fraud is not involved?
   a. Intent and reliance
   b. Commission and omission
   c. Remit and omit
   d. Remission and submission

7. A murder took place on a property you have listed. The sellers have insisted that you keep this information confidential. What is your duty to disclose?
   a. No duty to disclose; your duties lie with the seller.
   b. No duty to disclose; the murder does not physically affect the property.
   c. You must disclose; release the listing if the seller will not allow disclosure.
   d. You must disclose; but only if the buyer directly asks about the murder.

8. What is probably the best protection for consumers in business transactions?
   a. Real Estate License Act
   b. Deceptive Trade Practices Act
   c. Statute of Frauds
   d. Nothing—every law favors big business

9. What is the primary purpose of the Deceptive Trade Practices Act?
   a. To require all contracts to be in writing so they are enforceable
   b. To require all communications to be clear and understandable
   c. To protect consumers against false business practices
   d. To allow consumers to sue real estate brokers for overpricing listings

10. What is an action that takes advantage of the lack of knowledge of a person to a grossly unfair degree?
    a. Reasonable action
    b. Punitive action
    c. Express action
    d. Unconscionable action

Appendix

Buyer Client Questions

1. Why are you thinking of buying a home?

2. Are you currently renting or do you own a home?

3. How soon do you want\have to move?

4. Have you talked to a mortgage company yet?

5. Are you working with any other brokers?

6. Have you been through any other homes in the past 90 days? Why didn't you buy?

7. Describe your dream home if money was no object.

8. What are some things that you have seen/had in past homes (say your parents' home, for instance) that you liked?

9. What things have you seen in other homes that you know you do not want to have in your home?

10. Do you have any special needs, such as room for an RV or a boat? Does your house need to be wheelchair accessible? Would you like a sewing room?

11. What would it do to your plans if you are unable to find a home you want to buy?

12. If we find the perfect home for you today, will you buy it?

Buyer Prequalification Worksheet

Date _____

Appointment Date _____ Time _____

Name _____

Family size (children) _____

Address _____

Phone Residence _____ Office _____

Husband's Employer _____

How Long _____ Income $ _____

Title or job duties _____

Wife's Employer _____

How Long _____ Income $ _____

Title or job duties _____

Expenses (contract debt 10 months or longer) $ _____

Why do you want to buy? _____

How soon do you want to move? _____

How much will your initial investment be? _____

What price home are you looking for? _____

What monthly payment would be comfortable? _____

Bedrooms _____ Baths _____ Age _____

Fireplace _____ Laundry _____ Lot Size _____

Style _____ Sq. ft. _____ Garage _____

Floor _____ Carpet _____ Built-ins _____

Drapes _____ Roof type _____ Den _____

Service Porch _____ Pool _____ Fence type _____

Patio _____ Schools _____ Handicap _____

A/C _____ Other _____ Special needs _____

Additional Buyer Questions

- Will anyone else be living in your new home?
- How many bedrooms do you need? How will you use the third bedroom?
- Is a dining room important? May I ask why?
- Are there any special features you must have in your home?
- How soon will you need possession?
- Must you sell your present home to buy another?
- Are you currently renting? When does your lease expire?
- Have you seen any homes that you liked?
- Which area is that home located in?
- Tell me what you liked best about that home?
- Was there anything you disliked?
- Did you make any written offers?
- Are you working with any other real estate agents?
- Why are you moving?
- What do you like best about your present home? What do you like least?
- Do you have any special hobbies?
- How much of your savings do you plan to invest?
- What is your present income? Do you have any other income?
- What are your current monthly expenses?
- Are you a veteran?
- Is anyone else helping you with financing?
- How large is your family? What are the ages of your children?
- How long have you been looking for a home?
- What did you and your family like about your last home?
- Are there any specific features you will require in your next home?
- With whom are you associated, Mr. Client? Where do you work, Mrs. Client?
- Are you familiar with today's procedures for purchasing a home?
- Have you decided how you would like to finance your new home?
- Would you prefer a large down payment and small monthly payments, or a small down payment with larger monthly payments?
- Can you afford what you want?

Closing Checklist

BUYER(S) NAME(S) _____

Home Address _____

Property Address _____

Telephone (H)_____ (W)_____(Fax)_____

Selling Salesperson _____ Company Office _____

Company Address _____

Telephone (H)_____ (W)_____(Fax)_____

SELLER(S) NAME(S) _____

Address _____

Telephone (H)_____ (W)_____(Fax)_____

Listing Salesperson _____ Company Office _____

Company Address _____

Telephone (H)_____ (W)_____(Fax)_____

Title Company _____ File Number _____

Representative _____ Assistant _____

Address _____

Telephone (H)_____ (W)_____(Fax)_____

Lender _____

Representative _____ Assistant _____

Address _____

Telephone (H)_____ (W)_____(Fax)_____

Loan Type _____ Loan Number _____

Down Payment _____ Points _____ Fee _____

Interest Rate _____ Term _____

Lock-in Date _____ Closing Date _____

PEST CONTROL _____ Telephone _____

HOME INSPECTION _____ Telephone _____

HOME INSURANCE AGENT _____ Telephone _____

Contracts for a For Sale by Owner

(2) Copies Each of:

1. Assumption Purchase Agreement
2. Seller Finance Purchase Agreement
3. Conventional Purchase Agreement
4. VA Purchase Agreement
5. FHA Purchase Agreement
6. Unimproved Land Purchase Agreement
7. Deed
8. Deed of trust
9. Note
10. Survey
11. Loan Estimate/Closing Disclosure forms
12. Tenancy agreement
13. Rental agreement
14. Lease/contract
15. Farm and Ranch Purchase Agreement
16. Owner's title insurance policy
17. Homeowner's insurance policy
18. Modification agreement
19. Ways to finance property
20. Questions to make your home sell faster
21. Home warranty certificate
22. Competitive market analysis
23. Mortgage information request form
24. Intent to prepay letter
25. Quote sheets from mortgage companies
26. Contract for deed
27. Clause for wrap-around mortgage
28. Special contract clause
29. Contingency clause

30. Qualification form
31. Release of earnest money from title company letter
32. Release of earnest money from a seller letter
33. Amendment for repairs form
34. Notification of intent to purchase form
35. Seller's disclosure form
36. Bill of sale
37. Meditation agreement
38. Back-up a second contract form
39. Sellers net proceeds information letter

Documentation Needed at Loan Application

- Original sales contract
- Copy of earnest money check
- W2s or 1099s for previous two years
- Pay stubs
- Tax returns
- Five-year history of past residences
- Bank statement from most recent two months checking and savings, all pages
- Credit references (current obligations), company names, addresses, account numbers, balances
- Check for appraisal fee and credit report

The documentation is usually all that you will need to furnish at application. Always keep in mind that you will probably have to provide additional documentation, or you may have to write a letter for the file explaining some financial event or discrepancy. Remember that cooperation is paramount to a speedy closing.

Fair Trade Items (Seller)

1. Market analysis
2. Estimate of net
3. Tips on making the house salable
4. Advice on timing of sale
5. Methods of new financing
6. Estimate of repairs
7. Tips on showing a home
8. Tips on advertising
9. Reasons home didn't sell
10. Area competition
11. Salability checklist
12. Comparison flow chart

Comparison of FSBO and Broker

Advantages of Selling By Owner
1. No commission.

Advantages of Selling through Real Estate Broker
1. Maximum exposure to the open market.
2. Warning before all showings.
3. Screening of potential buyers by professional real estate salespeople.
4. Feedback or reaction of prospective buyers.
5. Comparison data on other sold properties in the area (CMA).
6. Protection from professional buyers who know how to damage an unsuspecting seller.

7. Priced to sell to get the most money for the property in the least amount of time.
8. All legal forms supplied by the salesperson.
9. Best available financing methods are used with the buyers.
10. Appraisals will be handled by the real estate salesperson.
11. Escrow opened and all documents properly recorded by the title company.
12. Buyer qualified by a professional real estate mortgage officer.
13. Property not "tied-up" by unqualified buyer offers.
14. Salesperson looks after the seller's best interest.
15. Salesperson has access to show home even when seller is not at home; seller does not have to wait for customers.
16. Salesperson prequalifies potential buyers for security purposes.
17. The FSBO is obligated to let in any one who comes to the door.
18. Eliminates possibility of problems arising from a homeowner allowing a stranger to enter home.
19. Salesperson furnishes advertising aids, signs, flags, newspaper ads, and so on.
20. Seller can't afford eye-catching ads in newspaper.
21. Salesperson knows how to help potential buyers make up their minds and close the sale.

Hamilton's Rules of Real Estate

1. The first offer is always the best offer.
2. If the buyer sees a personal item of the seller, the buyer wants it, no exceptions.
3. A seller is never in a hurry until the sign goes up.
4. A lease purchase is another name for no commission.
5. The real estate agent is always wrong. Corollary: The real estate agent is always at fault.
6. A real estate agent can choose his or her hours.

7. A commission on a transaction can be $2,500 at closing (or $2.73 per hour).
8. If a transaction is full of problems, it will close; if a transaction is smooth, it never closes. (This may be confusing to some agents because they have never had a smooth transaction!)
9. Always sell your own listings; it's the only way to ensure a competent agent on the other side.
10. If you go to closing, nothing happens. If you miss a closing, the entire transaction will fall apart over a minor problem that you could have handled if you had been there.
11. The more you use time-saving technologies and strategies, the less time you seem to have.
12. Doing something is always better than doing nothing.
13. We only get paid when we put buyers and sellers together. Everything else needs to be deleted, delayed to nonproductive times, or delegated.
14. Be the source of the source of the information.
15. Use TLC—They've got to **T**rust you, and they've got to **L**ike you before you can ever **C**lose.
16. The CMA is a tool, not a weapon
17. The Internet is a marketing tool; it is not your savior.

Keys to a Smooth Closing

Communication between the real estate agent and title company is essential.

Is the Contract Complete?
1. Have you chosen the right contract for the transaction? (Conventional, FHA, VA)
   Has the earnest money check been made out properly?
   Has the earnest money check been referenced on the contract properly?

2. Have you completed the "Option Fee" section correctly? If #1 has been chosen, has the fee been collected? Is the money to be credited to the buyer at closing? (Did you check the right box?)
3. Have all parties, including agents, signed the contract?
4. IMPORTANT! For sellers, buyers, agents, and lenders: Make sure you have legible, complete addresses, email addresses and phone numbers. In addition, for sellers: if available, make sure you have forwarding addresses.
5. Have all parties initialed all changes?
6. Do you have Social Security numbers for buyers and sellers?
7. Is the marital status of buyers and sellers shown?
8. Are full names of parties shown?

Information to Provide to Title Company

1. Single/married/divorced
    a. Marital status changes?
    b. Divorce involved? If so, is it pending or final?
    c. Where was the divorce filed?

2. Estate or probate?
    a. When and where was the will probated?

3. Lender information:
    a. Existing loan information needed in order to request pay-off: names, addresses, phone numbers, loan numbers, OR seller's current lender.
    b. Second lien information when applicable.
    c. New buyer lender information (if more than one lender, include all).
    d. Don't forget to ask about pool or home improvement loans.

4. Assumption Transactions:
    a. Homeowners/hazard insurance:
       Is the seller's present insurance transferable? Is the buyer securing new insurance?
       Need names and phone numbers of insurance agents.
    b. Important papers for seller to have available for quick reference:

Payment book, insurance policy, survey, seller's title policy, copy of note, and deed.

Getting Prepared for Closing

1. Is power of attorney to be used?
   a. Notify the title company and lender immediately. Both will need to approve the use of a POA and the form.

2. Will either party be out of town at the closing and need closing documents sent/scanned to them for signature?
   a. If so, notify title company immediately.
   b. Provide the title company with overnight delivery address (no PO boxes), telephone, and fax number.

3. Does lender or the contract require repairs? Has the title company been given repair bills?

4. Are utilities involved? Does the title company have utility bills?

5. Escrow agreements/repairs
   a. Are any funds to be given to buyer or escrowed for repairs?
   b. Obtain lender approval of new loan involved and notify the title company immediately.

6. Is pest inspection required? Has the title company been given the invoice and the original inspection report for signature and submission to the lender?

7. Does the lender require a survey? Has it been ordered yet?

At the Closing Table

1. The "good funds" rule:
   a. Has the buyer/seller been notified to bring funds to closing in the form of a cashier's check (the bank can also wire funds to the title company)?

2. Proof of identity:
   a. The buyer/seller must bring photo ID to the closing.

3. Does the buyer's lender fund the day of closing (table fund)?
   a. If not, does the seller know he/she won't be getting a check today?

4. Home warranty:
   a. Has home warranty already been ordered?
   b. Have you given the title company the invoice?

5. Termite inspection:
   a. Original report and invoice must be at the title company before closing.
   b. Are there conducive conditions or treatment required or shown on the report? If so, these probably need to be treated before closing, per lender requirements. Usually the new lender required a clear report before closing and funding.

In accordance with RESPA, make sure the title company receives CDAs (Commission Disbursement Authorization) prior to closing.

21 Steps to Marketing Your House

1. Order post yard sign.
2. Put listing in MLS.
3. Notify ALL agents and brokers active in the area (broker's open house).
4. Set up a preview for all the in-house agents after weekly sales meeting.
5. Prepare professional fact sheet/brochure with color picture.
6. Canvass neighborhood for possible purchaser (mail/hand out flyers to neighbors and follow up with phone call).

7. Continue promoting to other agents and prospective buyers as the situations warrant (inquiries on similar properties).
8. Put on company website.
9. Put on personal website.
10. Around-the-clock service from trained and professional office staff.
11. Give weekly feedback on all showings and market conditions (Sunday evenings).
12. Set up, promote, and conduct professional open house (one every six weeks).
13. Reduce all purchase proposals to writing (prequalified buyers only).
14. Represent you and your interest when negotiating in a co-broker situation.
15. After contracts are signed, be sure that deposit monies are collected at the designated time period.
16. Notify MLS of contracts signed.
17. Have the "SOLD" sign installed.
18. Get buyer's mortgage application started immediately (assist buyer through mortgage process).
19. Make yourself available.
20. Arrange for and be present at any engineering, termite, radon, appraisal inspections, certificate of occupancy, and any other meetings required to close escrow and title.
21. Scan and email all documents if needed to speed up closing of title.

Net Proceeds to the Seller

Financing type: _____   Yearly taxes: _____
Date prepared: _____   Commission rate: _____
Estimated closing date: _____   County: _____

The following data is for informational purposes only, and accuracy of the figures is not guaranteed. The actual costs with respect to each transaction will vary upon the circumstances.

Description	Cost
Sale price	
First mortgage payoff	
Second mortgage payoff	
Owner's policy of title insurance	
Prepayment penalty	
Escrow fee	
Recording fees	
Deed preparation	
Loan discount points paid by seller	
Home warranty	
Buyer costs paid by seller	
Real estate commission	
Miscellaneous	
Other expenses	
Seller's settlement costs	
Prorated taxes	
Prorated insurance	
Other prorations	
Prorations for seller	
Total cost to seller	
Estimated net to seller	

Newcomer's Packet Requirements

1. General maps of the entire area
2. Examples of listings (office listings)
3. Shopping information
4. Tax information
5. Preschool/secondary, schools/colleges/universities
6. Recreation information
7. Transportation possibilities (buses, trains, carpools, airports, etc.)
8. Churches and synagogues
9. Dentist, doctors, hospitals
10. Utility information
11. Demographics (if provided, be sure the information given does not violate fair housing laws)
12. Community profile (climate/community activities)
13. Area monthly magazine (listing weekend/monthly events)
14. Area personnel agencies
15. Cover letter
16. Information on you and your company
17. Local employment agencies
18. Mortgage lenders
19. Hotels
20. Sports centers, attractions
21. State information (contact state capital)
22. Referral publications
23. Any additional information specifically requested by the referral

Open House

Trigger Card
1. May I show you through the home?
2. Do you presently live in the area?
3. Are you presently looking at property with another broker?
4. What would be the best time to show your property: weekdays or weekends?
5. Would _____ at _____ or _____ at _____ be better?
6. And what was your name?

Checklist for a Successful Open House

Be sure to call owner one week in advance for approval to hold open house.

SALES MEETINGS—One week in advance

1. Decide who will be there.
2. Write newspaper ad.
3. Can it be run in conjunction with an open extravaganza?
4. Advertise open house on company, personal, and all other available websites.

PHONE CANVASS THURSDAY—Prior to open house

1. Call/email at least 25 homes in neighborhood.
2. Call/email at least 25 from your sphere of influence.
3. Call/email ALL of your hot prospects.

Put up "OPEN SATURDAY" or "OPEN SUNDAY" rider

PERSONAL CANVASS FRIDAY of the 25 neighborhood calls

CHECK EQUIPMENT FRIDAY

1. Signs and sign riders

2. Flags

3. Open House Kit
    a. Business cards
    b. Contracts
    c. Prospect inquiry sheets and guest book
    d. Brochures
    e. Feature sheets (special features of this home)
    f. Feature 5 × 7s
    g. Brochures of other company open houses in area
    h. Real estate section of newspaper
    i. Corporate hand-outs
    j. Balloons

4. Call owner to remind him or her of ways to make home look better. Remind them that it is important for them to leave during open house.

Arrive at House 30 Minutes Before Open House

1. Plan schedule for putting up signs.

2. Set up house.
   a. Lights on
   b. Garbage out of sight
   c. Refreshments (with owner's approval)
   d. Clean sinks
   e. Put up 5 × 7 cards highlighting special features of this home
   f. Soft music

3. Be sure you have the following memorized:
   a. Taxes
   b. Down payment needed and possible financing
   c. Monthly payments based on loan amount, including taxes and insurance
   d. Lot size
   e. Inclusions and exclusions
   f. Main room sizes
   g. School district

4. Clean up when through.

5. Leave note and call owners Sunday night for end report activity

6. Post open house activities

HANDOUTS:
>Brochures and special features
>Area maps
>Company information (Sold Brochures) Coloring books and crayons
>Mortgage schedules
>Referral
>Brochures on similar homes

17 Questions that Help Your Property Sell Faster

(Answers to these questions help you get more cash for your property, in a shorter period of time, and with the greatest of ease.)

1. What is the buyer's first impression of the exterior of our house? What can I do to improve it?
2. Shall I reseed the lawn and get my landscaping in top shape?
3. Does the house or any part of the house need painting?
4. Should I replace the door mats with new ones that omit our family's name?
5. What about the screens? What about the windows?
6. Should I give my sales associate a list of things my family likes about the house and the neighborhood?
7. What is the buyer's first impression of the inside of my house? What can I do to improve it?
8. Are pets under control at all times?
9. Does the carpet need cleaning or replacing?
10. Are all appliances in good working order?
11. Should I take items out of kitchen cabinets to make them appear more spacious?
12. Do any cabinets need to be touched up or refinished?
13. Is there any furniture I could store or dispose of to make rooms appear larger?

14. Because buyers will be looking in the closets, are there clothes I can take out to make them look roomier?
15. Should I remove any item(s) that a buyer may want as part of the house?
16. Are the garage and storage areas as clean and neat as they could be?
17. Are the price and terms offered going to appeal to most of the buying public in my price range?

Information Needed for a CMA

The following are samples of questions designed to get enough information to do a market analysis of the property and to get an idea of what the seller would like to net out.

- How many bedrooms are in your house?
- Is your house brick or wood frame?
- What style of house do you own?
- Tell me about the kitchen equipment you have.
- Do you have a family room?
- Do you have a wood-burning fireplace or a gas starter?
- How many baths do you have?
- Is your outdoor patio covered?
- Do you have a wood deck?
- What type of fence is on the property?
- Do you have a security system? An Intercom?
- Do you have a garage? Will it hold one or two cars? Do you have garage door openers?
- What type of heat do you have?
- Do you have a utility room?
- What is your lot size?
- Is your street paved?
- Do you have a septic system?

- Do you have a well?
- How much is owed on your house?
- What are your monthly payments?
- To whom do you make your monthly payments? (mortgage company, land contract, other)
- What do you think your home is worth?
- When was the house built?

Again, you want to find out as much information as you can. (Questions will vary depending on your area.)

Real Estate Services

- Member of Multiple Listing Service (MLS)
- Placement of push-in stake "For Sale" sign
- Placement of post "For Sale" sign
- Presentation of the property at the local board of Realtors® meeting for any of the attending Realtors® and their buyers
- Four-color photograph with descriptions of the property to be left in the house
- Black-and-white flyer containing a photograph of the house to distribute door to door
- Graphics box installation on yard sign
- Direct mail, email, or hand-deliver information to area residents
- Direct mail, email, or hand-deliver information to personnel directors of local companies
- Direct mail, email, or hand-deliver information to buyers currently in the market
- Direct mail, email, or hand-deliver information to cooperating real estate offices
- Presentation of the property at real estate office meeting for salespeople and their buyers

- Presentation of the property at cooperating real estate office meetings
- Tours of the home for office real estate salespeople to obtain their feedback
- Broker open house for cooperating real estate offices
- Broker luncheon for cooperating real estate offices
- Public open house
- Necessary contracts provided
- Explanation of forms and contracts
- Advice for buyers making a decision about buying property
- Home warranty plan for property
- Contract negotiation when an offer comes in on property
- Showing property to prospective buyers
- Property staging to make house show better
- Real estate advice
- Broker's price opinion and Competitive Market Analysis (CMA)
- Buyer qualification
- Seller's net proceeds from the sale estimated
- Meet buyer's inspector
- Meet property appraiser
- Verify insurance endorsement for buyer
- Meet buyer for final walk-through
- Follow-up for removal of contingencies
- Register with referral company
- Advertising
  - Main newspaper
  - Billboard
  - Bus stop benches
- Internet listing
- Copies of keys
- Lockbox
  - Electronic lockbox
  - Combination lockbox
- Prepare property profile book
- Telemarketing
- Set up buyer for purchase loan
- Set up property for title work
- Deliver your check at closing

Scripts for All Occasions

I have found the following scripts to be useful over the years. It's important, however, for you to feel good about the scripts you use, so modify them according to your personality and situation. If a script is not approved by your real estate commission, your broker, your manager, or your association of REALTORS®, do not use it.

I use the terms "Mr. and Mrs." regardless of whom I am conversing with to avoid showing favoritism and directing my attention to only one person. If only one of your customers gives an objection, you should address the script to that individual first and then to the other person. I also use the word "salesperson" throughout instead of "real estate professional" since the two are interchangeable.

Scripts for Overcoming Seller's Objections over the Telephone

Don't Like Real Estate Salespeople

Seller:
"We don't believe you can help."

Salesperson:
"If I were to show you how you could save time and money and get your house sold, would you be interested?"

Commission

Seller:
"We don't want to pay the commission."

Salesperson:
"And I would not want to pay a commission, either. I don't want to pay to get my taxes done, but I do. And what I

have found out is that my accountant actually saves me money because he finds deductions I never would have known. Doesn't it make sense to have me come out and at least see if I can sell your house and save you money while doing it?"

Seller:
"What is the industry's standard commission fee?" OR "What do you charge as a commission?" OR "Acme Realty said they would do it for less commission; will you?"

Salesperson:
"What I charge for a commission is based on the level of difficulty of selling the house. I can't determine that until I have actually seen the house. I could stop by at 2 p.m. or 5 p.m. if that would work for you."

Pricing

Seller:
"What do you think my house is worth?"

Salesperson:
"Well, I haven't seen your house, but I am available now or would later this afternoon be better to evaluate your house?"

Have a Friend in the Business

Seller:
"We will be selling through a friend in the business."

Salesperson:
"Great, let me ask you this: Doesn't it make sense to see what is offered by more than one company so you can make the best decision possible for you and your family? If it is with the friend then, great, you haven't lost anything. Now, I am

available at 4 p.m. or would 5 p.m. be better to show you our marketing concepts?"

Try FSBO

Seller:
"We are thinking of selling by ourselves for a while."

Salesperson:
"Are you prepared for all of the obstacles that could occur?"

Seller:
"Like what?"

Salesperson:
"Tell you what, I can come by and share a little about marketing a house and while I am there show you some things to be prepared for if you do want to try selling it yourself. Do you see how this can help you?"

No Hurry

Seller:
"We are in no hurry to sell."

Salesperson:
"Why are you selling?"

Seller:
"Because I am being transferred to Seattle in four months."

Salesperson:
"Did you know four months might not be enough time to sell the house?"

Seller:
"What do you mean?"

Salesperson:
"There is the marketing time, the processing time, and the closing time just to mention a few. I'll tell you what I can do. I can stop by and share with you a step-by-step walk-through of a real estate sale to give you an idea of timing. May I do that?"

Scripts for Overcoming Expired Seller's Objections over the Telephone

Try FSBO

Seller:
"We are going to sell it ourselves."

Salesperson:
"Understood. Do you mind if I stop by and give you some ideas to help make the selling process go more smoothly?"

Marketing

Seller:
"What makes you think you can sell it if the previous real estate salesperson couldn't?" OR "Why didn't you sell it while it was listed the last time?"

Salesperson:
"I am sure I can show you what it will take to sell your property, but I haven't seen it yet. I can be available in about an hour or will 6 p.m. be better to view the property?"

Scripts for Overcoming FSBO Seller's Objections over the Telephone

Don't Need a Broker

Seller:
"I don't think you can help us. We're doing fine so far. We just put it on the market."

Salesperson:
"Mr. Seller, it sounds like you've made up your mind about not using a real estate broker. Is that right?"

Seller:
"Yes."

Salesperson:
"Why is that, Mr. Seller?"

Seller:
"Well, I think I can do it myself."

Salesperson:
"So, in other words, you're not averse to paying a commission. You just feel 'If I can do it myself, I'll do it,' correct? Or, is it the commission?"

Seller:
"Well, we sold our last home by ourselves. I don't see any problem doing it again this time."

Salesperson:
"So, let me see if I understand: Are you saying you're not averse to paying a commission if I had a buyer?"

Seller:
"Not if you had a buyer."

Salesperson:
"Why are you trying to sell it by yourself?"

Seller:
"Well, a few years ago, when we sold our house, we originally had it listed with a Realtor®, and they didn't do anything. They just left us out to dry. I swore that I would never use a Realtor® again. So, we put it on the market ourselves and it sold."

Salesperson:
"How do you like selling your own house?"

Seller:
"Well I'd rather be playing golf."

Salesperson:
"We'll, let me ask you something. If I could help get you out on the golf course by doing three things: (1) getting you your money, (2) guaranteeing that if you shake my hand I'll get the job done, and (3) help you get into that new house in plenty of time, would you talk to me?"

Seller:
"Yes, if you could do all those things, I'd talk to you."

Salesperson:
"Well, let's do this: Find a time when I could stop over and take a look at your house. While I'm there, I'll do those three things for you, Mr. Seller. First of all, I'll prove to you that when we take a property, we sell it because of our marketing system. Second, I'll show you how I can get you out with more money than you can get yourself. And third, I'll assure you that I can coordinate the sale from beginning to end, so that you can buy the new home. The end result is you're on the golf course, I'm doing all the work, and you get the money. That's what you want, isn't it? So, should I come at 5:30 p.m., or would you like me to come a little later to see your property?"

Seller:

"I wasted six months with a real estate salesperson who did nothing. Not one offer. I can do a better job myself."

Salesperson:

"From what you've told me, I don't think that your salesperson did very much to market the property. I can show you my comprehensive marketing plan for the property with deadlines of when I'll complete each phase. That will make a huge difference. I am available now or would tonight be better?"

Lease It Buy It

Seller:

"Are you planning to buy it?"

Salesperson:

"No, I'm not. But I may find a client who is looking in that area and price range. I may want to show it to them. Would 3:00 tomorrow be okay for me to drop by?"

Seller:
"Why?"

Salesperson:

"I try to be very professional, and it's embarrassing for me to drive by your home with a client and not be able to tell them all about your house. I want to know as much as I can about the areas I'm showing homes in. May I drop by tomorrow at 4:00 to see your home or would 6:30 be better?"

Pricing

Seller:
"We are selling our home ourselves."

Salesperson:
"I understand. I am not calling to list your home. I would like to offer you a service free of charge that may prove to be a benefit to you. When a buyer places an offer on your home, odds are great that they, too, will have a home to sell. As a service to you and your buyer, I will prepare a market analysis on your buyer's home, which will show estimated market time and estimated net proceeds. This is information you would want, isn't it?"

Seller:
"Yes, but why would you do that?"

Salesperson:
"By providing this service, it is my hope that your buyer will give me the opportunity to compete for his or her business. May I come by and show you an example of a market analysis and estimated closing cost sheet that I have prepared on another property?"

Seller:
"Yes."

Close for an Appointment

Seller:
"No, just put it in the mail."

Salesperson:
"I could do that; however, I would like to go over the market analysis form with you. Perhaps tomorrow at 4 p.m. or would 6 be more convenient?"

Friend in Business

Seller:
"If we list it, it will be with our friend."

Salesperson:
"I'm glad you have an agent in mind; however, I show a lot of homes in your neighborhood and like to be familiar with all that are for sale. It's good business for both you and me if, when I drive by your home with a client, I can say, 'That home has three bedrooms, two baths, a lovely kitchen area. It is selling for $300,000.' My clients may wish to see your home. I can only do that if I have seen the home. Does that make sense?"

Commission

Salesperson:
"Why aren't you using a broker? I'm just curious."

Seller:
"Well if we want to get in the other house, we have to get every penny we can out of this one. And, if we had to pay a commission, I'm not so sure we could even do it."

Salesperson:
"So, it isn't a matter of you being against using a broker? You just need all the extra money you can get. Am I hearing you right?"

Seller:
"We don't have anything against using a Realtor®, no."

Salesperson:
"In other words, if the money were the same, you'd use a broker?"

Seller:
"I suppose if the money were the same, yes, I'd consider it."

Salesperson:
"Okay, then let's do this. Many times I find when I look at a property, for one reason or another, I'm able to get a seller

more money than he or she can get selling it alone. And I have a dozen different ways of doing that. Why don't I find a time when I can stop and look at your home? While I'm there, I'll let you know what I think I can honestly get you out with. One of two things is going to happen: Either it's not going to be enough money and you're going to ask me to leave, or you're going to get as much as you can get for yourself and you'll ask me to handle the sale. Does that sound fair to you? Now, I can't make it over to look at your property until probably later this evening, or I'm open tomorrow evening too. Which would be best for you?"

Salesperson:
"Selling your house yourself may seem like a money saver, but surveys say that homes sold by real estate professionals gross more dollars than those sold by the owners. So even with my commission, you'll do less work and probably come out with more money."

Scripts for Overcoming Seller's Objections at the Listing Appointment

Overpricing

Seller:
"Another real estate salesperson will list it for a higher price."

Salesperson:
"Why do you feel the other salesperson would do that? Maybe the other salesperson is trying to 'buy' your listing. Mr. and Mrs. Seller, do you know what I mean when I say 'buy' a listing? It is when a real estate salesperson tells the seller what the seller wants to hear so the seller will list with them. Then later, the salesperson hammers the seller for a price reduction after it is too late. Mr. and Mrs. Seller, I would like to tell you what it will take to sell your house. Will you let me do that?"

Salesperson:

"Mr. and Mrs. Seller, don't choose a broker based on price. Please do me and, more importantly, yourselves, a big favor by not selecting a broker based on who comes in here with the highest price. Remember that we're talking about your asking price, not our bid. A real estate salesperson coming in here with a price higher than the market will allow isn't offering to buy at that price. All of us have the same records; we're all Multiple Listing brokers. If you decide not to follow the market and price your house higher, I can do that too. And I'll back you 100 percent. I may not want to do it because I want to solve your problem. You have a need to sell here, so I may fight you a little bit on price. But please don't choose me based on pricing. Choose me for my professionalism, for my integrity, for my willingness to work, for my know-how, and for my honesty. The pricing we can work out."

Seller:

"My home is worth more than you want to list it for."

Salesperson:

"Mr. Seller, on what facts are you basing your price decision?" [Now listen to what the seller has to say.]

Salesperson:

"Mr. Seller, let us look at our Market Analysis." *[Emphasize the 'for sale' to show the competition and then the 'sold' to show the value. If the seller still feels their house is worth more, continue . . .]*

Salesperson:

"Mr. and Mrs. Seller, my job is to find a buyer who will pay top dollar for your house . . . perhaps you know something I am not aware of. What information do you have that leads you to believe that a qualified buyer will pay that much for your house?"

Salesperson:

"Mr. and Mrs. Seller, that is your decision to make, and I assure you that we will work very hard to get that amount for you. But I do want you to understand that no matter what you and I think your house is worth, the buyers are the ones that really decide the value of a house. You can't get any more for your house than a buyer is willing to pay. Someone looking at your house will view it in comparison to similar houses on the market. If we want to attract them to your house, we have to compete with the rest of the market."

Salesperson:
"Before you do that, consider this: Houses can get a reputation, usually within the first 30 days of their time on the market. After sales associates see an overpriced house in the Multiple Listing Service for two to three weeks, most will brand it negatively and won't show it. Even after the price is reduced, the notion persists that there is something wrong with the house. Let's not lose the impact of that first very important impression; it could make a lot of difference."

Seller:
"Don't you think we could get just a little more for it?"

Salesperson:
"Let me ask you this: Is that the only thing that's really bothering you at this point? That you want to get more for the house?"

Seller:
"Yes, that's it."

Salesperson:
"Remember when we discussed viewing your house as a product and how it's important that the product be priced competitively in order to sell?"

Seller:
"Yes."

Salesperson:
"I know that you need to be moved in four months. The figures I've shared with you about pricing are based on the prices of comparable houses in the neighborhood. If you price it too

high, it won't sell. All it will do is generate a flow of buyers who will look at it and purchase other properties."

Seller:
"Hmmm."

Salesperson:
"We'd all like to get more for our house, but I think you'd agree that based on the facts of record, this really is the right range for you."

Salesperson:
"I certainly want you to get as much for your house as possible. In fact, that is my job. But I don't want you to miss out on a buyer because of the listing price. It's true you can always come down later if your home doesn't move at $400,000, but there is also the danger that if you don't take advantage of the buyers presently waiting for a house like yours to come on the market, a later reduction won't solve the psychological stigma that will have surrounded your house."

Salesperson:
"It is your decision to make, but my professional opinion is that we should get as close as possible to your competitors' prices. How about putting your house on the market at a price closer to the other properties currently available?"

Seller:
"Another real estate firm said they could get me more for my home."

Salesperson:
"Did that salesperson show you a detailed Comparative Market Analysis of houses like yours, in this area, selling for that price recently? If you talk to enough people, I'm sure you will find someone who will take your listing at most any price. There is probably no limit on how high you could go and still find someone who will take your listing."

Salesperson:
"Sellers sometimes feel it is best to list with the real estate person who claims to be able to get the highest price. Actually, the best way to get top price is to be the most competitively priced house in your market, thus attracting the largest number of buyers. It's exposure to the largest number of qualified buyers that brings top offers, not an inflated asking price."

Salesperson:
"Mr. and Mrs. Seller, buyers determine how much you get for your house, not the real estate salespeople. All we can do is offer our opinions as to what buyers might be willing to pay. Sometimes salespeople will be overly optimistic about your house's value because of their desire to get your listing. I don't feel this is a service to you, and I don't think you do either. The Competitive Market Analysis on your house shows us what buyers have been paying for similar houses, doesn't it? Taking this into consideration, what do you feel your house will honestly bring?"

Salesperson:
"Let's try reversing positions, Mr. and Mrs. Seller, and look at your property from the standpoint of the buyer. We will pretend that you are that buyer and, for purposes of comparison, let us say there are six or seven other properties on the market of equal value to yours and just as desirable. Assume that I have shown you five of these: You like them all, and you are having a hard time deciding which one to select. However, one is priced at $275,000, another at $270,000, a third at $262,500, the fourth at $260,000, and the last at $252,500. All things being equal, which house would you choose?" *[Obviously, the seller would have to admit that his best choice would be the one priced at $252,500.]*

Salesperson:
"Mr. and Mrs. Seller, they can all be purchased for $250,000. The house priced closest to the market value will sell first in every case. Now, you say you want to sell, not have your

property used as a comparison to sell others, so why don't we start at $252,500?" *[If the seller remains adamant and refuses to lower the price, repeat how the Multiple Listing Service works and how you propose to induce other real estate salespeople to become interested in the sale of his property. Use the following dialog when doing so.]*

Salesperson:
"Mr. and Mrs. Seller, almost all of my listings sell quickly because I work harder than most salespeople to make this happen. Every Tuesday morning, I am at our weekly office meeting, along with many other top salespeople from my office. The average salesperson doesn't make an effort to attend these meetings. Next Tuesday I intend to place extra emphasis on the salability of your property when I talk about it. There are hundreds of other properties listed on the Multiple Listing Service, and I have found that it takes an extra effort to encourage other salespeople to look at and show one particular listing over another. I have excellent rapport and a good reputation with these other top salespeople, and they know when I talk about a listing, it will be one that is worth looking into. These top salespeople will jot down your address and possibly come by to see your property. The point is this, Mr. and Mrs. Seller: I cannot talk about an overpriced listing. If I do, the other salespeople will soon see my offerings as unrealistic, and they will not bother to write down the address, much less look at and show the property. Further, every salesperson knows that when I place a property on the office tour, it is a salable listing. Mr. and Mrs. Seller, please don't frustrate my attempt to put your property before every possible buyer. Give me the flexibility to talk about it with enthusiasm and get these other people to work on it with the same enthusiasm, as I am sure they will, if it is priced right. Let's set the listing at $250,000, or at the highest $252,500."

Seller:
"Let's price it higher at first, and we can come down on the price later."

Salesperson:
"I realize, Mr. and Mrs. Seller, that this approach to the problem does sound reasonable at first; the difficulty is that this practice tends to discourage those buyers who are now in the market for a home like yours. If you will remember our previous discussion, a high percentage of the properties we sell are sold during the first week of the exposure period. The mistake most homeowners make is to overprice the property at the beginning. When your home first comes on the market, it will be seen by many salespeople; if they feel the property is priced right for their prospective buyers, they will hasten to show it. Now, if either the salesperson or their prospects are discouraged by the price, no offers will be presented. Once we exhaust these buyers who are immediately available and interested in purchasing, we must start the long drawn-out process of advertising and looking for possible new buyers. This is what happens to most listings taken by salespeople who do not know what they are doing. A listing that stays on the market for a long time becomes shop worn, just like the merchandise in a store that has been picked over by many shoppers. The greatest opportunity for the sale of your home is when it first comes on the market. For this reason, I strongly recommend it being listed at a price of no more than $250,000." *[Now is the opportune time to talk about the amount of cash to be derived from the sale of the property at $250,000. If this amount is sufficient to meet the seller's needs in the purchase of another home, then you have taken his attention away from something he dislikes and focused it on something acceptable.]*

Salesperson:
"Mr. and Mrs. Seller, if I were interested only in getting a listing and tying up your property for 180 days, I would write it up at $275,000 or even $300,000. However, let's look at what would happen if I did so. Our Multiple Listing Service keeps very accurate statistics on properties sold. Those statistics show that when a property is listed above its market value, there is only slim chance that it will sell within a 90-day period. Now the point is this: No matter which price between the high of

$300,000 and the low of $250,000 the property is listed, it will sell eventually for no more than $250,000.

"Mr. and Mrs. Seller, there are no foolish buyers in the market. It may be that, if you list at the figure I suggest, a buyer who considers him- or herself a 'smart operator' will try you out with a lesser offer, but he will buy at $250,000. You say you want to sell—then I propose that we go after 100 percent of all buyers immediately with a $250,000 price, or at most—$252,500." [By concentrating on each property individually in comparison with the seller's house, you will eventually arrive at a figure very close to the true market value of his home as shown on the Competitive Market Analysis, which should be $250,000. You can now quote this directly to the owner, and at the same time draw comparisons of speculative price and term price in relation to market value, somewhat in the following manner.]

Salesperson:
"Based on these figures, Mr. and Mrs. Seller, I would say that your property should sell for right around $250,000, if we have an average buyer with an average down payment." *[If the seller has been convinced and answers your question directly, then your job of appraising is complete. If, on the other hand, they don't answer directly by saying, "Well, we still want more," then you still have a selling job on your hands. At this point, continue to ask questions and look for a break in the sellers' armor so that you might come to an agreement on price.]*

Company Too Large (or Small)

Seller:
"We don't like large companies. They are too impersonal."

Salesperson:
"Yes, Mr. and Mrs. Seller, I understand how you feel. It's not a comfortable feeling to imagine yourself to be just a number, is it? But wouldn't it be really great to do business with a locally owned company with salespeople who are all your neighbors

and still get the same national exposure that the largest corporations get?"

Salesperson:
"I understand. It seems what you're concerned with is whether my company can effectively market your home, correct? Let's review the marketing plan. Please stop me at any part that you don't understand."

Better Services/More Services

Seller:
"Acme Real Estate Company has better advertising than you do."

Salesperson:
"Mr. and Mrs. Seller, did you know that advertising only gets your home sold approximatcly two percent of the time? We offer a 21-point marketing plan to get your house sold. Let's take a look at it."

Salesperson:
"My office orchestrates a comprehensive marketing campaign designed to prompt potential buyers to call our office. This flow of buyers through the office can mean more potential buyers for your property and a greater chance of getting the right price for your property."

Salesperson:
"Mr. and Mrs. Seller, our company spends a great deal of money each year on national advertising. How does that benefit you? We are poised to have the strongest marketing campaign in the real estate industry, which in turn provides us the ability to capture interested buyers in the properties we market. What do those buyers do when they decide to buy? They call our office. Don't you think it would be prudent to have your property listed with the office that is getting all of those buyer calls?"

Seller:
"Acme Real Estate Company has more services than you do."

Salesperson:
"Really? What did they offer you that I failed to mention?" *[Virtually every service the seller was offered you can do too.]*

Seller:
"Will you advertise our property in the local newspaper every week?"

Salesperson:
"We have an ongoing advertising program, and your house will certainly be part of that marketing campaign until it sells. What we use in our office is . . ." *[Describe some specific things your office does, such as advertise in the newspaper, home guides, on television, and so on.]*

Seller:
"Will you hold our house open every weekend?"

Salesperson:
"Open houses can generate a flow of buyers, but rarely do those buyers purchase the specific house they saw open. Why don't we give my marketing campaign 30 days to produce results? Then if it doesn't, we can consider an open house."

Seller:
"We want you present at all showings."

Salesperson:
"What we have done in the real estate industry is cooperate. This means that a professional licensed real estate salesperson will escort each and every buyer that wants to view your property. This protects your house from the wrong people. It also allows me the time to actively market your house to get more people through."

Appendix 453

Seller:
"We don't want a lockbox because it will be inconvenient."

Salesperson:
"I understand your concern, but remember: It's important to be competitive. And being competitive means not only pricing the property properly and getting it ready to show, but also making it accessible to salespeople who may be working with the best buyer. How about if we use a lockbox and at times when you are there and don't want to be disturbed, you use your deadbolt or chain lock. Are you comfortable with that?"

Seller:
"We don't want a lockbox because we were once robbed."

Salesperson:
"Considering the problem you had with the robbery, it seems like there's really only a couple of alternatives. Either I can keep a key in the office and only give it out to licensed real estate salespeople who will show your property, or you will need to make arrangements to be here with a 10-minute notice anytime the property is going to be shown. Which will work best for you?"

Seller:
"We don't want a sign in our yard."

Salesperson:
"This is the most widely recognized yard sign in the real estate business. Buyers know it without ever being close enough to read it. This can mean more potential buyers for you. This is important since the largest number of potential buyers do come from yard signs."

Seller:
"We don't want a sign in our yard."

Salesperson:
"Is that the only thing we need to address?"

Seller:
"Yes."

Salesperson:
"I'm sure you have a very good reason. May I ask why?"

Seller:
"Because we don't want the neighbors to know we're moving. What would be the benefit to the neighbors knowing?"

Salesperson:
"In other words your neighbors will know your house is for sale, is that right?"

Seller:
"Right."

Salesperson:
"I understand how you feel, and you don't want them to know. However, they could be a major source of buyers for us. Your neighbors will want someone to move in that will be a good neighbor; they might know of someone interested right now. Since the neighbors can actually help us sell your home, let's put the yard sign up and enlist their help from day one."

Seller:
"We don't want a sign in our yard because we don't want our neighbors to know we have to sell."

Salesperson:
"I can understand why you want to keep your move from some of your neighbors. But you know, last year a great deal of the buyer inquiries into my office were generated by 'For Sale' signs. It's one of our most powerful tools for finding your best buyer. Without the sign, you limit your exposure in the marketplace, which means fewer potential buyers and ultimately, a longer time to sell. Buyers sometimes look in neighborhoods for houses, and if a 'For Sale' sign is not up,

they could pass it up. Also real estate salespeople need to be able to find the house easily when they are showing property."

Seller:
"We don't want a sign in front of our house because we are nervous about security."

Salesperson:
"I understand your concern about the sign. Security is not to be taken lightly, but the biggest producers of potential buyers that we have are from 'For Sale' signs. I wonder if we can find another way to work with the sign. I can certainly distribute flyers about your house. We can also use bulletin boards in the community to give it exposure. I wonder, though, would you be willing to have a portable sign that you just put out when you're home and take down when you go away? Would that make you feel more comfortable?"

Friend in Business

Seller:
"We have a friend in the business."

Salesperson:
"Mr. and Mrs. Seller, if you were convinced that another real estate professional could actually get you more money in the timeframe that is best for you, with the least inconvenience, would you still be committed to giving the listing to your friend?"

Salesperson:
"Tell me, do you feel an obligation because of the friendship or because you believe your friend will actually be able to get you the most money in the timeframe you desire with the least inconvenience?"

Salesperson:
"Mr. and Mrs. Seller, you owe me nothing, but you owe yourself the very best. In the real estate industry, 80 percent

of the property is sold by 20 percent of the salespeople. You have a tough decision to make, no matter who you hire to protect the equity you have built up in your home. One of us will be disappointed. Be sure you're not disappointed too."

Salesperson:
"Most sellers believe a house will sell for X amount of dollars, regardless of who sells it. That is not so. Statistically, real estate professionals can get more money for property than private sellers can, and some real estate people consistently get more for homes than other real estate people. Look at my record in the area."

Salesperson:
"I know just how you feel. Friendships are certainly valuable. Think a minute about your friend. We all know the old adage about not doing business with friends or relatives. By asking your friend to market your property, you put him in a delicate position. As your friend, he would be hesitant to give suggestions that might improve the marketing conditions of your property because he doesn't want to take a chance on hurting your feelings. It's very difficult to be objective when we are emotionally involved with an obligation of friendship. Actually, your friend might be relieved to have you list the home with someone more objective and not be placed in the position of being your employee. Your home is an important investment, and you certainly want to protect that investment by putting it the hands of an objective professional. Listing on the basis of friendship only sometimes proves costly in the sale and in the friendship as well. Certainly, it is something you should consider very carefully."

Seller:
"If we do list, we've got a friend in the real estate business."

Salesperson:
"Sure, when were you planning on listing?"

Seller:
"Probably in another couple of months."

Salesperson:
"If I could show you how I could perhaps do the same good job for you, but put more money in your pocket than your friend could, would you consider doing business with a *new* friend?"

Thinking of Going FSBO

Seller:
"I can sell my home without using a real estate professional."

Salesperson:
"Mr. and Mrs. Seller, at any given time there are a certain number of people in the market for a home who are well qualified and serious about buying a home. Do you agree? They look in the newspaper and discover that 91 percent of the homes for sale are in the hands of real estate professionals and only nine percent are for sale through private sellers. Tell me Mr. Seller, if real estate professionals have over 90 percent of the houses for sale, where do the serious, qualified buyers go? That leaves the private seller with bargain hunters, unqualified buyers, and weekend hobby lookers. That is the reason our company has sold so many homes in this market. We can expose your property to the greatest number of qualified buyers. Do you see how, by attracting the largest number of serious, qualified buyers to look at your home, we can help you net top dollar?"

Salesperson:
"Mr. and Mrs. Seller, tell me something. What is the number one advantage you hope to gain in selling your home directly to a private buyer? Save the real estate fee for service, is that right? Mr. and Mrs. Seller, put yourself in the buyer's shoes. What is the number one advantage to you as a buyer in buying direct from an owner? The number one advantage is to save the same commission you hope to save as a seller, isn't that so? Mr. and Mrs. Seller, can you see any possible difficulties you

may have in trying to save the real estate service fee? Research shows private sellers net four to six percent less by selling their home 'By Owner' than by selling through a real estate professional and paying a fee for service."

Salesperson:
"Mr. and Mrs. Seller, there are serious buyers, qualified buyers, and potential buyers. A potential buyer is anyone who might buy. A qualified buyer can buy. A serious buyer wants to buy. There are qualified buyers who are not serious and serious buyers who are not qualified. So the only kind of buyer that counts is a serious, qualified buyer. We in the real estate industry have well over 90 percent of the inventory of the homes for sale. Where do you suppose the serious, qualified buyers are likely to go to find a home? They will go to the professionals in real estate. Isn't that right?"

Seller:
"I don't want to list, but I will pay you a commission if you bring me a contract."

Salesperson:
"I understand how you feel. However, our company doesn't consider that fair to you. You shouldn't pay us for doing less than our best for you. Everybody's business is nobody's business. If we accept an open listing from you, you will be expecting action from us that we just can't give. When we accept the responsibility of finding the right buyer for your property, we are licensed and trained to accept the full responsibility of acting as your agent and using all our contacts and professional marketing tools to do that job. We have an obligation to all the owners who list their property in the Multiple Listing System to give exposure to their properties. We would violate the best interest of those owners to try to find a buyer for your unlisted property over theirs."

Seller:
"We have several people who are interested in the property, and we want to give them the time to make up their minds."

Salesperson:
"I understand how you feel. It seems there are often people who are interested in a property who are simply not qualified to buy it. Of course, it is difficult for you to find out about their financial capability, especially if they are friends. Yet, you must be careful not to limit your chances for a sale by keeping the property off the market for people who are not financially qualified to pay the top value. Mr. and Mrs. Seller, I suggest that you call the prospects and tell them the property is listed. If they are sincere prospects and they are qualified to buy, they will be motivated to draw up a contract immediately. If they are not serious, you need to know that now. We can exclude them from the listing agreement for one week."

Seller:
"We want to try a little longer ourselves."

Salesperson:
"Mr. and Mrs. Seller, how much longer will you wait? Do you agree that if you don't sell it in that time, we would be the company that can do the job for you? I'll be checking back with you in a week or two to see how things are going."

Seller:
"We want to sell by ourselves."

Salesperson:
"Why do you want to sell it yourself?"

Seller:
"I feel I can do the same job as a real estate salesperson."

Salesperson:
"What's your specific motivation for wanting to do the work yourself?"

Seller:
"I can save the commission for myself."

Salesperson:
"If I could show you how I could get you as much money as you could get yourself, would you be interested?"

Salesperson:
"Mr. and Mrs. Seller, if you expect to save the commission by selling at the fair market value, what do you think the buyer's attitude will be about this? Don't you think that they are also counting on saving the commission by dealing directly? Surely they are going to offer you a price minus the commission, and perhaps, an even larger discount for the property than your asking price. Otherwise, why would they be dealing with you? In contrast, wouldn't it be better to employ a skillful negotiator to work on your behalf, one who does this sort of thing every day and is being paid to have your interests at heart? If you will list your property for sale with us at its fair market value, we can use our skills and techniques acquired through experience to convince any buyer that he or she should pay the full fair market value."

Salesperson:
"Mr. and Mrs. Seller, if you try to sell the property yourself, you will have hundreds of people in the real estate business as your competitors; but if you list your property with us, you will have these same people working on your side to try to find a buyer. We are members of the Multiple Listing Service, and we are all pledged to work together."

Commission

Seller:
"The Acme Real Estate Company charges less commission."

Salesperson:
"Mr. and Mrs. Seller, I can see how a lower fee for service might sound good to you, but I don't believe it is in your best interest. Our company's fee is based on the amount of time and the kind of marketing it will take to sell your property. I

have demonstrated the marketing my company has to offer. What is Acme Real Estate Company offering?"

Seller:
"I want to negotiate your commission."

Salesperson:
"Fine, did you want to pay six, seven, or eight percent?" *[Explain the value of offering a higher commission to the selling real estate salesperson in the form of a bonus. Explain how a fee is split between the listing and the selling real estate companies and salespeople. Include cost of marketing, and so on.]*

Seller:
"Will you list my house for less commission?"

Salesperson:
"No. Any other questions?"

Seller:
"If we buy our next house from you, will you cut your commission on the sale of this house?"

Salesperson:
"The marketing of this house should not be contingent on the purchase of your next house. My services are complete as a seller's real estate professional and as a buyer's real estate professional. You do not want to limit my ability to get your house sold."

Seller:
"If my house sells in a week, will you cut your commission?"

Salesperson:
"Sometimes it happens like that. In those cases, what you find is that it didn't take just a week to sell the house; it probably took six months. Those are buyers who've been out in the marketplace, seen the house they wanted several times, and missed it, or they may have come in too low for a house they

wanted. Those buyers are ready. When they see the right house, they're going to buy it. Now, if I can find those buyers in one week's time, I believe I've done my job. Wouldn't you agree?"

Seller:
"Acme Real Estate Company will take my listing and sell it for a percentage less. Why won't you?"

Salesperson:
"Mr. and Mrs. Seller, Acme Real Estate Company knows the worth of its own efforts. My company and I will spend a great deal of time, effort, and know-how in the merchandising of your property, for which we expect to get paid. It will be worth your while to pay a little more and get the best service available than to save a little and perhaps suffer a greater loss in the long run! Believe me, Mr. and Mrs. Seller, we also know our worth, and we expect to give more than the value received!"

Wait to Make a Decision

Seller:
"We want to think it over."

Salesperson:
"Certainly, Mr. and Mrs. Seller. May I ask if there is anything in particular that is bothering you?"

Salesperson:
"I understand how you feel. Many people I work with feel the same way. In fact I've been in the same situation and felt exactly the same way. But what you are really telling me is that you have questions you still need to have answered before you go ahead. Isn't that correct?"

Salesperson:
"I can understand that. Selling your home is an important decision. Please help me understand. What is it that you need to think about?" *[After clarifying, respond to the actual concern.]*

Salesperson:
"Selling your home is an important decision. Just to clarify my own thinking, what is it that you're concerned about?" *[After clarifying, respond to the actual concern.]*

Seller:
"We'd like to sell, but we are going to hold off for a few months until . . ."

Salesperson:
"I can see why you would want to wait, but there might be some disadvantages to putting it off until later, if you know you're going to be making a move soon. Right now interest rates and the money supply are good. Within a short time a lot of homes will be coming on the market, and you will have to compete with them for a buyer. You also have to consider that it will take at least a few weeks to find a buyer for your home and secure financing. Doesn't it make sense to make the decision to sell now rather than later?"

Seller:
"We want to sell, but we want to wait."

Salesperson:
"No problem. How long were you planning to wait?"

Seller:
"Probably a couple of months."

Salesperson:
"Why were you thinking of waiting?"

Seller:
"We thought there would be more houses on the market in the spring."

Salesperson:
"Well, that's true. Let me ask you this. If I could show you how you might be able to put an extra thousand dollars in your

pocket by perhaps moving your plans up a little bit, would you consider at least talking with me about it?" *[Now you have to demonstrate the drawbacks to waiting.]*

Seller:
"We would like to think it over first."

Salesperson:
"I understand that this is a difficult decision. Are you wanting to think about the marketing of the home?"

Seller:
"No, the marketing is fine."

Salesperson:
"Is it our company that you want to think about?"

Seller:
"No, we like your company."

Salesperson:
"Is it me? Do you like and trust me?"

Seller:
"Of course, we like you."

Big Pause, then slowly . . .

Salesperson:
"Is it the price?" *[Generally the biggest objection from a seller is price.]*

Seller:
"Well, you know, it is less than we wanted to get."

Salesperson:
"I remember, let me ask you, if we could agree upon a price, would you list with me tonight?"

Seller:
"Well, I appreciate what you said. It's really interesting, but I need to think about it."

Salesperson:
"I can understand that. It's an awfully big decision. But just so I'm clear, will you tell me what it is that you need to think about?"

Seller:
"Oh, I don't know. I'm just sort of unsure."

Salesperson:
"Well, was it my marketing plan? Did you like what I had to say about how I'm going to market your house?"

Seller:
"Yes, I did. That was terrific."

Salesperson:
"Is the fee bothering you?"

Seller:
"No. Not really."

Salesperson:
"Is it the price?"

If the sellers would happen to say, "We want to pray about it," I choose not to handle this objection. I am very leery about challenging religious beliefs. Two of my friends have done so in the past and the following shows the results:

Scenario 1:

Seller:
"We want to pray about it."

Salesperson:
"Exactly, don't you think God sent me here tonight?"

Seller:
"Get out!"

Scenario 2:

Seller:
"We want to pray about it."

Salesperson:
"Fine, let's bow our heads."

Seller:
"Get out!"

Not what I call great results. I am not making a judgment here; I just choose not to counter this kind of objection. And that is the beauty of this business—choice.

Buy First

Seller:
"We don't want to put our home on the market until we find another home we like."

Salesperson:
"I realize your dilemma, Mr. and Mrs. Seller, but on the other hand, can you afford to buy a new home without first selling this one? Every homeowner faces this problem, but I assure you, I've never had a seller who had to move out into the street. I have to time the sale of your present home and the purchase of a new one so they coincide as closely as possible. The only way you can do that is to give your home exposure on the market while you're looking for another house. We can always arrange a possession date to insure that you have a home to move into. The opposite side of the coin is that you

find a home you want, but you aren't in a position to buy it because you don't have an offer on your present home. Then, while you try to sell your home, you take the risk of someone else buying the home you want. I'm sure you wouldn't want that to happen, would you?"

Seller:
"We don't want to put our home on the market until we find a place to move."

Salesperson:
"Yes, you certainly have to have a place to live. If I could show you how you could put your house on the market now and still have time to find another place to live, would you list with me tonight?"

Don't Like Salespeople

Seller:
"We don't want anything to do with real estate people."

Salesperson:
"I understand how you feel. In years past, and unfortunately, even today to a limited degree, there are salespeople who may not have had the benefit of thorough training and knowledge necessary to give the professional service you need to successfully sell your property. It is even true that the most common complaint about a real estate salesperson is, 'He listed my house, and I never heard another thing from him.' Fortunately, we have learned from others' mistakes. Our firm builds its reputation on the personal concern of well-trained salespeople who always work for your best interest. Let me give you the names and telephone numbers of some our satisfied clients who once felt the same way you do and then trusted our company to market their property."

Salesperson:
"In many cases, Mr. and Mrs. Seller, that is a very valid position. Our industry has been plagued with many unscrupulous and

unprofessional real estate salespeople. I am proud to say, though, that at our company we are truly your neighborhood professionals. We have some very sophisticated and highly effective methods available to help you sell your property and sell it right. That is my vow to both of you."

Salesperson:
"Mr. and Mrs. Seller, I dislike many of them, too. Unprofessional behavior is everywhere in our industry. What we have done is take the risk out of dealing with real estate people. You only have to deal with me, and I will take care of the rest."

Salesperson:
"Mr. and Mrs. Seller, that's understandable. Have I ever had a bad haircut at a hair salon? Of course, but did I quit getting my hair done? No, I did not. Seriously, Mr. and Mrs. Seller, we are highly trained to provide you with trouble-free service. Put me to work for you and let me prove my value."

Short-Term Listing

Seller:
"I don't want to tie up my property. Would you take a 30-day agreement?"

Salesperson:
"The average house in the area sold in 82.5 days. We like a little break on the average because we go to great expense putting a home on the market."

Salesperson:
"Our normal listing period is 180 days. Mr. and Mrs. Seller, I'm sure you can understand why we need that amount of time. We are going to spend a lot of money and time to attract buyers to your home. The average time it takes to sell a home in this area is much greater than 30 days. Now there is every possibility that your home will sell sooner than this, but we have to make sure we have an opportunity to bring you an

offer once we have put forth this much effort. We want to sell your home as quickly as possible too—make no mistake about it—because we don't get paid until we find you a buyer."

Salesperson:
"Mr. and Mrs. Seller, I am really glad you brought that up. You have probably heard all kinds of claims. I'll bet someone even told you they had a buyer who was looking for a home just like yours, right? Well, Mr. and Mrs. Seller, I am going to tell you something that might surprise you. I don't have a buyer for your house right now. I don't even guarantee I can find one in 30 days; no salesperson of great integrity would promise you that. But if I can show you that your chances of selling your home faster with the opportunity to receive more cash rests with our company, would you put faith in me and in my company?"

Salesperson:
"We probably could sell your home within 30 days, but we want to obtain fair market value for you, not a distress sale price. Our records indicate that it takes longer than 30 days to do this. Are you aware that most real estate activity takes place on weekends, and a 30-day listing limits us to only four weekends or eight effective sales days?"

Salesperson:
"Our normal listing period is 180 days. Mr. and Mrs. Seller, I am sure you can understand why we need this amount of time. I can also understand your concern that I might take the listing and do nothing. What I am promising is my commitment to do everything I can to find a buyer. And to prove it, I am willing to put my commitment in writing. It lists all our special services. The commitment releases you from the listing agreement should I fail to perform as I said I would."

Seller:
"I don't want to give you more than 30 days to sell our home."

Salesperson:
"Mr. and Mrs. Seller, we believe so strongly in quality service that we've put our commitment in writing. The commitment provides you with maximum peace of mind, wouldn't you agree?"

Salesperson:
"I would guess from what we've done tonight that you like what I've had to say, but you really don't know if I'm going to be able to deliver. How about if I put my promises in writing and give you the right to cancel the listing with 10 days if I don't do what I said I'd do? Would that make you feel more comfortable about a long-term agreement?"

Not in Area

Seller:
"You don't have an office in this area."

Salesperson:
"Mr. and Mrs. Seller, do you understand how the MLS system works and how actual location of an office is not as important as it was years ago? We can plug into a network of professionals all over town who also have groups of buyers that they're working with. Through the MLS, I'm able to expose your home to the maximum number of buyers, which can mean a faster sale for you."

Salesperson:
"My office is centrally located, highly visible, and attractive. It's easy for potential buyers to find and comfortable for them to walk into. That contributes to the flow of buyers through the office, and that can mean more buyers for you."

Interview Others

Seller:
"We are going to have another real estate company come out to talk with us."

Salesperson:
"That's totally understandable. Let me ask you, though: If I was to do all your homework for you and you were completely satisfied that I am with the best real estate salesperson, would you list with me right now?" *[Use the comparison chart of other real estate companies and point out where your company is always stronger.]*

Salesperson:
"I can understand your need to talk to another sales associate. Selling your home is a big decision, and it's important to select someone you can work with comfortably. Will you do me a favor, though? Will you call me after you've talked to that person? I'd like to have the opportunity talk to you again."

Salesperson:
"If you're feeling confident in my ability to sell your property, I think it might be doing him or her a favor to call and cancel the appointment. In fact, I'd be happy to do it for you. I've had calls like that and frankly, I've appreciated it."

BAD EXPERIENCE

Seller:
"I sold my house with your company in Alabama and had a bad experience."

Salesperson:
"Please elaborate on what happened. *[Listen to the sellers as they explain the situation.]* It does sound like that was a bad experience. Mr. and Mrs. Seller, if I was to guarantee my service to you and give you the option to fire me if I fail to perform, would you list with me tonight?" *[Use a seller's service guarantee, which guarantees your service if the seller puts the error in writing and gives you 10 days to correct the error.]*

Salesperson:
"Then you will appreciate the good experience you will have with me and my company. I'm only here to work for you and to get your home sold!"

Same Real Estate Salesperson

Seller:
"I bought my home from Brittany with Acme Real Estate; I think I will list with her."

Salesperson:
"Mr. and Mrs. Seller, do you understand my job here tonight and in the future is to get your house sold, not to sell it? There is a big difference between a professional marketer and someone with a buyer. I don't know Brittany, but I do know I am the best choice for getting your house sold for the most money in the least amount of time."

More Experience/New to the Business

Seller:
"Brittany with Acme Real Estate has a lot more experience than you."

Salesperson:
"Mr. and Mrs. Seller, what does the word 'experience' mean to you? Time in the business does not mean being the best at selling your house. If I would guarantee that my service to you is the best offered, would you list your property with me today?"

Salesperson:
"I am well-trained so you can be confident that I'll have the most up-to-date information to work with in the transaction."

Salesperson:
"I'm very well-trained in finding buyers, assisting with financing, working with transferees, developing marketing strategies, and providing quality service. I continue to attend real estate classes. That way my clients can have access to the most up-to-date information."

Salesperson:
"My office has sold many homes in this area over the past year. We've been in business for several years and are very well established in your neighborhood. You've probably noticed our yard signs. They're everywhere you look."

Salesperson:
"I really love my job. I enjoy working with people throughout the selling process and helping them with their move. And I view our relationship as a joint effort. We'll work together on this project until your house is sold."

Salesperson:
"You know, all the power of our company locally and nationally comes to bear on the marketing of your property through me. I've chosen to specialize in your neighborhood. As a matter of fact, I walk through this neighborhood every other week. Over the past few months, we've sold several properties here."

Seller:
"Are you new?"

Salesperson:
"I'm new to the business, so I'm very motivated, recently trained, and knowledgeable about the most current marketing techniques. When you hire me, I'll work harder and smarter than anybody else to get your house sold. In addition, my manager's been in the business for many years and stands behind me every step of the way." *[When you're new to the business, rely on the collective strengths of your office. Include yourself as part of your office's marketing team when describing its successes.]*

Disclosure

Seller:
"We don't feel it is necessary to tell about the murder on the property."

Salesperson:

"Why don't want to disclose that?"

Seller:

"We feel it will hurt our chances of selling."

Salesperson:

"I think I understand. My job here tonight is to protect you as well as get your house sold. We must disclose conditions with the house, but no one can force you to sell; you will always have the veto power if an offer is not what you want."

Third-Party Company

Seller:

"If we sell through the real estate company that our referral is offering, we get a rebate."

Salesperson:

"How much is the rebate?"

Seller:

"$350."

Salesperson:

"If I was willing to give you $350.00, would you list it with me now?"

Salesperson:

"How much is your monthly payment for this house?"

Seller:

"$1,450."

Salesperson:

"So, if it took even one month longer to sell through the other real estate company, how much would that cost you, less the rebate?"

Paying Closing Costs

Seller:
"We won't pay any buyer's closing costs."

Salesperson:
"You probably paid these costs when you purchased the house. If you pay closing costs for the buyers, you'll probably net about $4,000 less from the sale. But, paying them might make the difference between whether or not a buyer can afford to purchase your house."

Seller:
"I'm not paying for a title policy. If the buyer wants it, let them pay for it!"

Salesperson:
"Mr. and Mrs. Seller, let's not concentrate on the purchase agreement. Let's look at your bottom line: what you will walk away with." *[Review the net sheet.]*

Personal Property/Real Property

Seller:
"The buyers asked that we leave our hot tub, and we want to take it with us when we move."

Salesperson:
"Mr. and Mrs. Seller, how much is a used hot tub worth?"

Seller:
"$1,500."

Salesperson:
"Used, not what you paid for it."

Seller:
"Well, maybe $800."

Salesperson:
"Let's assume the buyers do not take our counteroffer if you don't give them the hot tub. Then we wait for four more months before we get another offer. During this time, you must keep this house in show condition. You must be ready at any given moment to leave for a showing. The lot you want to build on just sits there, and you continue to make monthly house payments on a place you no longer want. If we just take a look at your house payment of $1,385 times the four months, is it really worth the effort of moving that hot tub?"

Agency Listing

Seller:
"We want the right to sell the property ourselves and not pay a commission."

Salesperson:
"Why would you want to compete with me to sell your house?"

Seller:
"Well, maybe someone at my work might want to buy it."

Salesperson:
"Oh, I think I get it, you believe the only thing you're paying me for is to bring you a buyer. Let's review my services both before and after a written offer to purchase, and I think you will see I provide a great deal more than just a buyer."

Prequalifying Buyers

Seller:
"We don't want any old buyer traipsing through our home."

Salesperson:
"I prequalify buyers before I bring them through your property. That means less inconvenience for you and a better chance that your house is going to be affordable for the buyers that I show."

Salesperson:
"Today's sellers are more educated about real estate sales and the requirements most mortgage lenders ask of a buyer. Because of this knowledge, more and more sellers are asking that the potential buyers be financially pre-qualified before accepting an offer, and they are also requesting a preapproval letter rather than a simple prequalification. A preapproval carries a stronger, safer message that the buyers are truly qualified to purchase their home. Would you like me to get a preapproval letter from the buyer before we accept an offer to purchase?"

Managing All the Details

Seller:
"Part of the reason we would consider listing our property with you is not to be hassled with all the details in selling a home."

Salesperson:
"I want you to understand that I will stand in the middle of this transaction to make sure that everything gets done."

Service Guarantee

Seller:
"How can I be sure you will do what you promise?"

Salesperson:
"I will put my promises in writing and give you the right to cancel should I not perform. This provides you with maximum peace of mind."

Open Listing

Seller:
"I'll give an open listing and pay a commission to whomever brings the buyer."

Salesperson:
"An open listing limits what I can do for you. It means I can only work with those buyers I happen to be working with right now. With an exclusive listing, I can actively market and promote your home to all buyers."

Expired

Seller:
"You didn't show the house before."

Salesperson:
"Mr. and Mrs. Seller, you are paying me to be a marketing expert. That means I get houses sold. I might not actually sell it, but I will get it sold. The real estate salespeople that show houses are generally not the best marketing salespeople. We all have our specialties. My job is to find those real estate salespeople with buyers and get them to see your property. The last time your home was listed, it was not personally marketed to me, but we can change that. Are you ready to put me to work for you?"

Sell VA\FHA

Seller:
"I don't want to sell my property VA or FHA."

Salesperson:
"I understand. Would you do me a favor? At least look at all offers, and then together we can make the decision how to sell. You don't want to exclude a percent of the potential market, do you?"

Salesperson:
"Our company wants you to receive the quality service you deserve. Our company does more than just promise quality service. To be sure you are completely satisfied, you will receive a survey shortly after the sale of your property is completed. This survey allows us to measure our success. It acts as our

barometer and assists us in maintaining our dominance as the most preferred real estate company in the area. Does this type of confidence and follow-through convince you that my company is the right one to represent you in the sale of your home?"

Home Warranty

Seller:
"We are not going to pay for a home warranty for the buyer."

Salesperson:
"There are several ways to market your home to eliminate, or at least reduce, the competition. One of the most effective marketing tools I've used is not only a strong incentive to buy your property, but it's also a service that provides peace of mind for both you and the buyers. It's a home warranty. On average homes listed with a home warranty sell for a higher price and faster than homes without it. I think it would be prudent to protect your property with a home warranty, don't you?"

Seller:
"We are not going to fix a thing after closing."

Salesperson:
"If you're concerned about appliances that will break down or a furnace that quits the day you move out, let me tell you about home warranty plans. They provide you with the peace of mind you're looking for. They typically cover the items you choose and insures them against breakdown and the ensuing repairs with a low deductible fee to the buyer. Does this service sound like something you would like?"

Inspections

Seller:
"We are concerned about the condition of the property. We don't want to spend a lot of money on repairs."

Salesperson:
"Mr. and Mrs. Seller, if you feel there could be some issues with the property that may be found at the inspection, I would suggest you have your home inspected now to determine the best course of action for anything that may come up. I can give you the names of several inspection companies."

Salesperson:
"Mr. and Mrs. Seller, because you have an older home, it might be wise to have a company test for any lead paint issues. If so, the company will advise you on how best to eliminate the problem in the most efficient, cost-effective way. I can recommend a number of different companies."

Salesperson:
"Mr. and Mrs. Seller, I recommend that all seller clients have their properties inspected. Some problems can only be detected by a professional or by completing actual testing on such things as water and electricity. I can provide you with the names of several companies to choose from if you are interested."

Special Properties

Seller:
"We want a real estate company that appreciates our unique property."

Salesperson:
"Mr. and Mrs. Seller, some properties deserve special attention. Because you own a lakefront property, you can take advantage of our company's professional service and unique marketing that is designed to meet your home-selling needs and draw special attention to your home."

Salesperson:
"Mr. and Mrs. Seller, some properties require special attention. Because you're looking to sell a lakefront home, you can

take advantage of our recreational properties program. It is designed to market this type of property and will allow me to utilize a quicker reference to find the buyer for your house."

Internet

Seller:
"We believe the Internet is what it takes to sell property."

Salesperson:
"Mr. and Mrs. Seller, we have numerous technological avenues available to help you sell this house. We have a website where we list our properties. We have a community location with information listed about your neighborhood. If you're an Internet user, we'll have an additional means of communication by email. Do these technological advantages sound like the type of service that may create a shorter, easier avenue to finding a buyer for your house?"

Salesperson:
"Mr. and Mrs. Seller, we have the most comprehensive technological offering of any real estate company to market your property. We have a website where we can advertise your house, including a picture. We use a computer system to market your house through the Multiple Listing Service, and you can track the progress of your sale with email. All of these technological avenues allow us to generate leads at a greater rate than ever before. Does this sound like the type of marketing that may create a quicker sale of your property?"

Referral

Seller:
"We are concerned about where we will be moving to."

Salesperson:
"Mr. and Mrs. Seller, if you need assistance in buying out of the local area, I can refer you to one of our affiliate offices to

assist you at your next location. Would you like me to do that for you?"

Salesperson:
"Mr. and Mrs. Seller, should you need assistance moving out of the local area, I can refer you to one of many offices within the United States and abroad to assist you at your next location. If you're moving locally, I can help give your property exposure to buyers unfamiliar with this area. Is this a benefit you would like to take advantage of?"

Fair Housing Questions from Sellers

Seller:
"Which buyer is the contract from?"

Salesperson:
"This offer is from Mr. Jones, the computer salesman from Dallas."

Seller:
"Can I be sued if I refuse to sell to him?"

Salesperson:
"If you refuse to accept Mr. Jones's offer because he is a minority, you expose yourself to serious legal liability." *[The broker should document in detail that they have made this recommendation.]*

Seller:
"What color, religion, nationality, and gender are the buyers?"

Salesperson:
"I need to know why you asked that question. The listing agreement you signed provides that this property is offered without discrimination. If you intend to violate that agreement, I need to know now so I can protect myself and my firm."

Seller:
"What if I refuse to accept an offer from a minority?"

Salesperson:
"I presume you are interested in selling your property to a buyer capable of paying you the best price and offering the most favorable terms and conditions. Federal law requires that I present all offers, and it prohibits you from not considering them on the basis of discrimination."

Seller:
"What if I take my property off the market, and relist it at a later date when these people [minority] are no longer looking?"

Salesperson:
"If the property on which a 'protected class' has made an offer is to be removed from the market, the circumstances prompting such removal must be carefully and completely explained and documented by the listing broker and attested to by the seller. An offer from a minority is never a basis for the removal. If you insist the minority's offer is the only reason for the withdrawal, my firm cannot agree and we will have to terminate the listing."

Seller:
"Are you aware there is a bonus for selling my home to the 'right people'?"

Salesperson:
"I appreciate the offer of a bonus, but it would be unethical and illegal for me to accept an offer when it is conditioned on the race or the religion of the person submitting the offer."

Seller:
"Why must I sell my home to someone I don't like? What about my 'freedom of choice' and my 'rights'?"

Salesperson:
"I cannot answer these questions for you. If you believe you have these rights, you should talk to an attorney."

Seller:
"I want to list my property at $10,000 over its fair market value, but I will sell it to the 'right people' for $10,000 less."

Salesperson:
"When a property is overpriced, it tends to sit on the market without drawing any interest from any buyers. That is certainly not in your best interest."

Seller:
"Could you call and tell me who you are showing the property to?"

Salesperson:
"Of course, although I am not sure why you want me to bother you in this way. Most of our clients hire us to screen the buyers and only show to those who are qualified. Our experience shows that clients only want to be contacted when an offer is believed to be forthcoming."

Seller:
"What will you do if a minority wants to see my house?"

Salesperson:
"I will show your property to anyone who is financially qualified."

Seller:
"I am mad at my neighbors, and only want to sell to minorities."

Salesperson:
"Limiting the sale of your property to minorities is not an effective way to get revenge on your neighbors. A sale to minorities would not necessarily reduce the property values, any limitations on my marketing efforts will mean that your property is exposed to fewer buyers, and most importantly, any racial limitation on the sale of your property is illegal."

Seller:
"We don't want to sell to those people [any protected group]."

Salesperson:
"That's curious. I thought you wanted to sell this house."

Seller:
"We do."

Salesperson:
"Then why would you want to limit the market?"

Seller:
"Well . . ."

Salesperson:
"Doesn't it make sense to let me do my job and get your house sold to the most qualified buyer?"

Salesperson:
"I am sure you are aware of the legal limitations we are under according to the federal fair housing laws. This would cause way too many problems, so let's sell this property to the first qualified buyer, okay?"

Fair Housing Questions from Buyers

Buyer:
"What is the racial composition of the neighborhood?"

Salesperson:
"Since we do not maintain racial, religious, or ethnic statistics in our office, it would not be fair for me to guess at the demographics. If you wish to research this matter, you may contact the city planning department or the Census Bureau. They may have that information."

Buyer:
"We only want to see homes in a [protected class] neighborhood."

Salesperson:
"Let me identify a selection of homes that meet your other criteria, including size, price, schools, and so on. After you have seen them and weighed everything, you can make your decision."

Buyer:
"I am a [protected class]. Where would I feel most at home?"

Salesperson:
"Let's consider all of the features you are looking for in a home or neighborhood. Is there any particular subdivision you would like to start looking in?"

Buyer:
"Are the schools in the area integrated?"

Salesperson:
"Our office does not maintain statistics regarding the racial makeup of the student body. The only school I am really familiar with is the one my own children attend. They have many nationalities and religions represented there and have never had a problem."

Buyer:
"Do you sell a lot of homes to minorities?"

Salesperson:
"I don't separate classes of people. In the past few months I have sold six homes—all of them to wonderful people."

Buyer:
"Are racially integrated neighborhoods good investments?"

Salesperson:
"To the best of my knowledge, there is no correlation between property values and the race, religion, or nationality of the person who owns it."

Buyer:
"Who is considered a minority?"

Salesperson:
"Federal law prohibits discrimination based on race, religion, color, nationality, or gender. Thus, a large group of Hispanics could practice discrimination against a small group of Italians, and this would be considered discriminatory and illegal."

A Real Estate Transaction Step by Step: From Listing through Closing Summary

Step 1	Prospecting (continuous and ongoing)
Step 2	Prospecting finds suspects
Step 3	Need determination and qualifying of the suspects
Step 4	Suspects turn into prospects
Step 5	Loan application (at least prequalification)
Step 6	For sellers (listing presentation)
Step 7	For buyers (selection of property)
Step 8	Offers
Step 9	Negotiation (counteroffers)
Step 10a	Completed contract (completely initialed and signed option)
Step 10b	Distribute six copies
Step 11	Immediate property inspection (esp. with option)
Step 12	Repair renegotiation (amendment and/or termination)
Step 13	Appraisal
Step 14	Appraisal price possible renegotiation
Step 15	Amendment of contract (if necessary)

Step 16 Loan approval/title commitment/survey
Step 17 Verify walk-through acceptance of property
Step 18 Closing of purchaser and closing of seller
Step 19 Get commission check
Step 20 Happy buyers and sellers
Step 21 Follow-up produces referrals from past clients

Professionalism Checklist

The following is a professional checklist to help remind you of how you should act in the real estate business. This list is not all inclusive and may be supplemental by local custom and practice.

Always think of others first. Follow the golden rule.

Advise the clients of other brokers to direct questions to their real estate salesperson.

Communicate clearly; don't use jargon not readily understood by the general public.

Check your email and messages every two hours. Always respond promptly to inquiries and requests for information.

Schedule appointments as far in advance as possible; call if you are delayed or must cancel an appointment. Be sure to get lockbox information and find out if the property has a security system.

Always schedule property showings in advance.

If a prospective buyer decides not to view an occupied home, promptly explain the situation to the listing broker or the owner.

Communicate with all parties in a timely fashion.

Enter listed property first to ensure that unexpected situations, such as pets, are handled appropriately.

- Leave your business card if it not prohibited by local rules.
- Never criticize property in the presence of the owner.
- Inform sellers that you are leaving after a showing.

- When showing an occupied home, always ring the doorbell or knock before entering. Knock before entering any closed room.
- Present a professional appearance at all times; dress appropriately, and make sure your car is clean.
- Be aware of and respect cultural differences. Show courtesy and respect to the general public. Be aware of and meet all deadlines.
- Promise only what you can deliver, and keep your promises.
- Be responsible for visitors to listed property; never allow buyers to enter property unaccompanied.
- When the seller is absent, be sure to turn off the lights you turned on and lock doors that were locked after a showing.
- Don't use the seller's telephone or bathroom. If it is an emergency, ask the seller first.
- Tell buyers not to eat, drink, or smoke in the listed property.
- Use sidewalks; if weather is bad, take off shoes and boots inside the property.
- When a property is vacant, check that heating and cooling controls are set correctly; check the outside of the property for damage or vandalism.
- Call the listing broker to report the results of any showing.
- Notify the listing broker immediately if anything appears wrong with the property or a door to the exterior was left unlocked.
- Notify the listing broker if there appears to be inaccurate information of the listing.
- Share important information about property, including the presence of pets, security systems, and whether sellers will be present during the showing.
- Show courtesy, trust, and respect to other real estate professionals.

Basic Budget Worksheet for Personal Budgets

Category	Monthly Budget Amount	Monthly Actual Amount	Difference between Actual and Budget
INCOME:			
Wages Paid			
Bonuses/Dividend Income			
Interest Income			
Capital Gains Income			
Miscellaneous Income			
INCOME SUBTOTAL			
EXPENSES:			
Mortgage or Rent			
Utilities (gas, water, electric, trash)			
Cable TV			
Telephone			
Home Repairs/Maintenance			
Car Payments			
Gasoline/Oil			
Auto Repairs/Maintenance/Fees			
Other Transportation (tolls, bus, subway, etc.)			
Child Care			
Auto Insurance			
Home Owners/Renters Insurance			
Computer Expense			
Entertainment/Recreation			
Groceries			
Toiletries, Household Products			
Clothing			
Eating Out			

Category	Monthly Budget Amount	Monthly Actual Amount	Difference between Actual and Budget
EXPENSES:			
Gifts/Donations			
Healthcare (medical, dental, vision, incl. insurance)			
Hobbies			
Interest Expense (mortgage, credit cards, fees)			
Magazines/Newspapers			
Federal Income Tax			
State Income Tax			
Social Security/Medicare Tax			
Personal Property Tax			
Pets			
Miscellaneous Expense			
EXPENSES SUBTOTAL			
NET INCOME (INCOME LESS EXPENSES)			

My Goal Plan

Name: _____ Date: _____

Career Goal: _____

Career Goals:

1. Short-term goal (less than one year)
2. Intermediate goal (one year to five years)
3. Long-term goal (longer than one year)

Steps to Reaching Short-Term Goal	Timeline
1.	1.
2.	2.
3.	3.
4.	4.
5.	5.
6.	6.

Steps to Reaching Intermediate Goal	Timeline
1.	1.
2.	2.
3.	3.
4.	4.
5.	5.
6.	6.

Steps to Reaching Long-Term Goal	Timeline
1.	1.
2.	2.
3.	3.
4.	4.
5.	5.
6.	6.

Goals

1. Financial—_____
   _____

2. Career—_____
   _____

3. Family—_____
   _____

4. Spirit—_____
   _____

5. Physical—_____
   _____

6. Mental—_____
   _____

7. Education—_____
   _____

Answers to Summary Questions

Chapter 1
1. **D.** REALTOR®
2. **D.** All of the above
3. **A.** Doing something when you would rather be doing something else.
4. **B.** "Moral" and "character"
5. **D.** Golden Rule
6. **D.** Refer Kimberly to the policy manual and advise her to follow office procedures.
7. **D.** Assist the buyer with your current broker's permission and guidance. (You still work with the first broker)
8. **C.** Present your first offer and tell the seller another offer may be coming in. (all other answers are violations)
9. **C.** Consult your broker. (it is always best to consult your broker. Salespeople do not have the right to dispute others.
10. **A.** Selling your own property.

Chapter 2
1. **B.** 5 1/2
2. **A.** When agents keep personal items at their desks, books and files all around them, and enjoy sitting there instead of leaving the office to go prospecting.

3. A. Attainable and realistic
4. A. Loves people and uses money.
5. D. Do not allow your appearance to speak for you.
6. C. Organizational skills
7. D. Promise less and deliver more
8. B. Wear a nametag
9. C. The way you sell yourself
10. A. Real estate

Chapter 3
1. C. Enter them into a computer database.
2. A. To organize data on all of your people, listings and closings.
3. D. All of the above
4. C. Social media can allow you to connect with people.
5. D. 80% of your content is about things of interest to all people and 20% can be real estate related
6. A. Promoting the real estate salesperson
7. D. All of the above
8. B. They are a software program that carries out a set of instructions.
9. D. All of the above
10. B. To reduce expensive infrastructure.

Chapter 4
1. A. Don't fear competition
2. C. Persistence
3. D. All are things to be proud
4. B. You cannot generate enthusiasm, it must be natural.
5. A. To gain a balance between creating more value and making profit
6. A. Marketing Philosophy
7. D. All of the above are good ideas
8. C. Customer avoidance
9. C. Physical Effectiveness
10. D. Hunger

Chapter 5
1. C. Attention, Interest, Desire, Action
2. D. All of the above

3. A. Marketing Strategy
4. B. Marketing Plan
5. C. Marketing Project
6. D. Marketing Campaign
7. A. Name recognition
8. B. Prospect generating
9. B. Keep It Simple and Short
10. D. Familial Status

Chapter 6
1. C. Dual agency
2. D. $2,000
3. B. Lawful instructions of the seller.
4. A. Advice, opinions and advocacy are given to clients not customers
5. D. Represent the interests of his or her client
6. D. All the above
7. D. A relationship of honesty, integrity and expertise
8. A. Smorgasbord of services and the customer only pays for the ones he or she uses
9. B. Transaction fees
10. C. Rebate

Chapter 7
1. A. Call FSBO's
2. B. 12
3. B. Get an appointment to be face-to-face
4. C. Constantly
5. B. Send out a minimum of 12 mailings per year
6. A. No more than 100
7. C. Waifs
8. A. Geographic Marketing
9. B. Gold
10. D. Sells too fast.

Chapter 8
1. B. Residential Service Company (Home warranty)
2. A. Area or location
3. A. It should be priced above market.

4. **B.** Call friends over to increase the number of visitors.
5. **D.** Do client follow-up paperwork or computer work.
6. **C.** Put out one open house sign.
7. **C.** Homes that were foreclosed.
8. **B.** Three
9. **A.** On time
10. **C.** To establish rapport.

Chapter 9
1. **C.** Call until you get one.
2. **D.** Each of the above statements is true about buyers
3. **A.** Hold at least two open houses every weekend.
4. **C.** Allowing children to abuse the sellers' personal property
5. **B.** Ask the caller to come into the office.
6. **D.** Your sphere of influence
7. **A.** You lose control
8. **C.** To eliminate the property.
9. **A.** Hot buyers
10. **C.** A successful marketer says, "Yes" to everybody.

Chapter 10
1. **B.** Five
2. **A.** Needs and financial
3. **D.** Reanalyze the buyer's wants and needs
4. **C.** The buyer broker ultimately is paid through the agreement with the buyer.
5. **B.** The buyer presentation
6. **D.** The buyer's race
7. **B.** The conference room
8. **B.** A wants and needs analysis
9. **C.** Probing question
10. **B.** Keep cash money in your pockets, around your desk and in your car to look successful.

Chapter 11
1. **A.** True
2. **C.** "Trial"
3. **B.** Ask a lot of questions.

4. C. So what?
5. D. Taking notes on everything they say.
6. C. "If-Then"
7. D. "Appeal to the Higher Authority"
8. B. "Take Away"
9. C. "Good Guy, Bad Guy"
10. B. Develop an Objection Handling Worksheet

Chapter 12
1. B. Using the Internet
2. D. Twice a day
3. D. A monogrammed door knocker
4. A. Listening
5. B. Client management software on the computer
6. D. All of the above
7. C. E-Newsletters
8. D. Buy gifts that don't die or are consumed
9. A. Beer bash
10. B. It is a great time to get drunk with your fclients

Chapter 13
1. D. Including the clients weight
2. B. Contract law
3. D. All of the above are contracts
4. B. Earnest money
5. B. Competent parties
6. B. Voidable
7. A. Valuable consideration
8. C. Valuable consideration
9. B. Do not give originals only give copies of the contract
10. C. Be sure that addendums are added after acceptance of the contract.

Chapter 14
1. A. Lien theory
2. D. All of the above
3. A. Agreement
4. D. All offers should be presented

5. **D.** Any of the above
6. **C.** Mortgage Bankers
7. **D.** Mortgage Brokers
8. **D.** All of the above
9. **B.** Underwriter
10. **D.** All of the above

Chapter 15
1. **B.** Survey
2. **C.** Radon
3. **C.** The final walk-through
4. **C.** Licensed repair people
5. **C.** Previous owner's names
6. **D.** All of the above
7. **A.** It is unbiased
8. **B.** Environmental assessments
9. **C.** Get an inspector to do an air quality test
10. **D.** Pest inspection

Chapter 16
1. **C.** $1,540
2. **B.** $60,000
3. **B.** Ethnicity and gender
4. **C.** Insure loans
5. **A.** Conventional
6. **C.** Alienation clause
7. **B.** Balloon note
8. **D.** Assumption
9. **C.** Buy down
10. **B.** Buyer qualification

Chapter 17
1. **C.** Referral business
2. **D.** Giving a referral
3. **A.** Incoming referral
4. **B.** Outgoing referral

Chapter 18

1. **B.** There was no intent
2. **D.** Did not know and should not have known
3. **B.** Damages that are punishing
4. **D.** Laundry list
5. **C.** Did you know? Should you have known?
6. **B.** Commission and omission
7. **C.** You must disclose; release the listing if the seller will not allow disclosure
8. **B.** Deceptive Trade Practices Act
9. **C.** To protect consumers against false business practices
10. **D.** Unconscionable action

Glossary of Real Estate Terms

Accelerated Graphics Port (AGP)—a high-speed connection used by the graphics card to interface with the computer.

Adjustable-rate cap—a rate limit that protects the consumer from costly rate increases. Typically, the cap is two percent per year. The limit, or cap, is set by the lender.

Adjustable-Rate Mortgage (ARM)—a mortgage in which the interest rate is periodically adjusted based on the movement of a preselected index.

Amortization—the repayment of a mortgage loan by making equal, periodic payments of principal and interest over a stated period of time resulting in zero balance at the end of term.

Annual Percentage Rate (APR)—calculation disclosing total costs of financing including rate, points, and any other fees charged by the lender.

Appraisal—a report that gives an opinion of the value of the property being purchased: an estimate of value of real property.

Assumption—a situation in which a new buyer who purchases a house also takes over the responsibility for payment of an existing mortgage on that house.

Automated underwriting—a computer-based method of processing loan applications that enables the lender to process loans more quickly, objectively, and at less cost. Specific programs have been developed by Fannie Mae (Desktop Underwriter) and Freddie Mac (Loan Prospector).

Back-end ratio—the percentage of gross monthly income allowed for PITI, plus all other long-term debt.

Buydown—money advanced by a seller or builder to reduce the borrower's monthly payments on the mortgage; extra points to lower an interest rate.

Cable modem—Some people now use the cable-1019vision

system in their homes to connect to the Internet.

Canvassing leads—part of your listing farm or someone you found by using other prospecting methods.

Capital gains tax—tax charged on profit made from sale of investments.

Central processing unit (CPU)—the microprocessor "brain" of the computer system; everything that a computer does is overseen by the CPU.

Certificate of Eligibility—a certificate issued by VA that states the amount of entitlement available to a veteran in order to qualify for no-money down VA loan.

Certificate of Reasonable Value (CRV)—estimate of value of property for a VA mortgage loan.

Closing costs—money paid by the borrower to complete the closing of a mortgage loan. This normally includes an origination fee, discount points, title insurance and closing fees, attorney's fees etc., and such prepaid items as taxes and insurance escrow payments.

Cold buyer—a buyer who has no real need to buy.

Collateral—that which protects the rights of a lender in case of default on a loan. In real estate financing, the real property serves as collateral giving lender the right to obtain title to the property in case of default by the borrower.

Community Reinvestment Act (CRA)—enacted by Congress in 1977, this act requires lenders to provide full, credit service in the communities serviced by bank.

Compensating factors—positive features which may offset negatives, increasing the possibility that the borrower's application for loan be approved.

Conditions—additional information or documentation that must be provided to the underwriter before final loan approval will be granted.

Condominium—form of ownership granting fee simple title to individual unit plus undivided interest in the common areas.

Condominium fee—fee charged by the condominium association to cover costs of operation of the condominium, maintenance of the common areas, and financial reserves.

Conforming loan—a mortgage loan meeting the Fannie Mae and Freddie Mac guidelines.

Construction loan—a loan made for the purpose of constructing houses or other buildings. Funds are generally dispersed in increments called "draws" as various stages of construction are completed.

Conventional mortgage—a non-government mortgage, one that is not insured by the FITA or guaranteed by the VA or Farmers Home Administration; any mortgage loan not insured or guaranteed by any government agency.

Cost of Funds Index—common index used for adjustable rate mortgages (ARM) based on the average cost of borrowed funds by depository institutions.

Credit report—a detail of information regarding an applicant's credit history.

Credit score—numerical score based on statistics showing risk of default on loan; credit score becoming important factor in qualifying for all loans.

Debt-to-income ratio—ratio used to qualify a client for a mortgage. It compares the client's total monthly housing expense (the amount being paid out) with his or her monthly gross income (the amount coming in).

Deed of Trust—financing instrument giving legal claim to the property to a trustee designated by the lender who may exercise power-of-sale in event of default by borrower.

Default—failing to observe agreed upon terms of contract or financing instrument.

Department of Housing & Urban Development (HUD)—cabinet-level federal agency housing Federal Housing Administration (FHA) and Government National Mortgage Association (Ginnie Mae); also oversees Government National Mortgage Association (Fannie Mae) and Federal Home Loan Mortgage Corporation (FHLMC or Freddie Mac).

Department of Veterans Affairs (DVA)—federal agency providing assistance to veterans, including guarantee of VA mortgage loans.

Digital Subscriber Line (DSL) modem—a high-speed Internet connection that works over a standard telephone line.

Discount point—a charge by a lender to increase yield which reduces interest rate to borrower; one discount point equates to one percent of the loan amount.

Down payment—the difference between the sales price and the loan amount paid by purchaser; amount of down payment affects other terms of the loan.

Earnest money—money given by a buyer to a title company or a seller as part of the purchase price to bind the contract.

Equity—The difference between the market value of the property and the balance owed on the mortgage. The net value of an asset.

Escrow account—an impound account that is set up and maintained by the lender.

Monthly deposits are accumulated and annual payments of taxes, hazard insurance, and mortgage insurance are made from the account. Money held by third party on behalf of others; i.e., lender maintains funds in account to pay taxes and insurance on behalf of borrower.

Escrow settlement—in the western part of the U.S., settlement or closing on a loan and real property in done "in escrow."

Federal Deposit Insurance Corporation (FDIC)—insures accounts up to $100,000 for depositors in both commercial banks and savings associations.

Federal Home Loan Mortgage Corporation (FHLMC)—Nicknamed "Freddie Mac," this is term commonly used to refer to the Federal Home Loan Mortgage Corporation, a major investor of conventional mortgages. This stock-owned corporation was originally chartered to provide a secondary market for conventional mortgage packages.

Federal Housing Administration (FHA)—government agency providing insurance for FHA mortgage loans; managed by HUD.

Federal National Mortgage Association (FNMA)—Nicknamed "Fannie Mae," this is a major investor of conventional mortgages. It was originally chartered as government agency to provide a secondary market for FHA and VA mortgage loans. It is now wholly stock-owned.

Fee simple—unrestricted ownership interest in real property.

Finder's fee—payment made for procuring of purchaser for property, or borrower for mortgage loan.

First trust or first mortgage—the primary or original loan secured by real estate.

Fixed-rate mortgage—a mortgage in which the interest rate is set for the term of the loan.

Foreclosure—the legal process whereby lender receives title to real property with the right to sell the property to repay the mortgage lien.

Front-end ratio—the percentage of gross monthly income allowed for PITI.

Funding fee—percentage of loan amount charged on VA loans to provide a pool of funds for administrative costs; this fee has increased over time and is higher for subsequent use by veterans and for reservists and members of the National Guard.

Gift letter—a signed statement by a gift giver which explains that a cash gift used by the borrower to qualify for a loan need not be repaid.

Government loans—mortgages insured (FHA) or guaranteed

(VA) by government; may also include state-sponsored mortgages.

Government National Mortgage Association (GNMA)—Nicknamed "Ginnie Mae," a major investor in FHA and VA loans. The government agency was created in 1968 to facilitate a secondary market by insuring mortgage-backed securities.

Graduated payment mortgage—regularly scheduled payment increases on loan.

Graphics card—a device for translating image data from a computer into a format that can be displayed by the monitor.

Gross Monthly Income (GMI)—annual income before tax and other payroll deductions divided by 12.

Hard disk—a large-capacity permanent storage system used to hold information such as programs and documents.

Homeowners' Association (HOA) fee—fees paid monthly for maintenance and care of common facilities in a planned unit development.

Homeowner's insurance—a policy carried by the homeowner to protect the dwelling in case of fire and other hazards.

Hot buyer—a buyer who has been totally qualified and will buy within the next 30 to 60 days.

Index—financial indicator used as basis to calculate ARM rate. Most commonly used are treasury securities; also cost of funds index, LIBOR.

Integrated Drive Electronics (IDE) Controller—the primary interface for the hard drive, CD-ROM, and floppy disk drive.

Interest rate cap—a cap established by lender providing protection for borrower that interest rate cannot exceed stated limits.

Judicial foreclosure—a court procedure used to obtain title to real property after default on loan; after foreclosure property may be sold to repay debt.

Jumbo loan—any mortgage loan exceeding the Fannie Mae and Freddie Mac conforming maximum loan limit.

Keyboard—the primary device for entering information into the computer.

Lender Paid Mortgage Insurance—a program whereby the lender charges a higher interest rate instead of separate mortgage insurance charge.

Lien—a financial claim against the property, i.e., a mortgage.

Lifetime cap—the maximum increase in interest rate allowed over life of loan. A ceiling and floor set by a lender to restrict interest rate fluctuations on a mortgage. The cap is indicated either as a stated percentage rate or as five to seven percentage points more than the initial rate.

Loan-to-Value Ratio (LTV)—loan amount shown as percentage of the value of the property, i.e., 80 percent LTV represents mortgage of 80 percent of value. A percentage which compares the outstanding principal balance of a mortgage loan with the value or selling price of the mortgage property.

Local area network (LAN) card—a device used by many computers, particularly those in an Ethernet office network, to connect to each other.

Lock-in rate—the interest rate to which the lender formally commits; it is typically guaranteed for a specific time period up to the closing.

London Inter-Bank Offered Rates Index (LIBOR Index)—average rate major London banks charge each other for U.S. dollar deposits.

Low/Doc or No/Doc Loan—mortgage loan requiring little or no documentation from borrower; it generally requires large down payment.

Margin—the amount added to an index to determine the note rate on ARM.

Medium buyer—a buyer who will buy within the next six months; may have a home in closing or listed or may be transferred with a specific date by which he or she must move.

Memory—storage space used to hold data. Several specific types of computer memory include:

- **Random-access memory (RAM)**—used to temporarily store information that the computer is currently working with.
- **Read-only . . . memory (ROM)**—a permanent type of memory storage for important data that does not change.
- **Basic input/output system (BIOS)**—a type of ROM that is used to establish basic communication when the computer is first turned on.
- **Caching**—the storing of frequently used data in extremely fast RAM that connects directly to the CPU.
- **Virtual memory**—space on a hard disk used to temporarily store data and swap it in and out of RAM as needed.

Modem—a device used for connecting to the Internet.

Monitor—the primary device for displaying information from the computer.

Mortgage—the legal instrument by which real estate is pledged as security for the repayment of the loan.

Mortgage-backed securities—income producing securities based on mortgage loan packages.

Mortgage insurance—insurance protecting lender against default by borrower.

Mortgage Insurance Premium (MIP)—mortgage insurance charged on FHA loans; includes both an upfront charge which may be financed and monthly renewal fees.

Mortgagee—the lender of money secured by real estate.

Mortgagor—the borrower of money secured by real estate.

Motherboard—the main circuit board that all of the other internal components of a computer connect to. The CPU and memory are usually on the motherboard. Other systems may be found directly on the motherboard or connected to it through a secondary connection. For example, a sound card can be built into the motherboard or connected through PCI.

Mouse—the primary device for navigating and interacting with the computer.

Negative amortization—occurs when payments may not cover the total amount of interest due resulting in increase in loan balance, a problem with some ARM programs.

Net worth—the value of a client's assets minus the total of his or her liabilities; an amount used to indicate creditworthiness or financial strength.

Nonconforming loan—a loan that does not follow Fannie Mae or Freddie Mae conforming guidelines.

Nonjudicial foreclosure—a foreclosure that does not require court action; used with deed of trust.

Note—a legal instrument or written promise specifying agreement to repay debt on certain terms.

One-stop shopping—refers to an "umbrella" company that may own a real estate company, mortgage company, title insurance, and/or other entities providing income.

Origination fee—charge by a lender for costs of a originating mortgage (usually one percent of loan amount); fee earned by a lender to process and close a loan. This is usually part of the closing costs.

Parallel port—a connection point on a computer, commonly used to connect a printer.

Partial entitlement—the amount of guarantee after a veteran has used entitlement once; may be used for subsequent VA loans.

Payment cap—limitation on increases in payment rather than an increase in interest rate on some types of ARM loans; may lead to negative amortization.

Peripheral Component Interconnect (PCI) bus—the most common way to connect additional components to the computer. PCI uses a series of slots on the motherboard that PCI cards plug into.

Personal property—all property other than real property.

Points (discount points)—a fee charged by a lender to purchase a specific interest rate; one point one percent of the loan amount.

Portfolio lender—lender that retains a loan in its own portfolio rather than immediately selling it on the secondary market.

Power supply—an electrical transformer that regulates the electricity used by the computer.

Preapproval—an approval for a loan received prior to the borrower's selection of a home to purchase.

Prepaid—closing costs paid at the time of settlement that actually occur in the future; i.e., taxes, insurance, upfront interest.

Prepayment penalty—fee charge by the lender if a loan is paid off before end of its term.

Prequalification—a method of determining a borrower's potential qualification for a mortgage; does not guarantee commitment for a loan from the lender.

Presentation leads—people who you've talked to about selling but are not yet ready to make a move.

Principal, Interest, Taxes, and Insurance (PITI)—components of a mortgage loan including the escrow fund established to accumulate funds for payment of taxes and insurance on behalf of the borrower. This is usually referred to as the total monthly payment on a loan.

Private Mortgage Insurance (PMI)—mortgage insurance to protect the lender in case of default; required on loans with less than 20 percent down payment.

Processing—procedure from the time of the loan application through submission to an underwriter.

Rate factor—chart showing number of dollars required to pay off $1,000 of debt on a mortgage loan. Used to calculate PI mortgage payment and to determine the amount a borrower is qualified to borrow.

Ratio—see Back-end ratio; Front-end ratio.

Real Estate Mortgage Investment Conduit (REMIC)—a company formed to trade in investment pools made up of various types of mortgages.

Real Estate Settlement Procedures Act (RESPA)—federal law regulating settlement practices.

Real property—land including its improvements plus all legal rights attached.

Regulation Z—part of the Truth-in-Lending Act requiring full disclosure of all aspects of credit financing in advertising.

Removable storage—a device that allows you to add new information to your computer very easily, as well as save information that you want to carry to a different location. Some devices include:

- **CD-ROM (compact disc, read-only memory)**—a popular form of distribsution of commercial software. Many systems now offer CD-R (recordable) and CD-RW (rewritable), which can also record.

- **Flash memory**—based on a type of ROM called electrically erasable programmable read-only memory (EEPROM), Flash memory provides fast, permanent storage.

- **DVD-ROM (digital versatile disc, read-only memory)**—similar to CD-ROM but capable of holding much more information.

Resolution Trust Corporation (RTC)—formed to sell off assets of failed savings associations.

Reverse Annuity Mortgage (RAM)—mortgage that uses equity in real property to fund payments to a borrower; especially appropriate for the elderly who need cash but don't wish to sell their homes.

SCSI (small computer system interface)—pronounced "scuzzy," it is used to add devices, such as hard drives or scanners, to the computer.

Second trust (mortgage)—junior or secondary trust placed on property after first trust already established.

Secondary market—a market in which mortgage loan packages can be sold providing additional funds to primary market for mortgage lending.

Serial port—a connection point on the computer used to connect an external modem.

Servicing—when a lender collects monthly mortgage payments, forwards applicable portions of payment to investor, insurance, and taxing agencies.

Settlement agent—person or entity coordinating and conducting the closing of a loan and transfer of real property.

Sound card—a type of expansion board used by the computer to record and playback audio by converting analog sound into digital information and back again.

Survey—method of measuring boundaries of parcels of land, including improvements, easements, and encroachments.

"Teaser" rate—starting rate well below note rate (index plus margin) on ARM to entice borrowers.

Temporary buydown—a lower interest rate offered for fixed period of time.

Term—designated period of time for a loan.

Thrifts—another name for savings associations; financial institution established primarily for savings and providing home mortgage loans.

Title—ownership record of property.

Title insurance—insurance policy that protects the owner or lender against loss arising from defects in the title.

Title search—study of court records to verify a seller has clear title to a property.

Truth-in-Lending Act (TILA)—federal law requiring disclosure of all costs involved in financing, including APR.

Underwriter—person responsible for evaluating the risk of default by a mortgage loan applicant; grants approval or denial of loan.

Uniform Residential Appraisal Report (URAR)—form used by appraisers to estimate the value of properties for mortgage loans.

Uniform Residential Loan Application Form—loan application form required on Fannie Mae and Freddie Mac loans; generally used on all loan applications.

Universal Serial Bus (USB)—quickly becoming the most popular external bus for connecting peripherals to a computer; USB ports offer power and versatility and are incredibly easy to use.

VA (Department of Veterans Affairs)—federal agency providing assistance to veterans, including the guarantee of VA mortgage loans.

VA funding fee—fee charged on VA loans to cover administrative costs.

Very-high bit-rate IDSL (VDSL) modem—a newer variation of the Internet digital subscriber line (IDSL), it requires that your phone line have fiber-optic cables.

Index

A

abandoned clients. *See* real estate waifs
abbreviations
  ABR, 20
  ABRM, 20
  AIDA, 112
  ALC, 20
  AMO, 20
  ARM, 20
  CCIM, 20
  CIREI, 20
  CMA, 202–203
  CPM, 20
  CRB, 20
  CRE, 20
  CRS, 20
  DPTA, 400
  ERS, 228
  FSBO, 159–163
  GAA, 20
  GRI, 20
  IREM, 20
  KISS, 114
  LTG, 20
  MGM, 183
  MLS, 156, 160
  NAR, 20–23
  NAREE, 23
  NOO, 185–186, 257
  OBO, 114
  RAA, 20
  REBAC, 20
  REG Z, 117
  REO, 192
  RLI, 20
  RNMI, 20
  RRC, 20
  SIOR, 20
  SOI, 170, 171, 269
  TLC, 18
  WCR, 20
acceptance
  main discussion, 361–407
  appraisals and inspections, 362, 363
accountability, duty in agency relationship, 125
Accredited Buyer Representative (ABR), 20
Accredited Buyer Representative Manager (ABRM), 20
Accredited Land Consultant (ALC), 20
Accredited Management Organization (AMO), 20
Accredited Residential Manager (ARM), 20
accuracy, element of quality, 15
Act!, 324
action
  main discussion, 148–169
  action plans, 38
  active *vs.* passive salespersons, 148, 150
  four selling steps, (AIDA), 112
  prospecting for buyers, 260
  telemarketing, active areas, 150
active prospecting, 140
addendums to contracts, 332, 335
adjustable rate mortgage (ARM), 375
administrative assistants. *See* personal assistants
advance fees
  flat fees, 135
  for sale by owner (FSBO), 156
advertising. *See* marketing and advertising
advocacy for clients, 13, 18, 125
aesthetics as element of quality, 15

512   Index

affirmations
  main discussion, 9–13
  defined, 2
age
  competency of parties to contract, 333
  competitive market analysis, age of house, 204
  Deceptive Trade Practices Act, age of goods, 406
  fair housing, 116–117
agency law
  main discussion, 125–134
agency, defined, 125
agency disclosure form
  listing packet, 209
  for sale by owner (FSBO), 156
  alternative representative agreements, 129–134
  buyer listing appointments, 275
  reduced representation, 130
  "seller only with buyer representation," 128
  traditional agency, 125–134
agreements. *See* contracts
agricultural real estate investments, 50
alienation clause, defined, 371
"all cash," 274
alone time, 56
alternate-of-choice closes, 309
alternative representative agreements, 129–134
amenities and competitive market analysis, 204
Anderson, Rolf, 70
annual percentage rate, advertising, 118
anti-spam laws, 151, 325
ants and termites, 362, 363
apartment complexes
  prospecting for buyers, 260
  See also landlords and tenants
appeals to higher authority, technique for
  closing sales, 317, 308
appointments
appointment book, at open houses, 244
  listing appointments. *See* listings
  mail *vs.* appointment, sample discussion script, 434
  prospecting for buyer appointments, 257–270
  prospecting for seller appointments, 139–196
  showing appointments, 283
  telemarketing, 150
  tracking appointments per week, 49

  See also calendars
appraisals, 206, 207, 362
  compared to CMAs, 202, 202
  defined, 199, 361
area. *See* location
"as is"
  contracts, 335
  Deceptive Trade Practices Act, 405
Ash, Mary Kay, 7
assistants, 52, 56
assumable loans, 377
assumption, defined, 371
assumptive closes, 309–310
athletes, niche markets, 190
attention, interest, desire, and action (AIDA)
  four selling steps, 112
attitude
  main discussion, 5–9
  at conventions, 44
  defined, 2
  obscure, 6
  obvious, 6
attorneys
  agency model, 126
  and clients, 126
  contingency fee analogy, 16
  contracts and practicing law, 335
  lawyers, niche markets, 190
  referrals, 387
  trading services for legal advice, 133
auto dealers
  techniques for closing sales, 314
  See also cars
average sales prices, tracking, 49

B

babies. *See* children
balloon note
  defined, 371
  financing, 376–377
bankers
  niche markets, 190
  See also lending institutions
batteries
  laptops, 74
benefits
  definition, 292
  vs. features, 304
billable hours, 134
birthdays, 72
blanks in contracts, 334
Blaylock, Luella, 114
blind ads, 236

blog, 69–70
  See also social media
body language
  in negotiations, 341, 340
bonuses and agency relationship, 132
books
  guestbooks at open houses, 245, 326
  manuals. *See* manual
  reading for success, 42–43, 57
  real estate libraries, 43
boundaries, survey, 366
breach of security, explaining to sellers, 231
brochures, 119, 180
  high priced homes, 250
  prospecting for buyers, 262
  step-by-step process for selling property, 223
  Web site information, 185
brokers
  agency relationship. *See* agency law
  availability for advice, 267
  broker open houses, 246
  "buyer brokerage not buyer listing," 274
  "buyer's brokerage," 127
  definition, 126
  discussion of company or brokerage at buyer
  listing appointments, 277
  floor time
  objectives, 266
  mortgage brokers, 355, 356
  and time management, 52
budgets, 31, 46, 48, 110
  basic budget worksheet, 490, 491
  definition, 31
builders and new construction
builders market, 191
  fee for service type listing, 132
  prospecting for buyers, 258
bulleted statements in seller presentation manual, 209
Burke, Edmund, 9
Business and Commerce Code, 399–407
business cards, 112, 118, 119
  home phone numbers business cards, 55
  obituary clients, 168
  at open houses, 244
  prospecting for buyers, 258, 262
  for sale by owner (FSBO) prospects, 157
business luncheons, prospecting for buyers, 258
business marketing, 183

business plan, defined, 31
businesses owners, niche markets, 190
buy-down mortgages, 371, 377
buyers
  agency relationship, 128
  "all cash," 274
  appointment preparation, 274
  attitudes toward, 17
  "buyer brokerage not buyer listing," 274
  buyer objectives, 265–266
  Buyer Representation Packet, defined, 273
  buyer seminars, 269
    caveat emptor clauses under Deceptive Trade Practices Act, 405
  closings, 353–357
  dominant buying motive, defined, 274
  finding buyers, 256–269
  lifestyles, 277
  listing procedures, 273–287
  negotiating offers, 340–357
  qualification for financing.
    See qualifying buyers
  referrals, 381–390
  sample questions for, 412, 414
  as sellers, at open houses, 240
  types, 264
  See also clients
buyer signs, defined, 273

C

calculators
  buyer listing appointments, preparation, 275
  at open houses, 244
calendars
  daily planners, 46
  marketing plan, beginning and ending dates, 109–110
  open houses, appointment books at, 244
  promotional calendars, 181
"call now," effective advertising, 113
call-backs, client tracking techniques, 322–328
cameras. *See* digital cameras and pictures
caravan tours of open houses, 246
card files, client tracking techniques, 322
care, defined, 125
caring for clients, TLC, 18, 19
cars
  auto dealers, techniques for closing sales, 313, 314
  as bonuses, 132
  car signs, prospecting for buyers, 259, 263

driving for success, 42, 43
gas, 45, 56
parking. *See* parking
reading for success, 43
safety concerns, checking driver's license of buyer, 44
viewing and showing property, 283, 284
cash
"all cash," 274
as bonuses, 132
valuable consideration, 333
caveat emptor clauses under Deceptive Trade Practices Act, 405
CDs, listening for success, 43
cell phones
and safety, 46
See also telephone
center of influence farming, 170, 171
Certified Commercial Investment Member (CCIM), 20
Certified Property Manager (CPM), 20
Certified Real Estate Brokerage Manager (CRB), 20
Certified Residential Specialist (CRS), 20
character, 23
See also ethics
charities and public relations, 121
children
at appointments, 283
fair housing, 116–117
and goals, 55
greeting cards, 169
toys, safety concerns, 231
Christopher, Warren, 352
civic involvement
civil rights. *See* fair housing
clarity
clear-cut listing appointments, 143–147
defined, 140
classes. *See* education and training
classified ads, 112
cleaning, 232
staging property for sale, 252
clichés in advertising, 113
clients
advocacy, 13, 19, 128
in agency relationship, 128
buyers. *See* buyers
clinometer, 81
competitive market analysis (CMA), 199
contact manager software programs, 70–72
following up. *See* follow-up with clients

handling clients' objections, 292–318
keeping in touch with clients, 321–328
names. *See* names
past clients
keeping in touch, 321–328
prospecting for buyers, 258
rapport. *See* rapport
referrals. *See* referrals
sellers. *See* sellers
closets, organization, 219
closing the deal
buyer listing agreement, 280
"closing" the seller, 227
objection handling techniques, 292–318
and time management, 54
See also closings
closings
defined, 340
main discussion, 353–357
acceptance, 361–367
closing costs, good-faith estimates
gifts, 326
paying closing costs, sample discussion scripts, 434
preparation, 415, 420
seller's net sheet, 346–348, 425
step-by-step transaction, from listing through
clothing
dressing for success, 40–42
listing appointments, 201, 212
and personal safety, 46
prospecting for buyers, 258, 261, 262
shoes, removal at listing appointment, 212
cloud computing, 89
clutter, 219, 232
CMA (competitive market analysis), 202–204
clear-cut listing appointments, 146, 147
FSBO prospects, 161
overpriced listings, 227
sample questions, 431, 432
seller listing appointments, 201
closing gift, defined, 322
coffee refreshments at open houses, 242
cold buyers, defined, 257
cold calls
"do not call" laws, 149, 151
prospecting for buyers, 258
telemarketing, 150
color, discrimination based on, 116
colors in advertising, 116, 250

Commercial and Investment Real Estate Institute (CIREI), 20
commercial real estate investments, 50
commissions
  agency relationship, 126
  alternative representative agreements, 129–134
  budgets and commission checks, 47
  flat fees *vs.* commission fees, 137
  payment at closings, 357
  promissory notes for commission payments, 136
  referrals, 381–390
  retainer, defined, 126
  sample discussion scripts, 434–437, 457, 460
  and seller servicing, 234
  taxes, 50
commitment
  committing to the real estate business, 32
  goals, 38, 39
communication
  answering questions. *See* questions and answers
  direct mail. *See* direct mail
  e-mail. *See* e-mail
  in negotiations, 341–344
  telephone. *See* telephone
  See also letters
community involvement
  and psychology of marketing, 93
  by real estate professionals, 194
comparable properties
CMA. *See* CMA (competitive market analysis)
  market value, compared to CMA, 202
compensation
commissions. *See* commissions
  ratio of hours to income, tracking, 49
  referrals, 381–390
  taxes, 50
  "what you think equals what you bank," 7
competent, defined, 332
competition
  expired listings, 162
  fear, 94
  marketing plan, comparison with competitive plans, 109–110
competitive market analysis. *See* CMA (competitive market analysis)
compliments, at listing appointment, 212

computers and technology
  main discussion, 63–76
  cell phones and safety, 46
  computer printouts at open houses, 244
  contact manager software programs, 70–72
  databases, 70–72
  Internet. *See* Internet
  laptops. *See* laptops
  personal brochures, 119
  software and time management, 54, 324
  word-processed contracts, 334
condition, defined, 292, 295
condition of property, 207
  Deceptive Trade Practices Act, 406
  defects, overplaying problems, 285
  home warranties, 252
  professional inspections, 362, 363
  seller's disclosure statement, 404
  See also improvements; repairs and maintenance
conference rooms for buyer listing appointments, 275
conflicts of interest, 131
conformance to standards as element of quality, 15
confusion and Deceptive Trade Practices Act, 405
conscious brain *vs.* subconscious brain, 10, 11
consideration, defined, 332, 333
construction industry. *See* builders and new construction
consultants, nonagency agreements, 131
Consumer Protection Act, 399–407
contact information
  contact manager software programs, 70–72
  including in marketing plan, 109–110
continuing education. *See* education and training
contracts
  main discussion, 332–336
  alternative representative agreements, 130–135
  blanks, 334
  buyer listing agreement, 280
  competency of parties, 333
  definition of contract, 332
  listing packet, 209
  nonagency agreements, 131
  purchase agreements. *See* purchase agreements
  statute of frauds, 333
  writing contracts, 332–336

convenience, questions at listing appointment, 214, 217
conventional financing, 371, 373
  loans
    budget mortgage, 374
    fully amortized, 373
    partially amortized, 374
conventions, 44
  defined, 31
cookies at open houses, 242
cooperating brokers and bonuses, 132
copies of contracts, 334
corporate moves. *See* relocations costs. *See* expenses
Counselor of Real Estate (CRE), 20
counselors
  attorneys. *See* attorneys
Counselors of Real Estate (CRE), 20
nonagency agreements, 131
couples and fair housing, 117
creative financing, 371, 374
  seller, 374–375
credit. *See* financing
cupboards, organization, 219
customer orientation, 97

D

daily planners, 46
  open houses, appointment books at, 244
  See also calendars
damage caused by misrepresentation, 402
databases, 70–72
  sphere of influence (SOI) farming, 171
dates
  appointments. *See* appointments
  in contracts, 334
  See also calendars
dead-end streets, 236
deadlines in goals, 39
deaths
  obituary clients, 168
Deceptive Trade Practices Act
  main discussion, 399–407
defenses, 400–407, 403–405
definitions, 399
  seller's disclosure statement, 404
  waivers, 405
decisions of sellers, techniques for closing the deal, 291–318
defects. *See* condition of property
delay. *See* stalling

"delayed possession," 274
delegating tasks, 54
description of property in contracts, 334
designations, 20, 21
  defined, 2
desire and four selling steps, (AIDA), 112
direct mail, 112
  brochures, 119
  marketing plan, 109–110
  sphere of influence (SOI) farming, 171
directional signs for open houses, 237, 239
disabled persons, discrimination against, 20
disclosures
  agency disclosure form, 157
DocWallet, 79
dual agency, 131
driver's license of buyer, asking for, 44
  fair housing. *See* fair housing
"do not call" laws, 151
doctors, niche markets, 190
dominant buying motive, defined, 274
door-to-door marketing
  open houses, 242
  prospecting for buyers, 260
  prospecting for sellers, 151
down payments
  advertising, 118
  earnest money, 334
DPTA. *See* Deceptive Trade Practices Act
dressing for success, 40–42
  See also clothing
driver's license of buyer, safety concerns, 44
dual agency, 131

E

earnest money, in contracts, 334
economy
economic obsolescence, defined, 206
effect on price, 205
  fear, 94
education and training
  cassette tapes or CDs, educational, 43
  learnings from mistakes, 9, 32
  listening to educational cassette tapes or CDs, 43
  seminars and classes, 43
  See also seminars
efficiency, 30–62
ego, defined, 93

elderly. *See* older persons
electrical wire safety, 231
e-mail, 73–74
　business cards and e-mail addresses, 119
　client follow-up, 326
　geographical farming, 180
　junk or spam mail, 325
emotions
　in advertising copy, 114
　top salespeople, emotional balance, 34
employment transfers. *See* relocations
empty-nest buyers, 283
e-newsletters, 182
　defined, 322
engineers report, 366, 367
entering the profession, 4
environmental inspections, 366
equity
equity position, 168
　non-occupant owners (NOO) as prospective sellers, 186
ethickos,
　defined, 2
ethics
　main discussion, 22–26
　definitions, 2, 22
　in GREAT formula for success, 33
event, defined, 322
eWallet, 81
exaggeration in advertising copy, 114
exclusive agency listing, defined, 228
exclusive buyer broker contracts, 275
exclusive right to sell (ERS) listing, defined, 228
expenses
　and budgets, 30, 47, 48
　discussion at buyer listing appointments, 278
　expense reports, 73
　including in marketing plan, 109–110
　seller's net sheet, 346
　See also fees
expensive items in house, 233
expired listings, 162, 169
　sample discussion scripts, 435, 477
external stimuli and psychology of marketing, 93

F

Facebook, 65–66
　See also social media
facilitators, nonagency agreements, 131

failure
　being afraid to fail, 9
　learnings, 32
　See also mistakes
fair deal
　defined, 140
　FSBO prospects, 160–161
fair housing, 21, 208
　advertising, 116
　buyers, sample discussion scripts, 485
　driver's license of buyer, asking for, 44
　sellers, sample discussion scripts, 482
Fair Housing Act of 1968, 21–22
false advertising, 115
family and relatives
　children. *See* children
　fair housing laws, familial status, 20, 116–117
　indications of buyers' interest in property, 287
　pictures, 219
　referrals, 387
　sphere of influence (SOI) farming, 171
　time management. *See* work/life balance
farming (neighborhood servicing), 169
faxes and faxing
　business cards, fax number on, 119
fear
　competition, 94
　failure, fear of, 9
　sellers' objections, 295
features and services
　benefits *vs.* features, 304
　definition of feature, 3, 292
　element of quality, 14
　list of real estate services, 432, 433
　open houses, feature sheets, 244
　service guarantees, sample discussion scripts, 434
federal government
　financing, 372–373
　government information and Deceptive Trade Practices Act, 405
federal legislation
　anti-spam laws, 89, 325
　Deceptive Trade Practices Act, 399–407
　Fair Housing Laws. *See* fair housing
　FHA appraisal requirements, 206
　REG Z, Truth-in-Lending Act, 118
fees
　commissions. *See* commissions
　flat fees *vs.* commission fees, 134–135
　nonagency agreements, 131
　origination fees, 132

retainers, 135
for sale by owner (FSBO), 156
service type listings, 131
title companies, 355–356
transaction fees, 133
See also expenses
"female roommate," use of language in marketing materials, 116
Ferry, Mike, 153
fiduciary
    defined, 128
    See also agency law
files. *See* recordkeeping
filming of listing presentations, 229
financial planning
    applications, 76–77
    defined, 31
    financial balance of top salespeople, 34
    investments. *See* investments
financing
    main discussion, 370–378
    "all cash," 274
    competitive market analysis, 204
    creative financing, 371
    discussion at buyer listing appointments, 279–281
    financial institutions. *See* lending institutions
    monthly payment, advertising, 118
    mortgages. *See* mortgages
    owner financing, questions at listing appointment, 214, 217
    seller financing, 274, 374–375
    seller's net sheet, 346, 347
    See also loans
finding clients
    buyers, 257–269
    sellers, 139–196
    See also referrals
FindmyIphone, 79
fireplaces at open houses, 239
first impressions and dressing for success, 40
first-time homebuyers, 281
    niche markets, 190
fixed-rate loans, advertising, 118
flags at open houses, 237, 239, 244
flashlights at listing presentations, 210
Flickr, 68
    See also social media
flat fees, 135
fliers. *See* brochures
floor time, 188
    defined, 257
    getting buyers into office, 267

objectives, 266
prospecting for buyers, 263
referrals, 387
flyers. *See* brochures
follow-up with clients, 323–328
geographical farming, 180
real estate owned (REO) property, 192
Ford, Henry, 16
foreclosure property, 192
form letters
    prospecting for buyers, 261
former customers. *See* past clients
forms
    listing packet, 209
for-sale signs, 112, 248
    FSBO, 152
    multiple signs, 275
    prospecting for buyers, 258
    for sale by owner (FSBO), 156
    step-by-step process for selling property, 223
    things to bring to listing presentation, 209, 210
fraud
    definitions, 399
    See also Deceptive Trade Practices Act
frequency of moves, 168
friends
    attitude and friendship, 5
    friends in real estate business, sample discussion scripts, 439, 443
    indications of buyers' interest in property, 287
    sphere of influence (SOI) farming, 171
FSBO (for sale by owner), 159–162
    main discussion, 152–156
    builders market, 191
    comparison of FSBO advantages, 418
    expired listings, 165
    fee for service type listing, 131
    garage sales and potential real estate sellers, 169
    open houses, 241
    prospecting for buyers, 258
    referrals, 387
    sample discussion scripts, 436, 437, 436
    sellers' seminars, 193
fun in the real estate business, 6
functional obsolescence, defined, 206
future prospects, 150

G

gap analysis. *See* wants and needs analysis
gap analysis (wants and needs analysis), 33

garage sales and potential real estate sellers, 169
gender discrimination, 20, 117
General Accredited Appraiser (GAA), 20
geographical marketing, 172–195
  multiple geographic marketing (MGM), 183
gifts
  closing gifts, defined, 322
  free service, 14–16
  of real property, valuable consideration, 333
goals
  main discussion, 33–40
  business plan, 46
  children and goals, 55
  definition, 31
  floor time, getting buyers into office, 267
  motivation and commitment, 38, 39
  in negotiations, 337
  prospecting, 143
  sellers' goals, 208
  setting, 31
  specific, measurable, scheduled, action-oriented, realistic, and tangible, 38
  top salespeople, 33
  worksheets, 492, 493
  See also objectives
gold calls, telemarketing, 150
good consideration, defined, 333
good credit and financing, 372
good guy-bad guy closes, 314
government information and Deceptive Trade Practices Act, 405
Graduate, REALTORS Institute (GRI), 20
GREAT, formula for success, 33
guarantees, sample discussion scripts, 476
guestbooks at open houses, 245, 326

H

hammers, tools for open houses, 244
handheld computers
  laptops. *See* laptops
  handicapped persons, discrimination against, 21
handshake, at listing appointment, 212
handwriting
  legibility of contracts, 333
hard-to-reach streets, 236
  property brochures, 250

hardware devices
  digital camera, 87
  digital projector, 86
  mobile video, 87–88
  tablet, 87
headlines in effective advertising, 112
high-dollar properties
  brochures, 250
  nonagency agreements, 131
Hill, Napoleon, 10
historical information, multiple "for sale" signs, 275
holidays
  dates in contracts, 335
  hours of work, 94
home office telemarketing, 150
home warranties, 252
  brochures, 209
  sample discussion scripts, 479
honesty and ethics, 23–26
Hoover, Herbert, 36
Hopkins, Tom, 17
hospitality at open houses, 242
"hot buttons," viewing and showing property, 285
hot buyers, defined, 257
hotels, prospecting for buyers, 258
hours of work, 94
hourly fees, 134–135
house inspection, defined, 361
human behavior and psychology of marketing, 92–100
humor, sarcastic, 12

I

"if-then" closes, 307, 308
imagination and subconscious brain, 10
improvements
  discussion at listing appointment, 218
  questions at listing appointment, 214, 216
  tracking, 49
income, discussion at buyer listing appointments, 278
incoming referral, defined, 382
industrial real estate investments, 50
insect inspections, 362, 363
inspecting property. *See* professional inspections; viewing and showing property
Instagram, 67–68
  See also social media

Institute of Real Estate Management
  (IREM), 20
Insurance
  Errors and Omissions insurance, 404
  seller's net sheet, 347
  insurance rate cards at listing
    presentations, 210
intent, defined, 399
intentional misrepresentation, 402
interest
  conflicts of interest, 131
  four selling steps, (AIDA), 112
interest on loans, 353
  advertising interest rates, 118
  promissory notes for commission
    payments, 134
interior decorating, staging property
  for sale, 252
intermediaries and agency law, 131
internal stimuli and psychology of
  marketing, 93
Internet
  anti-spam laws, 76, 325
  client follow-up, 326
  defined, 322
  e-mail. *See* e-mail
  great source for prospects, 185
  online tax databases of non-occupant
    owners, 185
  property exposure, 248
  property sales via Internet, sample
    discussion scripts, 482
  prospective buyers, 264
  tax databases online, 185
  Web browsing, 73
investments, 50
  and budgets, 47
  financial planning, 31
investing, defined, 31
  researching properties for
investors, 192
  top salespeople, 34
invitations to open houses, 238, 243

J

"jailbreak," open houses, 246
jargon in advertising, 114
jewelry and valuables in house, 233
job transfers. *See* relocations
junk mail and anti-spam laws, 325

K

Keep It Simple and Short (KISS), 114, 106

keys
  tools to bring to listing presentation, 210
  viewing and showing property, 284
kick-backs, Real Estate Settlement
  Procedures Act, 192
kitchen table meetings, 212

L

landlords and tenants
  agency relationship, 128
  lease/purchase financing, 377
  questions at buyer listing
    appointments, 277, 281
landscaping, 219
laptops, 74
  digital pictures, 74
  at open houses, 245
  presentations, 74, 220
lawsuits
  home warranties, 252
  telephone communication
    logs, 55
lawyers. *See* attorneys
leadership
  in GREAT formula for success, 33
  Leadership Training
    Graduate (LTG), 20
leads
  finding buyers, 257–270
  finding sellers, 139–195
learning from mistakes, 9, 32
lease/purchase financing, 377
legal pads, at open houses, 244
legibility of contracts, 333
lemonade at open houses, 242
lending institutions
  banking and financial planning, 31
  real estate owned (REO)
    property, 192
letters
  e-mail. *See* e-mail
  form letters, prospecting for
    buyers, 261
  of recommendation, 221
  See also direct mail
libraries
  library cards, 43
  real estate libraries, 43
license examination, accomplishments, 95
licensed inspectors. *See* professional
  inspections
liens, 356
  payment at closings, 357
  See also mortgages

lighting
  at open houses, 239
  safety concerns, 231
  staging property for sale, 252
limited service, nonagency
    agreements, 131
lingering, as indication of buyers'
    interest, 286
LinkedIn, 66–67
  See also social media
listening
  five rules of, 342–344
listings
  buyer listing procedures, 272–287
  custom listing presentations, 73
  e-mail, 73–74
  expired listings, 162, 169
listing appointments
  clear-cut listing appointments, 143–147
  clothing, 201, 212
  preparation, 200, 274–275
listing book, 208
  presentations, 73, 202, 208–210
  prospecting, 143
  seller listing procedures, 198–253
  types of listings, 227, 228
loans
  main discussion, 353–357
  application, documents needed at, 417
  fixed-rate loans, advertising, 118
  interest. *See* interest on loans
  loan processors, 353
  defined, 340
  promissory notes for commission
    payments, 133
  seller's net sheet, 346
  Truth-in-Lending Act (REG Z), 118
  See also lending institutions
local economy, effect on price, 205
location
  advertising, 115
  competitive market analysis, 204
  geographical farming, 172–177
  office in this area, script for
    overcoming objections, 470
  open houses, 236
  planned prospecting campaigns,
    "neighborhood servicing," 169
  showing neighborhood features, 284
lock boxes, 249, 250
  listing presentation, things to
    bring, 210
  step-by-step process for selling
    property, 223
logging. *See* tracking techniques

long-range prospecting, 170
low offers, 286
  OBO, in advertising, 114
low-income homebuyers, niche
    markets, 191
loyalty
  defined, 125
  duty in agency relationship, 124, 125
  expired listings prospects, 163
luncheons, prospecting for buyers, 258
Lundquist, John, 180

M

MacArthur, Douglas, 36
magic plan, 82
mail
  direct-mail marketing. *See* direct mail
  e-mail. *See* e-mail
  prospecting for buyers, form letters, 261
  recommendation letters, 221
  vs. appointment, sample discussion
    script, 437
maintenance. *See* repairs and
    maintenance
mallets, at open houses, 244
management
  appeals to higher authority, technique
    for closing sales, 317, 308
  brokers. *See* brokers
manual
  seller presentation manual, 208, 209
marketing
  AIDA, 106
  analysis. *See* CMA (competitive market
    analysis)
  budget, 105
  buying motives, 99–101
  campaign, 105, 111
  customer satisfaction, 99
  defined, 105
  market value, compared to CMA, 202
  philosophy, 96–101
  planning, 98
  public relations, 106
  project, 105
  research, 97–98, 202
  specialization, 188
  strategy, 105
  ability, 107
  business, 107
  decision making, 108
  relationships, 107
  value, 199
marketing and advertising, 230, 423, 424

main discussion, 105–121
ad copy, 112
blind ads, 236
brochures. *See* brochures
Deceptive Trade Practices Act, 406
definitions
  prospecting, 140
  territory canvassing, 151
  warm and cold buyers, 264
direct mail. *See* direct mail
explaining advertising to sellers, 230
listing packet, advertising submission forms, 209
marketing plan book, 208
media and public relations, 120
  See also newspapers and newspaper ads
misleading advertising, 115
monthly payment, advertising, 118
name recognition, 106
networking. *See* networking
newsletters. *See* newsletters
newspaper ads. *See* newspapers and newspaper ads
open house advertising, 236, 246
price, 107, 113, 115
professional ad writing, FSBO prospects, 152
prospect generating, 106
promotional calendars, 181
prospecting for buyers, 258, 263
slogans, 116
step-by-step process for selling property, 223
strategy, 105–121
targeted advertising, 110
telemarketing. *See* telemarketing
Truth-in-Lending Act (REG Z), 118
mass mailings, 71–72
  See also direct mail
"maybe clients," stalling, defined, 296
measuring tools, for listing presentation, 210
media
  public relations, 120
  radio, listening for success, 43
  See also newspapers and newspaper ads
Mehrabian, Albert, 341
mental capacity, competency of contracting parties, 337
Microsoft Outlook, 323
military personnel, niche markets, 190
misleading information
  advertising, 115

Deceptive Trade Practices Act, 399–407
definitions, 399
Truth-in-Lending Act (REG Z), 118
misrepresentation, definitions, 399, 402
mistakes
  ethics and other peoples' mistakes, 23, 24
  learnings, 9
  See also failure
MLS (Multiple Listing Service)
  MLS input forms in listing packets, 209
  property exposure, 248
  for sale by owner properties, 156, 160
  status changes, 362
money management and financial planning, 30
monthly payment, seller's net sheet, 346
moral character, 22
  See also ethics
mortgage banker, defined, 340
mortgage broker, defined, 341
mortgage company, defined, 340
mortgages
  blanket, 376
  buy-down mortgages, 377
  foreclosure property, 192
  monthly payment, advertising, 118
  mortgage bankers, 355
  mortgage brokers, 355, 356
  mortgage companies, 353
  mortgage information letter, listing packet, 209
  mortgage partners and time management, 56
  mortgage schedules, at open houses, 244
  package, 375
  reverse annuity mortgage (RAM), 376
  See also financing; loans
motels, prospecting for buyers, 258
motivation
  dominant buying motive, defined, 274
  goals, 38, 39
  and subconscious brain, 10
move-down and move-up buyers, 281
muggings, 44
multiple "for sale" signs, 275
multiple geographic marketing (MGM), 183
Multiple Listing Service.
  See MLS (Multiple Listing Service)
multiple open houses in one area, 245
multitasking, 56

music
    listening for success, 43
    at open houses, 239
mutual assent, defined, 333

N

names
    in contracts, 334
    name recognition advertising distinguished from prospect generating advertising, 111–112
    remembering, 12
    and trust, 20
NAR. *See* National Association of REALTORS® (NAR)
National Association of Real Estate Exchanges (NAREE), 22
National Association of REALTORS (NAR), 20, 22, 23
    Code of Ethics, 22
    Deceptive Trade Practices Act, 406
    expired listings, regulations for contacting, 162
    promoting listings, 252
national economy, effect on price, 205
national origin discrimination, 20, 116
negative attitude. *See* attitude
negotiating offers
    main discussion, 341–353
    seller's net sheet, 346–348
neighborhood. *See* location
neighbors
    "introducing your new neighbor" cards, 177
    sphere of influence (SOI) farming, 171
nervousness
    indications of buyers' interest in property, 286
"nesters," defined, 54
net income, and budgets, 48
net listing, defined, 228
net sheet, seller's, 346–348
networking, 120
    defined, 106
    prospecting for buyers, 258
new construction. *See* builders and new construction
newsletters
    e-newsletters, 182, 325
    to keep realtor names front of prospects, 182
newspapers and newspaper ads, 112
    including in marketing plan, 111–112
    media and public relations, 120

obituary clients, 168
nonagency agreements, 131
non-occupant owners
    defined, 257
    prospective sellers, 185
    See also landlords and tenants
nonverbal communication
    defined, 340
    in negotiations, 341, 342
nonverbal communication in negotiations, 341
note pads at listing presentations, 210
notice
    defined, 125
    duty in agency relationship, 127, 128
notifying others of whereabouts, 46

O

obedience
    defined, 125
    duty in agency relationship, 127, 128
obituaries and prospective clients, 168
objections
    anticipated objections during sales presentations, 303
    defined, 298
    definition, 292
    objection handling techniques, 292–325
    questions *vs.*, 294
    rejections *vs.*, 294
    types of, 296
    See also goals
OBO, in advertising, 114
obsolescence, defined, 207
odors, 232
offers
    negotiating, 341–352
    presenting offers, 350–352
    seller's net sheet, 346–348
office tours
    defined, 199
    of open houses, 246
older persons
    empty-nest buyers, 283
    niche markets, 190
    widows and widowers, obituary clients, 168
omnifocus, 79–81
one-time listing, defined, 228
online. *See* Internet
open houses
    main discussion, 229–246
    checklist, 427, 428

prospecting for buyers, 258
referrals, 387
for sale by owner (FSBO), 156
signs, 237, 239, 244
special business cards, 119
open listings
defined, 227
sample discussion scripts, 477
opinions and agency relationship, 126
organization in effective advertising, 113
origination fees, 132
outgoing referral, 386–390
defined, 382
overplaying problems, strategy, 285
overpricing
expired listings, overpriced properties, 165
and marketing, 110
sample discussion scripts, 443
owner financing
questions at listing appointment, 214, 217

P

painting
staging property for sale, 252
touch-up paint, 219
paper trail. *See* recordkeeping
parking
at listing appointment, 211
viewing and showing property, 284
passive
passive side of real estate business, 169–188
past clients
keeping in touch, 321–328
prospecting for buyers, 258
referrals, 387
Patton, Rex, 203
pens
at listing presentations, 210
at open houses, 244
perceptions
element of quality, 15
sellers' objections, 295
performance
defined, 3
element of quality, 14
profit budgets, net income, 48
questions and answers, 44, 95
See also success
persistence, 95
personal assistants, 52, 56

personal property, sample discussion script, 474
pest inspections, 361, 364
pets, 229, 230
phone calls. *See* telephone
photos. *See* pictures
physical needs
balance, top salespeople, 34
and psychology of marketing, 93
pictures
in advertising, 113
buyers looking at pictures and not at house, 232
digital. *See* digital cameras and pictures
family pictures, 219, 232
seller presentation manual, 209
planned prospecting campaigns, 169
planners, 46
open houses, appointment books at, 244
See also calendars
police officers, niche markets, 190
portfolio, at open houses, 244
positive attitude. *See* attitude
possession
"delayed possession," 274
real estate owned (REO) property, 192
See also nonoccupant owners
prequalifying buyers. *See* qualifying buyers
presentation plan, step-by-step process for selling property, 223
price
adjustments, 250
average sales prices, tracking, 49
discussion at listing appointment, 218, 219, 224, 225, 227
dollar amounts per sale, tracking, 49
down payment. *See* down payments
economy, effect of, 205
high-dollar properties. *See* high-dollar properties
low offers, 286
marketing and advertising, 107, 113, 115
OBO, in advertising, 114
open houses, 236, 238
overpricing. *See* overpricing
price range goals, 40
questions at listing appointment, 214, 217
reductions, 250
sample discussion scripts, 434, 438
seasonal variations, effect on price, 205
supply and demand, 205

tracking, 49
See also CMA (competitive market analysis)
priorities, and time management, 52
privacy violations, 89
professional athletes, niche markets, 190
professional inspections, 362, 363
   Deceptive Trade Practices Act defense, 403, 404
   sample discussion scripts, 434
professionalism
   main discussion, 1–26
   buyer listing appointments, 276
   checklist, 488, 489
   competitive market analysis, 146
   definitions, 2–3
   ethics. *See* ethics
   listing appointments, 201
   for sale by owner (FSBO) prospects, 153, 157
   of top five percent of real estate salespeople, 34
profit
   budgets, net income, 48
promissory notes and commission payments, 133
promotional events, including in marketing plan, 111
property disclosure statement, 209
property graphics, 251
property inspections. *See* viewing and showing property
property knowledge, 188
property maintenance. *See* repairs and maintenance
property managers, prospecting for buyers, 259
property profile sheets, 251
property search, 84–86
prospecting for clients
   active, 140
   buyers, 257–269
   sellers, 140–195
   name recognition advertising distinguished from prospect generating advertising, 109–110
   prospecting, defined, 140
   reactive, 140
   tracking calls per week, 49
psychology of marketing, 92–101
public places and safety concerns, 44
public relations, 120
"public service" approach for new prospects, 177

punitive damages under Deceptive Trade Practices Act, 400
puppy-dog closes, 313
purchase agreements, 333
   blank agreements, at open houses, 244
   buyer listing appointments, 275, 280
   closings, 353, 353
   professional inspections, 363
   repairs required, 367

Q

qualified referral, defined, 382
qualifying buyers, 378, 378, 423, 433
   advantages of selling through broker, 419, 457
   "all cash," 274
   discussions, 278, 280, 476
   mortgage companies, 353
   worksheets, 245, 413
quality of service
   main discussion, 13–15
   aspects of quality, 14, 15
   defined, 3
questions and answers
   buyers, questions for, 412, 414
   close-ended questions, 302
   CMA (competitive market analysis), sample questions, 431, 432
   competitive market analysis, 146
   fast sales, questions for, 430, 431
   at listing appointment, 213, 214, 216
   at listing appointments, 280
   negotiations, 341, 342
   open-ended questions, 302
   seller presentation manual, 209
   and success, 44, 95
   vs. objections, 294
   See also scripts
quick sales, explaining to sellers, 231
quitting the profession, 5

R

racial discrimination, 20, 116
radio, listening for success, 43
radon, 361, 365
rapport, 18
   buyer listing appointments, 276
   office time, 267
   See also trust
reading
   for success, 43, 57
real estate agency law. *See* agency law

real estate applications
  financial planning, 76
  other, 83–84
  time management and organization, 77–83
Real Estate Buyer's Agent Council (REBAC), 20
real estate conventions, 43, 44
real estate industry support groups and associations, 195
real estate libraries, 43
real estate management software programs, 70–72
real estate office floor time. *See* floor time
real estate owned (REO) property, 192
Real Estate Settlement Procedures Act, 192
real estate waifs client follow-up, 327
  defined, 167
REALTORS® Land Institute (RLI), 20
REALTORS® National Marketing Institute (RNMI), 20
REALTORS® service mark, defined, 3
reasonable care, duty in agency relationship, 127, 128
rebates on commissions, 134
receptionists
  in real estate offices, 188
  See also personal assistants
recordkeeping
  contact manager software programs, 70–72
  databases, 70–72
  expenses, file and tax records, 57
  guestbooks at open houses, 245, 326
  referrals, 388
  relocation companies, market specialization, 188
  for sale by owner (FSBO) prospects, 159, 160
  and time management, 56
  See also tracking techniques
reduce-to-the-ridiculous closes, 312
referrals
  buyer, 384
  main discussion, 381–390
  definitions, 382
  outgoing, 386–390
  prospecting for buyers, 259
  Referral and Relocation Certification (RRC), 20
  rental, 384–385
  seller, 384
  specialists, great, 390–396
  tracking, 49

refreshments
  client follow-up parties, 328
  at open houses, 242
REG Z, Truth-in-Lending Act, 118
rejection *vs.* objection, 294
relatives. *See* family and relatives
reliability
  defined, 3
  element of quality, 14
reliance on misrepresentation, 402
religious discrimination, 20, 116
relocations
  FSBO prospects, 157
  hot buyers, 264
  market specialization and relocation companies, 188
  newcomers' packets, 426
  sample discussion scripts, 482
renters. *See* landlords and tenants
repairs and maintenance, 231, 367
  as-is property. *See* "as is"
  description in contracts, 336
  discussion at listing appointment, 218
  painting, 219, 251
  professional inspections, 363
  required by purchase agreement, 367
  See also improvements
Residential Accredited Appraiser (RAA), 20
residential real estate investments, 51
respect, in GREAT formula for success, 32
results
  See also performance; success
retainers, 135
retirement
  and buyers, 283
  planning, 52
retireplan, 77
return clients, 14, 15
Reverse Annuity Mortgage (RAM), 376
right or wrong. *See* ethics
room size, enhancing, 285
Roosevelt, Eleanor, 9
rushing into sale, 18

S

safety, 44, 51
  explaining to sellers, 231
  real estate offices, 267
salaries
  commissions. *See* commissions
  hourly wage, 39, 40

Index 527

regular fixed salaries, 47
sales price. *See* price
sales tracking, 49
sarcastic humor, 12
savings accounts, 51
scanners, 75
scannerpro, 82
schedules. *See* calendars
schooling. *See* education and training
scratch paper, at open houses, 244
scripts
    abandoned clients
        (real estate waifs), 167
    after viewing property, 286
    agency listing, 476
    alternate-of-choice closes, 309
    assumptive closes, 309–310
    bad experience, 471
    business marketing, 183
    buy first, 466
    buyer listing appointments, 281
    closed-ended questions, 303
    commissions, 434, 457, 460
    competitive market analyses, 146, 147
    dignifying sellers' concerns, 299, 301
    discussions at listing appointment, 223
    main discussion, 434–487
    don't like salespeople, 466
    door to door marketing, 151, 152
    expired listings, 163, 165, 437, 477
    fair housing questions from
        buyers, 485
    fair housing questions from sellers, 482
    feedback question closes, 310
    FHA, sale of property to, 477
    friend in the business, 439
    friends of sellers as listing agents, script
        for overcoming objections, 455
    FSBOs, 154, 155, 156, 160, 161, 436,
        437, 457
    garage sales and potential real estate
        sellers, 169
    geographical farming, 172–177
    handling ad calls, 269
    home warranty, 479
    "if-then" closes, 308
    inspections, 479
    Internet, property sales via, 481
    interview others, 470
    listing appointments, 223, 225, 281
    location, script for overcoming objec-
        tions to lack of office in area, 470
    mail *vs.* appointment, 442
    nonoccupant owners (NOO) as
        prospective sellers, 186
    open houses, 241, 244
    open listings, 477
    open-ended questions, 302
    paying closing costs, 475
    personal property, 475
    prequalifying buyers, 476
    pricing, 225, 439, 442, 443
    prospecting for buyers, 260
    reduce-to-the-ridiculous closes, 312
    referrals, 387, 388
    rephrasing sellers' concerns, 299
    service guarantees, 477
    short-term listing, 468
    similar situation closes, 311
    special properties, 480
    sphere of influence (SOI)
        farming, 171
    stalling, 297
    take away closes, 315, 317
    telemarketing, 150–151, 260
    telephone scripts, 434–437
    third party company, 473
    "tie-down closes," 307–308
    VA, sale of property to, 478
    waiting to make decisions, 462
searching for clients
    buyers, 257–269
    sellers, 140–195
seasonal variations, effect on price, 205
secretaries and assistants, 52, 56
security
    explaining to sellers, 231
    See also safety
self
    beliefs about yourself, 12
    self-fulfilling prophecy, defined, 8
    self-talk, 10
sellers
    absence of sellers at appointments, 284
    agency relationship, 128
    closings, 353–357
    disclosure statement, 404
    negotiating offers, 341–352
    referrals, 381–390
    seller financing, 274, 374–375
    seller listing packet, 199, 209
    seller presentation manual, 208, 209
    seller servicing, 234
    sellers' seminars, 193
    See also clients
seminars, 43
    definition, 31
    prospecting for buyers, 258
senior citizens. *See* older persons
septic system inspection, 364–365

service mark, REALTORS®, defined, 3
serviceability
　defined, 3
　element of quality, 15
services. *See* features and services
sex discrimination, 20, 117
shoes, removal at listing
　　appointment, 212
ShowHome, 82–83
showing. *See* viewing and showing
　　property
signing papers in listing packets, 228
signs
　car signs, prospecting for buyers,
　　259, 263
　for-sale. *See* for-sale signs
　open houses, 237, 239, 244
similar properties. *See* CMA
　　(competitive market analysis)
similar situation closes, 311
simple interest rate, advertising, 118
simplicity in advertising, 115
single persons
　fair housing, 116–117
single persons and fair housing laws, 20,
　　116–117
slogans, 116
smartphones, 74–75, 244
smells
　odors, 232
　open houses, 239
social media
　blog, 69–70
　defined, 64
　facebook, 65–66
　flickr, 68
　instagram, 67–68
　linkedin, 66–67
　personal website, 69
　tumblr, 68
　twitter, 67
　youtube, 68–69
Society of Industrial and Office
　　REALTORS® (SIOR), 20
soft drinks at open houses, 242
software. *See* computers and technology
spam laws, 325
special properties
　brochures, 250
　non-agency agreements, 131
　sample discussion scripts, 481
specialization
　industrial and office real estate, 20
　market specialization, 188
　niche markets, 190

sphere of influence (SOI), 170, 171, 269
spirituality
　spiritual balance of top salespeople, 34
square footage
　competitive market analysis, 204
staging property for sale, 252
stairs, safety concerns, 231
stalling, 296
　conditions, 295
　definition, 292, 296
　scripts, waiting to make decisions, 462
statistics, performance tracking, 49
statute of frauds, 337
stock market investments, 51
stocktwits, 76
stop-by appointments, 157
structural engineers report, 366, 367
subconscious brain, 11, 12
success
　dressing for success, 40, 42
　driving for success, 42, 43
　listening for success, 43
　persistence, 94
　prospecting for seller appointments,
　　140–195
　questions and answers, 44, 95
supplements to contracts, 333
supply and demand, 205
support groups for real estate industry, 194
survey, 361, 366

T

take-away closes, 314, 315
tape measures at listing presentations, 210
target buyers, 112
task analysis and time logs, 54
taxes, 50
　contact manager software programs,
　　generating reports, 70
　expense files, 57
　reports, 70, 73
　seller's net sheet, 347
　tax records
　　competitive market
　　　analysis, 205
　　online tax databases, 185
　　prospecting for buyers, 261
teachers, niche markets, 190
technology. *See* computers and
　　technology
telemarketing, 150, 257
　"do not call" laws, 151
telephone
　cold calls. *See* cold calls

"do not call" laws, 151
home phone numbers business
   cards, 55
prospecting, 263, 266
real estate office, answering calls.
   See floor time
safety, 51
sample discussion
   scripts, 434–437
seller servicing, 234
time management, 54
tracking techniques
advertising calls, 116
communication logs, 55
tenants. *See* landlords and tenants
tender loving care (TLC), 16, 18
termites, 362, 363
territory canvassing, defined, 151
things, 77–78
third party companies
   relocation companies, 189
   sample discussion scripts, 473
"tie-down closes," 307–308,
time
   appointments. *See* appointments
   delayed deals. *See* stalling
   goals, time frames for, 37
   on the market, tracking time, 49
   starting time, 56
   task analysis and time logs, 54
time management, 52–60
   applications, 78–83
   computers and technology, 73
   defined, 32
   family time. *See* work/life balance
timeliness
   defined, 3
   element of quality, 14
   wasting time, 54
   and telemarketing, 151
   See also calendars
title
   title companies, 355–356
   title insurance rate cards at listing
      presentations, 210
   title partners and time management, 56
TLC, 18, 19
   defined in real estate
      marketing terms, 18
to-do lists, 53
toodledo, 78
tools
   buyer listing appointments,
      preparation, 275
   top producer, 324–325

tote a note on commissions, 133–134
touching as indication of buyers' interest
   in property, 286
touch-up paint, 219
tracking techniques
   client follow-up, 323–328
   geographical farming, 173
   goals, 39
   referrals, 388
   telephone
   advertising calls, 116
   communication logs, 55
   See also recordkeeping
trade publications and reading for
   success, 43, 57
trading services, 133
training. *See* education and training
transaction fees, 133
transactional brokers, 131
Trulia.com, 86
trust
   advertising and inherent
      mistrust, 115
   attitude, 5
   buyer listing appointments, 276
   closing techniques, 307
   element of quality, 13
   in GREAT formula for success, 33
   privacy violations, 89
   sellers' objections, 295
   and TLC, 18–19
   See also rapport
truth
   Deceptive Trade Practices
      Act, 400–408
   misleading advertising, 115
   Truth-in-Lending Act (REG Z), 118
trying out the real estate business, 32
Tumblr, 68
   See also social media
Twitter, 67
   See also social media
types of listings, 227, 228
typewritten contracts, 334

U

unconscionable, defined, 399

V

vacations, as bonuses, 129
value
   comparative analysis. *See* CMA
      (competitive market analysis)

valuable consideration, defined, 337
valuable items in house, 233
See also appraisals; price
vehicles. *See* cars
verbal communication in negotiations, 342–344
veteran status, discussion at buyer listing appointments, 278
videotaping listing presentations, 229
viewing and showing property, 188
   final walk-throughs, 367
   listing appointment, property inspection, 213, 218
   number of properties to see, 284
   showing property, explaining to sellers, 231
   traveling, 283, 284
virtual tours, 245
visualization, 13
volunteer work
   leads, 72
   by real estate professionals, 194

W

wages. *See* salaries
waifs or abandoned clients. *See* real estate waifs
waiting
   expired listings, 165
   scripts, waiting to make decisions, 462
   warm and cold buyers, defined, 258
   See also stalling
waivers under Deceptive Trade Practices Act, 405
walkthroughs. *See* viewing and showing property
wants and needs analysis, 33
   definitions, 199, 273
   "hot buttons," 285
   at listing appointments, 213, 275, 276
warm buyers, defined, 258
warm canvass door, defined, 151
warm telemarketing calls, 150
warranties, 252
Web sites
   browsing, 73
   on business cards, 119
   See also Internet
weekends
   contract dates, 335
   hours of work, 94
wells, inspection, 365
widows and widowers, obituary clients, 168
women and fair housing laws, 20, 117
Women's Council of REALTORS® (WCR), 20
word-processed contracts, 334
work, defined, 4, 5
workday, hours of work, 94
work/life balance
   family appointments, 55
   home phone numbers business cards, 55
   of top five percent of real estate salespeople, 34
   "work at work and play at play," 54
worksheets
   budgets, 490, 491
   goals, 492, 493
   qualifying buyers, 245, 413
World Wide Web. *See* Internet
wrap-around financing, 376
Wrigley, R.J., 116
written documents
   contracts, statute of frauds, 334
   goals, 37
wrong or right. *See* ethics
WWW. *See* Internet
Wyatt, Patrick, 172

Y

yards
   signs. *See* for-sale signs
   staging property for sale, yard work, 252
YouTube, *See* social media

Z

Ziglar, Zig, 7, 19
Zillow.com, 85